Preserving Digital Information

Henry M. Gladney

Preserving Digital Information

With 43 Figures and 13 Tables

 Springer

Author

Henry M. Gladney
HMG Consulting
Saratoga, CA 95070, USA
hgladney@gmail.com
http://home.pacbell.net/hgladney/

Library of Congress Control Number: 2006940359

ACM Computing Classification (1998): H.3, K.4, K.6

ISBN 978-3-540-37886-0 Springer Berlin Heidelberg New York

Springer is a part of Springer Science+Business Media

springer.com

© Springer-Verlag Berlin Heidelberg 2007

Typeset by the author
Production: LE-TEX Jelonek, Schmidt & Vöckler GbR, Leipzig
Cover design: KünkelLopka Werbeagentur, Heidelberg

Printed on acid-free paper   45/3100/YL - 5 4 3 2 1 0

Dedicated to
My parents, who sacrificed much to obtain
the best possible education for their children,
And schools whose generosity admitted me to an education
I could not otherwise have afforded:
Upper Canada College, Toronto,
Trinity College, University of Toronto,
and
Princeton University.

Preface

What might this book offer to people already confronted with information overload? It is intended to help citizens who want to understand the issues around digital preservation without reading the technical literature. It is also intended to help scholars who want depth quickly find authoritative sources. It is for

- authors, artists, and university faculty who want their digitally represented works to be durable and to choose information service providers that are committed and competent to ensure preservation of those works;
- attorneys, medical professionals, government officials, and businessmen who depend on the long-term reliability of business records that are today mostly in digital form;
- entertainment industry managers, because their largest enterprise assets are old performance recordings;
- archivists, research librarians, and museum curators who need to understand digital technology sufficiently to manage their institutions, especially those curators that are focusing on digital archiving;
- citizens who want to understand the information revolution and the attendant risks to information that might affect their lives; and
- software engineers and computer scientists who support the people just mentioned.

Ideally, a book about a practical topic would present prescriptions for immediately achieving what its readers want—in this case a durable existence for monographs, articles, performance recordings, scientific data, business and government records, and personal data that we all depend on. Doing so is, however, not possible today because software and infrastructure for reliably preserving large numbers of digital records have not yet been built and deployed, even though we know what software would work and what services repository institutions need to provide.

The software needed includes tools for packaging works for long-term storage and for extracting information package contents conveniently for their eventual consumers. Many useful components exist, and some are in use. Others are not yet represented by specifications that must precede peer criticism, selection, and refinement within communities that have specialized applications. Some of the agreements needed will ultimately be expressed as information interchange standards. The products of such work could be deployed in five to ten years.

The infrastructure needed includes institutional repositories (digital archives) that share methods and digital content and whose characteristics are relatively well understood. Since large projects to create the required network and storage infrastructure exist in several countries (Australia, Germany, The Netherlands, the U.K., and the U.S.), the current book positions preservation within this infrastructure without describing the infrastructure in detail. It focuses on principles for reliable digital preservation and on what these principles teach about design for representing every kind of intellectual work.

Substantial deployment will not occur until interested communities achieve consensus on which proposed components to choose so that their clients, the producers and consumers of information resources, can share their works safely and efficiently. We intend this book to help the necessary discussions.

Trustworthy Digital Objects

The *Open Archival Information Systems (OAIS) Reference Model* and related expositions address the question, "What architecture should we use for a digital repository?" This is sometimes construed as all aspects of providing digital library or archive services—everything that might be pertinent to creating and managing a digital repository within an institution such as a university, a government department, or a commercial enterprise.

To address the *OAIS* question and the responsibilities of repository institution managers, doing so in the compass of a single monograph, seems to me a too-difficult task, partly because accepted best practices have not yet emerged from increasing research activities. In contrast, digital preservation is a tractable topic for a monograph. Among the threats to archival collections are the deleterious effects of technology obsolescence and of fading human recollection. In contrast to the *OAIS* question, this book addresses a different question, "What characteristics will make saved digital objects useful into the indefinite future?"

The book's technical focus is on the structure of what it calls a Trustworthy Digital Object (TDO), which is a design for what the *OAIS* international standard calls an Archival Information Package (AIP). It further recommends TDO architecture as the packaging design for information units that are shared, not only between repository institutions, but also between repositories and their clients—information producers and information consumers.

In contrast, most research articles addressing digital preservation focus on the structure and operations of archival repository institutions and research libraries—what they sometimes call Trusted Digital Repositories. A critic has called this distinction still controversial in the sense that TDO methodology is not widely accepted as the path that must be taken. In fact,

TDO architecture seems to have been mostly ignored since 2001, when current and former IBM Research staff members started to publish its description.

Most of today's digital preservation research literature focuses on a small segment of what is created in digital form—the kinds of information that research libraries collect. It pays little attention to the written output of governments and of private sector enterprises. It hardly mentions the myriad documents important to the welfare and happiness of individual citizens—our health records, our property records, our photographs and letters, and so on. Some of these are tempting targets for fraud and other misfeasance. In contrast, deliberate falsification does not seem to be a prominent problem for documents of primarily cultural interest. Protecting against its effects has therefore received little attention in the cultural heritage digital preservation literature.

The book therefore explains what I believe to be the shortfalls of preservation methodology centered on repository institution practices, and justifies my opinion that TDO methodology is sound. Its critique of the trusted digital repositories approach is vigorous. I invite similarly vigorous public or private criticism of TDO methodology and, more generally, of any opinion the book expresses.

Structure of the Book

The reader who absorbs this book will understand that preservation of digital information is neither conceptually difficult nor mysterious. However, as with any engineering discipline, "the devil is in the details." This motivates a typical engineering approach—breaking a problem into separate, tractable components.

Software engineers will recognize details from their own projects and readily understand both the broad structure and also the choice of principles emphasized. Readers new to digital preservation or to software engineering might find it difficult to see the main threads within the welter of details. Hopefully these readers will be helped by the Summary Table of Contents that can remind them of the book's flow in a single glance, the introduction that precedes each group of chapters, and also the summary that ends each chapter by repeating its most important points.

The book is laid out in five sections and a collection of back matter that provides detail that would have been distracting in the main text. The order of the sections and chapters is not especially significant.

The book proceeds from broad social circumstances to methodological details for preserving any kind of digital object whatsoever. It describes architectural abstractions without refinements that many people would demand before they called them designs. This choice is intended to emphasize what might be obscured by the detail required in design for implementations. Before it begins with technical aspects, it summarizes the soundest available basis for discussing what knowledge we can communicate and what information we can preserve.

Throughout, the book emphasizes ideas and information that typical human users of information systems—authors, library managers, and eventual readers of preserved works—are likely to want. Its first section, **Why We Need Long-term Digital Preservation** describes the challenge, distinguishing our narrow interpretation of digital preservation from digital repository design and archival institution management.

Preservation can be designed to require no more than small additions to digital repository technology and other information-sharing infrastructure. The latter topics must respond to subtle variations in what different people will need and want and to subjective aspects of knowledge and communication. In contrast to the complexity and subjectivity of human thinking, the measures needed to mitigate the effects of technology obsolescence can be objectively specified once and for all.

Chapter 2 sketches social and computing marketplace trends driving the information access available to every citizen of the industrial nations—access that is transforming their lives. These transformations are making it a struggle for some librarians and archivists to play an essential role in the information revolution. Their scholarly articles suggest difficulties with digital preservation partly due to inattention to intellectual foundations—the theory of knowledge and of its communication.

The second section, **Information Object Structure**, reminds readers of the required intellectual foundation by sketching scientific philosophy, relating each idea to some aspect of communicating. It resolves prominent difficulties with notions of *trust, evidence, the original,* and *authenticity.* It emphasizes the distinction between *objective facts* and *subjective opinions,* which is not as evident in information practice as would be ideal. The section core is a communication model and an information representation model. These lead to our recommending structuring schemes for documents and collections.

The third section, **Distributed Content Management**, sketches electronic data processing standards that are essential starting points. It continues by discussing repository infrastructure aspects that comprise context for preservation software. Since most of this material is well known and well handled in previous works, Chapters 7 through 9 are limited to sketching the aspects essential for preservation and to providing citations intended to help readers who want more detail.

The fourth section, **Digital Object Architecture for the Long Term**, suggests how to solve those preservation challenges that technology can address. Chapters 10 through 12 present the TDO approach in a form permitting objective and specific critiques. It depends on well known elements of scientific and engineering methodologies: (1) careful attention to the interplay between the objective aspects (here, tools that might be employed) and what is necessarily subjective (human judgments, opinions, and intentions that cannot flourish in circumstances controlled too tightly); (2) focus on the wants and actions of individual people that balances and illustrates abstractions such as authenticity, integrity, and quality; (3) identification of possible failures and risk reduction; and (4) divide and conquer project management with modest pieces that build on other people's contributions and that facilitate and encourage their future contributions to address weaknesses and provide missing elements.

Specifically, Chapter 10 teaches replication to protect against losing the last copy of any bit-string. Chapter 11 describes signing and sealing to provide durable evidence about the provenance and content of any digital object, and of its links to other information. Chapter 12 shows how to encode bit-strings to be interpretable within any future computing system, even though we cannot today know such systems' architectures.

In the **Peroration**, Chapter 13 suggests open questions and work yet to be done. The questions include, "Is every detail of what we call TDO methodology correct and optimal? Are there missing pieces? What would be the architecture and design of satisfactory implementations? How can we make these convenient for users with little technical experience?" Such questions lead to suggestions for projects to create lightly coupled software modules.

How to Read This Book

Precise communication is unusually important for this book's topic. Accordingly, its diction is particularly cautious. Nevertheless, definitions are not given in the text except for unusually sensitive cases. The careful reader is referred to the Glossary.

How an individual word or phrase is used differs from community to community. For key words, we signal what we intend. A word in italics, such as *model*, has a relatively precise, technical meaning that is so important that this word has a Glossary entry. A word or phrase between double quotes, such as "model," is used to quote a source. Single quotes enclosing a word indicate that the word itself is being discussed as an object—as a symbol for something other than itself.

Some readers will find their objectives best met by reading this book out of order. This should not be surprising in a topic as complex and subtle as human communication. First time readers are encouraged to ignore the references, especially those to other sections of the book.

Some readers might be impatient with philosophical discussions that seem to them to expound little more than common sense. Such readers might proceed directly from the introductory chapters to **Digital Object Architecture for the Long Term**, consulting the **Information Object Structure** chapters only if they start to wonder how to improve upon what the fourth section proposes, or whether the whole work is soundly based.

Some readers will prefer to understand where we are leading them before they join us on the journey. We suggest that such readers might prefer to start with Chapter 13, which is devoted to an assessment of the merits of the TDO digital preservation approach.

Some readers will want more detail, others less. For those who want an introduction to preservation issues and to technology that can help address its challenges, we recommend generally ignoring the footnotes and the citations. For readers who want technical detail, possibly because they are skeptical about what the main text propounds, the footnote citations attempt to identify the most authoritative works. These citations are selections from about three times as many books and articles considered. By consulting these and the literature that they in turn cite, the reader can quickly learn what other people believe about digital preservation.

Some readers will want to decide quickly whether or not to inspect a cited work. The footnotes and an accompanying Web page are designed to help them. The objective is that a reader will be able to decide from each footnote alone whether or not to look at the cited work, i.e., decide without looking at any other page. Web page citations include the Web address, and are not repeated in the formal Bibliography at the end of the book. Instead they will be provided as actionable links in a supporting Web page.[1] Footnote citations of hard copy works are abbreviations of formal citations included in the Bibliography; they begin with the last name of the author and the publication date to make finding their Bibliography entries easy. Every footnote citation includes enough of the work's title for the reader to decide how interested he is in this source.

A few works are cited so often that it has been convenient to indicate them by abbreviations.[2] A few phrases are used so often that it is conven-

---

[1] This Web page is available at http://home.pacbell.net/hgladney/pdilinks.htm. As a fixed Web address is likely to be ephemeral, we suggest that readers locate a copy by a Web search for "Preserving Digital Information citations" or for the ISBN "3-540-37886-3" or "3540378863".

[2] See Appendix A for the abbreviations LSW, NDIIPP, OAIS, PDITF, PI, PK, RLG, TLP, and W2005.

ient to represent them with acronyms. All these are tabulated in the Glossary.

The professional literature cited extends to autumn 2006. The reader will understand that work that appeared shortly before this cut-off could not be considered as thoughtfully as earlier work. Recent articles selected for citation are suggested for their insights beyond what the book includes.

When this book's manuscript was nearing completion, there appeared the final report and recommendations of the Warwick Workshop, *Digital Curation and Preservation: Defining the research agenda for the next decade*.[3] European experts across the full spectrum of the digital life cycle mapped the current state of play and future agenda. They reconsidered recommendations of a 1999 Warwick workshop and reviewed the progress made in implementing them. Their report concisely reflects the insights of many earlier discussions, making it a yardstick with which any reader can judge *Preserving Digital Information*. Appendix D uses its table of technical preservation components to assess TDO methodology.

Acknowledgements

I am grateful to John Bennett, Tom Gladney, Richard Hess, Peter Lucas, Raymond Lorie, John Sowa, and John Swinden for five years of conversation about topics represented in this book, including many suggestions for amendment of its draft versions. Their contributions and authoritative views are often acknowledged by the use of "we" in its text. I am particularly indebted to John Bennett for his patient inspection of several manuscript versions and his suggestions about how to communicate.

---

[3]   *Warwick workshop* 2005, http://www.dcc.ac.uk/training/warwick_2005/ Warwick_Workshop_report.pdf.

Summary Table of Contents

Detailed Table of Contents

Figures

Tables

Part I: Why We Need Long-term Digital Preservation

The question can be answered very simply: "If all that information is worth creating in the first place, surely some of it is worth saving!"

The principal legacy of those who live by and for the mind's work is literature: scholarly studies; multi-media recordings; business, scientific, government, and personal records; and other digitally represented information. These records convey information critical to democratic institutions and to our well-being. Every kind of human information is represented. The volume is enormous. As things currently stand, most of this material will become unusable in less than a human lifetime—some of it within a decade.

The people who support the information infrastructure deserve assurance that its best holdings will survive reliably into the future along with their social security records, building permits, family photographs, and other practical records. Without sound procedures beyond those in use today, they will be disappointed. The software currently available does not include good tools for saving digital originals in the face of rapid hardware and software obsolescence.

Information preservation has to do with reliably communicating to our descendants most of the history of the future. Choosing how to accomplish this without a sound intellectual foundation would risk systematic errors that might not be discovered until it is too late to put matters right, and perhaps also errors that are discovered earlier, but not before corrections would require expensive rework of the preserved content. The risks to communication quality are inherent in the transformations suggested in Table 2.

For these reasons, applying the best teachings is an ethical imperative whose importance cannot be better stated than Karl Popper did in 1967:

> [W]e may distinguish ... (A) the world of physical objects or of physical states; (B) the world of states of consciousness, or of mental states, or perhaps of behavioral dispositions to act; and (C) the world of objective contents of thought, especially of scientific and poetic thoughts and of works of art.
>
> ... consider two thought experiments:
>
> Experiment (1). All our machines and tools are destroyed, and all our subjective learning, including our subjective knowledge of machines and tools, and how to use them. But libraries and our capacity to learn from them survive. Clearly, after much suffering, our world may get going again.

Experiment (2). As before, machines and tools are destroyed, and our subjective learning, including our subjective knowledge of machines and tools, and how to use them. But this time, all libraries are destroyed also, so that our capacity to learn from books becomes useless.

If you think about these two experiments, the reality, significance, and degree of autonomy of world C (as well as its effects on worlds A and B) may perhaps become a little clearer to you. For in the second case there will be no re-emergence of our civilization for many millennia. [4]

As Popper suggests, the business at hand is preserving what is essential for civilization—what some people might call "knowledge preservation." The best intellectual foundation can be found in the writings of the scientific philosophers of the first half of the twentieth century.

Ten years have elapsed since the digital preservation challenge was clearly articulated.[5] Should we be surprised that it has taken so long to address the challenge effectively? Or should we be surprised that a solution has emerged so quickly? The answer depends on one's sense of timescale. From a modern engineering perspective, or from a Silicon Valley perspective, a decade is a very long time for addressing a clearly articulated need. From a liberal arts perspective, or from the kind of social and political perspective typified by "inside the Washington beltway," ten years might be regarded as appropriate for thorough consideration of civilization's infrastructure. From a historian's perspective, ten years might be indistinguishable from the blink of an eyelid.

Cultural history enthusiasts, participants in an interest group whose membership can be inferred approximately from the citations of this book and the list of supporting institutions of a UNESCO program,[6] have asserted urgency for protecting digital information from imminent loss. The value of long-term digital preservation is, in fact, much greater than its application to the document classes receiving the most attention in the publications and discussions of this cultural heritage interest group. It extends also to documents essential to practical services of interest to every citizen, such as his legal and health records, and to providing technical infrastructure for ambitious cross-disciplinary research.[7] Achieving a convenient and

---

[4]   *Knowledge: Subjective versus Objective*, Chapter 4 of Miller 1983, *A Pocket Popper.*

[5]   Garrett 1996, *Preserving Digital Information: Report of the Task Force on Archiving* provides the meaning of "digital preservation" used in this book instead of the broader sense adopted by some more recent authors, e.g., in the documents of the [U.S.] National Digital Information Infrastructure Preservation Program.

[6]   UNESCO, *Memory of the World*, http://portal.unesco.org/ci/en/ev.php-URL_ID= 1538&URL_DO=DO_TOPIC&URL_SECTION=201.html

[7]   O'Hara 2006, *Memories for Life.*

economical digital preservation infrastructure will benefit almost every citizen. (Table I)

Table 1: Why should citizens pay attention?

Why is digital preservation important?	Almost all new information is created first in digital form. Some of this is never printed. Every citizen depends on some of it, partly portions unique to him, for practical as well as cultural reasons. And some of that has long-term value.
Why is digital preservation suddenly urgent?	The U.S. Government recently granted a great deal of money to support it. However, the needed technology and infrastructure are not in place.
What kinds of challenge need to be addressed?	The challenges include legal, policy, organizational, managerial, educational, and technical aspects. Perhaps the most difficult challenge is selection of what to save.
Among these challenges, what are the technical components?	Only one difficult technical problem impeded digital archiving until recently—how to preserve information through technology changes. This has been solved, but the correctness and practicality of the solution are still to be demonstrated.
	The other technical challenges are engineering and solution deployment issues that have been discussed in many scholarly and trade press articles, so that elaboration in this book would be redundant.

Without action, much of what is created is likely to become unusable within a decade. Current preservation activities seem to be chaotic, uncertain, and sometimes confused, as is normal for any activity at an early state of its development and adoption. In part, this seems to be because scientific principles have not been heeded to full effect.

This book is about principles for long-term digital preservation, partly because it is not yet possible to point at complete and adequate implementations of the software that will be needed. It also seems premature to attempt to write a "best practices" manual for digital preservation.

The expression "digital preservation" has different meanings in the works of different authors. For instance, a UNESCO program defines it to be "the sum total of the steps necessary to ensure the permanent accessibility of documentary heritage."[8] This includes organizational, training, public information, selection, and funding activities outside the scope of this

---

[8]   UNESCO 2002, *Memory of the World: General Guidelines ...*, §3.2.

book, which focuses on the technology that can be brought to bear on the challenge. The UNESCO scope also includes routine and well-known library and computing center practices that are required to ensure that a work collected yesterday can be accessed without trouble today. In contrast, the current book focuses on what it calls "long-term digital preservation", by which it means processes and technology for mitigating the deleterious effects of technological obsolescence and fading human recall—effects which are usually apparent only some years after a digital object was created and collected.

There is, of course, overlap between custodianship for near-term access and what is required for the long term. This is most evident in file copying that computer centers have practiced almost from their first days, and that has now been implemented in software tools and hardware that any personal computer user can exploit almost automatically.[9] For long-term document safety, such tools and practices need only small extensions (Chapter 10).

Some modern opinion about preservation and authenticity holds that ensuring the long-term trustworthy usability of documents is better served by printed works on paper than by digital objects copied from place to place in computer networks. Such an opinion is hardly new. It has eerie similarities to sixteenth century opinions about the transition from handwritten copies on parchment to versions printed on paper. Five centuries ago, Trithemius argued that paper would be short-lived and that handwritten versions were preferable for their quality and because they eliminated the risk that printed inauthenticities and errors would mislead people because all copies would be identical.[10]

Management of the information recording human culture and business is a complex and subtle topic. Long-term digital preservation is a relatively simple component that can be handled once and for all, at least in principle. This is made possible by designing preservation measures so that they do not interfere with what might be necessary to deal with larger topics, doing so by implementing them without changing pre-existing digital repository software. For instance, this book treats only aspects of knowledge theory pertinent to preservation, and content management only as seems necessary for preservation support.

As outlined in the preface, the fundamental principles presented in Chapters 3 through 7 seem sufficient to design a reliable digital preservation infrastructure. The architectural principles presented in Chapters 9

---

[9]   Fallows 2006, *File Not Found.*

[10]   O'Donnell 1998, *Avatars of the Word: from Papyrus to Cyberspace*, pp.79–83.

through 12 seem sufficiently objective and clear so that competent software engineering teams could create everything needed without encountering difficult technical problems. Well known software engineering methods can be applied to make their implementations reliable. Readers can rapidly learn the most important of these principles by scanning the summary at the end of each chapter.

Specifically, each chapter's final section summarizes the driving circumstances for its recommendations—philosophical thinking and observations of economic, social, and technical environmental factors that cannot be altered by preservation technology. It also suggests principles for software design and for action by library and archive managers. Finally, several sections outline technical solution components. The summaries are deliberately silent about organizational and human measures that are handled extensively and well by other authors.

1 State of the Art

> Digital preservation consists of the processes aimed at ensuring the contin-
> ued accessibility of digital materials. ... To achieve this requires digital
> objects to be understood and managed at four levels: as physical phenomena;
> as logical encodings; as conceptual objects that have meaning to humans;
> and as sets of essential elements that must be preserved in order to offer fu-
> ture users the essence of [each] object.
>
> Webb 2003, *Guidelines for the Preservation of Digital Heritage*

Information interchange is a growing activity that is beginning to be
accompanied by attention to preserving digital documents for decades or
longer—periods that exceed practical technology lifetimes and that are
sometimes longer than human lifetimes. In the industrial nations, nearly
every business, government, and academic document starts in digital form,
even if it is eventually published and preserved on paper. The content
represents every branch of knowledge, culture, and business. Much of it is
available only in digital form, and some of this cannot be printed without
losing information.

Today's information revolution is the most recent episode in a long
history of changes in how human knowledge is communicated. Most of
these changes have not eliminated communication methods that preceded
them, but instead have supplemented them with means more effective for
part of what was being conveyed. However, they have stimulated, or at
least amplified, social changes to which some people have not adapted
readily, and have therefore resisted. A consequence has been that such
changes did not become fully effective until these people had been
replaced by their progeny. Much of the literature about today's information revolution and its effects on durable records suggests that this pattern
is being repeated.

The driving forces of information revolutions have always been the
same: more rapid transmission of content, more efficient means for finding
what might be of interest, and improved speed and precision of recordkeeping. Today's revolution is so rapid that it might startle an observer by
its speed. Part of what is communicated is technology for communication.
This helps those who want to exploit the new technical opportunities to do
so more quickly and with less effort then was needed in previous
information revolutions. The phenomenon is familiar to chemists, who
call it autocatalytic reaction.

The full infrastructure required to absorb revolutionary changes does not
all come into place simultaneously. People's enthusiasm for the most
obvious and most readily exploited aspects of new technology—in this
case the advantages of digital documents over their paper counterparts—

can cause them to change their habits before essential infrastructure is deployed—in this case services to preserve their digital works for as long as they might want. Perhaps people have not noticed and will not notice that there is no preservation infrastructure until they personally lose digital documents they thought would be accessible into the distant future. Prominent technical and operational issues that people might be assuming have already been adequately taken care of, but which have not, include management of assets called "intellectual property" and management of digital repository infrastructure.

1.1   What is Digital Information Preservation?

Almost all digital preservation work by scholars, librarians, and cultural curators attempts to respond to what is called for in a 1995–1996 Task Force Report:

> [T]he Task Force on Archiving of Digital Information focused on materials already in digital form and recognized the need to protect against both media deterioration and technological obsolescence. It started from the premise that migration is a broader and richer concept than "refreshing" for identifying the range of options for digital preservation. Migration is a set of organized tasks designed to achieve the periodic transfer of digital materials from one hardware/software configuration to another, or from one generation of computer technology to a subsequent generation. The purpose of migration is to preserve the integrity of digital objects and to retain the ability for clients to retrieve, display, and otherwise use them in the face of constantly changing technology. The Task Force regards migration as an essential function of digital archives.
>
> The Task Force envisions the development of a national system of digital archives … Digital archives are distinct from digital libraries in the sense that digital libraries are repositories that collect and provide access to digital information, but may or may not provide for the long-term storage and access of that information. The Task Force has deliberately taken a functional approach [to] … digital preservation so as to prejudge neither the question of institutional structure nor the specific content that actual digital archives will select to preserve.
>
> The Task Force sees repositories of digital information as held together in a national archival system primarily through the operation of two essential mechanisms. First, repositories claiming to serve an archival function must be able to prove that they are who they say they are by meeting … criteria of an independently administered program for archival certification. Second, certified digital archives will have available to them a critical fail-safe mechanism. Such a mechanism, supported by organizational will, economic means, and legal right, would enable a certified archival repository to exercise an aggressive rescue function to save culturally significant digital in-

formation. Without the operation of a formal certification program and a fail-safe mechanism, preservation of the nation's cultural heritage in digital form will likely be overly dependent on marketplace forces.

Garrett 1996, *Preserving Digital Information,* Executive Summary

Ten years old, this report still provides excellent guidance. However we have learned to modify two technical aspects of the quoted advice.

First of all, the task force report overlooks that periodic migration of digital records includes two distinct notions. The first, faithful copying of bit-strings from one substratum to a successor substratum, is simple and reliable. In fact, such copying functionality is provided by every practical computer *operating system.* The second, copying with change of format from a potentially obsolete representation to a more modern replacement, is a complex task requiring highly technical expertise. Even then, it is error-prone. Some potential errors are subtle. Preservation with the assistance of programs written in the code of a virtual computer, described in Chapter 12, minimizes such risks.

A second concern is that periodic certification of an institutional repository as satisfying accepted criteria cannot reliably protect its digital holdings against fraudulent or accidental modification that destroy the holdings' authenticity and might harm eventual users. Ten years after the report suggested the pursuit of reliable digital repositories, no widely accepted schedule of criteria has been created. A fresh attempt to do so began in 2005. In contrast, a widely known cryptographic procedure can protect any digital information with evidence with which any user can decide whether the information is reliably authentic (Chapter 11).

What will information originators and users want? Digital preservation can be considered to be a special case of communication—asynchronous communication which the information sent is not delivered immediately, but is instead stored in a repository until somebody requests it. An information consumer will frequently want answers that resolve his uncertainties about the meaning or the history of information he receives. Digital preservation is a case of information storage in which he will not be able to question the information producers whose work he is reading.

Digital preservation system designers need a clear vision of the threats against which they are asked to protect content. Any preservation plan should address the threats suggested in Table 2.[11]

---

[11] Adapted from Rosenthal 2005. *Requirements for Digital Preservation Systems.*

Table 2: Generic threats to preserved information

Media and Hardware Failures	Failure causes include random bit errors and recording track blemishes, breakdown of embedded electronic components, burnout, and misplaced off-line HDDs, DVDs, and tapes.
Software Failures	All practical software has design and implementation bugs that might distort communicated data.
Communication Channel Errors	Failures include detected errors (IP packet error probability of $\sim 10^{-7}$) and undetected errors (at a bit rate of $\sim 10^{-10}$), and also network deliveries that do not complete within a specified time interval.
Network Service Failures	Accessibility to information might be lost from failures in name resolution, misplaced directories, and administrative lapses.
Component Obsolescence	Before media and hardware components fail they might become incompatible with other system components, possibly within a decade of being introduced. Software might fail because of *format obsolescence* which prevents information decoding and rendering within a decade.
Operator Errors	Operator actions in handling any system component might introduce irrecoverable errors, particularly at times of stress during execution of system recovery tasks.
Natural Disasters	Floods, fires, and earthquakes.
External Attacks	Deliberate information destruction or corruption by network attacks, terrorism, or war.
Internal Attacks	Misfeasance by employees and other insiders for fraud, revenge, or malicious amusement.
Economic and Organization Failures	A repository institution might become unable to afford the running costs of repositories, or might vanish entirely, perhaps through bankruptcy, or mission change so that preserved information suddenly is of no value to the previous custodian.

These threats are not unique to digital preservation, but the long time horizons for preservation sometimes require us to take a different view of them than we do of other information applications. Threats are likely to be correlated. For instance, operators responding to hardware failure are more likely to make mistakes than when they are not hurried and under pressure. And software failures are likely to be triggered by hardware failures that present the software with conditions its designers failed to anticipate or test.

Preservation should be distinguished from conservation and restoration. *Conservation* is the protection of originals by limiting access to them. For instance, museums sometimes create patently imperfect replicas so that they can limit access to irreplaceable and irreparable originals to small numbers of carefully vetted curators and scholars. *Restoration* is the creation of new versions within which attempts have been made to reduce damage.[12] Because audiovisual (A/V) media are so easily damaged and because most A/V documents older than about ten years were recorded as analog signals, restoration is used by broadcasting corporations that plan to replay old material.

1.2   What Would a Preservation Solution Provide?

What might someone a century from now want of information stored today? That person might be a critic who wants to interpret our writings, a businessman who needs to guard against contract fraud, an attorney arguing a case based on property deeds, a software engineer wanting to trace a program's history, an airline mechanic maintaining a 40-year-old airframe, a physician consulting your medical charts of 30 years earlier,[13] or your child constructing a family tree.[14] For some applications, consumers will want, or even demand, evidence that information they depend on is authentic—that it truly is what it purports to be. For every application, they will be disappointed by missing information that they think once existed. They will be frustrated by information that they cannot read or use as they believe was originally intended and possible.

To please such consumers and other clients, we need methods for

- ensuring that a copy of every preserved document survives as long as it might interest potential readers;
- ensuring that authorized consumers can find and use any preserved document as its producers intended, without difficulty from errors introduced by third parties that include archivists, editors, and programmers;
- ensuring that any consumer has accessible evidence to decide whether information received is sufficiently trustworthy for his applications;
- hiding information technology complexity from end users (producers, curators, and consumers);
- minimizing the costs of human labor by automatic procedures whenever doing so is feasible;
- enabling scaling for the information collection sizes and user traffic expected, including empowering editors to package information so as to avoid overloading professional catalogers; and

---

[12] Hess 2001, *The Jack Mullin/Bill Palmer Tape Restoration Project*, illustrates restoration.

[13] Pratt 2006, *Personal Health Information Management*.

[14] Hart 2006, *Digitizing hastens at microfilm vault*, describes a family tree of unusual size and importance to the participants—the genealogical files of the Church of Jesus Christ of Latter Day Saints. Digitization is occurring primarily to provide ready access, rather than for preservation. However, some of the images are on acetate film, which is being rewritten to polyester film.

- allowing each institutional and individual participant as much autonomy as possible for handling preserved information, balancing this objective with that of information sharing.

Many institutions already have digital libraries, and will want to extend their services to durable content. They will want to accomplish this without disruption, such as incompatible change from their installed software.

Information producers will want to please consumers, and archive managers will want to please both producers and consumers. Archive managers are likely to have sufficient contact with producers to resolve information format and protocol issues, but will have personal contact with only a small fraction of their consumer clients.

Information consumers will decide whether to trust preserved information usually without conversations with producers or archivists. Each consumer will accept only a few institutions as origins in a trust graph—perhaps fewer than 20 worldwide for scholarly works. He will trust the machinery under his own control more than he trusts other infrastructure. He will see only information delivered to his local machine.

Digital information might travel from its producer to its consumer by any of several paths—not only using different Internet routes, but also involving different repositories. Which path will actually be used often cannot be predicted by any participant. Consumers, and to some extent also producers, will want the content and format of document instances they receive, or publish, to be independent of the route of transmission.

When a repository shares a holding with another repository—whatever the reason for the sharing might be—the recipient will want the delivery to include information closely associated with that holding. It will further want a ready test that everything needed for rendering the holding and for establishing its authenticity is accessible.

1.3   Why Do Digital Data Seem to Present Difficulties?

We can read from paper without machinery, but need and value mechanical assistance for digital content access for at least the following reasons:

- machinery is needed for content that paper cannot handle, such as recordings of live performances;
- much of every kind of information management and communication can be reduced to clerical rules that machines can execute and share much more quickly, cheaply, and accurately than can human beings;
- we are generating far more content than ever before, want to find particular information rapidly, and want to preserve more than ever before; and

- high performance and reliability depend on complex high-density encoding.

Digital information handling that many people older than 40 years find unnatural and difficult is accepted as natural and easy by many in the next generation. Many of us have personal experience with that. An anecdote might provoke a smile as it illustrates the point. A man was puzzled by a photograph showing six toddlers, each in a big flowerpot and wearing a wreath. He was amazed that every child was smiling and looking in the same direction. He mused aloud, "How did the photographer get them all to sit still simultaneously?" His teenage daughter looked over his shoulder. "Simple, Dad. They just clicked them in!"

A factor in comparisons between reading from paper and exploiting its digital counterpart is our education. We each spent much of our first ten years learning to write on and read from paper. Our later schooling taught us how to write well and interpret complex information represented in natural language. However, as adults we tend to be impatient with whatever effort might be needed to master the digital replacements. In contrast, many of our children are growing up comfortable with computing ideas.

In addition, our expectations for the precision and accuracy of modern information tend to be higher than ever before. Our practical expectations (for health care, for business efficiency, for government transparency, for educational opportunities, and so on) depend more on recorded information than ever before. All these factors make it worthwhile to consider structuring explicit digital representations of shared experience, language, world views, and ontologies implicit in our social fabric. The reliability and trustworthiness that can be accomplished with digital links are much better than what is possible in paper-based archives—an example of technology contributing to rising expectations.

Human beings accept a great deal of vagueness in their communication. This is partly because they have the opportunity to inquire whenever ambiguity proves troublesome. Such inquiry for computer programs is not usually possible, a fortiori not possible for preserved digital objects. For such information, if potential sources of confusion are to be avoided, this must be done before most users might want to ask questions. The care needed with digital technology has a reward, frequently bringing to light previously unnoticed ambiguities, omissions, and other problems, and teaching us to improve the precision with which we speak.

1.4   Characteristics of Preservation Solutions

> Whatever preservation method is applied, the central goal must be to pre-
> serve information integrity; that is, to define and preserve those features of
> an information object that distinguish it as a whole and singular work.
>
> Garrett 1996, *PDITF* p.12

The *Reference Model for an Open Archival Information System* (OAIS)
is a conceptual framework for organizations dedicated to preserving and
providing access to digital information over the long term. An OAIS is an
organization of people and systems responsible for preserving information
over the long-term and making it accessible to a specific class of users. Its
high level repository structure diagram is reproduced in Fig. 1.

This reference model, now an international standard, identifies responsibilities that such an organization must address to be considered an *OAIS*
repository. In order to discharge its responsibilities, a repository must:

- negotiate for and accept content from information producers;
- obtain sufficient content control, both legal and technical, to ensure
  long-term preservation;
- determine which people constitute the *designated community* for which
  its content should be made understandable and particularly helpful;
- follow documented policies and procedures for preserving the content
  against all reasonable contingencies, and for enabling its dissemination
  as authenticated copies of the original, or as traceable to the original;
  and
- make the preserved information available to the designated community,
  and possibly more broadly.

Almost every archive accepts these responsibilities, so that compliance
is seldom an issue. However, the quality of compliance is often a matter
of concern.

Fig. 1 tends to draw analysts' attention to activities inside repositories,
in contrast to drawing attention to the properties of communicated information that are suggested by Fig. 2, which identifies the content transfer
steps that must occur to consummate communication. Since the latter figure more completely suggests the potential information transformations
that might impair the quality of communication than the former, we choose
to focus on its view of digital object storage and delivery. A consequence
is that our attention is drawn more to the structure of and operations on individual preservation objects[15] than to the requirements and characteristics
of digital repositories.

---

[15]   Schlatter 1994, *The Business Object Management System.*

Information transmission is likely to be asynchronous, with the producer depositing information representations in repositories from which consumers obtain it, possibly many years later. For current consumers, the producer might also transmit the information directly. The transfer will often be between machines of different hardware and software architectures. Producers cannot generally anticipate what technology consumers will use, or by which channels information objects will be transmitted, nor do they much care about such details.

Figure 2 helps us discuss preservation reliability and suggests that, in addition to requirements outlined in §1.2, thinking of digital preservation service as an extension of digital information interchange will make implementations rapid and inexpensive. For a comprehensive treatment, we must deal with the entire communication channel from each Fig. 2 producer's knowledge **0** to each eventual consumer's perceptions and judgments **10**, asking and answering the following questions.

- How can today's authors and editors ensure that eventual consumers can interpret information saved today, or use it as otherwise intended?
- What provenance and authenticity information will eventual consumers find useful?
- How can we make authenticity evidence sufficiently reliable, even for sensitive documents?
- How can we make the repository network robust, i.e., insensitive to failures and safe against the loss of the pattern that represents any particular information object?
- How can we motivate authors and editors to provide descriptive and evidentiary metadata as a by-product of their efforts, thereby shifting effort and cost from repository institutions?[16]

Kahn 1995, *A Framework for Distributed Digital Object Services,* http://www.cnri.reston.va.us/home/cstr/arch/k-w.html.

Maly 1999, *Smart Objects, Dumb Archives.*

Pulkowski 2000, *Intelligent Wrapping for Information Sources.*

Payette 2000, *Policy-Enforcing, Policy-Carrying Digital Objects.*

[16] "… preservation in the digital age must be considered at the time of creation. Preservation cannot be an activity relegated to the expertise of libraries and archives, but rather must be seen as intrinsic to the act of creation." *NDIIPP Plan*, p. 52

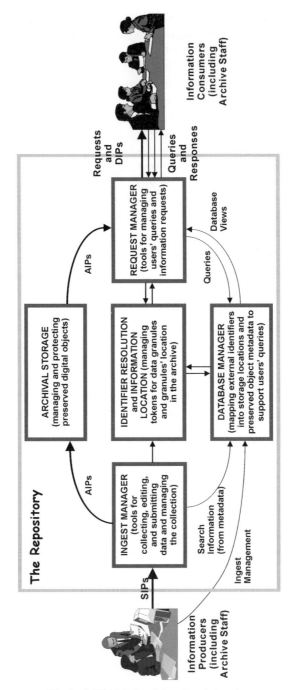

Fig. 1: *OAIS* high-level functional structure

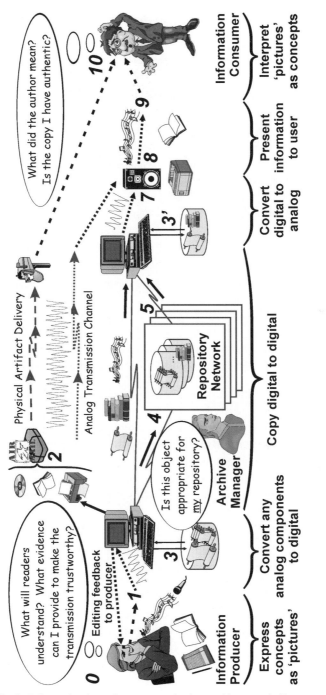

Fig. 2: Information interchange, repositories, and human challenges.
The numerals name input and output objects. Some of these are ephemeral.

Of particular interest in Fig. 2 are the steps that include transformations that might impair communication integrity, as suggested in:

Table 3: Information transformation steps in communication

0 to **1**	Create information to be communicated using human reasoning and knowledge to select what is to be communicated and how to represent it. This is a skillful process that is not well understood.[17]
1 to **2**	Encode human output to create artifacts (typically on paper) that can be stored in conventional libraries and can also be posted.
1 to **3**	Encode analog input to create digital representations, using transformation rules that can be precisely described, together with their inevitable information losses, additions, and distortions.
3 to **4**	Convert locally stored digital objects to what *OAIS* calls Submission Information Packages (SIPs).
4 to **5**	Convert SIPs to *OAIS* Archival Information Packages (AIPs).
5 to **3'**	Convert AIPs to *OAIS* Distribution Information Packages (DIPs).
3' to **7**	Convert digital objects to analog forms that human beings can understand.
7 to **8**	Print or play analog signals, with inevitable distortions that can be described statistically.
6 to **10** **9** to **10**	Convert information received into knowledge, a process called learning and involving immense skills that are not well understood.[18]

It will be important to persuade information originators to capture and describe their works partly because the number of works being produced is overwhelming library resources for capture, packaging, and bibliographic description. It is particularly important because originators know more about their works than anyone else. However, this is offset by the fact that they rarely will be familiar with cataloging and metadata conventions and practices—a problem that might be mitigated by providing semiautomatic tools for these process steps.

Digital capture close to the information generation is especially important for performance data in entertainment and the fine arts, because only producers can capture broadcast output without encountering both copyright barriers and signal degradation. Consider a television broadcast created partly from ephemeral source data collected and linked by data-dependent or human decisions that are not recorded but exist implicitly in the performance itself. Ideally, capturing performances for preservation can be accomplished as a production side effect. More generally, nontech-

---

[17] Ryle 1949, *The Concept of Mind*, Chapter II.

[18] Ibid., Chapter IX.

nical barriers embedded in the channels that connect data sources with a public performance might impede what would be best practice in ideal circumstances.

1.5 Technical Objectives and Scope Limitations

Technology informs almost every aspect of long-term preservation. It is not widely believed that ... solutions can be achieved solely through technological means. ... there is consensus around the following challenges: media and signal degradation; hardware and software obsolescence; volume of information ... urgency because of imminent loss; and ...

NDIIPP, Appendix 1, p.4

The *Open Archival Information Systems (OAIS) Reference Model* and related expositions address the question, "What architecture should we use for a digital repository?" This includes all aspects of providing digital library or archive services, including all important management aspects: management of people, management of resources, organization of institutional processes, selection of collection holdings, and protection against threats to the integrity of collections or quality of client services. Among the threats to collections are the deleterious effects of technology obsolescence and of fading human recollection. Efforts to mitigate these information integrity threats make up only a small fraction of what library and archive managers need to plan and budget for.

In contrast to the *OAIS* question, *Preserving Digital Information* asks a different question, "What characteristics will make saved digital objects useful into the indefinite future?" Such different questions of course have different answers.

Of the several dimensions of digital preservation suggested by the long quotation in §1.1, this book will focus on the technical aspects. We construe the word 'technical' as including clerically executed procedures, just as the word 'technique' spans mechanical and human procedures. Many topics that might appear in a more complete prescription of digital archiving have been thoroughly treated in readily available information technology literature. For such archiving topics, this book is limited to short descriptions that position them among other preservation topics, to relating new technology to widely deployed technology, and to the identification of instructive sources. For instance, digital library requirements and design are discussed only enough to provide context for changes that preservation requirements might induce.

The book is intended to suggest only document management aspects required for preservation, without getting involved with whatever mechanisms people might choose to manage related needs, and without commenting on proposals for satisfying such needs. It avoids most aspects of collection management, most aspects of librarianship, and most aspects of knowledge management. Such restraint not only avoids distracting complexity, but also tends to make the book's preservation recommendations architecturally compatible with installed software for these avoided areas, as well as with most of the literature discussing the other topics.

The book is motivated by the exponentially growing number of "born digital" documents that are mostly not tended by society's libraries and archives. Its technical measures of course extend without modification to works digitized from their traditional predecessors, such as books on paper. They are particularly pertinent to audio/visual archives. However, since the technology needed to maintain analog recordings is already well handled, we include it only by reference (§7.2.4).

Some topics to which the practitioner needs ready access are so well and voluminously described that the current work limits itself to identifying sources, discussing their relationships to the underlying fundamentals and their pertinence to digital preservation, and suggesting source works of good quality. Such topics are XML, with its many specialized dialects and tools, information retrieval, content management of large collections for large numbers of users, and digital security technology. Other prominent topics, such as intellectual property rights management and copyright compliance, are not made significantly more difficult by adding preservation to other digital content management requirements,[19] and are therefore treated only cursorily.

The solution, which we call Trustworthy Digital Object (TDO) methodology, addresses only the portions of the challenge that are amenable to technical measures. Of course, to accomplish this we must clearly distinguish what technology can address from what must be left for human skills, judgements, and taste. For instance, we do not know how to ensure that any entity is trusted, but do know many measures that will allow it to advertise itself as being trustworthy, and to be plausible when it does so. Thus, *Preserving Digital Information* must include an analysis of philosophic distinctions, such as that between trusted and trustworthy, in order to provide a good foundation for justifying the correctness and optimality of TDO methodology.

Many published difficulties with what is required for long-term digital preservation are digital content management issues that would exist even if material carriers, digital hardware, and computer programs had unbounded practical lifetimes. This book therefore separates, as much as possible, considerations of durable document structure, of digital collection man-

---

[19]   Gladney 2000, *Digital Intellectual Property: Controversial and International Aspects.*

agement, and of repository management. It says little about internal repository workings that relate eventual outputs to histories of inputs, but instead treats repositories as black boxes whose interior mechanisms are private to the staffs of repository institutions. This approach has the desirable side-effect that we minimize meddling in other people's business.

1.6 Summary

Digital preservation is critical to most of the history of the future.[20] This justifies every practical effort to ensure that the technical methodology used to accomplish it is sound and widely understood.

As business, government, and cultural records migrate from paper to digital media, the importance of digital archives will increase. Enterprises considering creating and managing repositories know that a document might be important five to 100 years later, and that technical obsolescence might by then make it irretrievable in any meaningful way. For instance, pharmaceutical development records must be held until the risk of lawsuits subsides many years after the drugs are sold. Doing this safely and inexpensively is not general practice today.

Consideration of the reliability of information on which we depend must include recognition that deceit can permeate agendas and transactions and that information flows so rapidly and in such great quantities that human errors are inevitable. Even if we had the resources to examine each saved record carefully, we would find it difficult or impossible to predict how it might be used and what risks its user might incur. Such circumstances motivate a strategy to protect all objects as if they were targets of attacks that destroy their integrity. A solution that is inexpensive in the document preparation needed for preservation, possibly with significant costs limited to the small fraction of objects that their eventual users decide to test, would be economical for all preserved data objects. Happily, such a solution exists (Chapter 11) and can be implemented to be an almost automatic side effect of saving documents that are being edited, or opening preserved documents for viewing.

We emphasize end user needs—what people acting in well-defined roles might need or want to accomplish specific tasks, rather than emphasizing how repositories might work. Preservation can be viewed as a special case of information sharing. It is special because consumers cannot obtain producers' responses for puzzling aspects or missing information.

---

[20] Cullen 2000, *Authenticity in a Digital Environment*, http://www.clir.org/pubs/reports/pub92/cullen.html.

Digital preservation is a different topic than repository management. The distinction is made particularly clearly in the program of the National Archives of Australia, which partitions its system into three components that share documents only by transported storage media: a quarantine server, a preservation server, and a digital repository.[21]

The book is limited to technical aspects of preservation, leaving social and managerial aspects of repositories and more general document management to other authors. It discusses digital repository design only to the extent necessary to provide preservation context—the technical infrastructure into which preservation software must be integrated.

Throughout, the book's focus is directed toward methods for preserving each intellectual work, leaving the management of repositories and social factors, such as training of archival personnel, to other treatments. The key novel challenges are:

- ensuring that a copy of every preserved document survives "forever";
- ensuring that any consumer can decide whether or not to trust a preserved document; and
- ensuring that consumers can use any preserved document as its authors intended.

---

[21]   Wilson 2003, *Access Across Time: How the NAA Preserves Digital Records,* http://www.erpanet.org/events/2003/rome/presentations/Wilson.ppt.

2 Economic Trends and Social Issues

> Digital technology ... has spawned a surfeit of information that is extremely
> fragile, inherently impermanent, and difficult to assess for long-term value.
> ... [I]t is increasingly difficult for libraries to identify what is of value, to
> acquire it, and to ensure its longevity over time.
>
> Never has access to information that is authentic, reliable, and complete
> been more important, and never has the capacity of ... heritage institutions
> to guarantee that access been in greater jeopardy. Recognizing the value that
> the preservation of past knowledge has played ..., the U.S. Congress seeks
> ... solutions to the challenges [of] ... preserving digital information of cul-
> tural and social significance.   NDIIPP *Plan*, p.1

We are in the midst of widespread changes in how people interact with
information, how it affects their lives, and how information will be managed in a networked world.[22]

In the digital environment, computer programming is codifying ideas
and principles that, historically, have been fuzzy or subjective, or that have
been based on situational legal or social constructs.[23]

2.1 The Information Revolution

> The new Information Revolution began in business and has gone farthest in
> it. But it is about to revolutionize education and health care. [T]he changes
> in concepts will in the end be at least as important as the changes in tools
> and technology. It is generally accepted now that education technology is
> due for profound changes and that with them will come profound changes in
> [institutional] structure. ... It is becoming clearer every day that these tech-
> nical changes will—indeed must—lead to redefining what is meant by *edu-
> cation.* One probable consequence: the center of gravity in higher education
> ... may shift to the continuing professional education of adults during their
> entire working lives. ...
>
> Everybody today believes that the present Information Revolution is un-
> precedented in reducing the cost of, and in the spreading of, information—
> whether measured by the cost of a "byte" or by computer ownership—and in
> the speed and sweep of its impact. These beliefs are simply nonsense.
>
> At the time Gutenberg introduced the press, there was a substantial in-
> formation industry in Europe. It was probably Europe's biggest employer.
> It consisted of hundreds of monasteries, many of which housed large num-
> bers of highly skilled monks. Each monk labored from dawn to dusk, six

---

[22] Mitchell 2003. *Beyond Productivity, Information Technology, Innovation, and Creativity.*
Perkings 2004. *Beyond Productivity: Culture and Heritage Resources in the Digital Age.*
See also a dozen articles in the Communications of the ACM 48(10), *The Digital Society*, 2005.

[23] Lessig 1999, *The Law of the Horse: What Cyberlaw Might Teach.*

days a week, copying books by hand. ... Fifty years later, by 1500, the monks had become unemployed. These monks (some estimates go well above ten thousand for all of Europe) had been replaced by a very small number of lay craftsmen, the new "printers," totaling perhaps one thousand, but spread over all of Europe.

Drucker 1999, Management Challenges, p.100

For many years newspapers and the computing trade press have talked about the "Information Revolution." Drucker suggests that in IT (Information Technology), the "T" part has occurred and the "I" part is yet to happen. Changes as disruptive as those induced by the sixteenth century invention of movable type do not yet seem to be complete. Ongoing, paradigm-changing information service developments[24] include:

- Personal communications to/from anywhere.
- Office tools enabling self-publication.
- Search and information retrieval functionality with steadily increasing sophistication and speed.
- Hypertext, reducing the drudgery of following bibliographic references.
- Digital storage cheap enough to save and share almost any data.
- Massive customized communication to select audiences.
- Intellectual property made more valuable, and also more at risk, by easy copying and distribution.
- Security and encryption, providing tools to control information access.
- Partnerships with more cooperation and sharing becoming essential for success and efficiency.[25]
- Student population shifts to include social groups that previously had not been much involved.
- Global awareness with rapid communication internationalizing all aspects of life.
- Political and social volatility enhanced by easier, faster information use and misuse.

This list reflects the writings, talks and informal conversation of librarians and scholars. Is it complete? Surely not. For instance, it does not hint at induced employment shifts. Even enterprise survival will sometimes be threatened by changes that are widely believed to be imminent.[26]

---

[24]   Neal 1998, *Chaos Breeds Life: Finding Opportunities for Library Advancement.*

[25]   IBM 2004, *Global Innovation Outlook,* http://t1d.www-306.cacheibm.com/e-business/ ondemand/us/pdf/IBM_GIO_2004.pdf.

[26]   Brown 1995, *Universities in the Digital Age.*

In the next five years, humanity will generate more data—from Web sites to digital photos and video—than it generated in the previous 1,000 years. Managing growing data collections is already a crisis for many institutions, from hospitals to banks to universities, that have not previously faced such a flood of data and the complexity caused by rising expectations.[27] In 1996, companies spent 11 percent of their IT budgets on storage, but that figure is likely to double to 22 percent in 2007.[28]

How much can this information be trusted? For what purposes? Perceptions of reports, especially when they become consensus opinion, can often mislead because they hide methodological failures. An indicident within IBM is illustrative. For a prospective business widely regarded with optimism, market estimates were scarce and new estimates would have been expensive and late. That problem seemed resolved by an unexpected consulting publication from a respected source whose estimates supported opinions within IBM. We were happy to pay $2,000 for the report, and launched product development. Months later, an analyst wondered about the consultant's estimates, and telephoned him to inquire how they had been developed. The answer: "Oh, I telephoned Mr. X at IBM HQ and asked how big he thought the market would be."

We do not have enough skills and resources to pursue all the manifest opportunities and challenges. If the evaluations alluded to are to be used to guide policy and action, they merit careful investigation to project their likely economic significance and implications for decisions about managing libraries.[29] We need to decide which designs have greatest leverage and will most please users—both end users and service personnel. We should make the critical choices in cognizance of quantitative estimates.

2.2   Economic and Technical Trends

Nevertheless, it is already clear that the usage patterns of digital records are challenging the traditional assumption that the value of the scientific record decays rapidly—far more 'older' content is being used than was previously the case. This is a function of the ease of access to large historical files at the desk top and through the same interface.

---

[27]   According to a trade article, Kodak manages more than 1 billion images for 23 million online users. In 2006, vendors are offering NAS stores larger than 500 terabytes (5×10^{14} bytes) and are pressed by customers for even larger fast storage arrays that are robust and easily managed. Apicello 2006, *The New NAS: Fast, cheap, scalable,* http://www.infoworld.com/article/06/06/15/78995_25FEnascluster_1.html.

[28]   From the International Technology Group of Los Altos, CA.

[29]   Wolf 1999, *By the Dawn's Early Light.*

Besides the economic value of building new ideas on the scientific record, there are equally examples of economic loss resulting from scientific records that have not been preserved and are therefore no longer accessible. Some research may be easy and inexpensive to replicate—in which case the costs of data preservation may be difficult to justify. Other research may be literally unrepeatable—or only repeatable at unacceptable cost.

Concerns about the robustness of the digital scientific record also create a major disincentive for libraries to switch from print to electronic in their collection development strategies and holdings. Maintaining a hybrid print and electronic collection within a library creates significant financial and organizational inefficiencies.[30]

Progress toward a digital commons has been accelerating.[31] Perhaps this is because key thresholds have been attained—an immense Internet and millions of WWW users, storage media so inexpensive that it no longer matters much how much storage space is required, a good start toward publicly available information digitally represented, and so on. Recent developments that will probably engender massive changes include:

- Emerging competition in inexpensive search services, which are extending to desktop search and services tailored for particular communities (such as Google for scholars). Only a fraction of the known search techniques have been exploited.
- Large collections of content not encumbered by intellectual property constraints.
- Open courseware such as that offered by The Massachusetts Institute of Technology.
- Advocacy group activity, such as those of the Center for the Digital Future and the Creative Commons.
- Inexpensive streaming media services for news and for music.
- "Grass roots" news services, such as WikiNews.[32]
- Increasing efforts to make running storage and application servers "as easy as turning on a faucet."[33]

---

[30]   European Task Force for Permanent Access to the Records of Science 2005, *Strategic Action Programme 2006–2010*, p. 8.

[31]   The Museum of Media History (http://www.broom.org/epic/ provides a compressed history of the next decade in the form of a video presentation, which starts, "The New York Times has gone offline. The fourth estate's fortunes have waned. What happened to the news?"
Bernard Golden provides whimsical open source predictions. http://oetrends.com/news.php?action=view_record&idnum=381.

[32]   Gillmor 2004, *We the Media.*

[33]   *Special Technology Report,* BusinessWeek, Nov. 9, 2004.

2.2.1 Digital Storage Devices

Falling prices of persistent magnetic storage—hard disk drives (HDDs)—will revolutionize how documents are stored, organized, and used. HDD improvements tend to affect document management shortly after they become available in the marketplace. The price trends most easily understood are those of PC components retailed to private consumers.

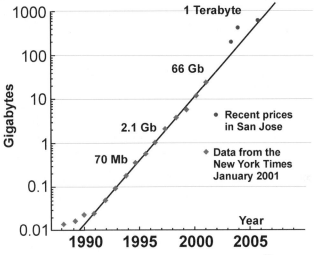

Fig. 3: How much PC storage will $100 buy? [34]

Fig. 3 suggests steady HDD cost lowering at approximately 28% per annum starting in 1991. (This graph is for "bare" PC HDDs. Storage configured as server arrays is about ten times as expensive, partly because it comes with hardware and software infrastructure for much higher reliability and performance.) Industry commentators suggest reasons to expect this trend to continue until at least 2010.[35] By 2009, $100 will buy over one terabyte, whose capacity is suggested by Table 3. Storage space in PCs will continue to increase, because no PC vendor can save money by reducing storage sizes below what about $30 will buy. This is partly because the manufacturing cost of HDD moving parts, electronics, and packaging is insensitive to recording density improvements. The marketplace effect is that PC vendors steadily increase the storage capacity of their PC offerings.

---

[34] For a review of the technical trend from 1956 to 1997, see Schechter 1997, *Leading the Way in Storage* and also Anderson 2003, *You Don't Know Jack about Disks.*

[35] Thompson 1999, *The future of magnetic data storage technology.*

In early 2006, one terabyte external storage units designed for home computers became available for about $700. These include software to make automatic file backup and recovery convenient. A computer user who wonders, "What would I ever do with that much space?" (Table 2) might be interested to hear that disk manufacturers have for more than twenty years asked, "How can we keep existing factories profitably busy?" Since then, capacity increases have been matched by new applications, and the dollar size of the storage industry has increased. Although nobody can be sure that interesting applications will grow as fast as manufacturing capacity, market projections continue to be optimistic.

Table 3: How much can be stored in one terabyte?

Feature movies	4 gigabyte each	250 films
Television-quality video	2 gigabyte/hour	500 hours
CD music	560 megabyte/disk	1,800 hours
Medical X-rays	10 megabyte each	100,000 pictures
Scanned color images	1 megabyte each	1,000,000 images
Scanned B/W images	50,000 bytes/page	20,000,000 pages
Encoded text	3300 bytes/page	300,000,000 pages

Backup tapes show similar price/performance trends, with up to 1.6 Terabytes on a single tape reel, at a street price of about 10¢ per Gigabyte.

Price trends of electronic components used in other machinery are more difficult to project because they are governed by pricing policies and business practices that embed consulting, software, and other service costs. Disk arrays configured for high performance and reliability (§9.3.1) can be an order of magnitude more expensive than PC HDDs.[36] However, their price trend is similar to that suggested by Fig. 3.

Telecommunications prices are particularly difficult to predict because transmission networks are deployed through massive, multiyear infrastructure projects and changing government regulations.[37] Just how difficult it is to track and estimate communication costs and prices was illustrated by the agonies of the fiber-optic network companies. They vastly overbuilt and much of the fiber will never be used, but simply be left to rot in the ground. Arguably, even those best positioned and motivated to know costs, applications, and markets "got it wrong." Accurate estimates would take into account the distortions caused by "winner take all" markets.

---

[36]   Gilheany 2000, *Projecting the Cost of Magnetic Disk Storage over the Next 10 Years,*
       http://www.archivebuilders.com/whitepapers/22011p.pdf.

[37]   Odlyzko 2003, *The many paradoxes of broadband.*

2.2.2 Search Technology

Today's most effective information discovery infrastructure is Internet catalogs and search engines—no longer the catalogs of research libraries.[38] Of course, research library catalogs are part of this and the *Dark Web*.

The ACM Special Interest Group on Information Retrieval[39] has tracked the vast search literature for about forty years. Three IEEE journals provide online numbers on recent technical developments[40] that include personalized research results and context sensitivity, geographically sensitive search, and enhancing user convenience with graphical maps of search "hits".

Tools similar to Web-search tools are appearing for individual consumers' local collections—PC files and electronic mail—and to limit search to Internet subsets, e.g., Google Scholar. Their usefulness is enhanced by quality ratings for periodicals.[41] In addition,

> Enterprise search engines ... unlike Web search engines, can search files no matter what [their] format ... or what repository contains them. ... [They] enable classification, taxonomies, personalization, profiling, agent alert, ... collaborative filtering, and real-time analysis, ... ability ... to add servers to scale up ..., metadata search, international [language] support, ... fault tolerance, ... security management for document access control and communication protocol encryption, ... and software development kits that let users construct search-enabled applications with no need for reengineering. The differentiating factor for enterprise search engines is how well these various features are deployed, as well as the relevance of the results they generate.[42]

In view of the current business and scholarly interest in information discovery, and the immense literature that has not been systematically exploited, we expect many practical enhancements.[43] These will include combining the best features of current separate offerings. Research groups are also investigating adding semantics to search engines that currently use

---

[38] Lossau 2004, *Search Engine Technology and Digital Libraries.*

[39] ACM Special Interest Group for Information Retrieval, http://www.acm.org/sigir/.

[40] *IEEE MultiMedia* looks at the growing amount of digital visual information, and asks, "Is It Time for a Moratorium on Metadata?" *IEEE Intelligent Systems* examines searching from cell phones. *IEEE Distributed Systems Online* addresses personalization and asks, "What's Next in Web Search?" The Digicult *Thematic Issue 6* treats the topic from the perspective of cultural heritage enthusiasts.

[41] Schwartz 2004, *How to Quickly Find Articles in the Top IS Journals.*

[42] Wang 2004, *Enterprise Search.*

[43] Asadi 2004, *Shifts in search engine development.*
Barrows 2006, *Search Considered Integral.*

only document keys and syntactic features, as well as administrative mechanisms to limit collection access to authorized users.[44]

2.3   Democratization of Information

The number of people who read, create, and update information is large and growing. It is larger than ever before, both absolutely and as a population fraction. This is only partly because of the amazing decrease in information technology costs. (These costs include the human time costs of learning how to use digital machinery and of exploiting it. In fact, human time costs are today the biggest economic constraint on adoption of digital services.) The number of information users is larger than ever before also because citizens are better educated, have more time for discretionary activities, and have easier opportunities for cultural involvement than ever before, especially in wealthy nations.

Technology and economics are changing the roles and methods of most knowledge workers and of all enterprises. Stenography has almost vanished as a profession, probably largely because authors now have tools to write better and more quickly without clerical assistance. Resources for whose effective exploitation most people used to need the help of specialists are increasingly accessible to almost anyone. End users' dependencies on professional mediation will continue to decrease. Even personal digital libraries will become practical within a decade[45] if they are not so already today.[46]

Internet activities do not seem to be decreasing people's enthusiasm for traditional libraries. My town library is probably typical. Serving about 30,000 people, it is occupied by 50–100 patrons at any time of day, and twice that number after school hours. The San Jose city library network, which serves about 900,000 people, reports similarly strong statistics for 2004–5: 5.4 million patron visits—more than the combined annual attendance at San Francisco Bay Area major league baseball games; 13.5 million loans, nearly triple the number of 1994–5; 2.1 million holdings pur-

---

[44]   Teets 2006, *Metasearch Authentication and Access Management.*

[45]   Beagrie 2005, *Plenty of Room at the Bottom? Personal Digital Libraries and Collections.*

Peters 2002, *Digital repositories: individual, discipline-based, institutional, consortial, or national?*

Tomaiuolo 2004, *Building a World Class Personal Library with Free Web Resources,* http://www.ccsu.edu/library/tomaiuolon/theweblibrary.htm.

[46]   The Greenstone Digital Library seems ready for this today. See http://www.greenstone.org/cgi-bin/library for a description and download.

chased in the last ten years; and 400 on-premises computers with Internet access available to the public.

2.4 Social Issues

We are generating material faster than we are taking care of it, without thought for the long-term value. The pace of technology means faster lock out of material. There is a high expectation by users in the networked world that they can use search tools like Google to locate information. Researchers are now becoming concerned about data management and are beginning to realise the value and need for personal archiving, reinvention, and replication. There is a lack of tools and education—for both professionals and researchers—coupled with a lack of review mechanisms for scientific and other digital archives. Academic literacy is changing and there is a growing democratization of the publication process. More requirements will be made of data from scholarly publishing.

W2005, p.10

In the *cultural history community,* how to absorb and exploit the digital revolution is replete with unresolved challenges, particularly when long-term preservation of digital artifacts is considered. Depending on what one considers to be the bounds of the topic, this community has addressed it with between 200 and 800 scholarly papers in the last ten years. These mostly describe the challenge without offering prescriptions for action.[47]

Data processing professionals seem mostly to have ignored the digital preservation concerns expressed in this literature, perhaps because most engineers are employed in the private sector. Computer scientists have paid little attention to long-term preservation of digital holdings, perhaps because they believe that it presents no deep unsolved problems. Computer scientists and engineers seem not to have heard any call to action for preservation of cultural heritage materials because its proponents are a tiny community.[48]

University and national research libraries and government archives have paid more attention to digital preservation than have business communities—even those in business areas that depend on information being available many years after it was first produced. On the other hand, the private

---

[47] "Although many aspects of digital preservation have received attention since the mid-1990s, most of the presentations and papers on the subject have ended with little more than general comments about the complexity and expense of the tasks, and ambiguity about responsibilities and roles."
Marcum 2003, *Research Questions for the Digital Era Library*

[48] The Research Libraries Group has approximately 100 members. If each of these has 10 employees dedicated to managing digital materials (a generous estimate), that's about 1000 people. However, only a small fraction of those express concern about digital preservation. In contrast, the software professionals' society, the ACM, has approximately 90,000 members.

sector seems to be ten years ahead of educational and cultural heritage institutions in exploiting digital content management technology. Digital
content management for business and government enterprises is both well
understood and a flourishing field of innovation. An exception is the topic
of long-term preservation, perhaps because businesses focus on short-term
benefits that include destroying records as soon as legally prudent.

A comment from library executives seems to epitomize a cultural heritage community consensus. "In summary, digital is not generally viewed
as a suitable long-term preservation archival surrogate for print. It is currently regarded more as an access medium. As a preservation medium, [it
is seen] as unstable, experimental, immature, unproven on a mass scale
and unreliable in the long-term."[49] This summation should not be accepted
without thorough examination of the context within which it was made.
Whose perspective is represented? What questions were the speakers
asked to address? Its source is a poll of the directors of 16 major libraries—mostly people with a liberal arts background, apparently without any
technical experts.[50] They were asked only about digital surrogates for content already held in older formats (on paper and other media), and only
about current practice, not about how means and controlling social conventions (including legal constraints) might evolve in either the near or the
distant future.

There are repeated calls for cross-disciplinary cooperation, such as,
"The ubiquity of the digital preservation problem speaks to the value of
collaboration and consensus building for resolving the challenges and uncertainties of managing digital materials over the long term,"[51] and "The
bed-rock of research in this area is to understand in more detail the sociol-
ogy of preserving and sharing information. This will include understanding better disciplinary differences, and in particular those requirements that

---

[49] British Library report, *Digital versus print as a preservation format – expert views from
international comparator libraries,* http://www.bl.uk/about/collectioncare/digpres1.html.
Compare the Trithemius story on page 4.

[50] Consider the implications of C.P. Snow's *The Two Cultures*, 1959. The slim volume documents
a 1995 Cambridge University lecture.

"as one moves through intellectual society from the physicists to the literary intellectuals, there
are all kinds of tones of feeling on the way. But I believe the pole of total incomprehension of
science radiates its influence on all the rest. That total incomprehension gives, much more
pervasively than we realise, living in it, an unscientific flavour to the whole `traditional' culture,
and that unscientific flavour is often, much more than we admit, on the point of turning anti-
scientific. The feelings of one pole become the anti-feelings of the other. If the scientists have
the future in their bones, then the traditional culture responds by wishing the future did not exist.
It is the traditional culture, to an extent remarkably little diminished by the emergence of the
scientific one, which manages the western world." (p. 7)

[51] Lavoie 2005, *Preservation Metadata,* http://www.dpconline.org/docs/reports/dpctw05-01.pdf.

are fundamental versus those that are primarily historical. For a cultural change to take place, it is important to involve key stakeholders and resource providers and for them to drive this process."[52]

The literature from which the foregoing librarians' viewpoints were almost surely derived never considers the business climate, particularly as it is influenced by the free enterprise system that has been chosen by Western European and North American countries.[53] The technology that creates better access to information to more people than has ever before been available is mostly created by private enterprise, whose rules of engagement emphasize responsiveness to markets.[54] Libraries have mostly not behaved like customers in their interactions with technology vendors.[55] Even if they acted differently, industry is unlikely to see museums, archives, and research libraries as promising sources of revenue. They are simply too few, and their collections are likely to be much smaller than business collections, at least for the next decade.

2.5   Documents as Social Instruments

Computers are "artifacts made by us and for us. You'd think that it would be part of our common heritage to understand them. Their insides are open to inspection, their designers generally understand the principles behind them, and it is possible to communicate this knowledge … 'But,' say the inquisitive, 'there must be more to it,' thinking that some deep problems inherent to computers force the outward complexity. … Superstitions grow rampant when testing is subjective, difficult, and (usually) not performed at all."[56]

> Books and paper documents set a useful precedent not only for document design, but for information technology design in general. In a time of abundant and even superabundant raw information, they suggest that the better path in creating social documents (and social communities) lies not in the di-

---

[52] W2005, p. 10.

[53] What follows might be seen as a polemic that inadequately considers the value of cultural collections, but this is not intended. Instead it is simply a reminder of well known economic facts that need to be considered by heritage institution managers.

[54] Some readers will protest with examples of inventions made by university employees. Such readers should consider the difference between invention and innovation, and what work is necessary to make inventions useful for the public at large.

[55] My source for this opinion is limited, but authoritative. During a decade of working on IBM's digital content management offerings, I often worked with representatives of major libraries. Their institutions thought of IBM as a partner, not as a vendor, and acted as if they expected IBM's products to be made available below the cost of producing them.

[56] Raskin, 2004, *Silicon Superstitions*.

rection of increasing amounts of information and increasingly full representation, but rather in leaving increasing amounts un[represented] or underrepresented. Efficient communication relies not on how much can be said. but on how much can be left unsaid and even unread in the background. And a certain amount of fixity, both in material documents and in social conventions of interpretation, contributes a great deal to this sort of efficiency.

Brown 1995, *The Social Life of Information*, p.205

Analyses of the historical and social roles of documents[57]—particularly documents represented on paper—and the pervasive importance of trust relationships guide what follows.

2.5.1 Ironic?

Avoiding small errors is helpful when the data being preserved represent natural language text, and essential if the data include computer programs. For about ten years, two approaches—*transformative migration* and *system emulation*—dominated the discussion of technology for information preservation, almost excluding any other thinking.[58] Extensive debates have neither resolved any of the issues that make them problematical, nor demonstrated that either method precludes errors.

> The emulation-versus-migration debate has largely played itself out. Neither approach provides a sufficient, general answer to the problem of digital preservation, and it has proven largely fruitless to debate the merits of these approaches in the abstract.[59] Instead, there is growing recognition that different kinds of information captured in different ways for long-term preservation will need various kinds of support.
>
> Waters 2002. *Good Archives Make Good Scholars*

In this, "growing recognition ... various kinds of support" seems futile, because Waters neither describes nor references specific measures for "different kinds of information." Furthermore, the statement suggests pessimism about invention of a single integrated set of measures—pessimism that we believe premature because inquiries are at an early stage, rather than a terminal stage.

---

[57] Brown 2002, *The Social Life of Information*.
Levy 2003, *Scrolling Forward: Making Sense of Documents in the Digital Age*.

[58] A third proposal has recently appeared in a Dutch project, and also in an Australian project. These consider XML as an alternative to migration and emulation. This is a curious approach, something like considering apple trees as an alternative to apples, because XML should be used together with other measures for complex data types, rather than instead of other measures.

[59] Waters calls this a "largely polemical debate on the relative merits of emulation and migration." For more balanced viewpoints, see Granger 2000, *Emulation as a Digital Preservation Strategy*.

Pessimism about digital preservation seems to have infected the research library and archive community.[60] Recent writings describe the circumstances as ironic, along lines illustrated in:

> The problem faced by [those] who aim to preserve history by preserving [digital] records is that [they] ... may be as ephemeral as messages written in the sand at low tide ... It is ironic that the primitive technology of ancient times has produced records lasting hundreds of years, while today's advanced electronic world is creating records that may become unreadable in a few years' time.
>
> The correct interpretation of records has always required knowledge of the language in which they were written, and sometimes of other subjects too .... Fortunately enough of this knowledge has survived that we can make sense of most of the records that have come down to us. ... Just as interpretation of the 1086 Domesday Book depends on the dictionaries and grammars for mediaeval Latin painstakingly compiled by long-dead scholars, interpretation of contemporary electronic records ... will only be possible if the necessary methods and tools are ... preserved now.
>
> Darlington 2003, *PRONOM ... Compendium of File Formats*

The putative statistic on which "ironic" is based involves an unreasonable comparison, viz., the fact that some old paper documents have survived compared to the fact that some digital documents might not survive. Consider also the following historical, technical, and economic factors.

- Beginning roughly 3000 years ago, society has built an immense paper management infrastructure. (The largest civilian bureaucracy in the U.S. is the United States Postal Service, with approximately 700,000 employees.) It has also invested heavily in education for using paper. We began to share digital objects only 20–30 years ago. It is hardly surprising that the infrastructure and education for handling paper have not yet been matched by that for digital equivalents.
- It being unnecessary, we are unwilling to work as hard on modern information as did the "long-dead scholars" who "painstakingly" compiled ancient dictionaries and grammars.

---

[60] Among symptoms of pessimism, the supposed high cost is noteworthy.

"Imagine a digital world in which [books] had recently been invented. You are head of information services for a major research university (providing all those services digitally ...), and have to persuade your Vice-Chancellor to invest in a new facility for [books], maybe a couple of million of them (only a fraction of the numbers of objects in your digital stores). You can probably script the interview yourself... 'You want a special building with 10 floors, with huge floor loadings and a special environment? You want 200 staff? You want how many million pounds? And after all that, the users have to go into the facility to access these books? You must be kidding me; get out of my sight!'"

Rusbridge 2006, *Some Digital Preservation Fallacies*

- The amounts of information under discussion today are orders of magnitude greater than those of information on paper. The Internet Archive has saved and indexed the text of over 10^{10} pages.[61] An IBM Research service called WebFountain has gathered a 500-terabyte database for analysis.[62] There is little a priori reason to doubt that such collections can be made to survive forever.

- WebFountain scours Web logs, newspaper stories, and other sources, and searches this content for patterns that the most dedicated librarian cannot find. Instead of just matching patterns, it analyzes a subject in 50 different ways (for instance, by noting how often two people's names are associated) to answer questions precisely.

- Today's data quality measures are much more rigorous (less than 1 undetected character error in 10^{10}) than those that have been and are still accepted as adequate for documents stored on paper.

- The marketplace has not yet asked for long-term retention.[63] Instead, what people have asked of digital technology is fast search, fast access from a distance, and immense capacity—qualities neither expected of nor delivered by paper. Today's commercial market for records management apparently wants controls and automation for discarding records as soon as the law permits and operational needs have been satisfied.[64] In recent years, that has been more urgent than preservation automation.

- Research libraries and archives are not an attractive market for software offerings, partly because there are so few of them, but even more because they seem to expect industry to provide technology below cost, e.g., by asking for donations at the same time as they try to acquire technology.

Arguably, digital preservation lags digital access because society values rapid gratification over enduring value. Perhaps Darlington calls the situa-

---

[61] The British Government recently archived many of its Web pages, ensuring preservation by way of a contract between the U.K. Public Record Office and the Internet Archive.

[62] Quint 2006, *IBM's WebFountain Launched–The Next Big Thing?* http://www.infotoday.com/newsbreaks/nb030922-1.shtml.

[63] Spedding 2003, *Great data, but will it last?* reports typical academic technical pessimism and marketplace optimism. See http://www.researchinformation.info/rispring03data.html.

[64] For an example of software industry response, see Miller 2004, *Coming Soon: E-Records*, http://www.db2mag.com/shared/printableArticle.jhtml?articleID=17602314. IBM's recently announced TotalStorage offering emphasizes managing records consistently with the data retention and corporate governance requirements of laws and regulations such as Sarbanes-Oxley, HIPAA, and SEC Regulation 17a-4.

tion "ironic" because National Archives personnel want quick gratification of their priority—durable copies. If so, that would be ironic!

Paper of durable importance is often unprotected because archiving it can be expensive. For instance, in 1991, an IBM Research group and a California Department of Transportation (DOT) department considered a digital library (DL) pilot for the construction and inspection records of thousands of bridges. While working on a proposal, they visited the records room of a DOT regional office. It was in a clay-floored basement, with 30-year old drawings, handwritten notes, and typescripts stored in cardboard boxes. A sprinkler system had been installed for fire protection. Imagine working with soggy, partially burned records!

That different opinions exist about preservation alternatives is illustrated by what an IBM team learned in conversations with California Government agencies in the early 1990s. At least one agency was planning to copy its digital records to microfilm for safety. At the same time the California Vital Records department was planning to create a digital library into which 60 years of birth, death, and marriage records were to be scanned. The Vital Records problem was that its microfiche cards could be read and reproduced only with deteriorating machinery whose vendor had vanished, so that spare parts were no longer available.

2.5.2 Future of the Research Libraries

The real question for libraries is, what's the 'value proposition' they offer in a digital future? I think it will be what it has always been: their ability to scan a large universe of knowledge out there, choose a subset of that, and gather it for description and cataloging so people can find reliable and authentic information easily. The only difference: librarians will have a much bigger universe to navigate.

Abby Smith in Wade 2005, *The Infinite Library*

The cultural heritage community works only sporadically across disciplinary boundaries. There is a hampering difference of social style. Scientists and engineers value criticism as a tool. Research librarians seem to hate it, valuing (the appearance of) consensus over almost every other expression of opinion about their business. The "not invented here" syndrome is rife. Preparation for digital preservation is uneven.[65]

"It has been almost universally true that established players were not the leaders in taking advantage of a new technology."[66] Research libraries and

---

[65]   Kenney 2005, *Cornell Survey of Institutional Readiness,* http://www.rlg.org/en/
page.php?Page_ID=20744#article0.

Lynch 2005, *Where Do We Go from Here? The Next Decade for Digital Libraries.*

[66]   Odlyzko 1997, *Silicon dreams and silicon bricks: the continuing evolution of libraries.*

archival institutions will not be leaders in determining their own digital futures unless they achieve significant changes in their internal attitudes, skills, and methods.

Information retrieval might be a harbinger of things to come. The initiative in search has moved from libraries and reference librarians to commercial search services and their software engineers. What is next? Storage and delivery of content? The leader in salvaging Web pages seems to be the Internet Archive (IA),[67] a not-for-profit business that is closely linked to a for-profit business.[68] IA has established partnerships with a few leading libraries.

Implementing a digital preservation solution within an existing information infrastructure can make nontechnical problems—social and organizational problems—vanish and perhaps later appear not to have been problems at all. This is feasible without disrupting existing repository service. Much effort and money could be saved by eliminating certain current activities. However, vested interests would probably oppose such a change.

Personal digital libraries are likely to contribute to some amount of disintermediation. What people want to preserve will include many more objects than traditional libraries can handle, and include works outside traditional library scopes. Self-archiving has already begun on a significant scale.[69] Tools to make packaging and durable descriptions convenient[70] are likely to be much improved from what is already available.[71]

As with other information services, skills previously found only among specially trained professional librarians are being acquired by many amateurs.[72] Many adults are uncomfortable with using computers except for the most routine clerical functions, but our children and their children are not. Some observers will surely argue in favor of professionally generated metadata—an argument with some merit. However, the fact that authors will be strongly motivated to make their works easily found largely offsets such arguments, particularly with tools likely to emerge in the next ten years.

---

[67]   *Internet Archive,* http://www.archive.org/.

[68]   *Alexa Internet,* http://pages.alexa.com/company/history.html.

[69]   Swan 2005, *Open access self-archiving,* http://cogprints.org/4385/.

[70]   Barton 2003, *Building Quality Assurance into Metadata Creation.*

[71]   Liu 2005, *Born-Again Bits,* http://www.eliterature.org/pad/bab.html.

[72]   Montfort 2004, *Acid Free Bits*: *Recommendations for Long-Lasting Electronic Literature,* "is a plea for writers to work proactively in archiving their own creations, and to bear these issues in mind even in the act of composition."

2.5.3   Cultural Chasm around Information Science

Top-down analysis is commonly used in the information technology professions, but might not be a comfortable method in other professions concerned with digital preservation.

A 1996 panel discussion drew my attention to conversation and debate style differences between graduates of arts and social science faculties, on the one hand, and scientists and engineers on the other. The organizers had structured a debate between what C.P. Snow called *The Two Cultures.* The debate topic, estimated prospects of *Documents in the Digital Culture,* was addressed by four social scientists and liberal arts representatives facing four scientists and engineers. Comments by each participant alternated across the gap.

Each social scientist began along the lines, "My scientific colleague talked about … a topic for which we must consider the relationship with … which itself cannot be understood without [the following broad context]." The more the speaker progressed from a narrow topic to a very broad spectrum, the more discomfort we saw among the scientists, who fought urges to interrupt the speaker.

The style of each scientist was along the lines, "The previous speaker dealt with … a topic too broad for me to say anything specific about. I'll deal with [thus and such] a small piece." Implicit in this was confidence that other scholars would address and integrate similarly small pieces, possibly not until years later, and that the whole would make a large addition to the state of the art. The further such a speaker progressed toward solving a small problem segment, the more discomfort we saw among the social scientists.

Effective communication, not easy for abstract topics even between people who know each other well, is made extraordinarily difficult between professions by differences of jargon, of expectations,[73] of conventional forms and manners, and of value priorities. Research librarians and their close associates seem to value consensus extraordinarily highly, and often seem uncomfortable with open debate.

In contrast, scientists tend to value their personal sense of correct and elegant design far more highly than consensus within any community. They often seek and welcome vigorous debate. They value exposing unproven propositions to criticism and believe this practice contributes to

---

[73]   Paepcke 2005. *Dewey Meets Turing: Librarians, Computer Scientists, and the Digital Libraries Initiative.*

progress. It works well when criticisms are directed at ideas rather than at the people that voice them.[74]

Software engineers share some of these values. They also exhibit another trait in contrast to librarians and information scientists. The latter favor surveys that attempt to discover what functionality might help and please their clients. Software engineers are likely to trust their own intuitions about what they themselves would want if they were clients, to build something that they recognize to be an imperfect trial version, and to make that available to learn what a small user population has to say about it. Many development efforts starting with such trials fizzle out, perhaps with their better features being incorporated into other development threads. A few threads eventually become marketplace successes.

Apparently neither group reads the literature of the other, or otherwise listens to the other.[75] There are few interdisciplinary citations in the literature of either group. Similar difficulties exist in other contexts with different players. Perhaps this is why it is hard to find evidence that user surveys directly influence the software that eventually dominates and is judged responsive to real needs.

Articles published in the best engineering and scientific periodicals[76] have been rigorously refereed for objectivity, novelty, and the quality of citations of previous work. Typically, each article has had three carefully chosen referees who make helpful suggestions that must be dealt with before the editor accepts for publication what is often an extensively modified version. Referees would reject a prospective article that does not identify what is new and how this is related to and advances specific previous work. Review and survey articles identify themselves as such, and usually appear in different periodicals than original research. Didactic and normative material also identifies itself as what it is and usually is published in different ways—mostly as textbooks and official standards

---

[74] The popular press is more interested in spectacular ad hominem attacks. See White 2001, *Acid Tongues and Tranquil Dreamers,* for celebrated impoliteness. In fact, much has been made of a ten-minute confrontation half a century ago between Ludwig Wittgenstein and Karl Popper. See Edmonds 2000, *Wittgenstein's Poker.*

[75] "Over the last thirty years, most ethnographers have gradually come to accept the idea that any claim to directly link fieldwork ... to the ethnography itself, unmediated or untransformed by narrative conventions, will not hold. No transparency theory can be confirmed by ethnography. Moreover, an author inevitably makes choices when composing an ethnographic work, and in fact, culture ... is created ... by the active construction of a text." (quotation marks omitted.)
Edminster 2002, *The Diffusion of New Media Scholarship*

[76] For software engineering, these include the *ACM Transaction* series, IEEE periodicals such as *Proceedings of the IEEE*, and conference proceedings such as the annual *Joint Conference on Digital Libraries* (JCDL). See Mylonopoulos 2001. *Global perceptions of IS journals.*

documents. A result is that the engineering research literature is well suited for the needs of readers trying to understand the state of the art.

Unfortunately, the information science literature addressing preservation seems to lack such rigorous practices. Its articles often repeat at length what can be found in earlier articles and rarely make clear what is new about they are trying to convey. Didactic text seems to be mixed with other kinds of material. A consequence is that engineers and scientists are likely to find this literature tedious and experience difficulty finding what is new. Its characteristics have made the book more difficult to write than should have been the case.

> Experts are both in awe and in frustration about the state of the *Internet*. They celebrate search technology, peer-to-peer networks, and blogs; they bemoan institutions that have been slow to change. ... The experts are startled that educational institutions have changed so little.[77]

As part of its "How to get there" tabulation, *W2005* recommends, "Work in partnership with commercial system providers and with key interested parties such as CERN and others, on error levels and developing affordable scalability." However, it offers few suggestions how this is to be achieved. Commercial system vendors have made rapid progress over several decades without much information science contribution, and seem likely to continue to do so for the foreseeable future. Partnership requires benefit to every involved party. Nobody has suggested specific help or expertise that the information science community and public sector repositories can offer to attract commercial partners.[78] Nor is it apparent what these might be.

2.5.4 Preservation Community and Technology Vendors

Inattention across the boundary between academic researchers and technology vendors is a sad tradition, evident in the digital library community from the earliest days. Product developers seldom publish in scholarly periodicals. Each academic community behaves as if what is not represented in its own literature does not exist. A search of the citations of D-Lib articles will reveal few citations of industrial work, even though much of it anticipated ideas published there. What is sad is that such inattention has permitted, and continues to permit, wastage of public funds. An example is the proposals funded by the first NSF Digital Library Initiative, which

---

[77] Fox 2005, *The Future of the Internet,* http://www.pewinternet.org/pdfs/ PIP_Future_of_Internet.pdf.

[78] Supplying cultural repositories is not an attractive business opportunity, perhaps because they have not tried to show it to be one.

included aspects that had been realized in commercial products and were already in use by many customers in 1995. For instance, several versions of the core digital library support described in §9.3.3 were commercially available for less than the development cost of versions funded by government research contracts. This pattern of inattention continues in the U.S. National Information Infrastructure Preservation Program (NDIIPP). Perhaps it is a simple continuation of academic inattention across disciplinary boundaries.

The information science literature about digital preservation pays less attention to economic factors and technical trends than to examining how current paper-based repository methods can be adapted to a digital world. There is a mismatch—a semantic dissonance—between the language and expectations of cultural heritage community spokespersons and technology vendors (e.g., with respect to "scaling" in the research recommendations above). Current emphasis among technology vendors is on system components, whereas cultural depositories want customizable "solutions".

For instance, what was offered at the 2005 LinuxWorld trade fair was confusing in the sense that no vendor at the show offered any broad system model for assembling into solutions the components it offered. Perhaps this is a passing problem, with "middleware" models yet to be invented— as has occurred repeatedly in the refinement of lower software layers. Several trade fair booths exhorted the need for layer interface standards.

Vendors' work on "solutions" is mostly in the custom contract business, which they call "services" and which is an immense business sector. Insights and design successes in this area are not published, but rather treated as marketplace advantages that companies nurture, hone, and propagate internally. This phenomenon contributes to another cultural mismatch: academic libraries are not emotionally, practically, or financially prepared to use such outside services, even though they do not seem to have sufficient internal skills for the middleware component of repository services.

> ... the reality of the situation we currently face. At this time, technologies frequently are designed and developed more for the benefit of vendors than for users, and persons concerned with digital preservation are expected to jump through whatever hoops are required by those technologies.[79]

This is an odd statement from an author who otherwise seems to believe that "collaboration structures" should include commercial institutions. It has the ring of left-wing political rhetoric, in contrast to my comparatively boring interpretation of a quarter century of observing the internal work-

---

[79]   Granger 2002, *Digital Preservation and Deep Infrastructure.*

ings of IBM's marketing and development teams for content management and database products.

Consider "persons concerned with digital preservation are expected to jump through whatever hoops are required."[80] The product managers that decide R&D investments mostly ignore the cultural heritage community, because it does not present itself as part of the market they are charged with addressing. We should expect such behavior in our private enterprise system, because its managers are appraised and rewarded primarily on achieving schedule and revenue targets. What you hear said among them is along the lines of, "If you don't make your numbers, nothing else counts!"

The lesson for anyone sympathetic to Granger's complaint is simple and direct: if you want a commercial vendor to meet your requirements, become a customer.

2.6   Why So Slow Toward Practical Preservation?

Historians will look back on this era and see a period of very little information. A 'digital gap' will span from the beginning of the widespread use of the computer until the time we eventually solve this problem. What we're all trying to do is to shorten that gap.

Danny Hillis, Disney Chief of Research and Development[81]

It is estimated that we have created and stored since 1945 one hundred times as much information as we did in all of human history up until that time![82]

Is the digital preservation in fact urgent? Is progress in fact slow? An eminent librarian once pointed out that "urgent" and "slow" have different meanings within the Washington beltway than they do in Silicon Valley.

Is it possible that the responsible managers believe that prompt action risks massive wasted effort because unsolved technical problems exist for some kinds of data? If so, they should tell the software engineering community specifically what these risks are and which data classes are affected. If nontechnical risks are the effective impediments, they should be specifically articulated for consideration by the best minds available.

Since the challenges were articulated in 1996,[83] many conferences have been held and many papers have been written on the topic. They include

---

[80]   A more balanced assessment is *The Political Economy of Public Goods* in Waters 2002, *Good Archives Make Good Scholars*.

[81]   Meloan 1998, *No Way to Run a Culture*, http://www.wired.com/news/culture/ 0,1284,10301,00.html.

[82]   *The Long Now Foundation*, http://www.longnow.org.

[83]   Garrett 1996, *Preserving Digital Information: Report of the Task Force on Archiving*.

reminders of urgency, because irreplaceable and valuable digital content is allegedly disappearing.[84]   Digital preservation is seen as "complex and largely uncontrollable. Preserving books and other cultural objects looks straightforward in comparison."[85] From librarians' perspectives the challenges include inability to determine where to start, lack of sufficient expertise, absence of easily obtainable and trusted tools, and unrealistic expectations about costs.   How much these and similar problems can be mitigated by librarian training is unclear.[86]

Sometimes a myth is repeated often enough that a community accepts it as fact, without questioning whether it is correct or pertinent. Contrasting the durability of paper with the ephemeral character of digital objects seems to be such a myth. It starts to sow confusion by its "apples to cows" comparison between paper (a substratum material) and digital content (a value or abstract pattern), as illustrated by the passage:

> In their seminal report of 1996, Waters and Garrett lucidly defined the long-term challenges of preserving digital content. Ironically, the questions and issues that swirl about this new and perplexing activity can be relatively simply characterized as a problem of integrity of the artifact. Unlike paper artifacts such as printed scholarly journals, which are inherently immutable, digital objects such as electronic journals are not only mutable but can also be modified or transformed without generating any evidence of change. It is the mutable nature of digital information objects that represents one of the principal obstacles to the creation of archives for their long-term storage and preservation.
>
> Okerson 2002, *YEA: The Yale Electronic Archive*, p.53

A professional myth that has been repeated so often that I overlooked its absurdity until lately is that "printed scholarly journals are inherently immutable." Paper is very mutable—easily burned, easily ripped, easily cut, and easily shredded. Its content is easily redacted and easily overwritten. What is true is that it is difficult to modify paper without making the changes to its inscriptions obvious, often to casual observers, but sometimes only to forensic experts. We do have an extensive infrastructure to protect certain printed objects—autonomous, widely dispersed library in-

---

[84] "The national approaches that are now being started ... can distract institutions from just going ahead and acting. Moreover, some organizations, national archives as well as national libraries, seem to be stuck in the requirements-specification stage and find it difficult to move forward to implementation, perhaps out of fear of making mistakes."

van der Werf 2002, *Experience of the National Library of the Netherlands*

[85] Webb 2003, *Barriers or Stepping Stones? Impediments to Digital Archiving and Preservation Programs*, http://www.clir.org/pubs/issues/issues34.html#webb.

[86] Wiegandt 2006, *ADBS Stages de Formation Continue,* http://www.servicedoc.info/Annonce-des-stages-de-Formation.html proposes such training.

stitutions with redundant holdings. These facts immediately suggest how to overcome the easy mutability of digital recording—build a worldwide network of repositories with redundant holdings, and represent digital objects so that their bit-strings cannot be altered without the fact of alteration being readily detected.

Furthermore, significant portions of our cultural heritage have never been stored on paper. Curators concerned with potentially premature conversion of paper records might, for the time being, look after their analog audio-visual collections stored on deteriorating magnetic tape and film.

Misunderstandings have contributed to ten years' delay between clear and widely known identification of the digital preservation challenge and its solution. We need to identify and root out the confusions that have impeded progress. The best intellectual foundation for accomplishing this is scientific philosophy summarized in this book's **Information Object Structure** section.

2.7   Selection Criteria: What is Worth Saving?

Patricia Battin, when President of the Commission on Preservation and Access and considering the deterioration of works on acid paper, observed that, "We faced very painful and wrenching choices—we had to accept the fact that we couldn't save it all, that we had to accept the inevitability of triage, that we had to change our focus from single-item salvation to a mass production process, and we had to create a comprehensive cooperative strategy. We had to move from the cottage industries in our individual library back rooms to a coordinated nationwide mass-production effort." [87]

Contrast this with the NARA opinion that preservation by triage may not be an option. "NARA does not have discretion to refuse to preserve a format. It is inconceivable ... that a court would approve of a decision not to preserve e-mail attachments, which often contain the main substance of the communication, because it is not in a format NARA chose to preserve."[88]

Perhaps a great deal of information will be lost. However, the information available will be much greater, much more accessible, and much easier to find than has historically ever been the case. It seems less likely that information wanted will have been irretrievably lost than that it

---

[87] Battin 1992, *Substitution: the American Experience,* quoted in http://www.clir.org/pubs/reports/pub82/pub82text.html.

See also *A Framework of Guidance for Building Good Digital Collections*, http://www.niso.org/framework/Framework2.html.

[88] Quoted in Talbot 2005, *The Fading Memory of the State,* http://www.technologyreview.com/articles/05/07/issue/feature_memory.asp.

will still exist somewhere in digital form, but will nevertheless not be found.[89]

2.7.1 Cultural Works

> One theme is the understandable reluctance of scholars to make choices because of the unpredictability of research needs. Scholars are loath to say, "this book will be more useful for future research than that one," because the history of their fields shows that writers and subjects that seem inconsequential to scholars in one era may become of great interest in the next, and vice versa. Moreover, discovery and serendipity may lead to lines of inquiry unforeseen.
>
> George 1995, *Difficult Choices*

Between 1988 and 1994, scholarly advisory committees considered content selection for History, Renaissance Studies, Philosophy, Mediaeval Studies, Modern Language and Literature, and Art History. Although this work was mostly done before digital capture was practical, its insights seem applicable today.

Selection seems to be difficult, but is not a challenge in the sense of being hampered by technical research issues. If the technical and organizational challenges are overcome, digital preservation is likely to become a routine activity with priorities set by each institution's resource allocation process. The funding challenges are likely to continue, because more content than research libraries can save will forever be generated. Copyright issues mostly involve conflicting interests that will not be quickly resolved.

Today's selection costs are exacerbated by the accelerating transformation from information scarcity to information overflow. It might today be neither possible nor desirable to save everything. Decisions will occur, either by default or with varying degrees of care and insight. For governments and ordinary folk, Lysakowski suggests looming disaster for office files in popular formats.[90]

Selection is much less challenging for old documents than for modern content. Writing and dissemination were relatively rare and relatively slow in earlier centuries. For instance, at the time of the American Revolution the British Departments of State had about 50 clerks; these clerks wrote longhand with quill pens. Their letters to North America took six to ten weeks to deliver and as long again to receive responses. Compare

---

[89] See MegaNet's *Online Backup Market Research* at http://www.meganet.net/pdfs/onlinebkresearch.pdf.

[90] Lysakowski 2000, *Titanic 2020: A Call to Action,* http://www.censa.org/html/Publications/Titanic2020_bookmarks_Jan-21-2000.pdf.

these circumstances to those of today's bureaucracies and to the tools the latter use to create and disseminate information. For old content, we benefit from de facto selection at the source—little was written.

In a 2003 posting to a Michigan State University discussion group frequented by fellow historians,[88] Eduard Mark wrote, "It will be impossible to write the history of recent diplomatic and military history as we have written about World War II and the early Cold War. Too many records are gone. Think of Villon's haunting refrain, *"Ou sont les neiges d'antan?"* and weep. ... History as we have known it is dying, and with it the public accountability of government and rational public administration. ... The federal system for maintaining records has in many agencies— indeed in every agency with which I am familiar—collapsed utterly." About the 1989 U.S. invasion of Panama, in which U.S. forces removed Manuel Noriega, Mark wrote that he could not secure many basic records of the invasion, because a number were electronic and had not been kept.

Even if this assessment were to be accurate, suggesting a discouraging prospect to some scholars, other communities will be easily satisfied. Students' wants are easier to satisfy than scholars', because the secondary school student or college undergraduate assigned a term paper will choose the first pertinent and interesting material that he encounters. Digitization can provide more interesting material than has been commonly available. It is becoming realistic for teachers to require students to find and work from original sources rather than from secondary opinions and other people's selections. The top issues for content usage by students are not availability or selection, but rather accuracy, authenticity, and balance of viewpoints.

2.7.2 Video History

Even for scholars, the prospect of permanently lost historical information is not nearly as worrisome as Eduard Mark's comments might suggest. For the facts about what actually happened, news reports surely provide as accurate an account as the missing government memoranda might have done. What the press does not report about the Panama crisis, the decision processes that led to the invasion, might be nice to have. However, information about modern events much exceeds that about similar and, arguably more significant, earlier historical events. It would be an interesting exercise to compare information available about the Panama episode, especially after some digging into private records and other nongovernment sources that will eventually become available, with information about the events and decisions leading to Napoleon's defeat at of Waterloo.

To some extent, Mark's concern is with the difference between what will be the case and what might have been the case had records retention circumstances been somewhat more favorable, rather than with what is needed by historical scholars. What is needed will often be a troublesome question. Shakespeare has the mad *King Lear* argue, "Oh, reason not the need. Our basest beggars are in the poorest things superfluous."

Multimedia information representations appeared only recently, but still earlier than the period for which doomsayers suggest records will be forever lost. Not only do the major television networks have immense archives that are being converted to digital formats,[91] but consumers have acquired large numbers of digital and video cameras, computers, HDDs, and writeable optical disks. And roughly half of the U.S. local police departments routinely use video cameras. Surely government agencies and private citizens are squirreling away a historian's treasure trove that, years from now, will be mined for what is of broad interest.

Only with fifty years' perspective does it become clear whose personal history might be worth saving in public records. For instance, Leonard Bernstein's childhood letters were acquired by the Library of Congress in the 1990s after a bidding war with the University of Indiana Library.[92] In 2005, copies of many Dorothea Lange photographs were discovered in a neglected personal collection. They had been retrieved from a San Jose Chamber of Commerce dumpster about 40 years earlier. Found when a daughter was clearing her deceased parents' house, the collection fetched a fortune in a Sotheby's auction.

2.7.3 Bureaucratic Records

The future archives of the U.S. government will undoubtedly be one of the largest and most complicated digital collections ever. "We operate on the premise that somewhere in the government they are using every software program that has ever been sold, and some that were never sold because they were developed for the government. The scope of the problem is … open-ended, because the formats keep changing."[93] Numbers that suggest the scale and complexity are approximately 40 million e-mail messages from the Clinton White House, approximately 600 million TIFF files from the 2000 census, and up to a million pages in a single patent application that might include 3D protein molecule models or aircraft CAD drawings.

---

[91]   Williams 2002, *Preserving TV and Broadcast Archives,* http://www.dpconline.org/graphics/events/presentations/pdf/DPCJune5th.pdf.

[92]   See the *Bernstein collection* at http://memory.loc.gov/ammem/lbhtml/lbhome.html.

[93]   Ken Thibodeau, director of the NARA electronic records program, quoted in Talbot 2005, *The Fading Memory of the State.*

Some business records will eventually be used by academic historians, in ways suggested by current use of sixteenth century galleon bills of lading held in Sevilla's Archivo General de Indias.[94]

In the public sector, the visible efforts toward preservation of "born-digital stuff" are focused on cultural content, on scientific data,[95] and on records of national significance. The literature makes few allusions to smaller political units, to educational priorities other than those of research scholars, to judicial systems, to health delivery systems, or to administrative collections of interest to ordinary citizens. (Among political issues, which include international terrorism, global warming, hunger and illness in Africa, and world trade rivalries, it would be naïve to expect most taxpayers to know or care much about their personal risks associated with disappearing documents.)

For about thirty years, some physicians have dreamed of the "longitudinal patient record"—a medical history accompanying each individual from birth to grave. Since the useful lifetime of uncurated digital records is much less than human lifetimes, preservation technology would be needed to fulfill this dream. (However, digital preservation is not the biggest challenge to realization of lifelong health records. Patient privacy, information standards, and medical system infrastructure are more challenging.)

A personal letter from a schoolmate illustrates other needs:

> Speaking of the [Immigration and Naturalization Service], we are trying to see if [my son] qualifies for [U.S.] citizenship on the basis of the fact that I did the border shuffle [between Canada and the U.S.] for most of my natural life. Now it is a question of proving I exist, it seems.
>
> [I am] trying to unearth papers to prove to the lawyers that I actually spent about half my time on either side of the border from birth until I married! Did you know that anyone who attended high school in the 1950s is clearly so far back in the Dark Ages as to be almost a non-person? Welcome to the real world. The schools in [city], where I attended the first three grades, tell me they have no records of any students born between 1931 and 1942; so much for that!
>
> The school board in [city] says [XYZ] school no longer exists. "If we had records, they would have been forwarded to the school you went to." The school fortunately had registered me as having come in from [XYZ] school, but kept no transcripts … And we haven't even been bombed or anything. No wonder half of people who lose their papers die of despair. Bureaucracy is immovable! Yet, a front page story about a restaurant on my block starts

---

[94] *Archivo General de Indias*, http://en.wikipedia.org/wiki/Archivo_General_de_Indias.

[95] Examples include the *2-Micron All Sky Survey* (10 Terabytes of data, five million images), the NSF Digital Library (preservation of curricula modules). The projects are driven by the research communities that use the data.

out with how the executive chef came to this country as an illegal immigrant from Mexico!

What might preservation priorities be if the public understood its risks?

2.7.4 Scientific Data

Awareness of the size and complexity of potential repositories for the digital records of science has increased greatly in recent years. Over the next ten years science projects will produce more data than have been collected in all human history. Some European research organizations are already each generating approximately 1,000 gigabytes of data annually. Approximately 15,000 academic periodicals exist; many of these are moving toward electronic versions. These circumstances are stimulating community efforts that are likely to replace fragmentary projects by individual research teams and institutional repositories, including the creation of a European Task Force to drive things forward quickly.[96] Potential economies of scale constitute a key incentive for creating a European infrastructure for permanent access.[97]

2.8 Summary

In less than a century we have progressed from an information-poor world to a world in which large populations are information-rich. Expectations have become very high for what technology can provide. While we each spend roughly a ten years learning how to mark paper to be intelligible to others (writing) and to interpret those marks (reading), we expect digital information to be intelligible without us having to extend our early schooling.

We encounter assertions that digital preservation is urgent if we are not to lose cultural heritage content—that we face inevitable loss if action is not prompt. The situation is neither quite so dire nor quite so simple. Bit-strings are saved helter-skelter on enterprise storage and in home collections that eventually are relegated to attics. Much of this might be lost, but much will also survive for long periods, and yield its treasures to hard working digital archeologists. The urgency is less a matter of imminent permanent loss than an economic urgency—that prompt action would be less expensive than leaving recovery to our descendants.

---

[96]   Presentation of *Task Force on Permanent Access*, http://www.dcc.ac.uk/training/warwick_2005/ TindemansWarwick07-11-05.ppt.

[97]   European Task Force for Permanent Access to the Records of Science 2005, *Strategic Action Programme 2006–2010*, p. 7.

Regrettably, the largely academic cultural heritage community apparently pays little attention to digital content that does not mimic university library collections inked onto paper, even though this material would mitigate some of its prominent concerns.

Physicists suggest that we perceive an order of magnitude change as a qualitative change. Declining computer hardware prices are precipitating institutional and social changes. Trends that will affect strategies include the following.

- The number of people with education, leisure, and interest in reading and writing is much larger than it has ever been, even as a fraction of the total population, and is growing.
- Our children are more comfortable with digital technology, and more skilled in its use, than we are.
- Automation is now inexpensive compared to human labor. A Swedish National Archives study supports the consensus expectation that the human administration is becoming the largest cost component for digital repositories.[98] Digital technology is even becoming affordable in less developed countries.
- It is reasonable to plan a home computer with a terabyte of storage!
- The amount of digital information that might be preservation-worthy is growing rapidly. Estimates suggest that the fraction represented by research library collections is small and shrinking.[99]
- The information management community is much larger than the combined staffs of all the research libraries and archives.
- The information quality and evidence of authenticity that people expect has increased steadily since early in the twentieth century (when radio broadcasts and music recordings became popular).

Large-scale digital preservation will be affordable only if we automate every human processing step that can be replaced by a machine procedure. It will be affordable partly because most of the software needed has already been developed and will be refined for daily use applications.

Part of what has delayed progress toward digital preservation is that the professional literature contains myths that are repeated, apparently without readers noticing that they are myths. An example is the assertion that information on paper is immutable. It would instead be accurate to say that

---

[98] Jonas Palm 2006, *The Digital Black Hole*, http://www.tape-online.net/docs/Palm_Black_Hole.pdf.

[99] Hey 2003, *The data deluge*.

Lord 2003, *e-Science Curation Report [for] the UK*, http://www.jisc.ac.uk/uploaded_documents/e-ScienceReportFinal.pdf.

information on paper is difficult to change without the change being detectable—sometimes readily and sometimes only by experts' experiments. As soon as this distinction is noticed, part of the digital preservation solution becomes obvious, viz., emulate the age-old practice of including provenance information and then signing and sealing.

Assessing what is known and what remains to be done to achieve practical digital preservation is made difficult by the style common in information science literature—style that does not clearly distinguish and separate didactic articles from research articles, that permits articles conveying little beyond what can be found in prior literature, and that rarely includes identification of and arguments for what is truly new and promising. This style contributes to alienation between the liberal arts and the technical communities.

Part II: Information Object Structure

> [T]he nature of the most important different object types and their distinctions can be characterized on the basis of the constructional system. ...   Of the autopsychological object type, we consider the experiences, their individual constituents, and the qualities (of sense impressions, emotions, volitions, etc.). Of the physical object type, we consider the physical things. Of the heteropsychological objects, we consider again experiences, their individual constituents, and the qualities; of the cultural objects, we consider the primary cultural objects and general higher-level objects.
>
> Carnap 1928, *LSW* §160

In this book, we look at digital preservation differently than most authors, perhaps unconventionally, building recommendations on a digital object model that exploits constructs suggested by the above *LSW* quotation.[100] For each object, someone must decide precisely what is to be preserved. We treat each repository as a *black box* whose input-output relationships are what we most care about. The book's main thread is based on the model of communication suggested by Fig. 2 and the model of information-carrying objects suggested in §6.3.

Choosing how to accomplish digital preservation without a sound intellectual foundation risks incurring systematic errors that might not be discovered until it is too late to put matters right, and perhaps also errors that are discovered earlier, but not before corrections require expensive rework of the preserved content.

We distrust unsupported common sense. This is partly because the digital preservation literature contains serious confusions and misunderstandings, and more generally because intellectual history is full of common sense assertions that later careful analysis demonstrated were incorrect or misleading. We need to clear this underbrush if we want to discern trunks strong enough to support sound methodological branches. For these reasons, we address digital preservation with a second unconventional way of thinking, building on philosophical theories of knowledge. Such treatment

---

[100]   As of late 2005, this approach might no longer be idiosyncratic. Shirky 2005, *AIHT: Conceptual Issues from Practical Tests* includes:

"[W]e have become convinced that data-centric strategies for shared effort are far more scalable than either tool- or environment-centric strategies. A data-centric strategy assumes that the interaction between institutions will mainly be in the passing of a bundle of data from one place to another—that data will leave its original context and be interpreted in the new context of the receiving institution. Specifying the markup of the data itself removes the need for identical tools to be held by sender and receiver, and the need to have a sender and receiver with the same processes in place for handling data."

responds to the need for an intellectual foundation asserted in a U.S. National Archives call for action:[101]

> The state of affairs [in digital preservation] in 1998 could easily be summarized:
> - proven methods for preserving and providing sustained access to electronic records were limited to the simplest forms of digital objects;
> - even in those areas, proven methods were incapable of being scaled to a level sufficient to cope with the expected growth of electronic records; and
> - archival science had not responded to the challenge of electronic records sufficiently to provide a sound intellectual foundation for articulating archival policies, strategies, and standards for electronic records.

The most troublesome published difficulties with preservation seem to be related to failure to understand the logic of our language. We need to examine the errors made to learn how to avoid repeating them.

For instance, I feel that "knowledge preservation" is too grand a term. Although the phrase has a satisfying ring, I prefer to describe the objective as "information preservation." This is because I do not believe that we can preserve the collective knowledge of any community. What its members communicate, and what can therefore be captured, is only a small portion of what they know. Philosophy teaches us to distinguish between information and knowledge. Information is what we write onto paper and speak into microphones. Knowledge is much more. It is part of what makes each of us more than what he writes or says. We use knowledge to write, to teach, to invent, to perform, to earn our livings, to care for our families, and to accomplish the myriad mundane and almost unnoticed things we do every day for safety, health, comfort, and amusement.

"Getting it right" depends on precision in language and in action. Whenever it is difficult to express an idea both simply and correctly, this book favors precision, accepting the view that simple does not justify simplistic.

Natural language is full of ambiguities. Language problems in digital preservation are a small of example of Wittgenstein's dictum, "Most of the propositions and questions to be found in philosophical works are not false but nonsensical. ... Most of the propositions and questions of philosophers arise from our failure to understand the logic of our language." (*TLP* 4.003) It is surprisingly difficult to avoid difficulties caused by imprecise or misleading use of ordinary language. For instance, "knowledge management" suggests a different meaning for the word 'knowledge' than the

---

101   Thibodeau 2002, *Overview of Technological Approaches to Digital Preservation.*

traditional one. We therefore begin with an introduction to knowledge theory and then apply that theory to digital preservation.

We find it helpful to distinguish three topics conceptually and architecturally as much as possible without introducing absurdities: (1) individual works as the proper targets of preservation attention; (2) collections of works that information providers choose to identify as being closely related, extended by such further works as are necessary to provide technical context for the interpretation of these conceptual collections; and (3) archival and library mechanisms—digital repositories—that are essential parts of the infrastructure for making accessible and preserving individual works and the information that binds individual works into collections.

An objective is to choose a structure sufficiently general to describe every kind of information. We choose the Digital Object (DO) model suggested in §6.3, the digital collection schema suggested in §6.4, and elaborations of these models. In fact, a single schema and model suffices for all DOs and also for digital collections. The chosen DO structure exploits ternary relationships recursively, object identifiers as references, and mathematical values. Our preservation model, the Trustworthy Digital Object (TDO) construction described in §11.1, is a modest DO extension. Our theory of knowledge and the models of its representations, particularly Carnap's *LSW*, support these models as being sufficient for any content collection, without any restriction to the information that can be described.

We believe that the TDO evidence of provenance and authenticity is as reliable as is feasible, as are the trust relationships essential to that evidence. This opinion is based on analyses of the subjective/objective distinction (§3.3), of the ethical value/fact distinction (§3.4), and of relationships (§6.5.2) and identifiers (§7.3).

We further believe that technology for preservation can be designed to be a small addition to software already deployed to support current and future information access services and other aspects of digital repository management. The inherent complexity of digital preservation software can be mostly hidden from its human users. To the extent that these objectives are achieved, the convenience, flexibility, and cost of digital archiving services will be optimized.

As much as I might want to wave some technical wand to preserve knowledge, I do not know how to do that. So I settle for information preservation.

3 Introduction to Knowledge Theory

> You know, Phaedrus, that's the strange thing about writing, which makes it truly analogous to painting. The painter's products stand before us as though they were alive: but if you question them, they maintain a most majestic silence. It is the same with written words: they seem to talk to you as though they were intelligent, but if you ask them anything about what they say, from a desire to be instructed, they go on telling you the same thing again and again.
>
> Plato, *Phaedrus*

The boundary between what can be mechanized and what must forever remain a human judgment or value decision is limited to the facts that language can convey. Work between 1880 and 1940 provides insights essential to identifying the boundary. Ludwig Wittgenstein, Rudolf Carnap, Ernst Cassirer, and Willard Van Orman Quine built on the work of Emmanuel Kant, Auguste Comte, Heinrich Hertz, Karl Weierstrass, Ernst Mach, Gottlob Frege, David Hilbert, Karl Kraus, and Bertrand Russell. William James and Charles Sanders Peirce represent separate but topically similar and compatible American lines of thinking.

These authors have been so successful in persuading Western scholars to accept and teach their views that their ideas and careful distinctions are often taken for granted as "mere" common sense, and too often then ignored. Wittgenstein's *Tractatus Logico-philosophicus* (*TLP*) can be seen to be a watershed in the theory of knowledge. It exposes problems in almost every earlier epistemological work. (This statement is fair only with respect to European philosophy. Until about the end of the nineteenth century, recognition of scholarly advances across the Atlantic Ocean occurred only slowly. There is little evidence that European philosophers knew the work of Charles Sanders Peirce or Willam James until after World War I, or that American philosophers paid careful attention to the *Tractatus* before Carnap, Quine, and Russell lectured in American universities in the 1930s.) Although *TLP* was completed in 1918, it was not published until 1921, and was noticed only by a handful of scholars before it came to the attention Moritz Schlick, the originator of the famous logical positivist group, the Vienna Circle, in 1926. That group analyzed it over the next two years, and later played a significant role in drawing the world's attention to the work. *TLP* affects almost every theory of knowledge later than 1925.

What any human being intends will forever be obscure and perhaps controversial. To make assumptions about people's objectives can be foolhardy. Furthermore, to tell people how to do their work would be ineffective, because people detest being told what to do. We therefore try to avoid normative statements by being explicit about results that someone might want and what methods might work for this. Instead of saying, "You should use rule set Y," we might say, "Should you want result X with properties Z under circumstances W, consider the method defined by rule set Y." Here, Z might be something like "with least human effort" or "with small likelihood of errors or failures" and W might include estimates of end user skills, such as "for undergraduates at your university." (This is little more than a prudent engineer's approach to an assigned task.)

Of course, such careful language can be tedious and can obscure a central message in a welter of contingencies. We therefore customarily take short cuts, but should always be ready to remind ourselves and listeners that more care might be needed.

Someone who frequently reads technical books or articles and is familiar with narrow definitions adopted for use primarily within their confines might be impatient with what follows in this chapter. To such a reader, we suggest skipping Chapter 3 until he questions whether TDO methodology described in the fourth section, **Digital Object Architecture for the Long Term**, has a sound theoretical foundation. He might also wonder whether so much care is in fact needed to avoid practical difficulties, such as those encountered in constructing ontologies for digital libraries or semantic browsing. We believe the care prudent because the potential cost of recovering from preservation technology weaknesses is very high.

Design for managing evidence of authenticity and for constructing metadata requires a keen sense of the boundary between facts and opinions. To discuss knowledge and information preservation, we must share what we mean by certain common words, such as *name, fact, value, objective,* and *subjective,* and also about a few arcane words, such as *ontology.*

3.1   Conceptual Objects: Values and Patterns

Of the information object classes suggested in Fig. 4, packages, performances, and data are probably so well understood that any reader could give examples that other readers would accept without any discussion or clarification. However, such acceptance without discussion is not likely for values and patterns.

> The word 'object' is here used ... for anything about which a statement can be made. Thus, among objects we count not only things, but also properties and classes, relations in extension and intension, states and events, what is actual as well as what is not.
>
> Carnap 1928, *LSW* §1

Following Carnap, we use 'object' for anything that can properly be referred to as a sentence subject, except that we often use 'value' for mathematical objects and 'pattern' for abstract relationships among objects.

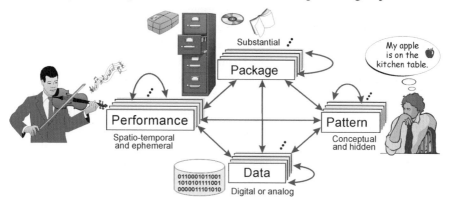

Fig. 4: Schema for information object classes and relationship classes

Figure 4 suggests that information can be classified by how it is represented: hidden thoughts in your and my brains; packages on physical media that might be stored in orderly collections; ephemeral performances that can be construed to include broadcast and networked signals; and digital representations stored persistently or only for the duration of some computing process. Each class has many types. The figure's double-headed arrows suggest both relationships between information instances and also transformations that create new information representations. Almost every kind of relationship and transformation depicted occurs in the information infrastructure. Each relationship class has many instances; this is, however, not shown in the figure because doing so would obscure patterns it suggests.

The entity that we call "3" or "three" undoubtedly exists and has useful relationships with other Fig. 4 entities. Is it real? What do we mean by saying, "3 exists"? Whatever the words 'real' and 'exists' mean, it is something different for "3" than for "the apple on my kitchen table" or for "the digital image of the apple on my kitchen table." But then, 'real' and 'exists' also mean something different for "the apple on my kitchen table" from what they mean for "the digital image of the apple on my kitchen table." If we wanted to challenge the reality or existence of the entity we call "3," we would be forced to say what we mean by 'real' and 'exists'—a topic for philosophers,[102] but not for this book.

---

[102] Hersh 1997, *What Is Mathematics, Really*, Chap. 5.

We call things like "3" *values* when we want to distinguish them from other Fig. 4 entities.

Similarly, the arrangement of boxes and arrows depicted by Fig. 4 exists whether or not Fig. 4 exists. The arrangement would continue to exist even if every Fig. 4 instance were destroyed. It is a different kind of value than 3—a kind of value sufficiently important that we have a name for it. We call it a *pattern*. That a pattern might have practical importance is illustrated by the legal fact that it can be protected by copyright.

Does a *value* or a *pattern* need to be what somebody is thinking about, as the Fig. 4 man is thinking about his apple on his kitchen table? Consider the situation in which Miss A calls Dr. B's office and asks the receptionist Mrs. C, "Do I have an appointment with the doctor?" and, after C consults a calendar, is told, "Yes, you have one on Tuesday March 3 at 3 p.m." In this case, neither A nor C knew of the appointment before C consulted the calendar, and B probably did not either. Nevertheless, we say that A had an appointment with B on Tuesday March 3 at 3 p.m., or that this appointment existed. Similarly, the crystalline pattern of table salt existed long before it was discovered by X-ray crystallography. A value or a pattern can exist even if nobody happens to know of it. We comfortably talk about such entities' existence without confusing anyone.

Patterns are at the core of intellectual property law. The claims of a patent application describe patterns of design for which the claimant is requesting a limited exclusivity of remunerative use, and such patterns are the core of what receives copyright protection. Patterns are also the essence of ontologies and of information schema.

3.2   Ostensive Definition and Names

We call very different things "names"; the word "name" is used to characterize many different kinds of use of a word, related to one another in many different ways; ... [I]n giving an ostensive definition for instance, we often point to the object named and say the name. And similarly, in giving an ostensive definition, for instance, we say the word "this" while pointing to a thing. And also the word "this" and a name often occupy the same position in a sentence. But it is precisely characteristic of a name that it is defined by means of the demonstrative expression "That is N."

Wittgenstein 1958, *PI* §38

Whenever we point at something and say, "This is W," the symbol 'W' is a definite description for the object (*LSW*, §13). If we instead say, "This

is an X," we mean the string represented by X to be the name of a class.[103]
Often the symbol 'W' will be a single word, but it might instead be a
phrase of any length whatsoever.

Pointing at an object and communicating a character string is the primitive *naming* operation. Given a starting set of names that we have agreed
on by exercising this primitive mechanism, we make a practice of defining
further names by conventional dictionary definitions. Such procedures are
an important part of how we teach language to young children.

Any object is likely to receive many names, with different names not
only in different contexts, but often even within a *context*, even by the
same speaker. For instance, I address my brother as "Tom," "Thomas,"
"bro'," or even "Heh, you!" My automobile has the appellations "VIN
QT2FF12Z4B075867," "Calif. 7BTU953," "grey whale," and "the 1996
Toyota Camry".

We might suppose that careful construction would allow us to avoid all
kinds of confusion. However, we would quickly find such optimism unjustified. Questions of granularity arise almost immediately. If I point at
an automobile you might not know whether I intend to indicate the entire
automobile, its engine, its carburetor, or some small part of the carburetor.
This difficulty is called a *correlation problem.*

Even supposing that we somehow magically avoid this kind of ambiguity—that correlation problems do not arise in the conversation of the moment, we will find that we have not evaded other difficulties. Suppose we
are trying to teach a four-year-old what we mean by "a ball." We show
him tennis balls, baseballs, and golf balls, occasionally interspersing another object that we call "not a ball." When we believe the child has
grasped the concept, we test him by showing a bowling ball. When further
examples and tests make us confident that the child has truly learned, we
show him a cantaloupe, and quickly learn that we should have helped him
distinguish between balls and spherical objects that are not playthings. After a long session of spherical object instruction which has engaged the
child's full attention, interest, and innate intelligence, imagine his perplexity if we show him an American football and say that that it also is a ball,
even though it is not spherical.

Such difficulties are not few or far between. Because the world has continuously infinite variety, whereas language is discrete and *atomic*, com-

---

[103] Language analysis starting with such simple notions is thoroughly treated in Quine 1960, *Word and object*

munication difficulties are the norm rather than the exception.[104]   In the face of such enormous challenges, we need to consider mathematicians' escape into formal languages that are not assumed to describe the real world.   And, as mathematicians do, we can shrug off the gibe that we might expend great effort to say a great deal about nothing whatsoever.

Suppose we retreat into formalism.[105]   Even then, we would be disappointed if we had hoped to eliminate all difficulties.   In the case of Euclidean geometry, it was observed that the world contained no perfect points or lines to act as ostensive starting points.   And if we carefully excluded circularity of definition, we would soon decide that we had no starting points for creating a dictionary.   The difficulty is illustrated by a difference between the early and the late Wittgenstein.   In the 1918 *TLP* he proceeded without apology as if readers understood what he meant by 'fact', 'world', and so on.   In the posthumous *PI* he wrote, "the meaning of a word is its use in the language.   And the *meaning* of a name is sometimes explained by pointing to its *bearer*."[106]   For instance, the seemingly uninformative quip, "physics is what physicists do" is not, in fact, tautological, but instead suggests how an observer can learn what is intended by "physics".

The only practical recourse seems to include abandoning attempts to ground our language—natural or formal—on starting points that are intuitively unambiguous.   This book necessarily does so, assuming that, magically, readers will sufficiently grasp what we mean by a few starting words, such as 'set', 'follows', and 'real'.   We concede that some readers might never understand our chosen words, no matter how diligently we provide examples and synonymous phrases.   Every use of language—a word, a sentence, a report, a book—is comprehensible only in the context of innumerable other communications.

---

[104]   For a careful exposition that identifies helpful primary sources, see Sowa 2004, *The challenge of knowledge soup*, http://www.jfsowa.com/talks/challenge.pdf, which includes the following example. "Overgeneralizations. Birds fly. But what about penguins? A day-old chick? A bird with a broken wing? A stuffed bird? A sleeping bird?"

[105]   In his intellectual autobiography, Carnap wrote, "In *Foundations of Logic and Mathematics* (1939, §§23–25), I showed how the system of science or of a particular scientific field, e.g., physics, can be constructed as a calculus whose axioms represent the fundamental laws of the field in question. This calculus is not directly interpreted. It is rather constructed as a "freely floating system," i.e., as a network of primitive theoretical concepts which are connected with one another by the axioms. On the basis of these primitive concepts, further theoretical concepts are defined. Eventually, some of these are closely related to observable properties that can be interpreted by semantical rules which connect them with observables."
Schilpp 1963, *The Philosophy of Rudolf Carnap*

[106]   The method with which the Oxford English Dictionary was created anticipated Wittgenstein. See Winchester 2004, *The Meaning of Everything.*

In view of the difficulties sketched, it seems amazing that we manage at all, let alone quite successfully.

3.3 Objective and Subjective: Not a Technological Issue

[T]here seems no reason to believe that we are ever acquainted with other people's minds, [as] these are not directly perceived ... All thinking has to start from acquaintance; but it succeeds in thinking about many things with which we have no acquaintance.

Bertrand Russell 1905, *On Denoting*

The greatest difficulties of communicating reliably have little to do with the use of technology. Personal thoughts, particularly those we call *subjective* (having to do with opinions, tastes, judgments, purposes or feelings) cannot be shared, except perhaps incompletely. However, someone can use words that, once they are spoken or written, are *objective* representations of his thoughts. If these thoughts are simple thoughts about empirical facts, scientific observations, or evidence, one might be able to convey them without misunderstanding. However, if the thoughts are about subjective matters, it is extremely difficult to communicate in such a way that either party can be certain that the listener understands the speaker's viewpoint precisely.

What someone intends—his purpose—is always subjective. You can know someone else's purpose only if he tells you what it is. Even then, it is often reasonable to doubt that you truly know it.

Every *atomic* assertion is either objective or subjective.[107] A complex assertion (one that can be analyzed into more primitive assertions) might correctly be said to be relatively objective or relatively subjective.

The "?" marks in Fig. 2 suggest these difficulties. We call the opaque steps **0→1** and **9→10** *subjective*. We sometimes call an assertion that we believe subjective a *value statement*.

Fig. 5, similar to Fig. 2 except that the communication machinery has been removed, illustrates that we should expect difficulties even if no digital machinery mediates the conversation. The figure deals with a case that

---

107 The boundary between objective and subjective is far from decided, even among philosophers. "It has been a central tenet of the pragmatists, no matter how great their other differences, that judgments of value are empirical in nature, and so have a cognitive or theoretical character amenable in principle to control by scientific methods. Stated in another way, the pragmatists have believed that judgments of value as well as the statements of science conform to the pragmatic maxim and are meaningful in the same sense. Carnap has certainly affirmed the opposite. He has maintained that we can deduce no proposition about future experience from the sentence 'Killing is evil,' and that value judgments, of which this is an example, are 'not verifiable' and so have 'no theoretical sense.'"

Schilpp 1963, *The Philosophy of Rudolf Carnap*, p.94

is much simpler than that of most shared documents—an empirical observation about a single relationship, the location of an apple. The speaker's assertion includes a common mistake—the definite article suggesting that only one table is pertinent. Our speaker can be excused; his context (suggested by the balloon above his head) includes only one table, because the small table is hidden by his desk and the large tablecloth. In contrast, the listener's context does include both tables, but only one apple, because the books on the large table hide the speaker's apple from him. So he infers something different (suggested by the balloon above his head) than the speaker implied. The problem is that, even for a very simple empirical statement, the speaker and the listener have different contexts.

Fig. 5: Conveying meaning is difficult even without mediating machinery!

Many listeners would not notice the speaker's small mistake, even if their context included both tables and both apples depicted by Fig. 5. Others would pass over it because asking or commenting would be a distraction from the main conversational thread. If either of the depicted individuals notices the confusion, perhaps because of something said later should the conversation continue, the pair might cooperatively overcome the difficulty by moving the pile of books and the small table so that the participants share sufficient context (facts observed about the contents of the room they are sitting in.)

Further difficulties arise in more realistic situations than Fig. 5 suggests. If the conversation were to be by telephone, sharing the same visual field would be unlikely. And for sharing information stored in and retrieved from repositories, dialog about the first message will occur only rarely. For information with a 50-year or greater lag from transmission to receipt, such dialog cannot occur. This is part of the reason that high quality metadata are so important in digital preservation.

If the conversation is not about empirically observed facts, but instead about a subjective topic, these difficulties become much greater—perhaps so great that they can never be resolved so that both participants know that they are resolved. Communication between human beings is usually uncertain in the way Fig. 5 suggests.

In general, the sign **1** in Fig. 2 might be deficient, omitting details needed to disambiguate the conceptual object **0** from similar objects. Writer's and reader's contexts are likely to be different in ways that are not evident to the information producer until some assertion about to be written is perceived as potentially ambiguous or otherwise incorrect, or to the information consumer at a much later time. Even if such elementary language problems are avoided, the listener neither has, nor can be given, a sure prescription for constructing his own conceptual object **10** to be identical to the speaker's conceptual object **0**. This is partly because shared contexts between information producers and information consumers are so difficult to provide that they are rare, although attempts to do so exist.[107]

Because we cannot find non-trivial examples that avoid such difficulties, we believe that communication steps illustrated by the **0→1** and **9→10** steps in Fig. 2 will usually embed uncertainty that cannot be removed by applied technology. Machine assistance can be applied at most to Fig. 2 steps starting with information objects **1** and ending with information objects **9**.

Human beings choose how to accomplish every Fig. 2 step, including choosing what technology or clerical method to use for the procedures from **1** to **9**. Each step might include a signal transformation chosen by some human being. These decisions are guided by information providers' and engineers' purposes, and are *subjective* choices whose reasons are rarely communicated to information consumers. They are based on human expertise that is mostly tacit.[108] However, after any such choice is made and implemented in a transformation, the transformation details can be described sufficiently objectively for assertions of authenticity.

3.4   Facts and Values: How Can We Distinguish?

What roused [Karl] Kraus's resentment ... was the mingling of opinion and fact involved in presenting news slanted by political interest. ... distorted in the free mingling of ... rational objectivity and subjective reaction that was the deliberate aim of the feuilleton. ... a subjective response to an objective state of affairs, ... laden with ... adjectives ... so much so, that the objective situation was lost in the shuffle. ...

For the bourgeois Viennese, with their passion for the arts, the feuilleton was the high point of all journalism ... in the Neue Freie Presse. To Kraus, however, the feuilleton destroyed both the objectivity of the situation de-

---

[108]   Polanyi 1966, *The Tacit Dimension*.

scribed and the creative fantasy of the writer ... prevent[ing] the reader from
making any rational assessment of the facts of the case.

Janik 1997, Wittgenstein's Vienna, p.79

A *fact* is a state of affairs in the world, or a state of affairs that might
have been, or might in the future come to be. The truth or falsity of any
fact can be observed; facts are empirical. That nobody might have observed a particular state of affairs is almost irrelevant to its being a fact or
to its truth or falsity.

The simplest facts, called *atomic* facts by some authors, are relationships such as, "My apple is on my kitchen table." A *value* is a mathematical entity (§3.1) or an ethical or aesthetic opinion that might motivate a
particular choice made by some human being, such as, "This kitten is play-
ful." (It is unfortunate that the word 'value' in natural English is ambiguous in the sense indicated here, and that both meanings are important for
the topics of this book. However, this ambiguity is so deeply engrained
that instead of choosing other words we will resolve it by modifiers when
needed.) In this context, *ethical* does not necessarily imply *moral*.[109]

Evidence, such as evidence of authenticity, consists of *facts, not value
judgments*. In connection with criminal law, we talk of eyewitnesses. The
word 'evidence', or more precisely 'evident' comes from the Latin 'ex vi-
dent', whose translation is 'out of [the fact that] they see'.

If we were to eavesdrop on audience conversations following a
performance of Beethoven's Violin Concerto, which exposes its soloist as
much as any other music composition, we would probably hear different
audience members voice similar critical opinions. What makes such
observations remarkable is that the opinions mostly come from speakers
who would insist that they lack music expertise.

What is probably occurring is that the opinions, themselves in the
domain of value judgments, are based on shared observations that range
from quite obvious facts, such as that the soloist played no incorrect notes,
to observations close to the boundary between facts and values, such as
that the soloist controlled his bowing technique so as to be highly
expressive. It is irrelevant to the point being made that the speakers might
themselves be unable to identify the particular facts that influence their
evaluations.

That objective factors might be difficult to discern is illustrated by
efforts to validate Rembrandt paintings.[110] The master's 40 pupils
emulated his style, sometimes even forging his signature, in pictures that

---

[109]   Instead it has to do with the kinds of distinction in Moore 1903, *Principia Ethica.*

[110]   Trevedi 2005, *The Rembrandt Code.*

dealers resold as the master's work. A century ago, about 700 works were attributed to Rembrandt. Since then, connoisseurs have identified nuanced features that distinguish master from student, eliminating about half the works from being considered authentic.

Imagine having to write an essay comparing Shakespeare's *Hamlet* to Lucas's *Star Wars*. Your statements might oscillate from one side to the other of the objective/subjective boundary—the boundary between what could be mechanized and what must forever remain a human value decision or judgment. The scope and limits of ordinary language are the subject of eloquent metaphor in:

> Positivism holds—and this is its essence—that what we can speak about is all that matters in life, whereas Wittgenstein passionately believes that all that really matters in human life is precisely what, in his view, we must be silent about. When he nevertheless takes immense pains to delimit the unimportant, it is not the coastline of that island which he is bent on surveying with such meticulous accuracy, but the boundary of the ocean.
>
> Engelmann 1967, *Letters from Ludwig Wittgenstein*, p.97

Readers are well served by authors who recognize that human communication is limited to the facts that language can convey, and who signal what is objective and what is opinion. How can we determine whether a sentence 'X is the case' purporting to be about the world expresses a fact or a value? Imagine an experiment in which we ask a large number of observers that we believe to be both competent and honest, "Do you see that X? Do you judge X to be a fact?" Here, X might be "an apple is on the table." 'Competent' should be understood to include both that the observer is physically capable of the observation called for and also that he can distinguish between what he sees and what he thinks. If nearly all the observers who say, "Yes, I see X," also agree that "X is a fact" is true, then almost surely X expresses a fact.

This is not to say that X is true. Every parched member of a desert expedition might say he sees a distant oasis that later proves to be a mirage. His statement would be factual, but incorrect.

One can almost always construct an objective statement of fact corresponding to a subjective expression of value, opinion, or choice. "On Monday, John Doe said, 'I believe P'" is objective, even if it happens to be false. Provenance metadata can usefully include such assertions, each conforming to the pattern, "X asserted S in historical circumstances Z." Something like this is a principal activity of government archives.

3.5   Representation Theory: Signs and Sentence Meanings

2.1	Wir machen uns Bilder der Tatsachen.	We make pictures of the facts for ourselves.
2.11	Das Bild stellt die Sachlage im logischen Raume, das Bestehen und Nichtbestehen von Sachverhalten vor.	A picture presents a situation in logical space, the existence and nonexistence of states of affairs.
2.12	Das Bild ist ein Modell der Wirklichkeit.	A picture is a model of reality.
2.13	Den Gegenständen entsprechen im Bilde die Elemente des Bildes.	In a model, the elements of the model correspond to the objects (of the reality).
2.14	Das Bild besteht darin, dass sich seine Elemente in bestimmter Art und Weise zueinander verhalten.	The picture's essence is that its elements are related to one another in a certain way.
2.15	Dass sich die Elemente des Bildes in bestimmter Art und Weise zu einander verhalten stellt vor, dass sich die Sachen so zu einander verhalten.	That picture elements are related to one another in a certain way represents that things are related to one another in the same way.

Wittgenstein 1921, *TLP*

The English translation of Hertz 1894, *The principles of mechanics* starts with, "We form for ourselves images or symbols of external objects and the form which we give them is such that the necessary consequents of the images in thought are always the images of the necessary consequents in nature of the things pictured." This picture theory, extended in *TLP* as just quoted, is the essence of representation theory. Almost every digital object that we can communicate is a *picture* or *representation* of something other than itself.

An *assertion* is a statement about something, expressed in marks on paper, or in some other manifestation that could be transformed to marks on paper by a finite sequence of mechanical steps—a picture. Wittgenstein's "ein Bild" is usually translated as "a picture." However, translating it as "a model" seems more likely to convey what Wittgenstein intended. It is a *symbol* for something other than itself—it stands for a fact or a concept.[111] Fig. 6 suggests what we might mean by *meaning*. The meaning of "ein Bild" is the worldly situation that it represents. We call a sign used this way a *representation*.

The picture of a situation is not the situation itself, even though the existence of such a picture in this chapter is itself a situation that could be depicted. However, Fig. 6 does not reflect the *TLP* model, because Wittgen-

---

[111]   "A word, or name, is not the image of an object; it is merely a sign standing for an object. But the proposition is an image of the depicted constellation of objects.

"An image, a picture, can represent anything except its own representational relationship to the depicted subject. (The rays of projection from the points of the original to those of the image cannot themselves appear in the picture.) If, then, the true propositions form a picture of the world, they can say nothing about their own relation to the world, by virtue of which they are its picture."   Engelmann 1967, *Letters from Ludwig Wittgenstein,* p. 101.

stein was striving to eliminate psychology from his theory of knowledge. Instead, a Wittgensteinian picture takes its meaning from its relationship to a situation in the real world. "An apple is on my kitchen table" has meaning even if no one knows whether or not the statement is true. Ideally, I could lead each reader to my kitchen to see the apple on the table for himself—obviously an impractical proposal.

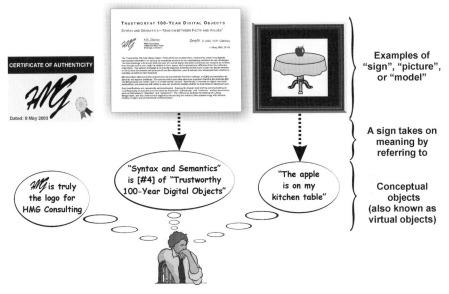

Fig. 6: A meaning of the word 'meaning'

Although showing readers a picture of an apple on a table, as in Fig. 6, would be a misleading interpretation of *TLP*, it does seem to correspond to what William James intended. His *How Two Minds Can Know One Thing*[112] suggests a relationship between the Fig. 4 conceptual objects and real-world relationships.

> [W]e confine the problem to a world merely 'thought-of' and not directly felt or seen. ... We find that any bit of [this world] which we may cut out as an example is connected with distinct groups of associates, just as our perceptual experiences are, that these associates link themselves with it by different relations, and that one forms the inner history of a person, while the other acts as an impersonal 'objective' world, either spatial and temporal, or else merely logical or mathematical, or otherwise 'ideal.'

> James 1904, *Does Consciousness Exist?* §III

---

[112] James 1905, *Essays in Radical Empiricism*, Chapter 4.

Frege deplored failures to distinguish symbols and what is symbolized.[113] The challenge is still with us.[114]

3.6 Documents and Libraries: Collections, Sets, and Classes

Every name or assertion has (at least) two senses (here 'sense' is almost, but not quite, a synonym for "meaning"): a $sense_1$ which is a relationship to the entity or entities (conceptual or real world) it names, and a $sense_2$ which is a relationship placing the name within the context at hand. The $sense_1$ both for the name 'the morning star' and also for the name 'the evening star' is the planet Venus. However, $sense_2$ for 'the morning star' might be "the brightest pinpoint of light in the sky in the wee hours," and similarly for 'the evening star'. It is an exercise in science and reasoning to recognize that the $sense_1$ corresponding to the two different names refers to the same real-world object.

This Venus example has to do with scientific fact. If we are talking about constructing something, such as a library collection or the works that should be cited by a scholarly paper, the import of the relationship between the $sense_2$ and the $sense_1$ of a collection description is prescriptive. Specifically, we ask whether the set of collected works (the $sense_1$) is adequately responsive to the $sense_2$ of the collection description and, if it is not, we attempt to identify the works that are missing.

Philosophers call the $sense_1$ of an expression or rule an *extension* of that expression. It is some number of objects—zero, one, two, or more objects—that mathematicians call a *set* of objects. Philosophers call the $sense_2$ of an expression its *intension* or *class*.[115] More widely used synonyms for extension and intension are, respectively, *denotation*[116] and *connotation*. For instance, 'the morning star' denotes a particular object—the planet Venus and connotes a certain procedure for observation. The predi-

---

[113] See the first chapter of Schilpp 1963, *The Philosophy of Rudolf Carnap*.

[114] "What most distinguishes human [being]s from other creatures is our ability to create and manipulate a wide variety of symbolic representations. This capacity enables us to transmit information from one generation to another, making culture possible, and to learn vast amounts without having direct experience. ... Although symbolic thinking is a hallmark of being human, it is not something infants can do. Instead children learn such thinking over several years. ... Only when children can see an object both as itself and as depicting something else can they start to think symbolically."

DeLoache 2005, *Mindful of Symbols*.

[115] For a careful analysis, see Davidson, *The Method of Extension and Intension*, in Schilpp 1963, *The Philosophy of Rudolf Carnap*. This essay is difficult reading because the notions involved are as subtle as they are important to any theory of language's meanings.

[116] Russell 1905, *On Denoting*.

cate portion of a *SQL* database query expresses an intension; the query evaluation result is, in the context of a particular database, its extension.

Starting in §6.4, this book discusses metadata to describe data that might be considered for preservation. Such metadata will describe the associated data and its role and position in the world—its genre, its name, its date of origin, other objects to which it is related, and so on. This is an example of a sense$_2$ or the articulation of an intension for the data being described. Ideally, such metadata will describe the object uniquely within its context, effectively naming the object. By packaging the metadata together with the data we will assert the reference to the same real world object mentioned above, and by sealing this package (§11.1) we will testify to this association for as long as some copy of the package survives—firmly binding a particular intension to the appropriate extension.

'Intension' and 'extension' are philosophers' jargon that is not used in other professions. Natural language has many words to denote "some number of related objects." *Collection*, *set*, and *class* are prominent. Each of these also has a technical meaning—a meaning used by some specialized community. Librarians use *collection* to denote copies of intellectual works that might be acquired to implement an institutional policy. Mathematicians use *set*, but do not usually try to define it, except ostensively (§3.1), because the words that might appear in a definition are often themselves defined in terms of *set*. Many professions use *class* to denote objects indicated by a natural language phrase, such as "spherical objects" or "balls," particularly when a speaker wishes to draw attention to the attributes connoted by the words, as in, "Most balls are spherical objects."

What the current book means by the noun 'set' is different from what it means by the noun 'collection,' even though the Oxford Thesaurus indicates that these are synonyms. It uses 'set' to denote what has been called extension above; more precisely, by 'set' this book means an entity of the Zermelo-Fraenkel set theory.[117] It uses 'class' to denote what has been called intension. It uses 'collection' to indicate the notion that librarians commonly intend. Specifically, what this book means by a *collection* is the set of entities denoted by somebody's designation of a class, as in "all books published before 1965 and mentioning the Carthaginian general, Hannibal" or "all digital objects cited by the document path:/A/B/C/doc.html, and by these objects recursively for three levels of indirection." In other words, a collection can be defined to be the result set of some query, which might be an SQL query. With this definition, the holdings of a repository are a special kind of collection, e.g., "all holdings of the University of California Library."

---

[117] *Set Theory*, http://plato.stanford.edu/entries/set-theory/.

Such care is necessary for clarity. While an aggregation might conform to what is intended by 'set', it might also conform to what is intended by 'class', or it might instead satisfy neither intension. Whether or not a specific class corresponds to a particular set is a matter either for careful inquiry, as evidenced by many mathematical and philosophical works written between 1870 and 1940, or for construction, as in creating a library collection.

A surprising number of the 1870 mathematical dilemmas are connected to the notion of infinity, but were resolved by about 1940.[118] These include notions of continuity and the entire basis of mathematical analysis (calculus). Although true infinities do not occur in physics or computing, mathematical formalism that admits infinity is convenient for analyzing situations with very large numbers of elements.

What value has all this, and the careful work of two or three generations of philosophers, for discussing digital preservation? An example of the value occurs for one topic we might want to discuss—what a librarian calls a "subject classification." We can relatively precisely describe a *subject classification* as, "a large set of class names in which each name has as its context the relationships with the other classes denoted in the subject classification." This description signals that each class name is meaningful only within the context of many other class names (the rest of the subject classification) and that each class name is to be associated with a set of intellectual works—respectively the intension and the extension of the class name.

3.7   Syntax, Semantics, and Rules

> [E]very use of language to describe experience in a changing world applies language to a somewhat unprecedented instance of its subject matter, and thus somewhat modifies both the meaning of language and the structure of our conceptual framework.
>
> Polanyi 1958, *PK,* p.104

Syntax is the relationship of sign components to each other. A *syntactic mapping* is the set of relationships of some signs to other signs. *Semantics* is the aggregated relationships of signs either to concepts or to real world objects, and the relationship of such sign meanings to each other.

In Fig. 2, the relationship of the nth intermediate representation to its successor is, for $1 \leq n < 9$, syntactic after the communication has occurred. However, its choice before the transformation is accomplished is a semantic decision, just as a spoken sentence is a semantic choice until it is ut-

---

[118]   For an elegant account of the subject, see Hilbert 1925, *On the Infinite.*

tered, but can thereafter be described by observations about its syntax. The kind of meaning suggested by Fig. 6 is useful for discussing digital preservation.

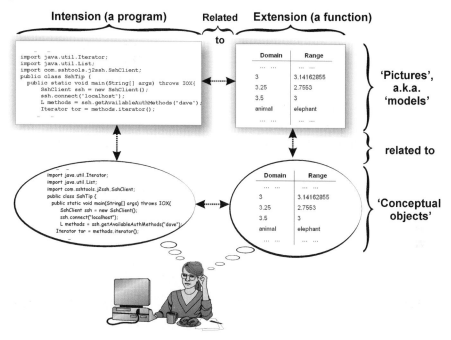

Fig. 7: Semantics or 'meaning' of programs
(illustrating the relationship between intensions and extensions)

In contrast, when a software engineer refers to the meaning of a computer program, he might have in mind the relationship of the program's outputs to its inputs—a functional table as illustrated on the right side of Fig. 7. This relates a kind of rule (an *intension*) and its associated *extension*.

Philosophical discussions of the role of *rules*[119] help toward working out a digital preservation methodology. Rules are used in many places in repository architecture—most prominently in semiautomatic control of software layers in storage hierarchies, and in potential metadata creation editors and validation processes within document ingest services, in which they help users conform to standard and wanted syntax.

Every formal theory can be represented by a symbolic system, using symbols that might be used without being formally defined. A symbolic system is likely to start with several axioms, which are symbol strings (lin-

---

[119] See *PI,* and also Kripke 1984, *Wittgenstein on Rules and Private Language.*

ear combinations) supplied without any justifying argument except after-the-fact justification that their consequences are interesting, perhaps because the symbolic system maps a set of empirical facts. In addition, symbolic systems contain *production rules* that regulate how new strings may be created. In mathematical symbol systems, these produced strings would be theorems, which can be associated with natural language assertions that have been proven to be true. In global symbol systems, the definition of theorems might not be so strict.

Almost every conceptual model can be abstracted. The interpretations of expressions and productions of this symbolic system—elaborations of the conceptual model—depend partly on tacit assumptions about symbol meanings, appropriateness of axioms, and the system's production rules. However, any expression of an intension "... X ..." might encounter the objection, "But you are assuming we understand what you mean by X."

A clerical or automatic *procedure* is a *rule*. A *computer program* is a procedure expressed in a formal language that a *compiler* or *interpreter* can prepare for execution on some machine by translating it to the *machine language* for the computer's architecture.

> Although I myself have completed only finitely many sums in the past, the rule [for addition] determines my answer for indefinitely many new sums that I have never previously considered. ... in learning to add I grasp a rule: my past intentions regarding addition determine a unique answer for indefinitely many new cases in the future.
>
> Kripke 1984, *Wittgenstein on Rules and Private Language,* p.7

Another meaning of program meaning is articulation in a formal semantics language, such as denotational semantics.[120] To explain program meaning to a reader in this way is like explaining the meaning of a Sanskrit passage him by giving its Latin translation even if he has no more than elementary Latin. This kind of meaning is not prominent in the current book, which instead uses the kinds of languages that information producers might use for metadata and for informal descriptions of preserved information.

3.8   Summary

> From where does our investigation get its importance, since it seems only to destroy everything interesting—that is, all that is great and important? ... What we are destroying is nothing but houses of cards, and we are clearing the ground of language on which they stood.

---

[120]   Gordon 1979, *The Denotational Description of Programming Languages.*

> The results of philosophy are the uncovering of one or another piece of
> plain nonsense ... that the understanding has got by running its head up
> against the limits of language.
>
> Wittgenstein 1958, PI §§118-9

Philosophers often write about what will not work, exposing notions
that are surely misleading.[121] What makes their analyses as valuable as
they prove to be is that eliminating inadequate methodologies, together
with insight into why each is unsatisfactory, helps us focus on achievable
objectives.

The notions of *extension* and *intension*[122] generalize patterns that have
many different labels. This is an example of a more general hypothesis,
that knowledge theory can be reduced to a surprisingly small number of
ideas[123] (§13.3) that common language denotes in many ways without
much attention to the fact its labels are often synonyms, or near-synonyms,
of one another. Some of these ideas are best framed as limitations or
bounds that no amount of ingenuity will overcome.

The current book tries to emphasize objectively decidable aspects, separating these from subjective factors. For any subjective factor, it is critical
to convey whose choice is represented.

Philosophical ideas that strongly influence the book's treatment of digital preservation include the following:

- Sensitivity to the limits of language and communication expressed in
  words.
- Sensitivity to the distinction between objective facts and subjective values, particularly as a guide to staying within the traditional engineer's
  role, not infecting technical recommendations with value judgments that
  clients find inappropriate.
- Conviction that the limits of what can be automated or specified as
  clerical tasks are rules that can be expanded into a finite number of steps
  to achieve the objectives at hand.
- Conviction that no document is comprehensible except in the context of
  many other documents.

---

[121] Hertz 1894, *The principles of mechanics*, p. 8.

[122] Carnap 1946, *Meaning and Necessity*, pp.25–32.

[123] To provide such a list explicitly would have been foolhardy in 1950, and is probably risky still
today. That it might be possible at all is the result of more than a century's analysis by the
world's most astute thinkers, starting with Emmanuel Kant and almost surely not yet complete.
Of course, even Kant drew on predecessors.

- Careful distinctions between *collection*, *set*, and *class*—synonyms in ordinary conversation—that help us convey what we mean about information collections more precisely than would otherwise be possible.

If a choice is subjective and needed for information sharing within a community larger than a few friends, it will not be settled quickly. It fact, it might never be settled to most people's unqualified satisfaction. This kind of difficulty plagues discussions of choosing metadata and of semantic interoperability. It is why electronic data processing standards discussions last for ten years or longer, and might result in competing standards that few people use as their authors intended.

4 Lessons from Scientific Philosophy

> Like chessmen, the symbols of pure mathematics stand not, or not necessarily, for anything denoted by them, but primarily for the use that can be made of them according to known rules. The mathematical symbol embodies the conception of its operability, just as a bishop or a knight in chess embodies the conception of the moves of which it is capable.
>
> Polanyi 1958, *PK, p.85*

Computers manipulate symbols that are surrogates for what they mean—symbolic representations of things and circumstances other than themselves. A computer model is good if its pattern follows the pattern of what it stands for. A *meaning* is a *relationship* between a symbol and some performance, package, concept, fact, or real world object.

What can we preserve of *meaning* for future generations? We might hope that information consumers understand exactly what producers intend to convey. The Fig. 2 arrows with question marks suggest that communicating intended meaning unambiguously is impossible in principle. The other arrows depict communications that can be restricted to purely syntactic transformations, including some between analog and digital representations.

We would like to explain how close we can come to communicating intended meaning. However, what we in fact do in the current chapter amounts to little more than identifying sources of confusion to avoid.

4.1 Intentional and Accidental Information

> My experiences and your experiences are 'with' each other in various external ways, but mine pass into mine, and yours pass into yours in a way in which yours and mine never pass into one another. ... Though the functions exerted by my experience and by yours may be the same (e.g., the same objects known and the same purposes followed), yet the sameness has in this case to be ascertained expressly (and often with difficulty and uncertainty) after the break has been felt.
>
> James 1904, *A World of Pure Experience*

Fig. 2 reminded us that every step of information sharing potentially involves representation transformation. The document **3** might have been generated from any combination of text, analog sound, images, videos, and computer programs. The transmission **0→1** involves semantics (representation of meaning with symbols) and the transmission **9→10** includes interpretation (trying to understand what meaning the signal's producers intended). After a communication has been completed, we can (at least in principle) describe precisely the transformation that occurred in each step of **1→9**. In contrast, we can say nothing objectively certain about the relationship of a conceptual input **0** or conceptual output **10** to any other object in the transmission channel.

We call a transformation that drops essential information irreversible. In this, *essential* is always to be understood to be relative to somebody's particular purpose. Both reversible and irreversible transformations are implicit in much of what follows, but occasionally need explicit attention. Reversible transformations are particularly useful. What *reversible* means depends on what the producer regards as essential to his message and what he considers accidental, and also on what can be inferred from the computational context.

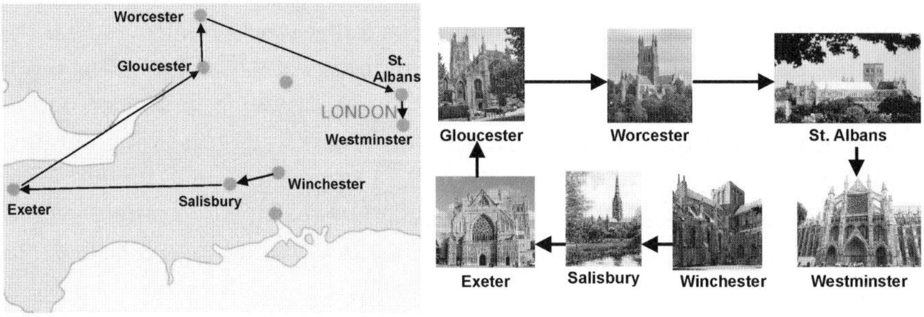

	origin	destination
Winchester to Salisbury to Exeter to Gloucester to Worcester to St. Albans to Westminster	Winchester	Salisbury
	Salisbury	Exeter
	Exeter	Gloucester
	Gloucester	Worcester
	Worcester	St. Albans
	St. Albans	Westminster

Fig. 8: Depictions of an English cathedrals tour

I know which conventions I am using to distinguish what is essential from what is accidental.[124] For instance, each Fig. 8 frame represents what I want to convey, a particular tour of English cathedrals. This information is represented first as a geographical map, then as a directed labeled graph, then as a sequence, and finally as a mathematical relation. Collectively, the four depictions do a better job of communicating the intended message than any single picture, because whoever reads them can see which aspects differ, and will know that these are accidental if he understands that I (the information producer) intend every one of the four depictions to convey the same information.

---

[124]   McDonough 1986, *The Argument of the Tractatus*, ch.viii.

This book's title is *Preserving Digital Information*. You might object that "digital" is not an essential attribute of what is to be preserved. Such an objection would have merit, but would still not persuade me to change the title. The core of the debate is that the word 'digital' has been my subjective choice. Although you are likely to guess correctly why I made this choice, to me this is less important than that it was my choice what to emphasize and what word to choose. These circumstances are similar to those that might cause me to say, "I hit him on the head with a big book." Again, "big" is probably not an attribute that you would include in describing what it means to be a book. However, it is essential to the picture of hitting that I want to convey. The points, already made above, are that what is *essential* and what is merely *accidental* is a speaker's subjective choice and that this choice is likely to be guided by what the speaker wants to convey.

4.2   Distinctions Sought and Avoided

In everyday language it very frequently happens that the same word has different modes of signification—and so belongs to different symbols—or that two words that have different modes of signification are employed in propositions in what is superficially the same way.

In this way the most fundamental confusions are easily produced (the whole of philosophy is full of them).

Wittgenstein 1921, *TLP* 3.323 & 3.324

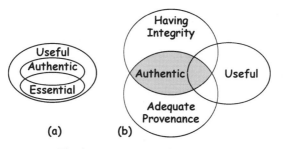

Fig. 9: Relationships of meanings;
(a) is unsatisfactory, (b) is helpful.

Confusion is all too easily generated by a hasty choice of key terms of reference. For instance, a problem with relationships suggested by Fig. 9(a) is that, if you say, "X is authentic," I might infer that X was also useful for whatever we were talking about. In contrast, Fig. 9(b) suggests that *authenticity* is made up of *integrity* and *provenance* qualities, that a useful object might not be authentic, and that an authentic object might not be useful.

In common usage, the words 'archive' and 'repository' are *overloaded* (ambiguous). Each of these is used to denote sometimes an institution, sometimes a service, and sometimes a preserved collection. For instance, Nelson's model of an archive[125] looks much like our §6.4 model of a document collection.

In contrast, we sometimes find it useful, or even essential, to ignore conventional distinctions. In particular, the usual distinction between 'document' and 'collection' conceals similarity that, if exploited, much simplifies the representation and management of records of all kinds, because almost all records identify other records that are helpful in, or even essential to, their correct interpretation.

Conventional English verbs such as 'read' and 'print', and nouns such as 'report', are often too narrow. Where their use would otherwise be ambiguous, the reader should construe them broadly. Similarly, information producers' topics and styles are mostly irrelevant to the methods and means of digital communication and long-term preservation. Thus, appellations such as 'author', 'artist', 'musician', 'composer', and so on are effectively synonyms for which we use 'producer' except when doing so would make the text stilted.

Allusions to people—appellations such as 'consumer' and 'manager'— and depictions of people in the figures generally denote the roles that these people assume in the transactions being discussed, rather than their professions or organizational positions and responsibilities. Almost surely there is at least one U.K. National Archives employee who participates in preservation-related activities sometimes as a producer, sometimes as a consumer, sometimes as an archive manager, and sometimes as an auditor.

Do '110010100' and '*110010100*' mean the same thing? What do we mean by "the same as"? The answer to this question is not as obvious as you might think. The answer must include, "It depends on the conversation we are having and, even within this context, you might have to ask me." [126]

Suppose a man takes two points and draws a line through them:

---

[125] Nelson 2005, *Archive Ingest and Handling Test: The Old Dominion University Approach*, §2.2.

[126] The long quotation that follows is an excerpt from Diamond 1976, *Wittgenstein's Lectures on the Foundations of Mathematics,* Chap. 24.

James 1905, *The Thing and its Relations,* Appendix C, also discusses the question.

He then shows me two points and tells me, "Do the same"; and I draw
this line:

Am I necessarily wrong? If he says, "No, I told you to do the same'", I
may say, "Well, this is the same."

Or suppose we take a circle and inscribe in it a pentagon, and then a
square, and then a triangle. And we now say, "Go on and inscribe a bian-
gle." He might perhaps draw a diameter.

"Now go still *further*, inscribe a monangle." He might draw some figure:

If we said, "But that is different," he might reply, "Well yes, of course.
But then the pentagon was different from the square, and the square was
different from the triangle." What is the continuation of that line, and
why shouldn't we say that this is?

Or he might say, "There is no such thing"—which would come to "I am
not inclined to call anything the continuation of that line."

Lynch writes, "The assignment of identifiers to works is a very powerful
act; it states that, within a given intellectual framework, two instances of a
work that have been assigned the same identifier are the same, while two
instances of a work with different identifiers are distinct."[127] Notice
Lynch's use of "the same." Consider "is similar to" and "the same" for the
simplest models, and "I am not inclined to call anything" the same as selections you might have made, as in the preceding quotation from Wittgenstein. Even elementary choices are subjective.

In ordinary conversation, we often use signs that look different to mean
the same thing. A word or phrase takes on meanings that we share within
a context as a matter of social convention. Even context boundaries are
social conventions. We choose particular shared meanings and shared
contexts because we find doing so to be useful. However, no matter how
much care we have taken during a conversation with our word choices, we
often find it necessary to backtrack, saying something like, "By ... I did not
mean ..., but rather ...".

---

[127] Lynch 1997, *Identifiers and their Role in Networked Information Applications*,
http://www.arl.org/newsltr/194/identifier.html.

4.3   *Information* and *Knowledge*: Tacit and Human Aspects

> I regard knowing as an active comprehension of the things known, an action that requires skill. ... Acts of comprehension are ... irreversible, and also non-critical. ... Such is the personal participation of the knower in all acts of understanding. But this does not make our understanding subjective. Comprehension is neither an arbitrary act nor a passive experience, but a responsible act claiming universal validity. Such knowing is indeed objective in the sense of establishing contact with a hidden reality; a contact that is defined as the condition for anticipating an indeterminate range of yet unknown (and perhaps yet inconceivable) true implications.
>
> Polanyi 1958, *PK* preface

"Knowledge management" has become a prominent topic.[128] Under various names, it has been considered by the artificial intelligence community for about thirty years and by archivists grappling with records and information discovery for about ten. Archivists use fonds to organize records into collections, partly for preserving the meaning of the terms that they use to support discovery of individual records. Some people argue that semantics management is archivists' principal responsibility.

Some authors have promoted their information management projects as "knowledge management," perhaps because the seemingly grander term helps them obtain enterprise support and funding,[129] for instance in a suggestion that university Information Science Departments should be renamed "Knowledge Science Departments".[130] This makes it necessary to remind readers of distinctions between "knowledge" as an objective topic (treating what can be known and communicated) and "knowing" as a psychological topic (discussing what some person or animal might know). Wittgenstein makes immense effort to treat objective knowledge, separat-

---

[128] The call for papers for a 2006 *Knowledge Organization Systems and Services* conference includes, "Knowledge Organization Systems (KOS), such as classification systems, gazetteers, lexical databases, ontologies, taxonomies and thesauri, attempt to model the underlying semantic structure of a domain for the purposes of retrieval. Traditionally the focus has been on construction of print-based resources. Possibilities for networked KOS-based services are emerging but pose new challenges in today's complex, interdisciplinary knowledge domains."

[129] 'Knowledge Management' (KM) is controversial. McElroy 2004, *How to Operationalize KM*, http://www.macroinnovation.com/How_to_Operationalize_KM.pdf, suggests a distinction between first generation KM and second generation KM. It starts with the view that there is a difference between producing and integrating knowledge in business—'Knowledge Processing' (KP) and systematic attempts to enhance processes by improving people's knowledge. Unlike KP, second generation KM addresses knowledge production, which it must do if it is to address first generation KM's *failure to distinguish between information [and] knowledge*. (The italics are McElroy's.)
  See also Maurer 2002, *On a New Powerful Model for Knowledge Management*.

[130] Private conversation with Chaim Zins of Bar-Ilan University, Jerusalem.

ing this as much as possible from subjective aspects. In contrast, psychology is embraced in the writings of William James.

The nature and content of knowledge has been a prominent philosophical topic at least since Kant shifted philosophical attention away from "reality" and "das Ding an sich" to human judgements about human perceptions.[131] It continues today as a topic of opinion and active inquiry.[132]

To discuss preservation clearly, we need an easily discerned boundary between what we mean by knowledge and what we mean by information. Without intending any critique of painstaking philosophical considerations or modern views about what common usage is or should be,[133] this book identifies *knowledge* as that which is contained in human memories and which, when used together with reasoning, enables action and communication. It uses *information* for what has been, or can be, communicated in speech, signals, pictures, writing, other artifacts, and perhaps even with body language. With these attributes, information is a proper subset of human knowledge.

Consider medical literature describing detailed procedures for open heart surgery. You could read and memorize such literature, but doing so would not in itself qualify you to perform heart surgery. Among critical factors is the distinction between "knowing about" and "knowing how to."[134] Part of "knowing how to" is immense implicit and tacit knowledge[135] that made it possible for the best medical authors to provide the articles you might have read. This tacit knowledge surely also includes surgeons' remembered sensations that guide their fingers, but that they would find difficult to articulate. Interpreting what they have written itself would involve shared experience, shared language, and shared world views—further implicit knowledge.

Popper's 'World 3' picture (p. 1) eloquently articulates the social value of the information we hold in libraries, separating that from "all our sub-

---

[131] Kant 1787, *The Critique of Pure Reason.*

Cassirer 1978, The *problem of knowledge: philosophy, science, and history since Hegel.*

Ryle 1949, *The concept of mind.*

[132] Magee 1978, *Talking Philosophy.*

Searle 1998, *Mind, Language and Society.*

[133] Conceptual boundaries suggested by Fig. 10 and §4.3 differ from those of other authors. Moore 2002, *Preservation of Data, Information, and Knowledge* starts, "Digital entities are images of reality, stored as data (bits) that must be interpreted … by applying information (semantic tags that provide the meaning of the bits) and knowledge (structural relationships defined by a data model)."

[134] Ryle 1949, *The concept of mind,* Chapter 2, "Knowing How and Knowing That".

[135] Polanyi 1966, *Personal Knowledge,* Part II.

jective learning" as suggested by the information/knowledge distinction in Fig. 10. For instance, this distinction is manifest in an analysis of what happens when a parent teaches bicycle riding to a child. What the parent can be seen to communicate does not include enough knowledge to ride without falling; what the child learns with the aid of trial and error somehow supplies the shortfall. We cannot confidently assert that the child's eventual knowledge for bicycle riding is identical to what the parent knew before the lessons began. Teaching and learning are complex processes that are suggested not only in Fig. 10, but also by the **0→1** and **9→10** steps of Fig. 2. We know so little about them that we do not attempt knowledge preservation, but address only its information preservation subset.

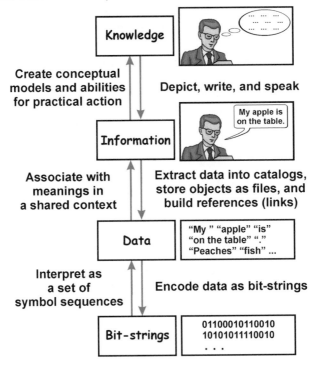

Fig. 10: Bit-strings, data, information, and knowledge
suggesting processes that we use to transform
among different ways of remembering

Figure 10 suggests the distinction by the difference between the "My apple is on the table" speech in its information example box and the incompleteness of the corresponding thought depiction in its knowledge example box immediately above.

We might have completed the Fig. 10 thought depiction similarly to the thought depiction at the right side of Fig. 4. The latter is how we would, and often do, depict a *knowledge* instance belonging to the subset we call *information*.

Some authors refer to knowledge management as a key component of digital preservation.[136] Of course they are free to choose whatever language they like. However, making exaggerated choices risks blurring the boundary with other scholarship. In contrast to the phrase 'knowledge management', the phrase 'knowledge worker' introduces no confusion because every knowledge worker acts on knowledge that he has but cannot communicate—the knowing how to.

Whenever a choice coincides with a widely used locution, but differs from how people use it in informal discourse, we risk misunderstandings and tedious explanations of how and why what we intend differs from what other people expect. An eloquent argument for careful language is Martin Gardner's comment on a *Through the Looking Glass* passage:

> 'I don't know what you mean by "glory,"' Alice said.
>
> Humpty Dumpty smiled contemptuously. 'Of course you don't—till I tell you. I meant "there's a nice knock-down argument for you!"'
>
> 'But "glory" doesn't mean "a nice knock-down argument,"' Alice objected.
>
> 'When I use a word,' Humpty Dumpty said ..., 'it means just what I choose it to mean—neither more nor less.'
>
> 'The question is,' said Alice, 'whether you can make words mean so many different things.'
>
> 'The question is,' said Humpty Dumpty, 'which is to be master—that's all.'
>
> Even in logic and mathematics ... enormous confusion often results from a failure to realize that words mean "neither more nor less" than what they are intended to mean. ... On the other hand, if we wish to communicate accurately, we are under a kind of moral obligation to avoid Humpty's practice of giving private meanings to commonly used words.
>
> Carroll 1872, The Annotated Alice, p.213

4.4 Trusted and Trustworthy

In the way it occurs in some digital preservation literature, "trusted" is likely to mislead anyone expecting ordinary English usage. "Trustworthy" would be more accurate. Whether or not you trust me is your decision. I can only behave in ways that encourage you to trust me. That is to say, I can try to be deserving of trust, i.e., trustworthy.

In contrast its use in phrases like "Trusted Digital Repository," 'trusted' in the following paragraphs denotes a controlled relationship.

---

[136] Ludäscher 2001, *Preservation ... with ... Knowledge-Based Archives*, is an example.

What is called a *trusted computing base* or *module* (*TCB* or *TCM*) is intended for reliable execution of arbitrary programs whose results cannot be independently validated, except perhaps by further expensive calculations. TCB architecture was designed in the 1970s for military intelligence and defense applications that must forestall security risks unlikely in civilian library applications. For instance, a military surveillance system needs to be safe from infiltration that modifies its software to hide potential targets. Archives are much simpler; they merely regurgitate what they were fed. They have only two critical kinds of output: search results and reproductions of deposited documents. Using TCB architecture would lead the library community into adopting systems, an infrastructure, and an internal methodology far more expensive than an alternative that can achieve the objectives tabulated in the cited study.

Computer manufacturers have begun to offer PCs and motherboards equipped with a TCM, a dedicated microchip enabled for security-specific capabilities. The *trusted personal computer* hardware platform[137]—running a secure environment rather than depending on software-only security measures—is emerging as a powerful tool for improving enterprise user authentication and data protection.

The critical distinction is that, for a TCB, the identity and logic of the trusting entity are known. Specifically, the trusting entity is software that is provided by a development team that works closely with the designers of the hardware and firmware security component that it depends on. It is usually an operating system that interacts closely with a sealed computer logic and memory component that is the TCB itself. The operating system code can be inspected and tested to determine precisely how it uses the TCB. In contrast, analogous examination of repository users would be ridiculous to suggest and impossible to perform.

4.5 Relationships and Ontologies

[I] aim to establish a "constructional system," that is, an epistemic-logical system of objects or concepts. … Unlike other conceptual systems, a constructional system undertakes more than the division of concepts into various kinds and the investigation of the differences and mutual relations between these kinds. In addition, it attempts a step-by-step derivation or "construction" of all concepts from certain fundamental concepts, so that a genealogy of concepts results in which each one has its definite place. … all concepts can in this way be derived from a few fundamental concepts, and it is in this respect that it differs from most other ontologies.

Carnap 1928, *LSW* §1

---

[137]   White 1987, *ABYSS: A Trusted Architecture for Software Protection.*

According to a story that might be apocryphal, in 1914 Wittgenstein read a traffic accident report illustrated with miniature vehicles and buildings.[138] He was impressed that this model was helpful not simply because its objects corresponded to real world objects, but that it was made informative by the positioning of the toy vehicles and buildings corresponding to an arrangement in the real world. According to the story, this revelation led him, in his *picture theory*, to emphasize relationships over individual objects and object classes.[139] (Wittgenstein seems to have been influenced by Hertz, whose *Introduction* to his 1894 monograph, *The principles of mechanics,* introduces picture theory on its first page.)

The *structure* of a part of the world that constitutes a domain of discourse is the set of relationships between its objects. An *ontology* is an organization of semantic labels—of names by which we know these objects and relationships. The word 'ontology' was adopted from philosophy, which had long used it to denote the study of or discourse about the nature of being. For instance, 'ontology' and its cognates are prominently used in Heidegger 1926, *Being and Time,* a massive effort to articulate the essential natures of being and of time. Ontology is sometimes used as a synonym of metaphysics, a broader topic than science because it includes theology.

Starting about twenty years ago, computer scientists and librarians started to use the word *ontology* for the meaningful relationships between semantic labels. We use many kinds of ontology: logical relationship sets called concept maps, procedural relationship sets called process maps or work flows, spatial relationship sets called atlases, and so on. An *ontological commitment* is a promise to use a specific vocabulary for shared concepts.

Subject classifications,[140] information taxonomies,[141] and thesauri[142] are closely related topics for which there is a wealth of publications. Excellent

---

[138] Peat 2002, *From certainty to uncertainty*, p. 76.

[139] "The world is the totality of facts, not of things." *TLP* 1.1

"If the elementary facts are known, all the possible composite facts follow. The logical relations between facts are depicted by corresponding relations between the propositions."
Engelmann 1967, *Letters from Ludwig Wittgenstein*, p. 102

[140] For instance, the *Library of Congress subject headings* at http://memory.loc.gov/ammem/awhhtml/awgc1/lc_subject.html.

[141] Delphi Group 2004, *Information Intelligence: Content Classification and ... Taxonomy Practice*, http://www.delphigroup.com/research/whitepapers/20040601-taxonomy-WP.pdf.

[142] For instance, the *UK Archival Thesaurus* at http://www.ukat.org.uk/

tools are becoming available for visualizing ontologies, for navigating among their nodes,[143] and for searching them.[144]

The content management literature includes assertions like, "Large ontologies such as WordNet provide a thesaurus for over 100,000 terms explained in natural language."[145] Such assertions suggest a blurry frontier between the concepts of ontology and thesaurus, as well as the librarians' term, 'subject classification', and the digital standards term, 'reference model'. The word *ontology* has other definitions, perhaps because it is in vogue; discussions of the Semantic Web and of "Knowledge Management" are full of it.[146] Its ambiguity is perhaps reason to avoid the word in our own writing, even while we strain to understand what other authors intend to convey with it.

A *reference model,* such as OAIS (§1.4) is an ontology extended by careful descriptions of processes for managing its components. How a reference model overlaps a requirements statement is illustrated in §6.5.

4.6   What Copyright Protection Teaches

[F]or Socrates (as for Plato) written forms are pale shadows of their human counterparts. They may speak, but they are incapable of dialogue, ... But [this] fails to get at what is most extraordinary about written forms. For it is exactly in their ability to ensure the repeatability of their talk [*sic*] that they are most powerful. The brilliance of writing—of creating communicative symbols—is ... a way to make things talk, coupled with the ability to ensure the repeatability of that talk. [*sic*]

Levy 1999, *The Universe is Expanding*

What makes an archived record of a 1950 law valuable is that the expression it carries was inscribed or printed to become the particular copy delivered to the archive in 1950 and that this process was managed to ensure the authenticity of the preserved copy. The 1950 physical carrier (paper) is valuable today only if the procedures and records of the archive make it unlikely that it has been tampered with. The value of the paper it-

---

[143] Fluit 2002, *Ontology-based Information Visualization.* See also *ADUNA Autofocus Products,* http://aduna.biz/products/autofocus/.

John Sowa (private communication) particularly recommends *CMAP software*, "This is one of the few concept mapping tools that seems to work in practice, with a special focus on collaborative modeling, and even better, completely free of charge." See http://cmap.ihmc.us/.

[144] One such tool is *Kowari*, an open source, special-purpose DBMS for metadata and ontologies, available at http://www.kowari.org/. Kowari is limited to storing ternary relations with 64-bit fields. These limitations enable high performance for unusually complex queries

[145] Moreira 2004, *"Thesaurus" and "Ontology".*

[146] For instance, several December 2005 *Communications of the ACM* articles, and also *What is an Ontology,* http://www-ksl.stanford.edu/kst/what-is-an-ontology.html.

self is created primarily by its evidentiary role. The paper and the archive exist in order to provide evidence for the conceptual abstraction—the pattern inherent in extant and potential replicas of the paper's content. A *pattern* is a Fig. 4 conceptual object. We see from the Levy quotation that these notions are ancient.

Much of the digital content whose owners claim copyright protection is also candidate for long-term preservation. To be eligible for copyright or for archiving, information must be fixed. For dynamic information, this is conventionally done in the forms of

- performance prescriptions, such as music scores, plays or librettos, mathematical proofs, computer programs, business procedures, and so on;
- performances proper, such as audio and video recordings, (computer) logs, (transaction) recovery logs, historical chronologies, business journals, and so on; and
- snapshots, such as video freeze-frames, instantaneous machine state information for program debugging, database snapshots, business balance sheets, and so on.

The essential core of copyright protection is that, if a work has once been represented in tangible form, copyright protects the originator's beneficial rights for using the symbolic pattern represented, rather than the ideas. A delightful fable identifies what can be protected, and therefore much of what is worth preserving.

> Fire swept through the converted grain silo that Naomi Marra has called home … Feared lost among the charred ruins is the last extant copy of her lyric ode, *Ruthless Boaz*. … [D]evotees hope that, following her many public declamations of the work, most or all of it may remain preserved in her memory. … Query: Is *Ruthless Boaz* still subject to statutory copyright protection?
>
> Nimmer 1998, *Adams and Bits*

With this hypothetical case, Nimmer analyzes the protection of intangible value—patterns inherent in the reproductive instances—extant and potential replicas of each document. The essential symbolic patterns of a document are those needed to allow it to be Levy's "talking thing."[147] (The word 'essential' is often misused by failing to be related to some identified purpose of identified individuals. Levy's usage is correct, being implicitly that the document speaks for its author(s), helping him (them) to convey intended meaning.)

---

[147] Levy 1998, *Heroic Measures: Reflections on the Possibility and Purpose of Digital Preservation.*

This is enough in principle, but not in practice if the content or ownership of a copyright is contested in litigation. A frequent and difficult litigation issue is the distinction between the pattern and coincidentally similar information that is part of the published instance. It is difficult because it is subjective, as discussed in §3.3 and §4.1. Questions of ownership are clearer, and can be resolved by evidence if a sufficient audit trail has been reliably protected against misrepresentation. For prudent protection of a digital information object, it should be tightly bound to metadata that describe who created it and when this was done—its *provenance* description.

4.7   Summary

[M]y mind has been growing into a certain type of weltanschauung. Rightly or wrongly, I have got to the point where I can hardly see things in any other pattern.

James 1904, *A World of Pure Experience*

For work depending on high precision or with significant risk from possible systematic error or institutional confusion, it is prudent to buttress common sense with searching analysis. For digital preservation, the analysis should be grounded in philosophical theories of knowledge, information, and communication.

Much of twentieth century scientific philosophy might seem to be no more than common sense. It would not have seemed so a century ago. Since then, its inventors have been immensely successful in persuading Western scholars to accept, use, and teach their views.

Some common sense is helpful, but other common sense is misleading. The best known case of being misled is that of Euclidean geometry, which for two millenia was thought to describe the structure of real space. Distinguishing model from empirical fact is a subtle task whose results can be controversial.   Creating today's professional consensus that separates mathematics from the physical sciences, which hold that space is curved, involved a half century's investigation and debate by the most profound thinkers of their times.

The most difficult technical preservation objective is ensuring that consumers can read or otherwise use each preserved object precisely as its producers intended. Accomplishing this is, in principle, impossible for at least some data types.[148] A prudent revision of the challenge is, "How can a producer represent preserved information to minimize each eventual consumer's misunderstandings of what he intended to convey?"

We might want structures and mechanisms that admit no misunderstandings. However, there is no proper and perfect starting point for defining any language—whatever language one might choose as the starting point cannot itself be defined without language. The best we can do is choose formal and natural language starting points for relatively simple data types, admit that we cannot fully avoid risks of misunderstanding, and use heuristics, redundancy, and examples to provide hints that might deflect misunderstandings.

Information schemata are abstractions of the worlds they model. Any Fig. 4 object might be related to each of any number of other objects in any number of distinct ways. The number of possibilities is so large that any choices we make are unlikely to be the same as those made by other analysts. It can, in fact, be difficult to demonstrate that two information models intended to correspond truly do so, or that two information instances express the same facts.

Polanyi emphasized that, "We can know more than we can tell."[108] In *Preserving Digital Information* we treat only what people can tell each other, choosing the Fig. 10 distinction between knowledge and information. We call the Fig. 5 relationships between data, performances, and packages "information." We call conceptual patterns and relationships to patterns "knowledge," whether or not they can be articulated.

The preservation action is creation of a symbol string related to the original pattern that is to be preserved. Separation of necessary from irrelevant information involves subjective choices that depend on producers' intended meanings, together with the nuances they consider important. Information producers that are concerned for the durable value of their work should avoid confounding it with irrelevant details of today's information technology—details that might be difficult to define, extract, and save completely and accurately.[148] The distinction between what is essential and what is accidental is particularly acute for artistic works.

Most archives are much simpler than secure computing environments. Few archives, if any, currently use a trusted computing base among their actions to make themselves appear to be trustworthy.

To be evidence, information must be fixed. Digital signature technology will make it easier to fix digital information than it is to halt detrimental changes of physical artifacts.

---

[148] Compare W2005 p. 8, "Preservation methodologies based on virtualization are now appearing; this involves the extraction of digital records from their creation environment and their import into a preservation environment. In the process, virtualization mechanisms are used to remove all dependencies on the original creation environment."

I have kept to three fundamental principles:

- always to separate sharply the psychological from the logical, the subjective from the objective;
- never to ask for the meaning of a word in isolation, but only in the context of a proposition; and
- never to lose sight of the distinction between concept and object.

Frege 1884, *Foundations of Arithmetic*

5   Trust and Authenticity

> There seems to be a sense that digital information needs to be held to a
> higher standard for authenticity and integrity than printed information. ...
> This distrust of the immaterial world ... has forced us to ... examine defini-
> tions of authenticity and integrity—definitions that we have historically been
> rather glib about—using ... verifiable proofs as a benchmark. ... It is much
> easier to devise abstract definitions than testable ones.
>
> Lynch 2002, *Authenticity and Integrity*

In casual conversation, we often say that a music recording copy is
authentic if it is "close enough to the original." But consider how signals
flow from an orchestral performance, with wall reflections to imperfect
microphones, followed by deliberate and accidental changes in studio
electronic circuits, and so on, until we finally hear the performance
reproduced in our homes. We cannot say with objective certainty which of
many different signal versions is the original.[149] Furthermore, it makes
little sense to assert that the only authentic rendition of a music work
would be as it was heard in its first performance.

The difficulty with *the original* is conceptual, rather than being caused
by any use of technology. It would occur for most works even if the signal
channels were perfect, because nothing is created in an indivisible act.
Easy editing of content destroys almost any a priori notion of the
boundaries between information versions.

The archival literature reveals uncertainty—even confusion—about
questions such as the following:

- What do we mean by "evidence for authenticity"?
- What kinds of authenticity evidence might be available for something at
  hand?
- How can producers create such evidence to be useful in the distant future?
- Is the authenticity evidence sufficient for the application at hand?
- For particular information genres (performances, reviews, written music,
  letters, and so on) and representations (on musty paper, photocopy,
  printed copy generated from a digital representation, and so on) what
  kinds of authenticity evidence would be valuable?

What makes the literature confusing is that it often fails to declare which
among these and other questions it is addressing at each point, and that it
makes unannounced shifts from one question to another.

---

[149]   Rusbridge 2006, *Some Digital Preservation Fallacies*, illustrates the uncertain identity of "the
original" with Walter Scott's *Kenilworth*.

Conspicuous by their absence in *Preserving Digital Information* are notions of morality or philosophical truth.[150] Applications of the idea of truth are limited to narrow questions about the validity of propositions addressing the quality of specific digital objects. Broader issues about the correctness of what preserved documents assert are outside curatorial scopes and responsibilities.

"It is worth noting that the authenticity of a record can usually be demonstrated without any knowledge of its contents (or even any means to access them)."[151]

5.1   What Can We Trust?

Trust is of fundamental importance in digital document management not only for scholarly work, but also for business transactions that include legal and legislative records, the supporting "paperwork" needed to satisfy regulatory requirements,[152] military and other government information,[153] and perhaps even private medical records. The computer science literature is rich in the discussion of security and trust models.[154]

Whenever misleading information might cause serious business damage or loss, its users should reject it in favor of reliable sources.[155] Information obtained through any channel not known to assure authenticity is not dependable for critical decisions. The World Wide Web is not reliable for important facts; they should be obtained or confirmed through other channels. For applications such as those involving contracts, it is prudent to be skeptical about e-mail from unverified sources or not signed and sealed for source verification.

---

[150] Compare O'Donnell 1998, *Avatars of the Word,* p. 141.

[151] International Council on Archives 2005. *Electronic Records: a Workbook for Archivists,* http://www.ica.org/biblio.php?pdocid=285, p. 34.

[152] Examples are pharmaceutical development records and airframe inspection records.

[153] Ongoing discussion about managing government records is monitored by American Library Association's Government Documents Roundtable; see http://sunsite.berkeley.edu/GODORT/.

[154] Gerck 1997, *Toward Real-World Models of Trust,* http://www.safevote.com/papers/trustdef.htm. Grandison 2001, *A Survey of Trust in Internet Applications,* provides a study starting point. The challenge to students is similar for security risks and mitigation mechanisms. See also National Research Council 1999, *Trust in Cyberspace.*

[155] The 10 July 2005 Manchester Guardian *Digital Citizens* article reported, "Paper records of births, deaths and marriages—the legal bedrock of individual identity—are to be phased out in England and Wales. Cradle-to-grave records will be stored on a new database—and the only proof of who you are will be digital." It continued with, "It is not something the government wants to trumpet."

The article quoted a British Library representative who reminded the public, "At present, there is no way of guaranteeing continued access and preservation of the digital version."

Human trust relationships come into existence only when one individual knows another sufficiently to be confident that some limited responsibility will be faithfully discharged or that certain specific risks will be avoided. Trust relationships are extended from individuals to corporate entities by agreements made with human agents of those corporations. They also tend to be more explicit, both in their scopes and their damage commitments, than those between individuals. Someone who breaches trust is likely to suffer adverse consequences. These might be explicit, but are often unspoken and indirect. For instance, if the babysitter ignores my wailing child, I will not employ her again.

Some people feel that in an environment pervaded by deceit, it will be necessary to provide verifiable proof for claims related to authorship and integrity that might be taken at face value in the physical world. Although forgeries are always a concern in the art world, one seldom hears consumers express concerns about mass-produced physical goods—books, journal issues, audio CDs—being undetected and undetectable fakes.

The most fundamental aspect of trust has to do with authenticating the professed identities of human or agent participants. All other trust relations, mechanisms, and system components are created to relate to this fundamental one.

Consumers' eventual tests of the trustworthiness of preserved information will depend on the correctness of the computing systems they use to perform these tests. Correctness of computer programs is notoriously difficult to test and almost impossible to verify. A significant research topic about 25 years ago, correctness verification proved to be feasible only for the simplest programs. It is partly for this reason that we recommend having each preserved object contain its own provenance and integrity evidence. By avoiding depending on what happens to information in any repository, apart from requiring that each stored bit-string be returned intact, we replace testing for integrity in environments over which consumers have no control whatsoever into with testing for integrity in environments where they either control or can choose from among competing suppliers.

5.2   What Do We Mean by 'Authentic'?

Because a record is assumed to reflect an event, its reliability depends on the claim of the record-maker to have been present at that event. Its authenticity subsequently depends on the claim of the record keeper to have preserved intact and uncorrupted the original memory of that event ... over time.

MacNeil 2001, *Trusting Records in a Post-Modern World*

A conventional dictionary definition for 'authentic' (see box) provides scant aid toward the objective analysis that authors might need to prepare records for readers who want to verify authenticity. We need an objective definition that is sufficiently precise to instruct software engineers and to explain to everyone what we are doing.

> *authentic* (adj.): 1. entitled to acceptance or belief because of agreement with known facts or experience; reliable; trustworthy: *an authentic portrayal of the past.* 2. not false or copied; genuine; real: *an authentic antique.* 3. having the origin supported by unquestionable evidence; authenticated; verified: *an authentic document of the Middle Ages; an authentic work of the old master.* 4. *Law.* executed with all due formalities: *an authentic deed.*
>
> *Random House Dictionary*

That *authentic* is used to describe quite different entity classes—written works, physical artifacts, performances, and fossils—suggests a shared conceptual base. A common element is that any assertion about authenticity compares some here and now entity with something that existed earlier. For digital and analog signals—information transmissions—the question is always about the authenticity of a replica. For material objects, the question is usually about comparison with some previous state of that object. For books and performance recordings we distinguish between the information written onto some material substratum and the substratum itself. For plays and music, we distinguish between prescriptions for performance, such as music scores, and performance recordings.

Fig. 2 suggests that authenticity can be articulated in terms of the relationship of each potential output instance to some specific input in its transmission history. We can describe the transformations that occurred in each part of the transmission channel that was used for the case at hand. *Authenticity* is typically discussed by comparing a **9** instance with a **1** instance. Instances denoted by **2** through **8** might be useful to discuss the origins and specific forms of signal degradation. If we know the technical characteristics of the transmission channel only incompletely, we can still speak objectively in terms of probabilities instead of certainties.

We are free to choose or devise our language symbols—its words and pictures—any way we find helpful. The following choice captures *authentic* in a way that can be used in a practical analysis of the transmission steps suggested by Fig. 2.

Given a derivation statement R, "V is a copy of Y (V=C(Y))"
   a provenance statement S,   "X said or created Y as part of event Z," and
   a copy function,   "C(y) = T_n (...(T_2(T_1(y)))),"

we say that V is a *derivative* of Y if V is related to Y according to R.

We say that "by X as part of event Z" is a *true provenance* if R and S are true.

We say that V is *sufficiently faithful* to Y if C conforms to social conventions for genre and for the circumstances at hand.

We say that V is an *authentic copy* of Y if it is a *sufficiently faithful derivative* with *true provenance*.

The derivation statement R says that some object V is a copy of some object Y. It further states that V is related to Y by some "copy" function $C(y)$ in "V=C(Y)," but does not in itself say what we mean by $C(y)$. Here "copy" means either "later instance in a timeline" or "conforming to a shared conceptual object."

In $C(y)$, each transformation $T_k(y)$ potentially adds to, removes from, or alters the information carried by its input signal. To preserve authenticity, the metadata accompanying the input in each Fig. 2 transmission step should be augmented with a description of the transformation function T_k. The metadata should identify who is responsible for each T_k choice and all other circumstances important to judgments of authenticity, perhaps as suggested by the Table 4 example of such information.

Table 4: Metadata for a format conversion event[156]

<migration ID="MIG1.0" TYPE="UPGRADE" DATE="2005-01-11T07:45:00">
<migration_process> format standardization </rulibadmin:migration_process>
<migration_agency> RUL Scholarly Communication Center
</rulibadmin:migration_agency>
<migration_environment platform="server"> Linux Redhat 7.2, Fedora 1.2
</rulibadmin:migration_environment>
<migration_software> (Open-source software -- version 1.0)
</rulibadmin:migration_software>
<migration_steps> Create datastream for JPEG2000 </rulibadmin:migration_steps>
<migration_specifications> See Migration Document 1.0
</rulibadmin:migration_specifications>
<migration_rationale> Create JPEG2000 datastream for presentation and standardize on JPEG2000 as an archival master format. </rulibadmin:migration_rationale>
<migration_changes> New digital object created by adding a new archival datastream. Re-ingest was not necessary </migration_changes>
<migration_result> Object verified visually and accessed through the PID
</migration_result>
</rulibadmin:migration>

The provenance statement S says that there was some person X who created some object Y in some historical context or event Z. The practical

---

[156] Jantz 2005, *Digital Preservation ... Technology for Trusted Digital Repositories*, table 1.

effect of this statement is that we are not willing to accept that the object V is authentic without explicitly identifying the past existence Y of V, the identity of the creator of Y, and the specific historical event Z within which this creation occurred.

These three statements are merely definitions of what we mean by V, Y, C, X, and Z. The rest of the mathematical language defines what we mean by *integrity*, *true provenance*, and *authentic*.

5.3   Authenticity for Different Information Genres

Authentic is simplest for digital transmissions, more difficult for analog transmissions, even more difficult for transmissions of artifacts (a manuscript on paper, a Louis XV chair), and problematic indeed when we speak of living things—so problematic that we do not usually use "authentic" to describe them, but choose other words that have similar meanings.

For digital objects, perfect copies are possible and often wanted.[157] For every other kind of transmission, imperfections are inevitable. In everyday usage of *authentic,* social conventions (subjective opinions) govern what is considered acceptable imperfection for each object class.   These conventions are usually tacit.

All the metadata and packaging discussed in §11.1.2 are expressed by the function C(y) of §5.2. Although we call C(y) a "copy function," it might describe a more complicated transformation than people usually understand "copy" to mean. The owner of a photographic portrait of his wife might write the date and her name on the front, further information on the back, and enclose it in a glassed frame. His wife would consider it her authentic portrait if the name and date are close to correct.

5.3.1   Digital Objects

For the case of digital objects the copy function C(y) can be the identity function I(y)—the transformation whose output is in every respect indistinguishable from its input. Given our digital object V, this means that its length and bit pattern are equal to those of the past digital object Y. For digital objects, and only for digital objects, what we mean by "having integrity" is that V is identical to Y.

---

[157] For a good introduction to the relationship of digital records to archives, see Currall 2001, *"No Going Back?" The final report of the Effective Records Management Project,* http://www.gla.ac.uk/InfoStrat/ERM/Reports/.

5.3.2 Transformed Digital Objects and Analog Signals

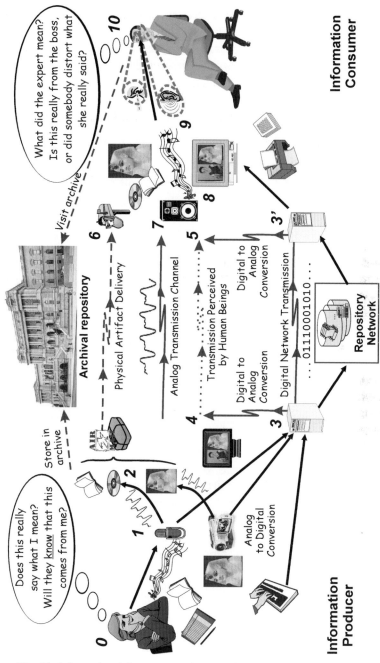

Fig. 11: Information delivery suggesting transformations that might occur

Without computed transformations, human users cannot easily interpret a digital representation such as the '11100010100' bit-string in Fig. 11. In it, the **4** to **5** arrow suggests a virtual transmission that reflects how human beings discuss their communications. The **3-4-5-3'** rectangle reminds us of machine support that is ubiquitous so that we rarely discuss it.

Suppose that an information consumer talked to its producer about a photograph of a King Tutankhamen alabaster bust that the producer had previously sent. The consumer might cause a binary image **3** in the producer's PC to be copied into an identical binary image **3'** in the consumer's PC. These people might then converse about the screen images **4** and **5**; **4** is a derivative object of **3**, created by software in the producer's computer, and **5** is a derivative of **3'** created by similar software in the consumer's computer. If the rendering software packages in the two machines are not identical, different pictures might be shown even though **3 ≡ 3'**. Even if this problem does not occur, it is unlikely that the color rendering by phosphors of two video monitors is identical.[158] Almost surely, the consumer will be shown something different from what the producer is shown. Language common in the literature suggests that a single information object occurs at each space/time location,[159] rather than two or more different objects that we might need to describe what is happening, such as **3** and **4** in the producer's PC. **5 = 4** would be difficult to achieve, and it would be almost impossible to demonstrate that it had been achieved. In contrast, **3' = 3** is easily achieved and demonstrated. Thus, Fig. 11 suggests how careful we must be in identifying derivative objects and explicating object interrelationships.

In the figure, **4** is a *derivative* of **3**. Derivative objects are common, for example, in the practice of the law. When an attorney consults case law, his source is usually a reference periodical quoting decisions, rather than an archival copy of decision paperwork. Of course, the reproduction is accompanied by a provenance statement alluding to the original from which it has been derived. Furthermore, any account of trial details is itself a derived work—a court reporter's quotation of what was said at the trial. The reporter's account is itself an excerpt constrained by customary rules. The attorney is likely to trust what he reads because the reference work has a history of faithful reproductions and because its publisher and the court reporter each have little motivation to mislead, and much to lose if their reputations for veracity and accuracy are impeached.

---

[158] *Physics Today*, December 1992, provides a good introduction to the physics of digital color.

[159] For instance, in Thibodeau 2002, *Overview of Technological Approaches to Digital Preservation,* see the paragraphs beginning with, "The ideal preservation system would be a neutral communications channel for transmitting information to the future."

For a digital derivative created with lossy compression, and for an analog signal that suffers accidental changes during transmission, the §5.3.1 notion of integrity is inapplicable. In everyday usage we say that such signals have integrity if their distortions are too small for human perception, or if we think we can distinguish the intended signals from the distortion (as we might do with a 78 rpm wax recording of Enrico Caruso). Such usage depends on opinion and tacit understanding, risking misunderstandings and disagreements.

Whenever such risks are not acceptable, we can describe the imperfections of the received message (**9** in Fig. 2) relative to what was sent (**1** in Fig. 2) probabilistically. Our careful definition of *authentic* would in this case weaken the §5.2 copy function, dropping the constraint on reversible changes.

Since the transformations T_k potentially add, take away, and alter the original Y, the metadata that is part of each transmitted object should contain descriptions of all the transformations performed, including identifying who is responsible for each transformation.

5.3.3   Material Artifacts

An old artifact is never unchanged from what it originally was; to see the change we merely need to look closely enough. For instance, the varnish on a Louis XV chair will have hardened as its solvent gradually escaped from the solid matrix. We mean something different by 'authentic' in everyday usage alluding to a famous painting, or to a Louis XV chair, than we mean when we describe signals. Instead, people require that many of the molecules, and their spatial layout, are the same molecules as were in the original many years earlier.

However, we do talk of "an authentic Gucci bag" even though the object at hand is not authentic in the sense we require for a famous painting. Instead, what we require is that it conforms to a certain reproductive pattern—integrity as discussed in §4.6—and that it has been manufactured by Gucci employees in a Gucci factory—acceptable provenance for a Gucci handbag.

Authentic illustrated by these examples conforms to the §5.2 formal definition if we concede that we can do no better than comparing today's artifact with another object. The latter could be either a conceptual object—what we imagine the artifact to have been on some past date, or else an information object that represents what the artifact was at that date. With such language, today's Louis XV chair is a "copy" of the Louis XV chair 300 years ago. If an auctioneer describes damage such as a deep scratch, he might have in mind a comparison with a particular conceptual object—the chair before the damage occurred many years earlier. In 2005, no Louis XV chair was identically the chair that existed in the eighteenth century, but an auctioneer would not risk a charge of fraud by calling one "an authentic Louis XV chair."

5.3.4   Natural Objects

We also often use "authentic" for natural objects that include dinosaur bones, fossils, and gemstones. We are comfortable with this for reasons similar to those for artifacts. However, fossils contain relatively few original molecules; instead, they embed the pattern inherent in extant and potential replicas. Just how far we seem to be willing to stretch the concept of authenticity is illustrated by the case of a gemstone, for which it is difficult to describe the creation event; instead, we often describe its provenance as the event of its being mined.

How much a natural entity can differ from its previous existence without losing the 'authentic' cachet is again a matter of social convention. When a speaker strays beyond what is familiar to his listener, he might be asked to explain why his use of "authentic" is appropriate. His answer is likely to include some description of the object's deterioration compared to a perfect conceptual object and might add something about its estimated history.

We even use "authentic" for human beings, as in, "He's an authentic Roman." We limit such usage to cases that the listener will understand to be comparisons to a conceptual model, or to examples to which he can relate. In other cases in which we might have used "authentic," we choose different words to express closely related notions. In a criminal proceeding, a witness might be asked, "Is this the man that assaulted you in March 1998?" and correctly say "yes," even though the man might be much changed in the intervening years. In the same trial, the priestly confessor of the defendant might truthfully say, "This is not the same man as five years ago. He's seen the error of his ways, and reformed!"

5.3.5   Artistic Performances and Recipes

> [I]t would have been ... amazing revelation to have heard [Bach's cantata] *Wachet auf* in Leipzig under Bach's direction [in] 1731, but no amount of wishing will make it happen.
>
> Leppard 1988, *Authenticity in music*

What is meant today by 'an authentic recording' was socially defined in the twentieth century when widespread quality broadcasts began and when long-playing records became inexpensive. Since then, archives have developed opinions about what constitutes "sufficient similarity" to originals for sound and video recordings. For valuable performances, what might be wanted is not mechanical fidelity to some early recording. Instead, what people want and expect is artistic fidelity in derived versions that are announced to their audiences as restorations.

People who judge whether or not an object is authentic make their own choices of what to use as the comparison standard for the object at hand. When we purchase "salsa autentica" in a California supermarket, we might think of an original Mexican recipe—a conceptual object.

5.3.6 Literature and Literary Commentary

Digital means are contributing to a new dynamic of literature that is quite different from what the preceding paragraphs discuss, but that has been anticipated in ancient manuscripts. Commentaries on a book are likely to appear in Web pages and blogs almost simultaneously with the book's publication, so that a full appreciation of the core work can depend on reading such commentaries. We can expect that, in the near future, someone will design an "instantly" popular construct that is used semiautomatically to complement each core book with its commentaries, and the commentaries with dissenting or elaborating commentaries.

Such constructs will have similarities to how, many centuries ago, the Hebrew *Torah* was first expanded by the commentaries of the *Talmud*, and then by those of the *Gemara*. I heard this idea about ten years ago in a Lanham lecture that showed how zooming into structure representations on computer display screens could be used to structure discussions in as much depth as anyone would want, with tools that would allow each reader to navigate wherever his interests took him and as quickly as he wanted.[160]

Of course, each piece of such a structure can be fixed as any other digital document is fixed. The entire structure would need to be handled as described above for databases.

5.4 How Can We Preserve Dynamic Resources?

There have lately appeared scholarly discussions expressing difficulty with preserving digitally recorded performances, such as:

> [T]the challenge … for ensuring the reliability and authenticity of records that lack a stable form and content. Ironically, the ease with which these records can be manipulated has given those who generate them … a new reason for keeping them: 'repurposing'. Makers and distributors of digital music …, for example, often obscure the meaning and cultural value of their records by treating their form and content merely as digital data to be

---

[160] Rhetorical communication is the topic of Lanham 2000, *The Electronic Word.*

manipulated to generate new records, decontextualizing them from the activity by which they were produced. The potentially wide dissemination of repurposed documents threatens the authenticity of the original materials, as well as their authors' moral rights.

Duranti 2004, *The Long-term Preservation of Dynamic ... Records*

It is not correct that "dissemination of repurposed documents threatens the authenticity of the original materials." It is, in fact, the availability of masters that Duranti questions. Releasing only derivative recordings is neither a new practice nor is choosing to do so a consequence of digital technology. It is a legal prerogative of an owner.

What is the underlying problem? Perhaps it is a misunderstanding of what 'dynamic' and related words mean. As far as we know, the authors expressing difficulty with digital recordings of performances do not have a similar difficulty with older analog methods for recording music or television performances, or with managing business records.

We can describe dynamic behavior either by a prescription of what should happen—a rule set for a business process, the text of a theatrical play, a music score, a computer program, or whatever prescription is customary for the genre at hand—or by a history of what has happened—a performance record, such as a business journal, a multimedia recording that might be sold on an optical disk, or a log of computing events.

We can describe any performance by a sequence—a function $P(t)$ of time t—which can readily be fixed. In engineering parlance, a repeat performance $R(t)$ of an earlier performance $P(t)$ is said to have integrity if it is a faithful copy except for a constant time shift, i.e., if $R(t) = P(t-t_{start})$ for some fixed starting time t_{start}. This seems simple enough and capable of describing any kind of real-world performance whatsoever, expressing what we mean for both digital and analog recordings. Its meaning is simpler for digital documents than for analog recordings or for live performances because digital files are finite representations and static nearly all the time, whereas real-world performances are continuous in time with transmission distortions associated with their analog representation, and require sampling decisions if they are to be recorded.

For fixing databases, an information producer has various possibilities—to save and fix one or more *snapshots* of the database state, a log (audit trail) of transactions that have occurred, and the current database programs (which might differ from what was first installed on the machine.) The first two options are functionality provided by the DBMS software. A current snapshot and a log can be combined to create a database snapshot for any past moment within the range of the log. The last option might present engineering and legal (copyright) challenges, but not conceptual difficulties.

The engineering task can be complex. A database might have several hundred tables whose relationships need to be preserved along with the tabular data if the database is to be reused with different DBMS software than that in its original environment. To recreate behavior without saving an entire DBMS (which would be more difficult than the method described by Heuscher 2004), the metadata must include descriptions of advanced DBMS features (constraint assertions, triggers, user-defined functions, access control rules, and so on). SQL could be used, if doing so seems attractive in the light of the facts that the *SQL:2003* standard is over 2,000 pages long, and that DBMS products conform with it to different extents.

The equivalent of a database snapshot in a conventional financial reporting system is a balance sheet. The analog of a log is a financial journal. The equivalent of a database management program is a set of rules for recording transactions.

A practical difficulty occurs in the case of information that changes more rapidly than snapshot construction, as can occur in the photography of automobile races. Something similar occurs for widely distributed and pseudorandomly changing information. To capture a snapshot of the instantaneous state of the World Wide Web is impossible because it consists of billions of pages and the fastest Internet sampling mechanisms can "touch" only millions of pages per minute. Search services such as Google and preservation services such as the Internet Archive[161] take several days or several weeks to sample the Web space that interests them, and accommodate the limitation by announcing to their users that what their data collections represent is only an approximation to any particular WWW state.

Apart from situations similar to those just described, preserving database states, sequences in time, or performances encounters no technical challenges beyond those encountered with any other data. The trick is simply to choose some instance or some sequence of instances to preserve. This works for any kind of signal or real-world situation. Its meaning is simpler for digital documents than for analog recordings or for live performances because digital states are static most of the time, whereas we think of real world performances as being continuous in time.

5.5 Summary

We trust at most what we ourselves perceive, or what someone tells us if we trust that person for the kind of information at issue.[162] In architecture

---

161 *Internet Archive,* http://www.archive.org/.

for preservation, we should always consider who decides to trust and when the decision is made.

What people consider to be an *original* or a valuable *derivative version* is their subjective choice, or an objective choice guided by subjectively chosen social rules.

Any *authenticity decision* is a comparison between an instance at hand and a specific previous instance associated with a historical event—a comparison based on (*approximate*) *integrity* and *true provenance*. To be authentic a document must be whole and not disturbed too much—that is *integrity*. It must have originated with the purported author as part of the purported event—that is *true provenance*. The language of §5.2 is attractive because we can use it for an empirical description of how the object at hand differs either from what it might have been earlier, or from a conceptual model of what we might wish it to be.

Information is often concurrently represented by several ephemeral physical states—such as patterns of magnetic bits, electronic circuit states, electromagnetic fields in space, and sound waves. Some of these patterns perfectly represent the original information, and are therefore called authentic. Others are imperfect representations, for which we can describe the deviations from perfection. Depending on what kind of object is under discussion, and on social conventions, we might still call such imperfect manifestations *authentic*.

Physical books, other paper-based information, and other analog forms cannot be copied without error and invariably contain accidental information that digital representations can avoid. Perfect digital copying contributes both to the challenge of preserving digital content and to its solution.

We regard communication machinery as perfect only if what the consumer perceives as **9** is a faithful copy of what the producer creates as **1**. Whatever errors make a representation **9** differ from the original input **1** might be such small changes that consumers do not notice them. If the errors are larger, a consumer might still understand enough to discount and tolerate them. The completeness of information and authenticity evidence are producers' responsibilities and ethical imperatives that require the exercise of judgment and taste.

An artifact is considered authentic if it corresponds to an accompanying provenance assertion. A curator's usual impulse will be to seek an object version corresponding to the creation event of each accession candidate. However, accomplishing this will often be impossible, or at least not affordable. The practical alternative is to adjust the provenance metadata to

---

[162] Denning 2003, *Accomplishment.*

Jordan 2003, *The Augmented Social Network.*

describe what is known and what is guessed about the history of the version held. Doing so would make the holding authentic!

Every kind of inscribed information—digital files, analog recordings, and works printed on paper—experiences dynamic episodes, but is static most of the time. Our information handling patterns have not been qualitatively changed by the advent of digital technology. Digital procedures are close analogs of time-honored methods for assuring that preserved information is authentic. A "dynamic object" is not a different kind of object than a "static object." Instead, "dynamic" merely refers to periods when the object described might be changing significantly. Plato quotes Heraclitus, "Everything flows, nothing stands still."

Who is to decide what evidence is important and what tests are worth applying? This has to be the end user—the person for whom the document in question is preserved and who assumes risk by using it. The decisive act will invariably be an economic decision—a weighing of the cost of evidence testing against the costs of a wrong decision. A role of technology is to minimize these costs.

6 Describing Information Structure

All scientific statements are structure statements.

Carnap 1928, *LSW* §16

If I ask a pupil, 'What are the elements of which the world is composed, from which it is built up?' ... he is likely to reply: 'The world is composed of objects such as trees, houses, human beings, tables; and all objects together are the world.' But this is not correct. ... For without a knowledge of the combinations which relate objects to one another, no reconstruction ... can be effected. In reality the table only occurs in combinations, as in the propositions: 'The table stands in the room,' or 'The carpenter has made the table,' etc. It is not the table, then, but the table's standing in the room, which is one of the elements constituting the world.

Engelmann 1967, *Letters from Ludwig Wittgenstein*, p.100

What do philosophical ideas teach us about structuring and managing preserved information?

A preservation method should allow us to represent whatever authors want to express, within the limits of what language can express. This includes any information relationships whatsoever. However, a goal mentioned by some authors—completeness of collections—is ill defined for most cultural topics. In contrast, the completeness of archival collections built from bureaucratic records can be objectively defined by comparison with the business agency collections from which they are derived.[163]

A durable infrastructure-independent representation for collections is needed.[164] A common information model should make accessible the attributes associated with collection members and collection organization. We want data models that are both simple and also able to model all practical information structures. Our choices in this chapter are not the simplest possible, but are, instead, compromises to facilitate analysis and discussion.

A *blob* (binary large object) is a closely associated agglomeration of data that is managed as a single entity. The term 'blob' is used to signal that neither the blob's meaning nor its internal structure is relevant within the discussion at hand. A *bit-string* is a linearized form of a *blob* suitable for sending over a simple communication channel. A *file* or *dataset* is a blob's storage form, in which the content might be represented in noncon-

---

163 A collection can sometimes be defined by rules for semiautomatic maintenance. Such a rule is likely to be described as "authoritative" by those information consumers.

164 W2005, p. 10, urges the community, "Develop collection-oriented description and transfer techniques. Develop data description tools and associated generic migration applications to facilitate automation. Develop canonical intermediate forms with sets of coder/decoder pairs to and from specific common formats."

tiguous segments on a magnetic or optical storage volume or on a set of storage volumes. The storage layout is chosen and managed by a file system in order to provide better reliability, economy, performance, and flexibility than is likely to be provided by a simple, contiguous layout. It is irrelevant at higher layers of typically layered software. A file system usually includes a programming interface to provide any file in bit-string format. The word 'file' is often used when the less well known term 'blob' might be more apt.

6.1   Testable Archived Information

The clients of any repository will care more about the quality of information it delivers than about internal aspects of how it is managed. This book therefore emphasizes an archival document representation scheme, trying to ensure that it can express everything pertinent that admits unambiguous, objective, and testable representation—and as little as possible beyond that. Whether or not a document so represented and saved will be trusted will remain a value judgment that each information consumer must make for himself.

A good archival methodology will avoid value judgments whenever possible, will identify as being subjective those it cannot avoid, and will expose its mechanisms for peer criticism. How diligently archive managers and information producers might pursue such objectives will, of course, depend on their estimates of the probative value of the content at hand and of the risks of accidental and deliberate falsification.

Being testable is critical. Every important property of each archived document, and also of each archiving system component, should be explicitly specified (asserted), and the archived data should include whatever is needed to test these assertions. Such testing should be possible without permission from or personal assistance by archiving institution personnel.

Such test results and procedures—what certified public accountants call audit trails and audit tools—must be firmly bound to each sensitive information package. These assertions will nearly always need to identify who is responsible for each piece of information. Such provenance information might itself be represented in distinct documents or document portions that require their own audit trails. This collection of documents and procedures is what we mean by *external evidence* of authenticity and provenance, and in combination with *internal evidence*—content of the document itself—is what can make the information trustworthy.

An eventual user will trust a document if its associated evidence is accessible, reliable, and sufficient for the use that he intends to make of the document content. This might seem a prescription for endless tests that themselves must be tested. However, the providers of evidence can readily arrange that its audit trails converge on a few disinterested public assertions.

6.2 Syntax Specification with Formal Languages

Regular expressions are used for defining the syntax of relatively short character strings, such as identifiers. The *extended Backus-Naur format* is used for defining the syntax of programs and complex documents, such as XML documents. *ASN.1* is used for defining many information processing standards. The set of context-free languages is a restricted formalism to which most computer programming languages conform. It is coextensive with recursive functions. The set of regular expressions is a still more restricted formalism that excludes recursive definitions. It is useful for describing families of mathematical expressions and formal grammatical expressions.

Formulae such as those of either regular expression definitions or of *BNF* (Backus-Naur Form) definitions are called *rewrite rules*.

6.2.1 String Syntax Definition with Regular Expressions

Regular expressions are a context-independent syntax that can represent a wide variety of character sets and character set orderings. While regular expressions can be interpreted differently depending on the current locale, many features, such as character class expressions, provide for contextual invariance across locales.

A *regular expression*, often called a *pattern*, supports mechanism to select specific strings from a set of character strings. Regular expressions were the core of an elegant programming language, SNOBOL, in the 1970s. One is often used to describe a string set, without having to list all elements. For instance, the set containing the three strings *Handel*, *Händel*, and *Haendel* can be described by the pattern "H(a|ä|ae)ndel." Another way of saying this is, "the pattern *matches* each of the three strings".

The origin of regular expressions lies in automata theory and formal language theory (both part of theoretical computer science). These fields study models of computation (automata) and ways to describe and classify formal languages. The theoretical computer scientist Stephen Kleene described these models using his mathematical notation called *regular sets*. Ken Thompson built this notation into the editor *QED*, and then into the Unix editor *ed*, which eventually led to *grep*'s use of regular expressions. Regular expressions are widely used in Unix and in well known Unix-like utilities including *expr*, *awk*, *Emacs*, *vi*, *lex*, and *Perl*.

The precise syntax for regular expressions varies among tools and application areas.[165] Many textbooks provide definitions,[166] and others can be found on the WWW.[167] Both Basic Regular Expressions (BREs) and Extended Regular Expressions (EREs) are supported by the Regular Expression Matching interface in the System Interfaces volume of IEEE Std. 1003.1–2001 under *regcomp*, *regexec*, and related functions.

6.2.2   BNF for Program and File Format Specification

The *Backus-Naur Form* (*BNF*)[168] is a formal language for defining the grammar of a context-free language. The Extended Backus-Naur Form (EBNF) adds the syntax of regular expressions to the BNF notation in order to allow very compact specifications. Numerous BNF variants have been defined, and almost every programming-language textbook and standard identifies the version it uses.[169] While a BNF notation can be specified in a few sentences, the proper definition of EBNF requires more explanation. Often only BNF is used although the result is less readable.[170]

Each rule of a BNF grammar has the form: **symbol ::= expression.**

symbol	if defined by regular expression: initial capital, lower case otherwise
expression	right-hand side of rule which has the syntax shown below to match strings of one or more characters
#xN	matches the character specified by the Unicode code point corresponding to **N**, a hexadecimal integer
[a–zA–Z], [#xM–#xN]	matches any character with a value in the range(s) indicated (inclusive)
[^a–zA–Z], [^#xM–#xN]	matches any character with a value outside the range indicated
[^abc], [^#xM#xN#xP]	matches any character with a value not among the characters given
'text' or **"text"**	matches the literal string given inside the single (double) quotes

---

[165] An example is provided by Hosoya 2005, *Regular expression types for XML.*

[166] Denning 1978, Machines, Languages, and Computation, p. 161.

[167] For instance, *Regular expression,* http://en.wikipedia.org/wiki/Regular_expression#Syntax.

[168] Garshol 2003, *BNF and EBNF,* http://www.garshol.priv.no/download/text/bnf.html#id2.3.

[169] The ISO 14977 standard defines EBNF syntax. A final draft version (SC22/N2249) of the standard is available online at http://www.cl.cam.ac.uk/~mgk25/iso-14977.pdf .

[170] Anderson 2004, *CL-XML: Common Lisp support for the 'Extensible Markup Language,* links examples of BNF used in XML parsers. See http://pws.prserv.net/James.Anderson/XML/.

These symbols may be combined for more complex patterns as follows, where **A** and **B** represent expressions:

(expression)	expression is treated as a unit and may be combined as described in this list
A?	matches **A** or nothing; optional **A**
A B	matches **A** followed by **B**
**A	B**	matches **A** or **B** but not both
A – B	matches any string that matches **A** but does not match **B**
A+	matches one or more occurrences of **A**
A*	matches zero or more occurrences of **A**
/* ... */	comment
[wfc: ...]	*well-formedness constraint*; this identifies by name a constraint on well-formed documents associated with a production
[vc: ...]	*validity constraint*; this identifies by name a constraint on valid documents associated with a production

6.2.3   ASN.1 Standards Definition Language

The Abstract Syntax Notation (ASN.1) is used to express syntax of objects and messages.[171] Its Basic Encoding Rules (BERs) enable abstract data value specifications to be represented in concrete form as an array of bytes. Although programmers may choose to work directly with the encoding of ASN.1 types, generally encoder/decoder routines are used to translate between the coded form and the native types of the programming system. ASN.1 DER (Distinguished Encoding Rules) and BER-encoded data is largely platform-independent, helping to make the byte-stream representation of a standards definitions document that uses it easy to transport between computers on open networks.

Non-developers only need to know that an ASN.1 Abstract Syntax is usually a specification of a list of typed elements that are either primitive (such as integers or octet-strings) or constructed (such as sets and sequences of additional elements). A type hierarchy is a collection of data type declarations, normally organized in modules that manage declaration scoping. Sequences of message elements forming a message to be transferred often take the notational form of a list of identified fields, e.g., "ver-

---

[171] This section is a synopsis of Kaliski 1993, *A Layman's Guide to a Subset of ASN.1, BER, and DER,* http://luca.ntop.org/Teaching/Appunti/asn1.html.

sion", and their data type, e.g., "Version". The following listing illustrates
the appearance of ASN.1 syntax specifications:

```
SignedData    ::= SEQUENCE {
    version           Version,
    digestAlgorithms  DigestAlgorithmIdentifiers,
    contentInfo       ContentInfo,
    certificates[0] IMPLICIT ExtendedCertificatesAndCertificates  OPTIONAL,
    crls        [1] IMPLICIT CertificateRevocationLists OPTIONAL,
    signerInfos       SignerInfos        }
```

Being abstract, a type such as **SEQUENCE OF INTEGER** is not limited to
the built-in capabilities of programming platforms; the list of integers is
logically infinite, as is the length of integer values. Pragmatic designers
set constraints to limit the generality of such types.

ASN.1 has been widely used to describe security protocols, interfaces,
and service definitions, such as the X.500 Directory and X.400 Messaging
systems, which include extensive security models. An example of language specification to aid the specification of security mechanisms occurred during the specification of the Secure Electronic Transaction (SET)
standard. With terms formulated in response to business, technical, and
security requirements and using PKCS security constructs as the underlying connectives, the notation enabled precise specification of the security
mechanism for protecting bank-card-based payment protocols. The resulting language of structured security primitives enabled security analysis as
the design took shape.

6.2.4   Schema Definitions for XML

Schema define the record structure for any data type of interest, and are
particularly prominent in the use of XML to package information of various data types.[172] Typically a schema is expressed as a set of properties
with an associated type. For instance, an informational schema description
for a customer database would be something like: (1) Name: string of up to
80 characters; (2) Customer ID: number of up to 10 digits; (3) Orders: a
list of Order records. Some schemas conform to standards such as Dublin
Core. Others are recommended by software suppliers to facilitate the use
of their offerings, or might be defined by institutional records managers for
designated communities or professional communities.

Three schema description languages are prominent: XML Schema,[173]
RDF Schema,[174] and Document Type Definition (DTD).[175] Applications

---

[172]   See the *XML Schema Tutorial* and related tutorials at http://www.w3schools.com/schema/.

[173]   *XML Schema Part I*, http://www.w3.org/TR/xmlschema-1/.

might use them together. XML might be used to lay out document meta-data, extended by RDF to describe the people who have approved the document. This is because RDF provides a *bag* structure convenient for the approval list.

6.3   Monographs and Collections

Every document refers to other documents that are essential to its interpretation and to provenance evidence. We represent such references as citations, links, or pointers. Not all references are explicit. In fact, in human communication, most references are implicit, consisting of "shared social context."[176]

For all but the simplest works, particular programs and schema information will be needed if they are to be correctly rendered for human intelligibility or executed as intended by their providers. This ancillary information should be as accessible as the primary works. Each such ancillary data unit is likely to be needed for many primary object instances, making it convenient and efficient to preserve it as a distinct archived work. This recursive pattern can be made to converge to being grounded in a small collection whose descriptions are humanly intelligible and usable without recourse to archival collections.

Some authors treat the concept *collection* as a property of a library. It seems more productive to exploit the fact that any collection can be defined by a document that tabulates or otherwise identifies the collection members. A traditional library catalog defines such a collection. This way of construing *collection* is even more powerful for a digital library than it is for a traditional library in which each physical holding is, at any moment, necessarily in only one physical collection—a restriction that is almost meaningless for its digital counterpart.

With this paradigm shift, almost every document defines a collection—the set of documents and other objects that it references, as suggested by the arrows leaving the DO box in Fig. 12. In practical implementations, XML will be used as "glue" between blobs.[177] Any of the depicted substructures could be an empty, or null, object.

---

[174] *RDF Schema Specification,* http://www.w3.org/TR/1999/PR-rdf-schema-19990303/.

[175] *IEEE Standard DTD,* http://xml.coverpages.org/ieeeStandards.html.

[176] How human natural language copes with references is carefully analyzed in Quine 1960, *Word and Object* §§12, 22, and 30.

[177] Compare ISO 2001, *MPEG-21 Overview: Coding of Moving Pictures and Audio,* Fig. 1. Compare also §4.1 of Risse 2005, *The BRICKS Infrastructure.*

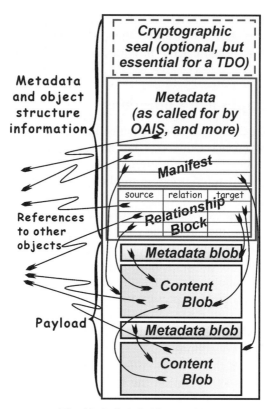

Fig. 12: A digital object model.

The kinds of references that are particularly prominent in Fig. 12 are similar to the main content of what librarians call *finding aids*.[178] For instance, at the Biblioteca Apostolica Vaticana (the Vatican Library) you can see a room containing finding aids that include nineteenth century works describing sixteenth century collections.[179]

In a mid-2006 draft, Priscilla Caplan communicated that the Florida Center for Library Automation had substantially implemented the Fig. 12 structure in the DAITSS component of its dark archive; see *Florida Digital Archive,* http://www.fcla.edu/digitalArchive/.

[178] The Yale University Library makes accessible a search service into its finding aid collection. See http://webtext.library.yale.edu/finddocs/fadsear.htm. See also *Archival Finding Aids at the Library of Congress,* http://www.loc.gov/rr/ead/. The EAD Document Type Definition (DTD) is a standard for encoding archival finding aids using XML.

[179] Mintzer 1996, *Toward On-Line Worldwide Access to Vatican Library Materials.* Samples of the marvelous collection can be seen at http://www.research.ibm.com/journal/rd/402/mintzer.html. See also Mintzer 1999 *Developing Digital Libraries of Cultural Content for Internet Access.*

Every catalog describing a collection is an object that could include its own description, as well as descriptions of relationships among the objects referenced in its core, represented by the Fig. 12 Manifest.

Similarly, every ontology is an object whose core is the kind of Relationship Block suggested by Fig. 12. Any ontology is likely to have its own descriptions, which might best be part of the same object that represents its relationships (to make management as easy as possible by keeping the complete ontology representation together within stores and for network transmissions), and every piece of information mentioned is likely to have associated metadata.

The differences that create distinct genres for intellectual works and business information objects—texts, diagrams, multimedia objects, catalogs, invoices, organizational diagrams, and all other kinds of information—are, in the Fig. 12 model, represented by different content block encodings that might be supported by different metadata blob structures and/or different values within metadata fields.

6.4   Digital Object Schema

Engineers are most comfortable with assignments whose technical constraints force a single best answer to every important design question. Key features of abstract digital object schema exhibit this behavior. The following conditions are easily accommodated.

- Every digital content piece requires a linear representation for storage and for transmission.
- Some information is needed for so many works that it should be packaged independently and referenced.
- Accessioned content should not be altered, but might be made more helpful with more outbound references than those its producers provided.
- All structures can be described by a single fundamental construct—a ternary relationship.
- References occur in few structurally distinct forms.
- Recursive reuse of a few construction principles is common. Any Fig. 12 content blob could itself be a DO.

Every digital object consists of a *payload* and *metadata*. The payload consists of zero or more content and metadata blobs provided by people we call authors, editors, or artists—*information providers*. To this content, some preservation agent might add metadata conforming to widely recognized schema, a manifest identifying the boundaries of each payload blob, and a relationship block describing connections among DO contents, and between DO contents and external objects. The XML Formatted Data Unit (XFDU) draft specification[180] recommends structure for the metadata called for by *OAIS*.

The Fig. 12 *relationship block* contains a ternary relation that can be represented by a graph such as that in Fig. 13. This structure seems to be sufficient to be a schema for current ontology and digital collection structure proposals. For instance, Lagoze's Information Network Overlay model is a special case of what Fig. 13 depicts.[181] The Fig. 13 schema is sufficient for digital representation of any kind of intellectual work, of any kind of collection, and of any ontology.

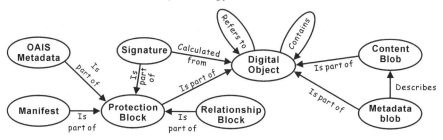

Fig. 13: Schema for documents and for collections
without showing the many "refers to" arcs from manifests, relationship blocks, and content blobs to digital objects and content blobs.[182] Compare Fig. 12.

6.4.1   Relationships and Relations

The elementary descriptor for *structure* is a relationship. Any set of one-to-one relationships can be represented by a set of binary relations. This is true not only for relationship sets that are bounded, but also for infinite sets—even for sets that are uncountable. However, because digital systems are always bounded, we can avoid the subtle issues associated with infinite sets.[183]

A *unary relation* is a set. A *binary relation* is a set of ordered pairs. A *ternary relation* is a set of ordered triples. A *tuple* is any element of a rela-

---

[180]   CCSDS 2004, *XML Formatted Data Unit (XFDU) Structure and Construction Rules*,
http://www.ccsds.org/docu/dscgi/ds.py/GetRepr/File-1912/html.

[181]   Lagoze 2006, *Representing Contextualized Information in the NSDL*, http://arXiv.org/abs/cs/0603024, Fig. 1.

[182]   Compare the structure described in Lagoze 2005, *Fedora: an Architecture for Complex Objects and their Relationships*, and also that specified in *The Open Archives Initiative protocol for metadata harvesting* at http://www.openarchives.org/OAI/2.0/openarchivesprotocol.htm.

[183]   The applicable formalism is the *Zermelo-Fraenkel Set Theory*. See http://plato.stanford.edu/entries/set-theory/ZF.html.

tion; this word is used for a finite sequence whose length is either irrelevant or obvious in the context at hand.

A (mathematical) *function* is a relation whose first elements constitute a proper set.[184] Specifically, if this relation is *n-ary,* i.e., if it relates *n* elements, its extension can be represented by an *n*-column table whose individual rows express instances of the functional relationship. If every m-tuple from the first *m* columns of this table is distinct, with $m < n$, then this set of m-tuples is a *set.* In this case, the first *m* values are called an instance of the *independent variables* of the function and the remaining *m - n* values are called the *dependent variables.*

Ternary relations prove to be more convenient structure descriptors than binary relations, without being more expressive.[185] This is partly because ternary relations are naturally depicted by labeled directed graphs.[186] For instance, each of the top two frames of Fig. 8 is an example of a directed unlabeled graph that represents either a binary relation or a ternary relation in which the second element of each relationship might be either an empty string or a null object. Fig. 13 is a directed labeled graph used to depict a ternary relation. A ternary table can represent any number of binary tables.

We choose to order ternary relationships corresponding to structure description sentences with the first element of each tuple representing the sentential subject, the second element representing the verb articulating the type of relationship, and the third element indicating the sentential object. We would map "Harry owns his own hammer" with "Harry," "owns," and "his own hammer" in first, second, and third positions respectively. Fig. 13 illustrates that this choice maps naturally onto the source (starting object), label, and target (end object) of each directed arc of a corresponding graphical representation.

With the identifier scheme of §7.3.3, any tuple element—even the second one—can identify any of the following:

- a scalar value, such as 'Charlie Chaplin',
- a set of versions of preserved information,
- any external object of any type whatsoever (Fig. 4) either by its UUID or by its location (e.g., URL), even though such links might not be durably reliable,

---

[184] Stanat 1977, *Discrete Mathematics in Computer Science*, ch. 3 through ch. 5.

[185] Ternary relationships are the core data of the RDF standard, perhaps for the same reasons that we find them the most convenient structuring primitives. See W3C 2001, *Resource Description Framework (RDF)*, http://www.w3.org/TR/1999/REC-rdf-syntax-19990222/.

[186] Rodrigues 2006, *A Multi-Graph to Support the Scholarly Communication Process*, http://arxiv.org/ftp/cs/papers/0601/0601121.pdf.

- a content blob or metadata blob within the object at hand, or within any external object instance,
- a bookmark or location in an instance of any of the above blobs,
- an extent in an instance of any of the above blobs, or
- a structured value set.

A second reason for the convenience of ternary relations is their natural mapping onto relational database schema and SQL queries, which avoids limitations that the simple natural mapping of binary relations encounters. In an SQL query of the form "select X from TABLE where COLUMN = Y" embedded in a high-level language program, the predicate expression Y can include a program variable whose value is calculated as part of the execution of the enclosing program. This is not true either for table names such as TABLE or for column names such as COLUMN.

Consider a description of capital cities tabulating their populations and their countries. We might represent this with a relation mapping each city to its population and its nation. This would support queries such as "Which countries have capital cities whose population is less than 500,000?" Suppose now that we wanted to extend this database to support queries about national languages, such as "In which capital cities with population greater than 300,000 is French the national language?" For this, we would probably want to add a column holding the national language names. To set this up, we probably would need to enlist the help of a database administrator, thereby encountering significant delay and administrative nuisance.

In contrast, with a single ternary table whose second column was configured to contain any short character string, any user with update privilege could immediately add triples such as "Washington, language, English" and formulate a suitable query. By mapping what might have been many binary relations into a single ternary relation, with the values in the second column of the ternary relation being mappings of the binary relation names, we make it easy to write programs whose end users choose the kind of relationship between each first column and third column entity. In contrast, we cannot easily help users choose arbitrary binary table names when they execute our programs.

6.4.2 Names and Identifiers, References, Pointers, and Links

The problem of identity arises only because it is not the case that each object has only one name (in the widest sense). The problem is to determine when two or more different expressions designate the same object. That there are several different expressions for the same object is not just an empirical shortcoming ... Rather, a multiplicity of names is logically brought about by the fact that, for each object, we may have not only a proper name (more than one proper name is superfluous), but that we also have definite descriptions; in fact, always several of them.

Carnap 1928, *LSW* §159

A *name* is a character string intended by its user to indicate a particular object within some context, but which in fact might be ambiguous, being associated with more than one object. An *identifier* is a name intended to be unique in the context at hand. If this context is the space of all contexts and if the identifier also qualifies as a *Uniform Resource Identifier* (URI), it might be called a *Universal Unique Identifier* (UUID). A *Uniform Resource Name* (URN) is a kind of URI.[187]

A *context* is a set of objects and their relationships (Fig. 4) together with such verbs as might be used to describe their changes, and perhaps also the language used to talk about these objects. Any conversation or information collection constitutes a context.

A digital *locator* is a character string indicating a specific address within a computer system or within a network. Today's best-known digital locator type is perhaps a World Wide Web (WWW) *Universal Resource Locator* (URL).[187] A URL is a kind of *Universal Resource Identifier* (URI), which is a particular formal kind of identifier.

A *naming scheme* is a rule set for creating and assigning names and unique identifiers that conform to a specified syntax. There are many computing naming schemes. A *resolution system* is a network service that stores identifiers and maps them to locators. For design flexibility we separate naming and name resolution by having *registries* identify name *resolvers* for any naming scheme that might be used. Registries might or might not be automated. How to find root registries must be published for implementers of network software.

A *reference* is a character string identifying a document, a particular place in some document (which might be the document at hand), or a contiguous extent in some document. Ideally, a reference is also an identifier.

A *pointer* is a reference to a particular location within an address space. An *address space* is a set of locations in which each location is identified by a unique number or character string. An example is the main memory of a computer. Another example is an HDD surface. Pointers are commonly used to make information rapidly accessible.

A *link* is a locator or a reference within a document. It is either visible as part of the link character string or otherwise explicitly known to the process at hand. Frequently, a document-embedded link is hidden, becoming evident to a human user only when a display cursor position coincides

---

[187] W3C 2001. *URIs, URLs, and URNs*, http://www.w3.org/TR/uri-clarification.

with a certain part of the displayed document, or partially hidden, being hinted at by some form of string highlighting such as underscoring and/or color changing in a visible presentation of the document. Perhaps the best known digital links are WWW pointers.

A *bookmark* is a marked and perhaps hidden document location intended to help human beings or computer processes rapidly locate specific content within its blob. All mature word processing software supports bookmarks.

6.4.3   Representing Value Sets

To help convey any information structure whatsoever concisely, what is depicted in Fig. 12 allows metadata elements that are not only scalars, but alternatively extensible value sets that might include references (links) and substructures such as vectors and lists.

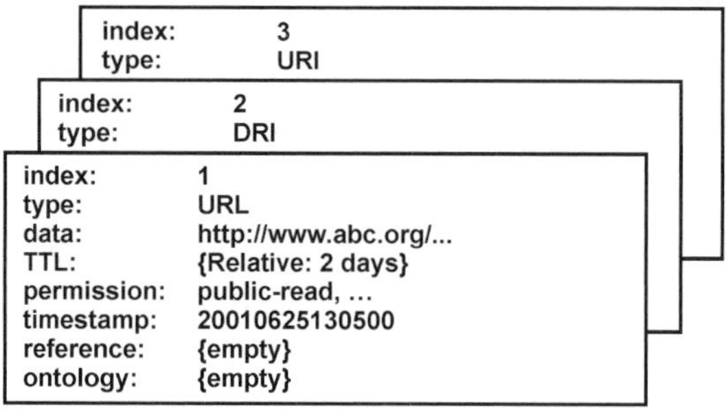

```
index:        3
type:         URI

index:        2
type:         DRI

index:        1
type:         URL
data:         http://www.abc.org/...
TTL:          {Relative: 2 days}
permission:   public-read, ...
timestamp:    20010625130500
reference:    {empty}
ontology:     {empty}
```

Fig. 14: A value set, as might occur in Fig. 12 metadata[188]

Fig. 14 illustrates such an indexed value set.[189]   Its schema is reminiscent of data structures found in 1970's programming languages, such as PL/1. Such value sets are not strictly essential, but rather merely convenient for communicating complex data structures.

In this structure, each value is itself a labeled structure with a unique index, a data type name (a literal element indicating the value's syntax and semantics), and any number of other fields whose labels and interpretations are alluded to by the literal element. In addition to predefined types, such as 'URL', 'DRI', 'URI', and so on, further types can be defined as architectural extensions. A definition might include administrative information such as TTL (time to live) and access permissions. A value

---

[188]   For instance, a recent European project is using this structure. See Fig. 5 of Risse 2005, *The BRICKS Infrastructure - An Overview.*

[189]   IETF RFC 3651, 2003, *Handle System: A general-purpose global name service ...* provides detailed field descriptions.

can also convey semantics using ternary relations. Suggested is an ONTOLOGY data type whose data field could identify a Fig. 12 object whose only content is a Relationship Block. Among things of interest for audit trail and historical purposes, a value set element describing a link might record who created that link.

6.4.4   XML "Glue"

XML is firmly established as the language for conveying the layout and other external details of the blobs in compound objects. Roughly a hundred standard XML schema definitions have been agreed on, e.g., MathML for mathematics and XBRL for business reporting. More are being considered for standardization. XML schema are poised to supersede DTDs because they are extensible, written in XML, support data typing, and support XML Namespaces.[190]

An XML document represents a labeled and ordered tree that can include data tags. Its content can be anything that can be represented with Unicode text—relational data, object-oriented data, schemas, procedures, or geographic information. An XML document can also embed bit-strings that do not conform to XML rules.

Much attention has been given to the use of XML as a technology-independent format. The idea is to extract from the original format all data elements and to tag them with mnemonics. The complete information would then be encoded in an XML string. The argument is that the XML string will remain readable in the future. A drawback of this approach is that XML brings with it a potentially large increase in file size. Recent measurements of the efficiency of transforming XML into browser-ready HTML resulted in 95 and 87 percent overhead rates. Only 5 percent and 13 percent, respectively, of the servers' capacities were left to run the program, a number considered by some to be unacceptable.[191]

XML strings will be used in the gaps between the blobs in realizations of Fig. 12 and also within its metadata, structure, and cryptographic blobs. The schematic limitations of a family of XML documents can be defined by XML Document Type Definitions (DTDs)—which themselves are regular expressions. Richer information models are emerging. An XSchema[192] object defines the structure of XML documents, including:

- the elements and attributes that can appear;

---

[190] *Namespaces in XML Adopted by W3C,* http://www.xml.com/pub/a/1999/01/3namespace.html.

[191] Goth 2006, *XML: The Center of Attention Up and Down the Stack.*

[192] *XML Schema Tutorial,* http://www.w3schools.com/schema/.

- the hierarchy and order of elements, and the number of each kind of child element;
- whether or not an element can be empty or can include text;
- the data types for elements and attributes; and
- default and fixed values for elements and attributes.

Since XML is thoroughly documented in many books[193] and WWW reports,[194] including standards definitions, not much needs to be said about it in this book. Only a small portion of standard XML will be needed within digital objects to be preserved. There is little doubt that the rules for XML portions needed for preservation are documented in forms that will survive anticipated technological obsolescence.

6.5   From Ontology to Architecture and Design

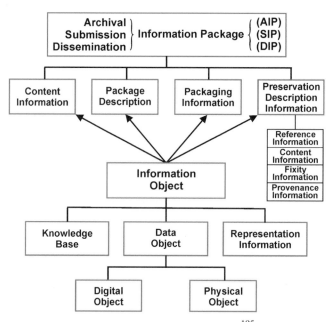

Fig. 15: *OAIS* digital object model[195]

OAIS is widely accepted as a framework for sharing archival notions. It outlines repository administration, ingest (i.e., accession), archival storage,

---

[193] For instance, Morrison 2000, *XML Unleashed.*

[194] The *Cover Pages*, at http://xml.coverpages.org/, provide a good entry to this literature.

[195] Holdsworth 2000, *A blueprint for Representation Information in the OAIS model,* http://www.personal.leeds.ac.uk/~ecldh/cedars/ieee00.html.

data management, access, and planning. An *OAIS* archival holding corresponds conceptually to a Fig. 12 content object—a set of information that is the original target of preservation. It is comprised of one or more constituent bit-strings and secondary information related to these data objects' representation.[196] Its Fig. 15 information model separates long-term bit-string storage from content structure management. An *OAIS* Content Information object itself is encapsulated in an Information Package that holds and binds the Content Information object components.

OAIS distinguishes between what is preserved, an Archival Information Package (*OAIS* AIP), what is submitted to the archive, a Submission Information Package (*OAIS* SIP), and what is delivered to archive clients, a Dissemination Information Package (*OAIS* DIP). This distinction is needed to talk about the fact that some repository submissions have insufficient information for meeting the objectives of that repository.

Critical discussions suggest reasons for making DIP bit patterns identical to those of corresponding AIPs, e.g., Beedham 2005. A counter-example might be the U.S. NARA collections, in which the number of small objects is so large and the organization into logical file folders is so compelling that each ingestion (SIP) and repository holding (AIP) might be such a folder containing many hundred individual memoranda or completed forms. If so, information requests and deliveries (DIPs) would conveniently permit specification of a range of objects from one or more AIPs.

6.5.1   From the OAIS Reference Model to Architecture

To understand the distinction between a reference model and an architecture,[197] consider the Fig. 16 *OAIS* ingest processes[198] and a similarly structured fragment of a reference model for *residences,* suggested by the Fig. 17 processes of a Kitchen structure. This fragment suggests how we might map much of the *OAIS* model onto our residence model. Each *OAIS* process would correspond to a room or other space in a residence. The wording of the following paragraphs closely mimics *OAIS* paragraphs.

A residence may contain one or more areas called Kitchens. The Receive Groceries process provides storage space and an entrance to receive

---

[196] Bekaert 2005, *A Standards-based Solution for the Accurate Transfer of Digital Assets.*

Giaretta 2005 *Supporting e-Research Using Representation Information*, http://eprints.erpanet.org/archive/00000100/.

[197] *Shortcomings of [OAIS],* http://www.ieee-tcdl.org/Bulletin/v2n2/egger/egger.html, reminds readers that the 2002 version of OAIS emphasizes, "This reference model does not specify a design or implementation."

[198] This subsection simply rewrites some of *Reference Model for an Open Archival Information System (OAIS)* 2001, §4.1.1.2.

a grocery shipment. Its execution represents a legal transfer of ownership of the groceries, and may require that special controls be placed on the shipments. It provides the Grocer a *receipt*, which might accompany a *request to send* missing items.

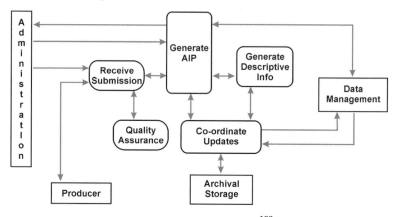

Fig. 16: *OAIS* ingest process[199]

The Quality Assurance process validates correct receipt in the unpacking area. This might include tasting a sample of each received item, and the use of a log to record and identify any shortfalls.

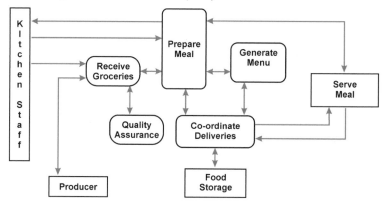

Fig. 17: Kitchen process in a residence

The Prepare Meal process transforms one or more packages into one or more dishes that conform to *culinary and health standards*. This may involve boiling, frying, baking, or blending of contents of grocery shipments. The Cooking process may issue *recipe requests* to a cookbook to

---

[199]   Adapted from CCSDS 650.0-R-2, *Reference Model for an Open Archival Information System*, Fig. 4-2, http://www.ccsds.org/documents/pdf/CCSDS-650.0-R-2.pdf.

obtain *descriptions* needed to produce the menu. This process sends *sample dishes for approval* to a critic, and receives back an *appraisal*.

Likewise, the Generate Menu and other processes have their own rules.

This reference model helps toward building a residence by providing builders and prospective residents a shared vocabulary. Each builder further needs instructions about what kind of residence to construct: a single family home, an apartment building, a military barracks, or a college residence. Just as our reference model says what it means to be a place to live—a *residence*, *OAIS* articulates what it means to be a place to hold information—a *library* or *archive*. Each is in the form of an *intension*. Like most definitions, each is incomplete.

The kitchen model above does not specify architecture. A builder's instructions should include dimensions, location, and other factors. Such detail would not appear in our reference model, just as *OAIS* does not distinguish between a research library, a state government archive, a corporate archive, or a personal collection. Missing in each case is a high-level design differentiating structural alternatives; quantifying spaces, resources, and flows; describing materials and visible appearances; specifying utilities and safety factors, and so on.

How much qualitative and quantitative detail must an architecture express? The customer decides. He will often accept conventional levels and styles of description, but might also want to inject his own notions about what is important. A satisfactory architecture would describe every aspect on which the customer insists, and these would be essential elements of a prudent construction contract.

6.5.2 Languages for Describing Structure

Discussions of structure occur at various levels and with different styles:

- For syntactics—formal structure, language, logic, data, records, deductions, software, and so on.
- About semantics—meanings, propositions, validity, truth, signification, denotations, and so on.
- In pragmatics—intentions, communications, negotiations, and so on.
- Relative to social worlds—beliefs, expectations, commitments, contracts, law, culture, and so on.

In a knowledge theory that includes relations as primitive constructors, graphs can be considered a derivative notion.[200] There are many graphical languages for expressing roughly the same information. They include dif-

---

[200] Sowa 2000, *Knowledge representation*.

ferences of aspects shown or suppressed in order to make their depictions comprehensible at a glance. Directed graphs with labeled nodes and arcs constitute graphical languages for depicting ternary relations

Schema are models, and may themselves require further models that explain by reminding readers how words are used. The explications of schema are called *reference models*.

Semantic intentions can be conveyed by a knowledge management language that is used for expressions that accompany the information. Ternary relations and information identifiers in fact comprise a sufficient knowledge management language. In particular, they are sufficient for an elegant representation of any information collection.

6.5.3   Semantic Interoperability

A model is created for a specific purpose. It is a simplified representation of part of the world. This simplification should help us analyze the underlying reality and understand that. Many groups are working to map ontologies, subject classifications, and thesauri to each other. While significant progress has been achieved in system, syntactic, and structural/schematic interoperability, comprehensive solutions to semantic interoperability remain elusive.[201] Yet, trends in software technologies continue to bring focus on semantic issues.[202] For instance, in late 2005 a W3C working group was created to define a business rules language for interoperability—a rules interchange language.[203]

What is being attempted is scientific observation to relate subjective opinions to objective assertions about social behavior (§3.3). However, it would be unrealistic to expect comprehensive convergence to schema that fully satisfy all the members of any interest group. Recent literature related to the failure of Artificial Intelligence to achieve its early "pie in the sky" objectives is instructive.[204]

Models with graphic languages such as UML[205] and OWL[206] have advantages over XML markup. They are more readable and convey semantic intensions. One glance at a model can convey a rough idea of the num-

---

[201] In the Semantic Web literature, "the Holy Grail of semantic interoperability remains elusive."

[202] Ouksel 1999, *Semantic Interoperability in Global Information Systems.*

[203] *Rule Interchange Format,* http://www.w3.org/2005/rules/.

[204] Lemieux.2001, *Let the Ghosts Speak: An Empirical Exploration of the "Nature" of the Record,* "a case study of record-keeping practices illustrates … many valid conceptualizations arising from particular social contexts."

[205] *Unified Modeling Language,* http://www.omg.org/technology/documents/formal/uml.htm.

[206] *OWL Web Ontology Language,* http://www.w3.org/TR/owl-features/

ber of object classes under discussion and the complexity of their relationships.

6.6 Metadata

Metadata—structured data about other data—have been used in libraries for more than a century. Digital metadata have become a central paradigm.[207] Existing metadata types have been augmented, new metadata types have been proposed and adopted for digital objects, and metadata concepts have been applied to creating community-specific ontologies.[208] In digital collections, metadata fulfill a variety of tasks, including

- identifying items uniquely worldwide;
- describing collection items (e.g., author, creation date), including their contexts;
- supporting retrieval and identification;
- grouping items into collections within a repository;
- recording authenticity evidence, including historical audit trails;
- helping protect item integrity against improper change and unintentional corruption;
- recording access permissions and other digital rights information;
- facilitating information interchange between autonomous repositories; and
- recording technical parameters describing items' representations.

Embedded metadata can make a digital object *self-documenting* and well positioned for long-term preservation and access. That ownership, custody, technology, legal restrictions, and other circumstances are likely to change over time can be handled by a nesting scheme for version management. This idea—that each data package should embed its most important supporting information, its metadata—has a history that became distinct and explicit in "object-oriented programming" research in the late 1970s—research that included calls for *persistent objects*.[209]

---

[207] Gradmann 1998, *Cataloguing vs. Metadata: old wine in new bottles?*

Lazinger 2001, *Digital Preservation and Metadata,* provides a good introduction to this topic.

[208] Warner 2002, *Metadata & Taxonomies for a More Flexible Information Architecture,* http://www.lexonomy.com/presentations/metadataAndTaxonomies.html, is a quick tutorial.

Metadata ... Primer, Cataloging and Classification 40(3/4), 2005, provides tutorial articles

[209] Shepard 1999, *Universal Preservation Format.* UPF is an object encapsulation proposal.

Boudrez 2005, *Digital Containers for Shipment into the Future,* http://www.expertisecentrumdavid.be/docs/digital_containers.pdf.

Encapsulation has, in fact, an even longer practical history. Identifiers are a special kind of metadata. Requiring people to carry identification papers started in some parts of the world at least a century ago. Including provenance information in books is of similar vintage. Serial numbers are stamped on handguns and automobile engine blocks for much the same reasons that we include identifiers in TDO metadata.

6.6.1 Metadata Standards and Registries

There are few objective criteria for choosing which metadata scheme to use for any particular situation. Each profession emphasizes variant aspects. Each repository institution has different circumstances from most other institutions, and its own ideas on how to serve its designated community.

Whenever semantic choices are necessarily subjective and also essential for sharing information, we may expect lengthy debates before even uneasy agreements are achieved. This is seen nowhere more prominently than in choices of metadata content and format. In contrast to semantic choices, syntactic standardization is well in hand. The *ISO/IEC 11179* specifies basic aspects of metadata element composition for sharing among people and machines.[210]

A *metadata registry* is a database service that identifies and describes features of metadata schemas. Among the many initiatives to define metadata schemas for different information objects, the instantiation process has revealed many ways to describe them. Some seem to bury key information in ancillary documents. Specification documents sometimes assume an understanding of the purpose, scope, and perspective of the schema and launch straight into metadata element description. This is not helpful toward trying to assess whether a particular schema exists to meet one's needs. Pilot instantiations reveal a proliferation of encoding schemes, such as controlled vocabularies from which element values are sourced or standardized data representations for elements.[211] A need to analyze relationships amongst these schemes has been asserted.

Initiatives like the *Australian Recordkeeping Metadata Schema* and *ISO 23081* assume that much of the metadata required for recordkeeping is available in the business systems in which records are created and kept. At issue is whether the metadata are reliably connected to each record to which they pertain and whether the authenticity, accuracy, and reliability

---

[210] ISO/IEC 2001, *Information technology—ISO Framework for the Specification and Standardization of Data Elements.*

[211] For example, *ISO 8601, Data elements and interchange formats - Information interchange - Representation of dates and times.*

of the metadata are maintained. Recordkeeping professionals are beginning to believe that automatic capture of metadata is the only sustainable
method of metadata creation.[212]

There is much ongoing activity. Over a million Web pages with "Metadata" in their titles were updated during 2005. More than 100 books with
"Metadata" in their titles are in print. This vast literature surely contains
every plausible best practice recommendation. It would make little sense
for us to add comments, apart from recommending a starting point for
readers not familiar with the literature,[213] and to quote Weibel: "The idea
of user-created metadata is seductive. Creating metadata early in the life
cycle of an information asset makes sense, and who should know the content better than its creator? Creators also have the incentive of their work
being more easily found—who *wouldn't* want to spend an extra few min-
utes with so much already invested? The answer is that almost nobody
will spend the time, and users are unlikely to have the knowledge or pa-
tience to do it very well. Our expectations to the contrary seem touchingly
naïve in retrospect."[214]

6.6.2 Dublin Core Metadata

The Dublin Core metadata set is intended to support WWW resource discovery.[215] It consists of 15 elements (Table 5) whose names suggest their
semantics. It was originally an attempt to overcome a widely perceived
problem—that authors often did not provide orderly metadata that every
repository manager needed to address his responsibilities. It receives a
great deal of attention, but remains problematic.[216]

---

[212] Evans 2004, *Describing and analyzing the recordkeeping capabilities of metadata sets,*
http://www.slais.ubc.ca/PEOPLE/faculty/tennis-p/dcpapers2004/Paper_27.pdf.

[213] NISO 2004, *Understanding Metadata,* http://www.niso.org/standards/resources/
UnderstandingMetadata.pdf.
NISO 2002, *NISO Guide to Standards for Library Systems,* http://www.niso.org/standards/
resources/RFP_Writers_Guide.pdf.

[214] Weibel 2005, *Border Crossings: Reflections on a Decade of Metadata Consensus Building.*

[215] National Information Standards Organization 2001, *The Dublin Core Metadata Element Set,*
ANSI/NISO Z39.85, http://www.techstreet.com/cgi-bin/pdf/free/335284/Z39.85-2001.pdf.
Duff 2003, *The Dublin Core and Its Limitations,* http://www.digicult.info/downloads/
dc_info_issue6_december_20031.pdf.

[216] There is an annual Dublin Core Conference. That the Dublin Core standard presents difficulties
is suggested by the fact of too much discussion about something intended to be very simple and
easy to use, and by large efforts to design more complete metadata schema. The difficulties are
touched on in Lagoze 2006, *Metadata aggregation and "automated digital libraries,"* http://
arXiv.org/abs/cs/0601125, §5.

Table 5: Dublin Core metadata elements

Title	Creator	Subject
Date	Description	Publisher
Contributor	Type	Format
Identifier	Source	Language
Relation	Coverage	Rights

6.6.3   Metadata for Scholarly Works (METS)

The Metadata Encoding and Transmission Standard (METS)[217] is a packaging scheme for drawing together potentially dispersed but related files and data. It uses XML to provide a vocabulary and syntax for expressing structural relationships, and has Java packaging assistance.[218] It is beginning to be widely used and illustrates aspects found in other schemes, including relationships to *OAIS*. It is intended to be a flexible, yet tightly structured, container for all metadata necessary to describe, navigate, and maintain a digital object. It conforms both to *OAIS* and to the scheme discussed in §6.4. A METS document consists of the following:

- Header information to convey the dates of content creation and latest modification, status, names of information providers, and alternatives to supplement the primary document identifier.
- Structural mapping to outline a hierarchy of DO components, with links to content files and metadata representing each component, and to record hyperlinks between components.
- Behavioral information for recording how components should be rendered for human viewing.
- Administrative metadata to convey provenance and property rights.
- Descriptive metadata that might hold both internal descriptions and also pointers to external information.
- File information similar to the Manifest suggested by Fig. 12.

METS accommodates autonomously specified specialized extensions. Although the METS editorial board does not specify such extensions, it does recommend some to render a METS record more readily interchangeable between institutions. These include MODS (Metadata Object Description Schema) and MARC-XML for descriptive metadata,

---

[217]   *Metadata Encoding and Transmission Standard,* http://www.loc.gov/standards/mets/.

[218]   *METS Java Toolkit,* http://hul.harvard.edu/mets/.

and MIX36, METSRights and TextMD for administrative metadata.[219]
PREMIS preservation metadata[220] are intended to be a METS extension.[51]
A program offering, docWORKS/METAe, automates conversion of
printed documents into tagged METS objects.[221]

6.6.4 Archiving and Preservation Metadata

Examples of heritage institutions' efforts to develop broadly useful preservation metadata prescriptions abound. The National Library of New Zealand (NLNZ) designed a schema intended to balance between the principles of the *OAIS* Information Model and practicalities as it saw them. Its
model allows plug-in components for describing data-type-specific aspects, such as the resolution and dimensions of an image file. The NLNZ
model is said to have greatly influenced younger schemas, such as LMER
of the Deutsche Bibliothek.

6.7   Summary

No one should be surprised either that the solution to an information technology challenge is an exercise in software engineering or that analyses of
proposed solutions draw on philosophical theories of knowledge.

We cannot partition the world's collections into unconnected partial collections. We can neither define an impervious boundary between cultural
documents and business records, nor segregate picture collections from
text files.

Some formal languages—regular expressions, BNF, and ASN.1—are so
widely used to describe document structure that they are permanently dependable as starting points for representation.

Ternary relations are particularly convenient for communicating structure—more convenient than binary relations. This is partly for a technical
reason: in SQL, table names are not first-class variables, i.e., they are not
conveniently manipulated in table administration or query formulation
commands.

Choices of ontologies and of metadata schema are subjective, often being made in the light of local objectives different from those of seemingly

---

[219] Littman 2006, *A Technical Approach and Distributed Model for Validation of Digital Objects*
describes why and how the Library of Congress's National Digital Newspaper Program is using
METS, MODS, MIX, and PREMIS standards in combination.

[220] Bolander 2005, *Data Dictionary for Preservation Metadata*: Final Report of the PREMIS
Working Group, http://www.oclc.org/research/projects/pmwg/premis-final.pdf.

[221] *Automatic Conversion of Printed Documents into Fully Tagged METS Objects*, http://
www.loc.gov/standards/mets/presentations/od2/gravenhorst.ppt.

similarly projects. Many different approaches (Table 6) are used to describe similar aspects.

Table 6: Closely related semantic concepts

Thesaurus	Subject classification
Topic map	Semantic network[222]
Data dictionary	Ontology

What metadata is essential for each document? Phrases such as "the essential attributes of the information object" are common in the literature. Essential to whom? For what? That depends on what the eventual users of the document will want to accomplish with its content. Producers can only guess what this is. The metadata choices people will eventually settle on as standards will involve community consensus, will probably converge on more standards than would be ideal, and are likely to remain subjects of debate for five to ten years. There is probably nothing that anyone can do, or should attempt to do, to hurry the discussions or push them toward some ideal number of standards.

Much effort has been expended on metadata for describing library and archives records, with emphasis on methods that can be used within the time and effort that writers, publishers, and libraries are willing to invest. However, the published recommendations have not resulted in commensurate practical implementation.[223]

We use the same patterns over and over again:

- Patterns of description in language;
- Patterns in our pictures;
- Patterns of reasoning; and
- Patterns of behavior.

A single model is sufficient for digital representation of any intellectual work, of any collection, of any ontology, and perhaps the structure of any digital information whatsoever.

---

[222]   Sowa 2002, *Semantic Networks,* http://www.jfsowa.com/pubs/semnet.htm.

[223]   Bulterman 2004, *Is It Time for a Moratorium on Metadata?*

Duff 2003, *The Dublin Core and Its Limitations.*

Greenberg 2005, *Final Report for the AMeGA (Automatic Metadata Generation Applications) Project,* http://www.loc.gov/catdir/bibcontrol/lc_amega_final_report.pdf.

Shankaranarayanan 2006, *The Metadata Enigma.*

Part III: Distributed Content Management

People need common bases for their messages and shared information to know how these should be interpreted, managed, and maintained.[224] They need communication conventions and standards. They also need network infrastructure (Fig. 18) that conforms to other standards.[225] In fact, such standards and infrastructure are today so widely used that their users might notice them only when they fail either catastrophically, as in the New Orleans Katrina disaster,[226] or in small incidents, such as a file being inaccessible. Only a small fraction of this technology needs to be included in a discussion of content preservation.

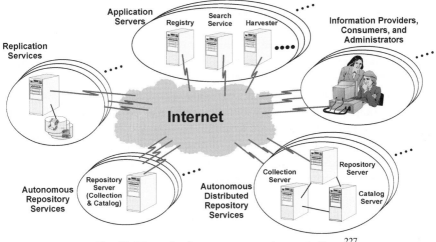

Fig. 18: Network of autonomous services and clients[227]

We have networks of interoperating repositories. From a preservation perspective, redundancy of content storage and access paths might be this infrastructure's most important application. Viable preservation solutions will allow repository institutions and individual users to exploit already deployed and future software without disruption, conforming to interface

---

[224] For instance, Arthur 2004, *Recognizing Digitization as a Preservation Reformatting Method,* identifies about 40 Web sites working toward such a common basis.

Greene 2006, *How to Digitize a Million Books,* http://www.technologyreview.com/InfoTech/wtr_16434,300,p1.html.

[225] Besser 2002, *Moving from Isolated Digital Collections to Interoperable Digital Libraries.*

[226] Entlich 2005, *Too Close for Comfort? The Case for Off-site Storage.*

[227] Cf. Fig. 2 of Risse 2005, *The BRICKS Infrastructure.*

conventions that permit "mixing and matching" components from competing providers—software that, over time, will be improved over today's versions. Scarcely a week goes by without new offerings with improved scaling, reliability, security, and cost. Furthermore, the standards involved will allow each institutional and individual participant much autonomy in handling preserved information, balancing this objective with that of information sharing. This might include an institution's managing autonomous repositories combined with a software layer that presents their content as if from a single repository.[228]

University libraries and other cultural heritage institutions began to explore widespread application of such technology only recently. "Institutional repositories are being positioned decisively as general-purpose infrastructure within the context of changing scholarly practice, within e-research and cyber-infrastructure, and in visions of the university in the digital age."[229]

To establish starting points for encoding complex data types (Chapter 12), our main concern must be primary encoding standards, rather than other standards that we can define with these. We choose primary standards conservatively. The eventual choices will be community decisions that depend on more detailed deliberations than this book can include. Happily, the standards essential for durable encoding are limited to ASCII, Unicode, UTF-8, methods of describing computer programs, and core portions of XML. Additional standards are useful to bypass obstacles associated with proprietary data formats, such as the formats of Microsoft Office files.

We use "divide and conquer" tactics, as is common throughout software engineering. Individual digital object structure is almost entirely divorced from archival repository design. A repository should "see" each digital object mostly as a bit-stream from which it might extract information, e.g., for search indices that support information retrieval services.

A collection is an entity specified either by a list of its members (extensively) or by a query predicate (intensively). Such a collection might be housed in a single repository, but need not be. A set of repository holdings is merely a special case of a collection.

A recent book suggests,

> It is possible to re-imagine archival systems of the future that: manage the records of multiple groups and individuals beyond the boundaries of the personal or corporate archive; represent multidimensional contexts of creation, capture, organization, and pluralization—juridical, organizational, func-

---

[228] Liu 2005. *File-based storage of Digital Objects and Constituent Datastreams.*

[229] Lynch 2005, *Institutional Repository Deployment in the United States.*

tional, procedural, technological and recordkeeping; provide multiple views of parallel recordkeeping universes; continuously and cumulatively weave relationships between records and related people, organizational structures, functions and activities to assist in preserving their evidential value and [to] enable multiple access paths to records and their meanings; and keep records relating to all recordkeeping and archiving processes persistently linked to the records they form and transform.

Such archival systems would have great potential utility in relation to the preservation and accessibility of electronic records of continuing value, as well as to the management of current records. The locus of the archives system might exist as an interface to archival records held by an archival institution, but it might also link to all records, publicly available or not, of continuing value or not [of continuing value], still maintained in the recordkeeping systems of individual agencies. In this sense, the collective archives could be preserved and made accessible in virtual space. Custodial arrangements and issues of where the record is physically located would cease to be of prime importance.

McKemmish 2005, *Archives*

This is written as if talking about a future possibility. Perhaps this is because universities have not asked those who could have done so to package the technology discussed in Chapter 9 for university requirements. However, we have long known how to provide such infrastructure[230] and have deployed it widely in business enterprises for about ten years.[231]

---

[230] Nelson 2005, *Shared Infrastructure Preservation Models.*

[231] Lynch 2005, *Institutional Repository Deployment in the United States.*

7 Digital Object Formats

All documents to be shared must conform to widely known structural schema. Information protocol and representation standards are also critical. Many such standards are used to facilitate interchange between otherwise autonomous individuals and agencies.[232] However, having too many standards can present more difficulties than having too few. For instance, the National Alliance for Health Information Technology identifies more than 450 mandatory and voluntary standards, more than 200 organizations with standards working groups, and more than 900 standards publications!

Conventions that are widely adopted in the marketplace without public body endorsement are known as *de facto standards*.[233] RSA Laboratories' Public Key Cryptography Standards (PKCS) are widely accepted de facto standards. In contrast to de facto standards, *de jure standards* are formally established by official bodies such as International Organization for Standardization (ISO), and the Internet Engineering Task Force (IETF). An example of a de jure standard is *ISO/ITU–T X.509* for digital security.

It is difficult to predict which standards will themselves be deemed well preserved in a few decades—or in a century or two. The current chapter discusses a small set that is sufficient for an economical and practical preservation solution. This set is not the minimum needed to ensure future interpretability of saved documents, because using only a tiny subset might make the proposed solution cumbersome. It is also not the much larger set that community processes will probably accept sufficiently for use in content preservation.

XML is addressed by many standards, but only a few of these are needed for a sufficient working base.

7.1 Character Sets and Fonts

Information in digital machines is represented as strings of zeros and ones (or on and off indications, or true and false indications—different ways of saying the same thing). Such strings can be viewed to be binary encodings of numbers; for instance, 11100_{binary} is the same number as $28_{decimal}$.

---

[232] See the lists of standards and protocols found in the U.K. *e-Government Interoperability Framework*, accessible via http://www.govtalk.gov.uk/interoperability/egif.asp.

[233] Miller 2004. *Toward the Digital Aquifer,* discusses current efforts by UK agencies to collaborate on a Common Information Environment (CIE) that meets the diverse needs of consumers of digital content and services.

These numbers are mapped into alphanumeric characters by *character coding* or *character encoding*. Unicode/UCS provides for encoding most printed characters. ASCII is a much older standard that Unicode has incorporated as a subset, and is widely used, including for writing the definitions of other standards.

7.1.1   Extended ASCII

ASCII, the American Standard Code for Information Interchange, is a seven-bit code standardized in 1968.[234] The ASCII set consists of 128 natural numbers (each represented by a seven-bit pattern) ranging from zero through 127. Each integer is assigned to some letter, numeral, punctuation mark, or one of the most common special characters. For instance, in response to the numbers $65_{decimal}$ (01000001_{binary}) and $97_{decimal}$ (01101110_{binary}) in a print stream, the characters 'A' and 'e' will be printed.

An extension of 128 code points, using the full eight bits of the byte, is mapped to mathematical, graphic, and foreign characters.

7.1.2   Unicode/UCS and UTF-8

Unicode characters are sufficient to represent the written forms of all the world's major languages.[235] 'Unicode' is an informal name for the *ISO 10646* international standard defining the Universal Character Set (UCS).[236] Files containing only seven-bit ASCII characters are unchanged when viewed with Unicode UTF-8 encoding, so plain ASCII files are already valid Unicode files. Relative to all other character standards, UCS is a superset guaranteeing round-trip compatibility. (No information will be lost by converting a text string to UCS and then back to the original encoding.) Conceptually, UCS is simple.

The *meaning* of a character and its *picture* are distinct. There may be many pictures for the same character—even several for each font. For instance, "the first letter in the Latin alphabet" (a meaning) can be depicted by any of the glyphs "A," "A," "A," "*A*," "*A*," "A," or by the $65_{decimal}$ code

---

[234]   Later ASCII standards include ISO 14962-1997 and ANSI-X3.4-1986 (R1997). *Extended ASCII tables* are available in textbooks and on Web sites. E.g., http://www.lookuptables.com/.

[235]   Unicode currently defines almost 100,000 characters; see http://www.unicode.org/charts/ and http://www.unicode.org/charts/charindex.html. *The Online Edition of The Unicode Standard Version 3.0*, http://www.unicode.org/book/u2.html, points to the latest versions.

[236]   Järnefors 1996, *A short overview of ISO/IEC 10646 and Unicode*, http://www.nada.kth.se/i18n/ucs/unicode-iso10646-oview.html.

Korpela 2001, *A Tutorial on Character Code Issues*, http://www.cs.tut.fi/~jkorpela/chars.html, provides comprehensive citations to Unicode resources and explanations that include descriptions of idiosyncrasies and pitfalls of character representation.

point from any of several hundred other fonts. The principal notions in an articulation of character coding are indicated in the following list.

Unicode/UCS   is a function from natural numbers in $[0,2^{31}\text{-}1]$ (31-bit integers) to characters.

A code point   is the number or index that uniquely identifies a character.

A glyph   is a picture for displaying and/or printing a visual representation of a character.

A font   is a set of glyphs for some Unicode subset, with stylistic commonalities in order to achieve a pleasing appearance when many glyphs combine to represent a text.

UTF-8   is the most popular of several ways of representing Unicode text to take less storage space than would be required if each character was represented by a 32-bit word (4 bytes).[237]

Unicode defines a function from code points (integers) to names (ASCII character strings), as illustrated by the first two columns of Table 7. It is silent about how the integers should be represented by binary code in computers, about how the characters should be depicted by glyphs, or about how they should sound when spoken. Digital representations are specified by standard encoding rules, such as UTF-8, and glyphs are defined in font tables.

Unicode character names (column 2 of Table 7) are surrogates for conceptual objects. They are also mnemonics by virtue of being well known English phrases. A character takes its meaning from how it is used, not from the appearance of any glyph. For instance, a 'PARENTHESIS, LEFT' signals the start of a delimited string. Provided that a glyph used in formatted text is understood to mean 'PARENTHESIS, LEFT', it is almost irrelevant whether it looks like '(', '(', or '('.

Different characters might, in some fonts, have identical glyphs. ASCII contains characters with multiple uses; for instance, its 'hyphen' is used also for 'minus' and 'dash'. In contrast, Unicode defines 'HYPHEN' and 'MINUS' among its dash characters. For compatibility, the old ASCII character is preserved in Unicode also (in the old code position, with the name 'HYPHEN-MINUS').

Why do we distinguish between 'HYPHEN' and 'MINUS' even though their glyphs are identical in many fonts? Although the distinction might be unimportant for print and display appearance, it is almost surely critical for sorting and searching. When we search for minus signs, we would prefer not to be distracted by hyphens.

---

[237] Yergeau 1996, *UTF-8, A Transformation Format for Unicode*, http://www.ietf.org/rfc/rfc2044.txt.

Kuhn 2001, *UTF-8 and Unicode FAQ for Unix/Linux*, http://www.cl.cam.ac.uk/~mgk25/unicode.html.

Table 7: Samples illustrating Unicode, UTF-8, and glyphs

Code point (hexadecimal)	Unicode name (surrogate for a meaning)	Storage representation (UTF-8 encoding)	Rendering (sample glyphs)
002D	HYPHEN-MINUS	000101100	-
2010	HYPHEN	11100010 10000000 10010000	-
2013	EN DASH	11100010 10000000 10010011	–
2212	MINUS	11100010 10001000 10010010	—
00E9	LATIN SMALL LETTER E WITH ACUTE	01101001	é é é
01A9	LATIN CAPITAL LETTER ESH	11000110 10100101	Σ
03A3	GREEK CAPITAL LETTER SIGMA	11001110 10100011	Σ Σ Σ Σ
2211	N-ARY SUMMATION	11100010 10001000 10010001	Σ **Σ** Σ Σ
0633	ARABIC LETTER SEEN	11011000 10110011	س

When a text file is sent to an application, how is it known what character coding is being used? Applications that support Unicode typically require that their input files have header records that identify the encoding. The encoding is a kind of metadata that is so important that some standards demand that it be explicitly named. The header record itself is usually required to be ASCII-encoded. For instance, a proper XML header record is:

```
<?xml version="1.0" encoding="utf-8"?>
```

Text for which no encoding specification is identified is almost always represented with ASCII encoding.

7.2   File Formats

In the numerate disciplines and bioinformatics in particular, researchers have made use of the ever-increasing capabilities of computers to process both very large and very rich information sources. Moreover, an individual electronic document can contain embedded spreadsheets, graphics, audio and video clips, as well as internal and external links to these resources. Researchers tend to push the boundaries of these multimedia capabilities, in order to use the full power of the computer technology to express their ideas. This use of a variety of multimedia types in a single document is gathering pace and spreading to other fields.[238]

A *file format* is a rule set that specifies, for some kinds of data, which bit-sequences are permitted—its syntax, the information needed to write and print that kind of file.[239] A file format is called *open* if its specification is publicly available without requiring users to pay fees or to observe usage restrictions. Only open formats are likely to work for preservation without unacceptable risks. This is because the owner of a proprietary format might in the future vanish or choose to charge unaffordable fees.

Archives are assessing their practices for specific formats.[240] The archival community has more than once changed its collective opinion about which information representations are good enough for preservation.[241] However, it is not clear how important such opinions might be, since some archives feel they must prepare for whatever formats their data sources provide. File format specifications and related tools are not centrally managed.

Much of the painstaking work needed to handle any file format properly is likely to have been provided by contributors with idiosyncratic interests and priorities.

7.2.1 File Format Identification, Validation, and Registries

Identification, validation, and characterization of a file format are frequently necessary for routine document operations and repository man-

---

[238] European Task Force for Permanent Access to the Records of Science 2005, *Strategic Action Programme 2006-2010,* http://www.knaw.nl/cfdata/epic/announcerechts.cfm#212.

[239] For suggestions on how to deal with many file formats, see http://www.stack.com/file/extension/.

[240] Abrams 2005, *The role of format in digital preservation.*

Clausen 2004, *Handling File Formats,* http://www.netarchive.dk/Web site/publications/FileFormats-2004.pdf.

University of Leeds 2003, *Survey and assessment of information on file formats ...,* http://www.jisc.ac.uk/uploaded_documents/FileFormatsreport.pdf.

Lawrence 2000, *Risk Management of Digital Information: A File Format Investigation.*

[241] Levy 1998, *Heroic Measures: Reflections on the Possibility and Purpose of Digital Preservation,* comments: "Within the archival community, whose focus ... has been on paper, microform, and [so on], the predominant answer to ["preserving what?"] has shifted over time. ... [I]n the early nineteenth century, archivists took their mission to be the preservation of the information contained in documents rather than the original documents themselves. ... It was only ... in the twentieth century, that advances in preservation theory and practice ... made ... possible ... preserving ... original materials. The pendulum thus swung from ... preserving the information content of documents to ... preserving the artifacts themselves."

Beedham 2005, Assessment of UKDA and TNA Compliance with OAIS and METS Standards, p. 89, presents a U.K. viewpoint.

agement. This is because policy and processing decisions about object in-gest, storage, access, and preservation depend on the type of object being handled. For efficiency, repositories need to automate these procedures as much as possible.

The JSTOR/Harvard Object Validation Environment (JHOVE) imple-ments format-specific identification, validation, and characterization of files.[242] JHOVE scope is controlled by plug-in output handlers so that the file types covered can be extended. It already includes handlers for ASCII and UTF-8 encoded text; GIF, JPEG, and TIFF images; AIFF and WAVE audio; PDF, HTML, and XML text files. *OAIS* representation information produced by JHOVE includes the file's pathname or URI, its last modifi-cation date, byte size, format, format version, MIME type, format profiles, and optionally, MD5, and SHA-1 checksums. Additional media type-specific representation information is consistent with the *NISO Z39.87 Data Dictionary* for digital still images[243] and the AES metadata standard for digital audio[244] illustrated in Table 8.

Table 8: Sample AES metadata[245]

<didl:Statement mimeType="text/xml; charset=UTF-8">

<dc:creator xmlns:dc="http://purl.org/dc/elements/1.1/"
    xmlns:xsi=http://www.w3.org/2001/XMLSchema-instance
    xsi:schemaLocation="http://purl.org/dc/elements/1.1/
    http://dublincore.org/schemas/xmls/simpledc20021212.xsd">
    Jhove (Rel. 1.0 (beta 2), 2004-07-19)</dc:creator>

<dc:description xmlns:dc="http://purl.org/dc/elements/1.1/"
    xmlns:xsi=http://www.w3.org/2001/XMLSchema-instance
    xsi:schemaLocation="http://purl.org/dc/elements/1.1/
    http://dublincore.org/schemas/xmls/simpledc20021212.xsd">
    Jhove (Rel. 1.0 (beta 2), 2004-07-19) Date: 2005-04-30 20:50:51 EDT Representa-tionInformation:
    file:%2Fhome%2Fspace%2FsampleArchive%2Farchive%2Flc_email27%2Etxtl
    ReportingModule: ASCII-hul, Rel. 1.0 (2004-05-05)
    LastModified: 2005-04-10 20:25:35 EDT Size: 6206
    Format: ASCII Status: Well-formed and valid MIMEtype: text/plain; charset=US-ASCII ASCIIMetadata: LineEndings: LF
    Checksum: 76c99b38 Type: CRC32 Checksum: 52217a1bcd2be7cfd4cdc9cf
    Type: MD5 Checksum: 6d51599d4d978e5d253e945a7248965ddc3616
    Type: SHA-1
    </dc:description>   </didl:Statement>

---

[242] *JSTOR/Harvard Object Validation Environment*, http://hul.harvard.edu/jhove/.

[243] *NISO Z39.87-200x Data Dictionary - Technical Metadata for Digital Still Images*, http://www.niso.org/standards/standard_detail.cfm?std_id=731.

[244] *AES metadata standard for digital audio* via http://www.aes.org/publications/standards/.

[245] From Nelson 2005, *Archive Ingest and Handling Test: The Old Dominion University Approach*.

Digital library and archival communities have asked for a durable, global registry of file formats because the current MIME Media Types registry[246] provides neither sufficient granularity of format typing nor sufficient standardized representation information.[247]

The U.K. National Archives is building PRONOM, a repository of information about the file formats, software products, and other technical components for long-term access to digital objects of cultural, historical, or business value. By 2003, its database identified approximately 550 file formats, approximately 250 software products, and approximately 100 vendors.[248] However, a sampling of a few popular file formats suggests that PRONOM entries need much more work before they will be useful to software developers.[249] Another project, Harvard University Libraries' *Global Digital Format Registry* (GDFR), began in late 2005.[250]

For its own storage and services, a format registry is best managed simply as a repository whose content types are constrained, and whose contents are preserved similarly to any other record types.

7.2.2   Text and Office Documents

The Adobe PDF (Portable Document Format) format is intended for sharing text-based documents so that details of their page layouts are seen by recipients exactly as their senders wish. It achieves this so well that no competitors exist for this function. (The total size of the surface Web has been estimated as about 200 terabytes, with about 9% of that occupied by PDF documents.)

A subset called PDF/A has been standardized[251] to enable organizations to save electronic documents ensuring the preservation of their content and visual appearance over an extended period, independently of the tools used for creating and rendering their source files. This standard has been rapidly accepted for its intended purpose. However, since any electronic

---

[246] Internet Assigned Numbers Authority, *Mime Media Types,* http://www.iana.org/assignments/media-types/.

[247] Abrams 2003, Towards a global digital format registry.

[248] Darlington 2003, PRONOM—A Practical Online Compendium of File Formats.
Brown 2005, Automating Preservation ... in the PRONOM Service.

[249] As of 2005, the information for ".xsl" and for ".tif" files was incomplete.

[250] *Global Digital Format Registry,* http://hul.harvard.edu/gdfr/.

[251] ISO 19005, *Document management – Electronic document file format for long-term preservation* at http://www.iso.org/iso/en/commcentre/pressreleases/2005/Ref974.html.
Gilheany 2000, *Permanent Digital Records and the PDF Format,*
http://www.archivebuilders.com/whitepapers/.

document, even one that contains no pictures, is likely to contain more information than is conveyed by its print image, PDF/A is far from a complete document preservation solution.

The most heavily used formats for word processing documents are proprietary and not accompanied by detailed publicly available format specifications. In an effort to ensure that digital office files remain perpetually accessible, OASIS[252] has sponsored development of the OpenDocument file format (ODF) for text, spreadsheets, and presentations,[253] and released a specification. This OASIS Standard[254] may be used by anyone without a fee. The free, open-source OpenOffice application suite[255] conforms to OpenDocument.

7.2.3   Still Pictures: Images and Vector Graphics

Archive Builders provides a good introduction to image formats and image preservation.[256] The Technical Advisory Service for Images provides excellent guidance for image format choice for specific tasks, as well as much more information.[257]

Two-dimensional vector and mixed vector/raster graphics are addressed by the Scalable Vector Graphics (SVG) standard, a modularized XML dialect.[258] For instance, the package used to prepare this book's figures, CorelDraw, has an option to create SVG output.

Manufacturing information, such as product data that might include CAD (computer-aided design) drawings, is subject to similar considerations. STEP, the *Standard for the Exchange of Product Model Data (ISO 10303)* describes how to represent and exchange digital product informa-

---

[252] OASIS is a not-for-profit industry-sponsored consortium promoting standards for Web services, security, and e-business in the public sector and application-specific markets.

[253] Fioretti 2005, *Everybody's Guide to OpenDocument,* http://www.linuxjournal.com/article/8616.

[254] OASIS 2005, *The OpenDocument Format for Office Applications (OpenDocument) v1.0 Specification.* In May 2006, this was approved by the International Standards Organization, with the same name, as ISO/IEC 26300.

[255] *OpenOffice free office suite,* http://www.openoffice.org/, which is described at http://home.iprimus.com.au/ozcolour/open_office.htm.

[256] *Archive Builders White Papers,* http://www.archivebuilders.com/whitepapers/.

[257] Technical Advisory Service for Images, http://www.tasi.ac.uk/.

[258] W3C 2003, *Scalable Vector Graphics.*

tion.[259] Consideration of preservation of CAD and CAM (computer-aided manufacturing) is just beginning, at least in the U.S.[260]

7.2.4 Audio-Visual Recordings

> [Since 1997], the price of raw disk storage has dropped ... from $180 to under 50 cents per gigabyte, and more than 25 million broadband connections have been added in the U.S. alone. It is now possible to store every broadcast, and to offer Internet access to television archives ... all over the world. ... The Library of Congress currently has over 1.1 million moving image items in its collection, and over 314,000 television titles.
>
> Ubois 2005, *New approaches to television archiving*

As of 2004, there was "little or no available technology for enterprise-level archiving of all components of the digital output from a broadcaster. In particular, there [was] little support for archiving interactive content and other ancillary components, which are playing an increasingly important role in the viewer proposition."[261]

Modern multimedia recordings—audio and video recordings—are digital files that can be fixed for preservation. Older recordings in analog formats include perceptible imperfections. Good technology to convert these to digital derivatives is affordable even for hobbyists, and extensive literature teaches us how to deal with imperfections.[262] The digital formats are controlled by standards that are widely used to ensure portability of recorded tapes and disks for presentation with machines from competing vendors. In fact, these standards are so effective that people might come to consider multimedia recordings in certain formats fit for long-term archiving. However, the circumstances under which this might be prudent, instead of using something like the UVC mechanism described in Chapter 12, have not yet been sufficiently considered for this to be accepted without question.

---

[259] *Standard for the Exchange of Product Model Data*, http://www.steptools.com/library/standard/.

A new European initiative is considering such data: *LOTAR - LOng-term Archiving and Retrieval of digital technical product documentation.* http://www.aecma-stan.org/Lotar.html.

[260] This perception is from a NIST (National Institute of Standards and Technology) March 2006 workshop on *Long-term Knowledge Retention: Archival and Representation Standards.*

[261] Chisholm 2004, *Archiving Interactive Digital Television*, describes research into the archiving of as-transmitted interactive content. See http://www.bbc.co.uk/rd/pubs/whp/whp096.shtml.

[262] Calas 1996, *La conservation des documents sonores.*

Pohlmann 2000, *Principles of Digital Audio.*

The IMAP Web site[263] outlines key issues of media arts preservation and provides specific information and access paths to resources for video, audio and digital media preservation. It is targeted at archivists, artists, broadcasters, choreographers, composers, conservators, curators, distributors, filmmakers, librarians, media manufacturers, musicians, producers, registrars, scholars, and other caretakers of media collections.

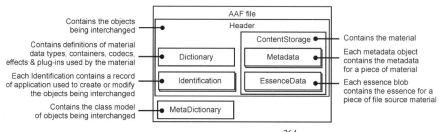

Fig. 19: Objects contained in an AAF file [264] (cf. Fig. 12)

The Advanced Authoring Format (AAF) is an industry-driven, cross-platform, multimedia file format that will allow interchange of compositional information between compliant applications (Fig. 19). These applications are primarily content creation tools. AAF is intended to simplify project management and to preserve metadata that is otherwise often lost when transferring media between applications.

For the sound and video tracks themselves, the new MPEG-A Multimedia Application Format[265] integrates elements from different MPEG standards into a single specification that is useful for a few widely used applications. Examples are delivering music performances, photographs, or home videos. It uses elements from MPEG-1, MPEG-2, MPEG-4, MPEG-7, and MPEG-21.[266] The most recent addition to digital audio standards is MPEG-a ALS, which provides a high-speed *codec* algorithm for lossless compression. Its compression performance is superior to that of ZIP file format in reducing download time, offering operational modes with varying speeds and performances. Implementations typically decode ten times faster than the music playback.

---

[263] *Independent Media Arts Preservation,* http://www.imappreserve.org/. Its *Preservation 101* summarizes processes for video, audio, and film.

[264] Figure 2 of AAF Association 2001, *AAF Object Specification,* http://www.aafassociation.org/html/specs/aafobjectspec-v1.1.pdf.

[265] ISO N6823, *Coding of Moving Pictures and Video,* available via http:// www.chiariglione.org/mpeg/standards/mpeg-a/mpeg-a.htm.

[266] Bekaert 2003, *Using MPEG-21 DIDL to Represent Complex Digital Objects.*

As is true for other modalities, the simplest part of sound preservation involves technology and its application.[267] The complexities and uncertainties have to do with a mix of political,[268] social, legal, and financial issues. The social issues include how preservationists with limited engineering, computing, and other technical training can evaluate competing claims and risks. The legal issues include copyright and the risks that an institution may choose to take about what constitutes fair use and preservation copying. The financial issues include the quality of preservation an institution can afford for each collected item. Happily, for digital audio representations, the last issue is rapidly disappearing as a problem.

For existing audio and video collections that might include movie films, the largest practical problem that money can address is that relatively old holdings have been recorded in analog format. "A running joke among video archivists is that there is no such thing as video preservation, since there is no reliable format which can be trusted to be playable for more than two decades."[269] There is little doubt that uniquely valuable analog recordings should be converted to digital form in the near future to avoid further distortion and noise than they already suffer.[270] The technical parameters for doing so are well understood.[271] The cost of handling each saved tape and disk might be the largest barrier, because the collections are huge.[272] This explains why the Library of Congress has started to use a ro-

---

[267] Edmonson 2004, *Audiovisual Archiving.*

[268] Mann 2002, *Why the cybergurus are wrong about libraries.*

[269] Gracy 2004, *The Preservation of Moving Images,* also comments, "If the lack of standards for video preservation makes conservation-minded information professionals uneasy, the state of digital preservation is likely to incite a full-fledged panic attack. No longer are we merely coping with the chemical instability of the recording media; the obsolescence of the recording formats takes precedent [*sic*] as the new preservation challenge. And in the last twenty years, we have seen a staggering array of digital formats—with more being developed on what seems like a weekly basis."

[270] Teruggi 2004, Can *We Save Our Audio-visual Heritage?*

[271] Seadle 2004, *Sound Preservation*, §II.C.

Media Matters 2004, *Digital Video Preservation Report of the Dance Heritage Coalition,* http://www.danceheritage.org/preservation/Digital_Video_Preservation_Report.doc.

[272] Williams 2002, *Preserving TV and Broadcast Archives,* communicates that the BBC holds about 1.7 million items of film and videotape, about 800,000 radio recordings, four million items of sheet music, three million photographs, and 22.5 million newspaper clippings.

See also Wright 2004, *Digital preservation of audio, video and film.* Wright communicated that the BBC collection occupies about 100 kilometers of shelves. Its video media formats include 2," 1," 3/4" = UMatic, BetaSP, DigiBeta, D3, DVCPRO, DVCAM tapes. Its audio media formats include 78, 33, 45 rpm discs, 1/4" tape, CD, and minidisks in various encoding formats, Moving films occur on 35 and 16 mm tape, some black-and-white and some color, with several kinds of sound tracks (optical, magnetic; on the same carrier as the images or separate) on several kinds of film stock.

botic tape system to help convert its audio-visual collection. This automated migration system will automatically supervise quality control and document the conversion process while gathering metrics about collection health. Its output is a lossless compressed Motion JPEG 2000 copy of each master tape.

7.2.5 Relational Databases

Relational databases present the conceptually simplest preservation challenge. They are close to ideal because a normalized database is free of inessential information.[273] This is because relationships are the most primitive descriptive constructs. In fact, it is this circumstance that led Codd to propose that relations be used to construct databases.[274] This was so successful after initial performance disadvantages were overcome that relational databases eventually superseded the hierarchical and network databases that dominated in the 1970s.

The database object to be saved is a *snapshot*. For information consumers' convenience, this snapshot should include at least part of the administrative tables maintained by the DBMS as a side effect of database administrator commands. These tables, called the *database catalog* by members of the DBMS community, include table and column names, integrity constraint rules, index definitions for query performance enhancement, and access control rules. Information providers might want to preserve only a subset of the tables and columns of a database, and perhaps to limit this to records that were changed only within a prescribed time interval. Such conditions might be complex, especially if the database contains a large number of tables.[275] Preserved database snapshots might be much larger than other kinds of preservation objects, and therefore require more careful planning than might be needed for other blob types.

Just as for any other kind of information, comprehensive interpretation of a relational database will depend on a great deal of contextual information. Future users might be interested in the most important applications of any preserved database, and this might depend on procedures that effectively extend SQL and that are stored within the database. This context is likely to be less obvious than the corresponding context for scholarly articles which provide their own citations and whose representations conform

---

[273] Fagin 1977, *Multivalued dependencies and a new normal form for relational databases.*
See also Ashley 2004, *The preservation of databases.*

[274] Codd 1970, *A Relational Model of Data for Large Shared Data Banks.*

[275] Heuscher 2004, *Providing Authentic Long-term Archival Access to Complex Relational Data,* describes a prototype interactive interface to help manage these choices

to well known formats. Additionally, its preservationist might consider saving the SQL statements used to construct and manage a database, even though these are not essential, because doing so might save future users time and effort to restore the database to service within a DBMS environment. A diligent information provider would think carefully about such information consumers' interests.

7.2.6 Describing Computer Programs

Computer programs usually contain portions which include no redundancy whatsoever, so that errors of translation cannot generally be detected by inspecting the translated version alone (i.e., without the source.) For this reason, the preservation version of a computer program must be expressed with a representation that is perpetually and correctly comprehensible in every detail.

The syntax of any computer program can be completely specified with *BNF*. However, for its eventual consumer, a textual description is something that every responsible preservationist would include. BNF is widely understood and widely used, and is therefore likely to be useful in describing for preservation any programming language and therefore any program.

The semantics of any computer program can be precisely specified in one of several ways: denotational, algebraic, and operational. Unfortunately, these languages are so seldom used for practical programs that their role in preservation is likely to be small.

7.2.7 Multimedia Objects

Usually a single work will be represented by a set of several files of diverse types. A medical history or a real-estate contract might require both text and image bit-strings, and all preserved objects will require metadata that includes provenance information. This need is so common that it has recently been addressed by a packaging standard.

The MPEG-21 ISO standard[276] is intended "to define a normative open framework for multimedia delivery and consumption for use by all the players in the delivery and consumption chain." Although it comes from entertainment industry enterprises, the MPEG-21 framework is a packaging protocol for any kind of complex digital information, including scholarly texts, periodicals, scientific data, engineering and product records, and

---

[276] A Cover page tracks progress toward completing the *MPEG-21 Standard* definition. See http://xml.coverpages.org/ni2002-08-26-b.html.

so on. The Standard is described in 12 parts, which include some that are particularly important in the preservation context, viz.:

- Part 2 – Digital Item Declaration Language (DIDL), detailing the representation of complex digital objects,
- Part 3 – Digital Item Identification Language, detailing the identification of complex digital objects and their contained entities,
- Part 4 – Intellectual Property Management and Protection, detailing a framework to enforce rights expressions,
- Part 5 – Rights Expression Language (henceforth referred to as REL), detailing a language to express rights pertaining to complex digital objects and their contained entities,
- Part 10 – Digital Item Processing detailing the association of processing methods with complex digital objects and their contained entities.

Bekaert provides a ready exposition of the XML syntax that comprises much of MPEG-21.[266]

7.3   Perpetually Unique Resource Identifiers

A *Universal Unique Identifier (UUID)* is a bit-string intended to be a perpetually unique name for some resource or, more generally, anything that might exist in any sense suggested by Fig. 4. Specifically, a UUID is chosen in some way to make very improbable an identifier *collision*—an accidental equality with an independently chosen bit-string that might be used as a resource name.

Often people insist on zero collision probability. However execution of a conforming service can become expensive and error prone. If the condition is relaxed to "very improbable," an inexpensive, reliable choice of conforming identifiers is possible. Moreover, it is possible to design this so that the collision probability is smaller than any number someone might choose, for example, to less than 10^{-10} that one or more collisions will occur in a pool of 10^{10} identifiers.

Identifiers have a long and subtle background. Their topical literature is extensive.[277] Their essential simplicity is sometimes confounded with technical detail for specific application domains—aspects that are not universally necessary and of little interest for long-term asset preservation.

In addition to its main purpose—helping readers separate core ideas from technical details, the current section has three purposes: (1) commu-

---

[277] Vittiello 2004, *Identifiers and Identification Systems;* Dack 2001, *Persistent Identification Systems,* http://www.nla.gov.au/initiatives/persistence/PIcontents.html; and W3C, *Naming and Addressing: URIs, URLs, ...,* http://www.w3.org/Addressing/.

nicating what is essential for an identifier to be perpetually useful; (2) describing a scheme that will permit any document producer to refer unambiguously to any set of resources whatsoever; and (3) reminding readers of identifier resolution optimizations that might become worthwhile as Internet exploitation expands.

Some of the abstractions are illustrated below with two identifier systems: DRIs and "info" URIs. A new OASIS proposal, the EXtensible Resource Identifier (XRI), seems to be a comprehensive packaging scheme for all other identifiers, but also seems more elaborate than needed.[278]

A UUID security extension is taken up in §11.1.3, after sufficient groundwork has been laid.

7.3.1 Equality of Digital Documents

Digital content management needs the concept of *same document*. Users must be able to determine what works have been archived, distinguishing these from similar documents, and identifying them in distributed repositories which might preserve those particular works. A preservation scheme should help answer, to the extent that doing so is feasible, whether a particular file presented for preservation has already been preserved.

Deciding whether two files purporting to represent the same document in fact do so is surprisingly difficult. (In fact, the challenge is not limited to information objects; consider, human identities as discussed in §5.3.4.) There has been little research on formal identity conditions—logical rules consisting of predicates on the representing bit-strings—for a pair of digital objects which might be intended to represent the same work. As a result, progress on a number of important problems—including preservation, conversion, integrity assurance, retrieval, federation, and metadata comparisons—has been hindered.

In the absence of a theory of document identity, preservation strategies typically fall back on treating the bit-stream as a surrogate for the document. Problems with this approach are well known. The subsequent recovery and presentation of the document from an archived bit-stream is problematic and there is no theoretically sound way to tell what document has been preserved or whether two saved bit-strings preserve the same document, except if their representations are identical. In the case of migration-based preservation strategies, which require multiple conversions over the years, these problems are permanent features of the preservation environment. This situation is at least in part a consequence of not having an adequate conceptualization of what a document is.

---

[278] OAIS 2005, *XRI 2.0 FAQ*, http://www.oasis-open.org/committees/tc_home.php?wg_abbrev=xri.

Syntactic schemes called *canonicalization*[279]—adjustments of accidental representational features, such as the number of blank characters between parameters in XML documents, to conform to some rule—prove to be impractical because the possible equivalent representations (§4.1) are difficult to predict. Exploration of document semantics has just begun,[280] but is not promising because determining that two autonomously developed ontologies have the same meanings is difficult. The root of the difficulty is the impossibility of reliably knowing what someone else means by the words he chooses. Furthermore, what someone means by "the same as" is subjective and might be different for different speakers, and even for single speaker at different times. (§4.2)

At least for the time being, the only sure basis for communicating the essential identity for any Fig. 12 DO is to bind its own identifier, using the same unique identifier for all objects whose originators assert are versions of each other.[281] Perhaps this is why we find serial numbers on almost every kind of valuable artifact.

7.3.2   Requirements for UUIDs

The seminal note specifying how identifiers should work asserts, "The same URN will never be assigned to two different resources." [282]   Although this anticipates every kind of resource, digital services based on it seem to assume that if two blobs are associated with the same identifier, then these two blobs must be identical. This assumption is appropriate if the referent is a program that manages real-time battlefield intelligence and has versions that work differently. On the other hand, it is conventional to refer to different printings of a book using the same ISBN, even if later versions correct errors and add material to their predecessors.

A common unannounced assumption is that each resource is entirely in one place. However, a resource might consist of distributed pieces, as with the British fleet or the *Encyclopedia Britannica*. We often use a singular substantive such as 'fleet' to refer to sets with moving, changing, distributed parts. Even the set membership might change over time, such as when ships of the fleet are built or scrapped.

---

[279] Lynch 1999, *Canonicalization ... to facilitate preservation ... of digital information.*

[280] Renear 2003, *Toward Identity Conditions for Digital Documents,* http://www.siderean.com/dc2003/503_Paper71.pdf.

[281] Less rigorous methods are problematic. For example, see Lagoze 2006, *Metadata aggregation and "automated digital libraries,"* §7.2.

[282] Sollins 1994, *Functional Requirements for Uniform Resource Names,* http://www.ietf.org/rfc/rfc1737.txt.

Even experts are confused about the distinction between 'URN' (Uniform Resource Name) and 'URI' (Uniform Resource Identifier). A contemporary prescription[283] identifies the class URI as permitting namespaces and as including both URNs and URLs. In other words, "urn:" is also a URI scheme; it defines nonintersecting subspaces, called "namespaces." For instance, the set of URNs of the form "urn:isbn:x-xx-xxxxxx-x" is a URN namespace. "http:" is a URI scheme that identifies a resource by an access path, rather than by some other attributes it may have.

Table 9: Reference String Examples

3	Within the current TDO, the third content block
2#175	Within the current TDO, the 175th byte of the second content block
3#435#4500	In the third content block of the current TDO, the block from byte 435 through byte 4550
DRI:abc123	The resource set whose name is abc123
DOI:10.1000.10/123456789	A Digital Object Identifier [284]
ISBN 1-861003-11-0#23-45	Pages 23 to 45 in the physical book denoted by the ISBN number shown
US_SSN:456-8765-123	U.S. Social Security Number denoting a particular human being
TEL:1(408)867-5454	An international telephone number
urn:oid:1.3.6.1.2.1.27	URN (Uniform Resource Name) registered at 'OID'
http://www.google.com/	URL (Uniform Resource Locator)
book:Dante's "Paradiso"	Title of a literary work
urn:path:/A/B/C/doc.html	

Table 9 illustrates naming schemes using different formats. Many divide the name into two parts, a naming authority set off by punctuation such as a slash or a colon, followed by a string unique within the context defined by the naming authority. For instance, the handle "cnri.dlib/august95" consists of a naming authority, "cnri.dlib" followed by a unique string, "august95." The URN "/A/B/doc.html" consists of a naming authority "path," a path "/A/B", and a string, "doc.html", which should identify a unique file.

It is common to signal which identifier scheme is in use with an identifier prefix. This is sometimes not done for material objects with firmly at-

---

[283]   W3C 2001. *URIs, URLs, and URNs,* http://www.w3.org/TR/uri-clarification.

[284]   Paskin 2003, *The DOI Handbook,* http://www.doi.org/hb.html.

tached identifiers, because the type of object and/or the identifier context is obvious to human users. For instance, the string "0123 4567 8901 2345" embossed at a certain place on a 53 mm × 85 mm plastic card with a magnetic stripe on its back would almost certainly be a credit card number.

We assert the following requirements for perpetually useful and universally unique identifiers.

- The identifier syntax must subsume every kind of reference that might occur within the documents that use it, including WWW locators and conventional bibliographic citations.
- The identifier syntax must provide for every known legacy identification scheme, avoiding collisions, possibly by adding a prefix that disambiguates identifiers belonging to independently administered schemes.
- Whoever defines an identifier should be able to avoid collision with any previous identifier.
- Whoever defines an identifier should find it easy to register its mapping to the resource it identifies.
- Developers of identifier assignment and resolution services should easily be able to optimize for increasing numbers of objects and to provide access to autonomous network communities.
- For reliability, copies of each information object might be stored in several autonomous repositories. Resolution protocols must support returning multiple answers to a request for the location of a copy.
- If a bibliographic citation unique, it can be used as an identifier. For instance, the string "Russell, Bertrand, 1905. *On Denoting,* Mind 14, 479-493" is an unambiguous identifier. And in 2005, the string "http://cscs.umich.edu/~crshalizi/Russell/denoting/" was a good locator for a copy of this classic essay.

7.3.3   Identifier Syntax and Resolution

Identifier patterns are defined by the regular expression:

identifier   ::= **family* resource segment?**   **Rule 0**

This suggests a hierarchy of resolution contexts (family*), the name of a resource in context (resource), and optionally something within the resource (segment?). A context is both a language (such as the set of all possible URLs) and infrastructure services to provide access to its named resources. A resource name identifies a set of objects within the innermost context. A segment identifier provides granularity—either a place within the resource or some portion of the resource.

A more detailed description is as follows:

identifier   ::= **(domain separator?)* main suffix**   **Rule 1**

domain	::= alpha alphanumeric*	**Rule 2**
separator	::= "://" | ":" | "/" | " "*	**Rule 3**
main	::= bit-string	**Rule 4**
suffix	:= {see below}	**Rule 5**
bit-string	::= byte+ | alphanumeric+	**Rule 6**
alpha	::= [a-z A-Z]	**Rule 7**
alphanumeric	::= [a-z A-Z 0-9]	**Rule 8**
byte	::= [#x0000-#xFFFF]	**Rule 9**

A domain identifies a context for the remainder of the identifier, and is interpreted by resolution services as a hint for directories mapping the identifier to the resources it denotes.[285] Whether or not this will work in some particular computing environment depends on implementations: whoever created the identifier must have caused a record relating it to the location of the identified resource to have been stored in some widely accessible resolution server; and the identifier invocation environment must find that resolution server.

The main part of an identifier is often chosen to be a mnemonic, but it can be a randomly chosen alphanumeric string of sufficient length for at most a tiny probability of collision with any independently chosen identifier.[286] The latter approach avoids implying any semantics for the designated object. Its individual identifiers can be chosen without network message overhead or the nuisance of maintaining an address-choosing network service. (A random string of 20 ASCII characters chosen from the lower case Roman alphabet and numerals has probability less than 10^{-23} of colliding with any of a billion similarly chosen identifiers, and no chance of colliding with any shorter or longer identifier. It also satisfies the limitations suggested by the next paragraphs.)

The suffix part of an identifier provides for referencing either a location, such as a bookmark, or a contiguous extent, such as a paragraph, within the document referenced. Both the syntax and the semantics of this optional indicator—its separator character and its locator—might be a function of the data type of the object from which it selects a location or a portion.

Rules 1 through 9 are idealized to emphasize the generic syntactic pattern, but are sufficient for teaching students how identifier schemes are put

---

[285] Sollins 1998, *Architectural Principles of Uniform Resource Name Resolution,* http://www.ietf.org/rfc/rfc2276.txt.

[286] Rivest 1996, *A Simple Distributed Security Infrastructure (SDSI),* http://theory.lcs.mit.edu/ ~cis/sdsi.html, teaches that the public keys of asymmetric key encryption could be used as identifiers.

to work. They omit details forced by limitations of the practical world and to reduce errors that human users might make.[287]

- Identifiers that are to be printed or typed should be limited to byte patterns that correspond to printable glyphs. Identifiers that are to be used only in hidden system applications can safely be any bit-strings, except that it is usually prudent to limit their lengths to multiples of 8.
- Identifiers that are to be printed or typed anywhere in the world are best limited to the printable portion of the ASCII character set. For identifiers to be typed by human beings, it is best to avoid case sensitivity (the difference between "a" and "A").
- Some applications require that an alphanumeric identifier begin with an alphabetic character. In contrast, a credit card number has only numeric characters, and in its usual context is printed without separators.
- Characters permitted in an identifier portion might include more than alphanumerics, except that this should be limited to prevent ambiguity with punctuation, such as the ":" in the separator above.[288]

For a name to be useful, there must be a mapping service to lead to the named resource—a *resolver,* and also a way of finding that mapping service—a *Resolver Discovery Service* (RDS). The latter must be by way of locally stored hints, such as the URN of a resolver service that may further resolve the URN, the address of such a service, or a location at which the resource was previously found.[289]

Such hints are merely hints; they may be out of date, temporarily invalid, or only applicable within a specific locality. They cannot guarantee access. Some combination of software and human choice is needed to choose which hints will be tried and in what order. However, an RDS is expected to work with reasonably high reliability, and therefore may result in increased response time. A possibility that has not yet been investigated is to use widely accessible search services, such as Google, to provide the RDS functionality. Having found a resolver, the application at hand must invoke it to find the resource wanted (Fig. 20).

Notwithstanding a call for persistent name resolvers,[290] this would be convenient, but not strictly necessary, as their data can be reconstructed

---

[287] These details are part of what can make a normative syntax specification difficult to read, as in OAIS 2005, *Extensible Resource Identifier (XRI) Syntax,* V2.0, draft.

[288] Berners-Lee 1998, *Uniform Resource Identifiers,* §2.3 describes these limitations. See http://ftp.ics.uci.edu/pub/ietf/uri/rfc2396.txt.

[289] An implementation is sketched in Van de Sompel 2005, *aDORe: a Modular, Standards-based Digital Object Repository,* §2.2 and §4.

[290] W2005, §2.1.

from repository catalogs. Doing so would be facilitated if each object package included the object's identifiers.

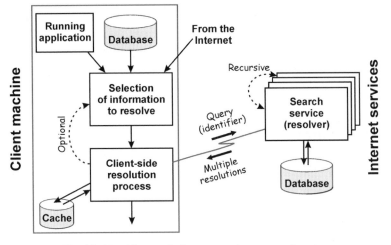

Fig. 20: Identifier resolution, suggesting a recursive step

7.3.4 A Digital Resource Identifier

In addition to internal links, almost every TDO will need external references to standards specifications and schema objects. It might also need references to authenticity evidence, such as authority descriptions of its human editors. A reference can have two parts: a prefix and a suffix (Rule 1 in §7.3.3). The *prefix part* would be a resource identifier. The *suffix part* would indicate either a place in that resource (as an offset from the start point) or an extent in that resource (such as the bit-string portion between a beginning and an ending offset). The external resources identified can be static or dynamic, and can be either digital, such as e-mail addresses, or physical, such as land parcels. For resources that are likely to have long-lived versions, it is helpful to have an identifier for distinguishing the set of all versions of a work from the version at hand.

Each TDO has at least two embedded self-identifiers—its own URN and the *Digital Resource Identifier* (DRI) for a set to which the object is more intimately related than to other objects, typically to the set of all its versions. A TDO can embed any number of self-identifiers. Several DRIs might be used to identify several classes to which it belongs. DRIs have the prefix, 'DRI:', which is different from the prefixes used for other URI classes and long enough to be a search engine eye-catcher. The producer of a new TDO may choose whether it is to have new identifiers or reuse existing ones to signal that the object is a version of some other object.

7.3.5 The "Info" URI

Formal URI syntax and resolution rules have not until recently provided for legacy identifier schemes with namespace authorities—agencies that issued identifiers for physical resources such as automobiles and legal resources such as passports. A scheme is needed whereby such resources can be uniquely referenced within digital records. This scheme must avoid calling for any change to how legacy namespace authorities conduct business or how legacy resources are labeled or refer to outside objects.

As is often done in computer science, this is accomplished by adding a level of indirection to a previous scheme—URI syntax. This solution has recently been formalized[291] with the following syntax:

info-URI	= "info:" info-identifier ["#" fragment]
info-identifier	= namespace "/" loc-identifier
namespace	= ALPHA *(ALPHA | DIGIT | "+" | "-" | ".")
loc-identifier	= *(pchar | "/")
pchar	= unreserved | pct-encoded | sub-delims | ":" | "@"
fragment	= *(pchar | "/" | "?")
unreserved	= ALPHA | DIGIT | "-" | "." | "_" | "~"
pct-encoded	= "%" HEXDIG HEXDIG
sub-delims	= "!" | "$" | "&" | "'" | "(" | ")" | "*" | "+" | "," | ";" | "="

The main things to notice are that a prefix, "info:", has been registered as belonging to a new URI class and that the next substring, namespace, identifies a preexisting naming authority. For instance, this is chosen to be "lccn" for Library of Congress Control Numbers, a choice registered with a new "info" naming authority.

The rest of the BNF definition allows almost any sequences to be used for loc-identifier, a name chosen by the pre-existing naming authority, and for the optional suffix—the "#" fragment. The only exceptions seem to be inclusions of a few reserved punctuation characters, such as "#" and "%".

7.4   Summary

A few relatively simple standards—specifications for character coding, for file formats, and for a small portion of XML—are a sufficient starting point for durable long-term encoding. Other standards specifications can be written with these.

A few relatively complex standards (such as parts of MPEG) are so heavily used that conforming blobs might be considered preservation-

---

[291] Van de Sompel 2005, *The "info" URI Scheme for Information Assets with Identifiers in Public Namespaces*, http://www.ietf.org/internet-drafts/draft-vandesompel-info-uri-04.txt.

ready. This possibility has, however, not yet been sufficiently considered for a firm recommendation.

Binding metadata firmly to the content it describes can convert a document of uncertain historical significance into an evidentiary document, and is an efficient way to transmit content safely. Retrieving a specific holding from a repository will be possible only if the information consumer has previously received its unique identifier from some machine or human agent, perhaps within a digital document, or as part of a query response into that repository's catalog.

The digital library community has long grappled with ensuring that identifiers and referents are correctly associated. This problem is artificial; its solution is natural: embed in each object a copy of its own identifier. Stout rivets ensure that a vehicle identification number stays firmly connected to the correct automobile; imprinting on the copyright page of a book ensures that no ISBN comes adrift without this being manifest to anyone who cares to check. The lesson is plain.

8 Archiving Practices

Digital preservation can be accomplished with no more than small extensions over information interchange and digital library (DL) technologies that are already widely deployed. Most of the software technology needed is already available, or soon will be, and is being standardized. This includes cryptographic tools for sealing information against surreptitious change, encoding rules for multimedia (e.g., MPEG[292]) and for scientific data, XML syntax for packaging digital objects, and semantic models encoded as sets of triplets.

This is not to say that repository software is fully satisfactory; it is not. However, the most pressing repository extensions have to do with day-to-day service rather than with overcoming the effects of technology obsolescence and media degradation. Specifically, today's repository metadata implementations are far from ideal.[293]

The professional literature about repositories falls into categories that do not contain as many cross-references as might be desirable. Archivists' articles tend to focus on management and control issues that often ignore the nature of the subject materials and their audiences.[294] Librarians' articles pay much more attention to the topical value of materials and the interests of specified reader communities.[295] Business and other communities express other interests, and software engineers do not say much about what information is served, as long as the service is quick, trouble-free, and easy to use.[296]

8.1 Security

Digital security technology is a highly developed field.[297] For digital preservation, no new security technology is needed. Only a few of the many

---

[292] Hunter 1999, *MPEG-7 Behind the Scenes.*

[293] Gill 2002, *Re-inventing the Wheel? Standards, Interoperability and Digital Cultural Content.*

[294] For instance, Millar 1999. *The Spirit of Total Archives.*
Koltun 1999, *The Promise and Threat of Digital Options in an Archival Age.*

[295] Greenstein 2002, *Next Generation Digital Libraries*, http://www.vala.org.au/vala2002/2002pdf/01Grnstn.pdf.
Lougee 2002, *Diffuse Libraries*, http://www.clir.org/pubs/reports/pub108/contents.html.

[296] Fox 2002, *Digital Libraries.*

[297] Dam 1996, *Cyptography's Role in Securing the Information Society.*
Menezes 1997, *Handbook of Applied Cryptography.*
Naor 2004, *Theory of Cryptography.*
Schneier 1996, *Applied Cryptography.*

available digital security tools[298] will be used. In contrast, repository content protection against improper change sometimes merits rigorous application of the latest and strongest security measures, and regular human vigilance to detect and mitigate unauthorized activities.[299]

Access to personal information must be easily controllable by the owner. Privacy concerns suggest that, by default, others should not have access to the content. However, those of us with public Web sites need to be able to map information in personal repositories onto a variety of increasingly public sites without having to maintain an array of separate sites.

Cryptography has a long and exciting history.[300] Authoritative books teach the essentials of methods to secure digital works.[301] Additional books provide detailed descriptions of software whose need is implied below.[302] Because of continued and increasing mischief on the Internet, a vigorous cryptographic community is refining methods and inventing new tools.[303] Furthermore, the IEEE has defined new standards for encrypting data on tapes and disks[304]—standards for which industry observers expect complying products soon.

8.1.1 PKCS Specification

One mark of a mature technology is that, with little change, it can be applied to different problems and operate in different environments. The Public-Key Cryptography Standards (PKCSs) are a suite of well-documented specifications used by many offerings. They are frequently referenced, reused, and refined in public specifications addressing certificate-based security systems. They fit the definition of maturity.

---

[298] Atkins 1996, *Internet Security Professional Reference*.
Schäfer 2003, *Security in Fixed and Wireless Networks*.
Vacca 1996, *Internet Security Secrets*.

[299] Anderson 2001, *Security Engineering*.

[300] Bauer 2002. *Decrypted secrets: methods and maxims of cryptology*.
Kahn 1967, *The Codebreakers*.
Singh 1999, *The Code Book*.

[301] Menezes 1997, *Handbook of Applied Cryptography*, §1.5.

[302] Eastlake 2002, *Secure XML*.
Fegghi 1998, *Digital Certificates*.
Knudsen 1998, *Java Cryptography*.

[303] W3C 2002, *XML-Signature Syntax and Processing*, http://www.w3.org/TR/xmldsig-core/.

[304] IEEE P1619, *Security for Storage Data at Rest*, http://www.t10.org/ftp/t10/document.04/04-146r0.pdf.

PKCS standardizes algorithm details. The elements of the series translate raw mathematics into interoperable implementation schemes. Using X.509 notation, they formally declare algorithms, associated data formats, processing conventions, and identifiers. The series also specifies algorithm-independent security mechanisms, interchange syntaxes, and programming techniques for interfacing computers to crypto peripherals.

PKCSs are written in a highly structured form with a minimal ASN.1 notation. Their message syntax descriptions are accompanied by annotations stated in highly technical English, which describe the procedures that applications are expected to use to handle the specified data objects, and which often define the intended semantics.

8.1.2 Audit Trail, Business Controls, and Evidence

The principal security objective for digital preservation technology is to make evidence available to any consumer who might be put at risk by improperly changed information. Ideally, such evidence would consist of an incontrovertible fact set that, taken as a whole, demonstrates that each digital object is what it purports to be. Such evidence will consist of an audit trail describing who did what to the object at hand for a sufficient number of significant events in the object's history.

In this requirement, 'audit trail' means almost the same thing to members of different professions, including lawyers, forensic accountants, archivists, and software engineers. The concerned professions consider it axiomatic that audit trail design should be considered from the very first deliberations leading to a new processing system (manual, semiautomatic, or automatic), and that such consideration needs to include estimates of the likelihood of risks (accidental failures or deliberate misbehaviors) to the dependents on such systems.[305]

A financial control principle—that every likely opportunity for misbehavior should be structured to involve at least two participants unlikely to collude in fraud—can be adapted for creation of provenance evidence. This motivates the handover of a sealed record by its custodian to another custodian who also seals it.

8.1.3 Authentication with Cryptographic Certificates

After a digital object has been ingested into the repository network, we want reliable evidence that it was not later modified even slightly, because in some cases even a single changed bit can radically alter the meaning of

---

[305] Bearman 1998, *Authenticity of Digital Resources: Towarda Statement of Requirements.*

text or the behavior of a program. Digital certification based on hashing and public key encryption is the right technology to create evidence.[306]

This approach would be similar to what has been used earlier to bind a user's name securely to his public key for user authentication.[307] The application receiving such a certificate could answer the question, "who wants to access the service?" (*authentication*), but could not answer the supplementary question, "what (level of) service is this user allowed to access?" (*authorization* or *access control*) without recourse to additional, usually internal, access control information. *ISO/ITU–T X.509 v.3* certificates[308] include information for these questions.

A *message-digest algorithm* takes a arbitrary length message as input and produces a fixed-length digest as output. The fixed-length output is called the *message digest*, a *digest*, or a *hash*. A message-digest algorithm is also referred to as a *one-way hash algorithm*, or simply a *hash algorithm*.

The mapping from a message to its digest is chosen to be a *one-way function*—a function for which it is believed an inverse cannot be found. To be cryptographically secure, the mapping must have three properties. First, it must be infeasible to determine the input message based on its digest. Second, it must not be possible to find an arbitrary message that has any particular digest. Third, it should be computationally infeasible to find two messages that have the same digest. Other properties of well-designed message algorithms are that the mapping from a message to a digest appears to be random, and that changing even one bit of the message results in a new, uncorrelated digest.

A *message authentication code* (MAC), sometimes called a *message integrity code* (MIC), is a fixed-length data item that is sent together with a message as evidence of the message origination and integrity. A MAC is basically an encrypted message digest. The encryption can be effected either with a *symmetric-key algorithm* (or *secret-key algorithm*) or with *public-key cryptography* (or *asymmetric-key cryptography*).[309] Only the latter interests us because publication is for unknown readers for whom confidentiality is not an objective.

---

[306] Gerck 2000, *Overview of Certification Systems*, http://nma.com/papers/certover.pdf.

[307] Lampson 1992, *Authentication in Distributed Systems*.

[308] ISO Network Working Group 1999, *Internet X.509 Public Key Infrastructure Certificate and CRL Profile*, http://www.ipa.go.jp/security/rfc/RFC2459EN.html.

[309] Ibid. §1.8.

Originator   Recipient

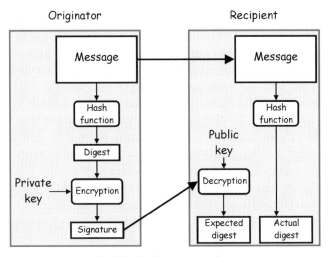

Fig. 21: MAC creation and use

These ideas have been combined to provide a method for document authentication. Suppose that Alice calculates the digest of her message and uses her private key to encrypt (sign) it, as suggested in Fig. 21. She transmits her message and its signed digest to Bob. Bob decrypts the signature using Alice's public key, computes the digest of the message, and compares the two values. The message surely comes from Alice if they are equal. Mary, who wants to impersonate Alice, cannot generate the same signature because she does not have Alice's private key. If she decides to tamper with the message while it is in transit, the tampered message will hash to a different value than the original one, and Bob will be able to detect that. Alice will find it difficult to repudiate the fact that she sent the message because the digest of the message is signed by her private key. However, Alice can argue that her private key has been compromised and used by someone else to sign the message.

If the fixed-length output of a message digest has m bits, one must inspect approximately 2^m messages to find a message with a desired digest, and inspecting $2^{m/2}$ messages to find two messages that have the same digest. Among popular digest algorithms, MD5 (Message Digest 5) creates a 128-bit output. Some people feel that this is too short in view of immense and improving computer power.[310] The U.S. government's SHA-1 (Secure Hash Algorithm 1) creates a 160-bit digest, making it preferable.

The key used for encryption (called the *private key* or *signing key*) is different from, but functionally related to, the key used for decryption

---

[310] Gauravaram 2006, *The legal and practical implications of recent attacks on 128–bit cryptographic hash functions.*

(called the *public key* or *verification key*). These two keys are chosen together, in a way to make it computationally infeasible to guess the second key—the verification key—from the value of the first key—the signing key. A message encrypted with the first key can be decrypted with the second key, but with no other candidate key, not even the first key. This enables the recipient of a message encrypted with the privatet key to verify that it was indeed sent by the purported author, provided that this author has kept this private key secret and has made the public key value available. Because it is not feasible to forge a party's signature without the possession of its signing key, the signer of a message cannot later repudiate the fact that he has signed the message. A new method for choosing easily remembered asymmetric encryption keys seems promising.[311]

The above description of electronic signing is somewhat oversimplified in that it insufficiently protects signatures that will be used over long periods. Detail for syntax in which extra layers provide extra protection, associated processing routines, and careful jargon definitions for signing and certificates is provided by IETF RFC 3126 and other normative documents on which it depends.[312] It describes procedures for packaging a time stamp certified by an autonomous authority as part of a signature, together with ancillary certification information to help the recipient test signature validity. A signer can choose to use a Fig. 22 Electronic Signature, or a Time-stamped Electronic Signature, or the entire Fig. 22 information, depending on the value of and risk to what is being certified. As usual, the choice needs to be an information provider's tradeoff between cost and value.

Timestamped Electronic Signature

Electronic Signature

Fig. 22: Cryptographic signature blocks

311   HP 2003, *Identifier-Based Encryption*, http://www.hpl.hp.com/research/ssrc/security/id/ibe/tutorial/briefs/IBE_tutorial.pdf.

312   Integris 2001, *Electronic signature formats for long-term electronic signatures*, http://www.ietf.org/rfc/rfc3126.txt.
     Buchman 2006, *Perspectives for Cryptographic Long-Term Security*.
     Apvrille 2002, *XML Security Time Stamping Protocol*, http://citeseer.ist.psu.edu/apvrille02xml.html.

8.1.4 Trust Structures and Key Management

To enable §8.1.3 certificates, it is necessary to distribute and preserve public keys in a way that securely associates each key pair with the human or institutional entity that signed the authenticity certificate. This requires that each such key be certified as belonging to the purported entity, creating a recursive relationship that must be grounded in widely known and widely accessible information about a small number of institutions that are trusted to be honest agents for the authentication of less trusted institutions' identity-to-public-key relationship. A data and processing discipline and network implementation that provides this service is called a *Public Key Infrastructure* (PKI).

The idea is to share each individual fact and test among many objects, and to end each recursion with facts that are widely known and *trusted*. Suppose that the *New York Times* (*NYT*) annually changed the public/private key pair with which it signed its digital news, that the Library of Congress published the full set of the *NYT* public keys, and that many people frequently used these keys to test *NYT* articles. Then any key in the published set would be widely known and trusted in the sense intended here.

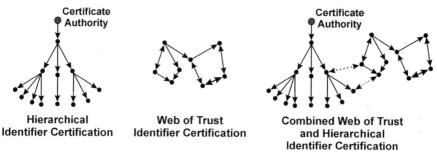

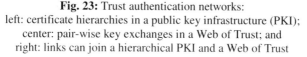

Fig. 23: Trust authentication networks:
left: certificate hierarchies in a public key infrastructure (PKI);
center: pair-wise key exchanges in a Web of Trust; and
right: links can join a hierarchical PKI and a Web of Trust

The best known PKI depends on commercial *certificate authorities* (CAs) as the roots for certificate hierarchies. Each such certificate asserts the relationship of some computer user (usually a human being) or group (often an enterprise) to a particular public key, as suggested by the graph on the left in Fig. 23. Flaws have been identified in this scheme.[313] One is that a CA might not check sufficiently thoroughly to eliminate imposter

313 Gerck 2000, *Overview of Certification Systems.*
     Ellison 2000, *Naming and certificates*

certificate applicants, because the CA's fees are too low to finance thorough checking. Since impersonation may be the most important threat to content authenticity certification, we should not accept this kind of risk.

Consumer unfamiliarity with the use of digital certificates for electronic authentication and transactions has further exacerbated the problem. Many certificate users have little technical or legal understanding of how digital certificates work and what the associated risks are. This creates an incentive for opportunistic behavior by some CAs to underinvest in technology and operational procedures, possibly compromising the certificates' quality. More generally, despite years of intensive effort within the computer science and legal communities, establishing trust service interoperation remains a key e-commerce challenge.[314] Early reviewers hoped that PKIs would provide the basis for establishing trust in secure electronic transactions. Such early aspirations now seem too optimistic.[315] The use of PKIs has in fact been limited.

Signatures need to be certified for long periods.[316] While the longevity of the document itself depends only on the preservation of its readability, multiple factors impact the reliably useful longevity of digital signatures, making them likely to have relatively short lifespans. The keys used are at risk from determined attacks by cryptanalysts. Common CA practice limits endorsement to one or two years for certificates based on a 1024-bit RSA key pair. Signing keys may be otherwise compromised, or the algorithms used for signature creation may be broken, rendering the signature of a document vulnerable to modification attacks. Other risks are that information needed for the verification of a digital signature, such as digital certificate chains and the certificate revocation status, may become unavailable, and that the CA that binds each public key to a specific identity may cease existence. Although breaking a 1024-bit key cannot currently be accomplished in a two year period, the evolution of technology is unpredictable. Also long-lived keys are more probable to be lost or stolen.

The participants in many commercial transactions are not acquainted before their transactions. However, the situation is more favorable in an information producer chain. Since its participants are usually personally acquainted, sometimes by way of face-to-face meetings, we can expect "web

---

[314] Burmester 2004, *Is Hierarchical Public-Key Certification the Next Target for Hackers?*

[315] Ellison 2000, *Risks of PKI.*

[316] Birrell 1986, *A Global Authentication System without Global Trust.*
Integris 2001, *Long-term electronic signatures.*
Lekkas 2004, *Cumulative notarization for long-term preservation of digital signatures.*

of trust" methods[317] to work well in creating record authenticity and provenance evidence (Fig. 23). Each step of preparing a scholarly document ends in the current producer collaborating with the producer who will execute the next step, as in a bucket brigade. We exploit this by requiring each such collaborating pair to exchange public keys personally. For any later communication in which impersonation would jeopardize the safety of the transaction, the partner at risk can reliably test incoming messages signed by the other partner. Specifically, for TDO safety, a producer should certify as correct only the content that he is confident was asserted reliable by the producer that the incoming TDO identifies, or that he has himself generated.

8.1.5 Time Stamp Evidence

For some evidentiary documents, to lie about the date of signing can be advantageous to originators.

An originator can provide a reliable earliest possible date by quoting from a readily accessible periodical, for example with the table of contents of a recent *Harvard Law Review* number. If the document for which date evidence is wanted happens to be cited by a work from some indubitably independent author, this would provide a credible latest possible date. However, to depend on this would not be certain enough for authors of document types not commonly cited. Even if such a document were cited, its eventual users would probably not know of or find the citation.

Thus, the challenge is to define a method whereby a document originator can generate evidence that eventual readers would accept as proving that the document was written before some specified date. In the world of paper, this is routinely accomplished by having the document signed and notarized, preferably with disinterested witnesses who could vouch for its authenticity. This challenge is created by networks of pervasive, clever deceit that might include bogus notarization.[318]

Such notarization has been adapted for digital documents by proposing Internet time stamping services that would act as uninterested witnesses.[319] However, a decade after the proposal, such agencies do not seem to exist. Perhaps the Trustworthy Institutions discussed in §11.2.1 might serve, but doing so would be a different and more intensive task than what §8.1.4

---

[317] Caronni 2000, *Walking the Web of Trust.*

[318] Just 1998, *Some Time stamp Protocol Failures.*

[319] Bayer 1993, *Improving the Efficiency and Reliability of Digital Time Stamping.*
Cipra 1993, *Electronic Time Stamping.*

calls for. Moreover, notarization has not been justified as reliable for periods significantly longer than the availability of the notary and witnesses.

Two other possibilities should be considered. The originator of a sensitive document might embed in his document an announcement that he will publish its name, identifier, and message authentication code to appear on a certain date in a well known newspaper, such as the *Financial Times*, and accomplish this by paying for a classified advertisement constructed immediately after sealing the document. Secondly, a repository service might collect the same information for every record accessioned in an announced period (e.g., the latest quarter year) to construct and seal a document containing these records. Such a corporate document would be accepted as timestamp evidence by any reader who trusted the repository to be an honest broker for this service.

8.1.6   Access Control and Digital Rights Management

Access control is functionality that limits the kinds of use permitted to each individual client of repository (or other) resources. Each level of a §9.1 storage hierarchy might include access control limitations.

Typical access control services implement rules expressed in triples with the schema {user_identification, action_requested, resource}. Such schema might be extended to represent organizational hierarchies of users and sets of resources, such as "all the files in directory xyz/a/b." Some access control services used in military systems either replace or augment this by associating security levels both with users and with resources for control according to rules such as "reading top secret documents is permitted only to people with top secret clearance."

Digital Rights Management (DRM) functionality is an access control extension with more complicated rules, such as what might be needed to control the use of copyright materials, possibly including the imposition of pricing.[320] Stimulated by entertainment industry concerns, it has become a topic of intense attention in recent years, both in the business press and in cultural heritage community articles.

Even seemingly simple questions create difficult dilemmas. For instance, it is difficult to identify the rightsholder for a work whose representation does not include his embedded identification, and difficult to verify that the purported rightsholder is in fact the true, legal owner. This di-

---

[320]   Ayre 2004, *The Right to Preserve.*

Coyle 2005, *Descriptive metadata for copyright status.*

Rust 1998, *Metadata: The Right Approach.*

DRM Watch at http://www.drmwatch.com/ monitors digital rights management issues and news.

Communications of the ACM, April 2003 contains seven DRM articles.

lemma evokes immense complexity. If one were to need permissions for each holding in a collection of thousands, it would probably be unaffordable. And it would be impossible in collections of millions of holdings. The problem is that, if one omits obtaining permission for some protected right before using it, the owner might announce himself with a lawsuit. For cultural heritage repositories, DRM remains a topic in which many questions are repeatedly asked, and few are answered.[321]

So much for current collection management. No one has addressed access control or rights management for the long term, i.e., for periods long compared to the periods in which human beings are incumbent in particular jobs, let alone periods of a century or longer. We might ask what should be done as specific access control rules become obsolete because people's roles change. Perhaps *role-based access control*[322] will provide part of what is needed. However, it would be premature to think about mechanisms before we have some understanding about the policies that might be acceptable.

8.2   Recordkeeping Standards

The ISO records management committee TC46/SC11, started in 1997, has seven working groups: (1) Metadata for records; (2) RM relationships and guidelines for stating records management requirements; (3) Access rules and guidance for rights management, privacy, and security; (4) Self-assessment and compliance guidelines; (5) Review of *ISO 15489*; (6) Work process analysis, to transform the Australian standard for work process analysis (*AS 5090:2003*) into an international standard; and (7) Digital records preservation, emphasizing specific requirements for long-term preservation. One of the objectives is to establish requirements for file formats to make them sustainable over time, instead of developing archival standards for each format, such as PDF.

Its best-known records management standard is *ISO 15489*.[323]   ISO 22310 provides guidelines for stating records management requirements in standards. *ISO 23081, Information and documentation—Records management processes—Metadata for records—Part 1: Principles*, provides a benchmark for the development of best practices for recordkeeping metadata attributes and values, and criteria against which metadata schemas can

---

[321]   Marcum 2003, *Keepers of the Crumbling Culture.*

[322]   Sandhu 1998, *Role-based Access Control.* See also http://csrc.nist.gov/rbac/.

[323]   Data Capture Solutions 2005, *ISO 15489—The Essentials,* http://www.datacapture.co.uk/pdf/ISO-15489-White-Paper.pdf?=SID.

be assessed in terms of their recordkeeping and archiving functionalities.[324] It defines a framework for creating, managing, and using these metadata and discusses the underlying principles, extending *ISO 15489* and explaining what is necessary to ensure the authenticity and integrity of records.

Each of the many metadata set definitions has a different purpose that must be understood in order to see how any record set may or may not connect to or be used in other contexts. Although different business contexts require different approaches, some basic principles can be identified. One is that metadata explaining a record's business context need to be captured together with the record itself to fix it in time and space (i.e., in the domain in which the record was created). Similarly, whenever a record is updated metadata about the change should be captured. §11.1.3 suggests how this might be handled.

Related is also the desirability to avoid duplication in work—recreating metadata again when documents or records are received by another organization. For instance, the current Australian Clever Recordkeeping Metadata project[325] is exploring how metadata created in one domain can be easily (re)used in another, often for different applications (repurposing). These issues span organizations and communities and may require shared services, such as metadata schema registries. We will need automated tools for extracting metadata and translating metadata elements between schemas from different environments (cross-walks), and also a thorough understanding of the metadata schemas.

The [U.K.] National Archives (TNA) has published an updated National Archives Standard intended for archivists and characterized as "the recognised benchmark for caring for records and providing access to them" and providing "guidance on the preservation of digital records."[326] An accompanying framework document relates a range of standards and best practice guidelines for many aspects of recordkeeping.

The ISAD(G) standard provides general guidance for the preparation of archival descriptions, saying that, "the purpose of archival description is to identify and explain the context and content of archival material in order to promote its accessibility [by means of] accurate and appropriate representations organiz[ed] in accordance with predetermined models."[327]

---

[324] McKemmish 2004, *Smart Metadata and the Archives of the Future*, http://www.ifai.org.mx/ica/presentaciones/04.pdf.

[325] Evans 2005, *Create once, use many times*. http://www.ifai.org.mx/ica/presentaciones/04.pdf.

[326] National Archives 2004, http://www.nationalarchives.gov.uk/archives/framework/repositories.htm.

[327] ICA 1999, *ISAD(G): General International Standard Archival Description*, http://www.ica.org/biblio/cds/isad_g_2e.pdf.

ISAD(G) processes enable "the intellectual controls necessary for reliable, authentic, meaningful and accessible descriptive records to be carried forward through time."

At least as long as an item is held by an archive, its ISAD(G) information "remains dynamic and may be subject to amendment in the light of further knowledge of its content or the context of its creation." Its descriptions do not depend on the forms or media of the archival material. Nor does ISAD(G) give guidance on the description of special materials such as seals, sound recordings, or geographical maps, because manuals for such topics are available from other sources.

8.3 Archival Best Practices

Recent guidelines, advisories, and statements of repository best practices extend the tradition and style of predecessors for paper-based and microfilm archives. These published statements are mutually consistent, illustrating community consensus about what archival repositories should achieve and roughly how they should do so.[328] They typically start by asserting that each repository should publish its statements of mission, acceptable document classes, and intended accession sources. Many of their statements are of the form, "A repository will follow documented policies and procedures which ensure that information is preserved against all reasonable contingencies."[329] This illustrates that they often specify objectives rather than attributes for which compliance can readily be validated by independent auditors.

The National Archives of Australia and the National Library of Australia have thought long and carefully about preservation. Their publications are recommended.[330]

Currall teaches repository service aspects in ways that are ready to be applied,[157] discussing

- identifying the roles and responsibilities of records creators;

---

[328] International Council on Archives 2005, *Electronic Records: a Workbook for Archivists*, http://www.ica.org/biblio/Study16ENG_5_2.pdf.

National Archives of Australia 2004, *Digital Recordkeeping Checklist*, http://www.naa.gov.au/recordkeeping/er/checklist.html.

Records Management Society 2005, *Code of Practice for Records Managers and Archivists*, http://www.rms-gb.org.uk/resources/140.

Shepherd 2002, *Managing Records*.

[329] Greenstein 2000, *Minimum criteria for an archival repository of digital scholarly journals*, http://www.diglib.org/preserve/criteria.htm.

[330] *Recordkeeping*, http://www.naa.gov.au/recordkeeping/, and *National Library of Australia Preservation Policy*, http://www.nla.gov.au/policy/pres.html.

- creating, using, disseminating, and eradicating digital records;
- training users in digital record management practice;
- improving retrieval speed for documents and elements within them;
- increasing accuracy for items within a document and individual document choice from a collection; and
- reducing organizational risk from unmanaged records.

The sections relating digital record practices to their paper counterparts are particularly helpful. Palm[331] presents an example teaching how to estimate the costs of digitizing audio-visual content and paper materials and long-term storage in a national archive.

8.4   Repository Audit and Certification

Archives of physical objects usually require a client to come to their facilities to inspect any holdings, and often impose constraints that help make the object safe. For instance, in the U.K. Public Record Office (PRO), a reader sits in a room under the surveillance of a uniformed overseer (often a retired military man). The PRO also records who handled each holding. Familiarity with such practices might lead archivists to state their requirements in terms of the physical integrity and history of a document instance and of the premises and procedures of the archival institution.

A collection of durable digital documents is easily held safely in a repository network, because the collection definition can itself be represented by a digital document. This depends on ensuring that references (links) can be made reliable in the sense that, if a link referent can be found, its authenticity can reliably be tested. For document collections that include self-identifying metadata, we can automatically build library catalogs that are as good for information discovery as the metadata inherently permit.

RLG explores procedures intended to engender clients' trust that a repository will deliver only authentic information,[332] declaring that, "to meet expectations all trusted repositories must:

- "accept responsibility for the long-term maintenance of digital resources on behalf of its depositors and for the benefit of current and future users;
- "have an organizational system that supports not only long-term viability of the repository, but also the digital information for which it has responsibility;

---

[331] Jonas Palm 2006, *The Digital Black Hole*, http://www.tape-online.net/docs/Palm_Black_Hole.pdf.

[332] Research Libraries Group 2002, *Trusted digital repositories.*

- "demonstrate fiscal responsibility and sustainability;
- "design its system(s) in accordance with commonly accepted conventions and standards to ensure the ongoing management, access, and security of materials deposited within it;
- "establish methodologies for system evaluation that meet community expectations of trustworthiness;
- "be depended upon to carry out its long-term responsibilities to depositors and users openly and explicitly;
- "have policies, practices, and performance that can be audited and measured."

The first four of these exhortations amount to "extend conventional research library objectives to whatever digital collections they hold." The fifth and sixth exhortations are subjective, suggesting neither specific prescriptions for action nor measures for which independent observers would surely reach identical conclusions. The final exhortation leads RLG to its first recommendation: "Develop a framework and process to support the certification of digital repositories. A certification framework and certification process for repositories are crucial and their absence has been an impediment to assigning trust. Model processes, including checklists for certification reviews, should be developed incorporating the community-approved attributes of trusted digital repositories."

How can a repository protect its content against improper changes? RLG calls for certifications that might lead to a public announcement that an institution has correctly executed sound preservation practices. However, to execute partly human procedures faithfully over decades would be difficult and expensive without technology and business controls that few archival institutions can afford or manage well. Repository-centric proposals have unaddressed weaknesses:

- They depend on an unexpressed premise—that exposing an archive's internal procedures can persuade clients that its content deliveries will be authentic. Such procedures have not been defined; nor is it obvious that creating them is feasible.
- Certifying procedures is inherently more expensive for their institutions[333] and less reliable than basing an archive on stored objects that individually embed their own audit trails.
- Periodic audits will not provide a consumer with good evidence for the authenticity of documents he might depend on. The reader of a century-

---

[333] The expense can be estimated from the cost of providing National Research Council 2000, *A Digital Strategy for the Library of Congress*, or of a similar study currently underway for the National Archives and Records Administration.

old document would have to assume that, during the entire time the archive held the document, no lapse in the exercise of management controls permitted the key content to be improperly modified. For information of critical importance with risks to this consumer, this might not be a prudent assumption.[334]

- To convene a truly independent audit committee would be difficult. Librarians would be reluctant to criticize their professional colleagues, especially if the procedures at issue resemble procedures in their own institutions.[335] Nonlibrarians that are not professional auditors might not find procedural weaknesses and remedies quickly.

- RLG did not consider technology trends that favor data replication or other design possibilities, such as sources of trust that are different institutions from those managing repositories.

Since the appearance of the RLG proposal, Jantz has proposed computing a digital signature for each preserved document and storing it in the technical metadata of the object, and then computing a signature for the complete object and storing that signature externally to the repository.[336] As part of the proposed authentication architecture, a background process would periodically recompute the hash for each object and compare it with the originally computed hash. Any differences would be reported and off-line storage or mirrored repositories would be used to restore the integrity of the object.

8.5   Summary

Increasing numbers of library and archival commentaries suggest the need for advances in standards and best practices to ensure that displayed items have not been damaged. Work in progress adapts principles from a paper-dominated world to a digital world.

A small fraction of proven digital security technology is sufficient to protect preserved information against surreptitious modification. How to manage intellectual property rights in long-term archives is not known.

OAIS and RLG pay more attention to the structures for and the processes within an archive than to the archival service as seen by clients.

---

[334] Casey 2006, *Investigating Sophisticated Security Breaches.*

[335] This is a side effect of the high value that librarians place on consensus, as well as the small size of their professional community. The National Research Council 2000, *A Digital Strategy for the Library of Congress,* a scathing assessment of digital technology in the Library of Congress originated primarily from the outsiders among this report's authors. (The Librarian of Congress, Jim Billington, had great courage in inviting an outside audit of his institution.)

[336] Jantz 2005, *Digital Preservation ... Trusted Digital Repositories.* Compare this to Chapter 11.

Managing an enterprise to high standards is difficult. It is even more difficult to demonstrate to auditors and to users that internal procedures are sufficient to ensure trustworthy output—particularly because this might depend on proper execution of institutional procedures from the time a document was deposited until a user requests it 50 years later. Feasibility has not been demonstrated and, at best, will take many years to demonstrate.[337] However, accomplishing this is neither necessary nor sufficient to achieve reliable long-term preservation for sensitive information whose improper modification might damage future information consumers.

This opinion is not intended to imply that audit and certification of document repositories (traditional or digital) are without value. A relatively independent audit might, in fact, be an inexpensive measure towards enhancing the quality of both service delivery and of the content delivered. The point at issue is narrower, having to do only with the information consumer who might be damaged significantly by falsification of a document that he assumes authentic. Audits would provide insufficient evidence for his confidence that any particular repository holding was authentic.

---

[337] Ross 2005, *Audit and Certification of Digital Repositories*.

9 Everyday Digital Content Management

> For the first thirty years of digital preservation, archives managed their digital collections with … a simple storage system and … a catalog database. Although the fundamental design of a digital archive system has remained the same … a contemporary digital archive needs more than [storage] for magnetic tapes and a [database] for the catalog. The rapid growth of digital material in both volume and complexity [and] rising expectations of archives' users … have all contributed to the redefinition of digital archive functions.
>
> Beedham 2005, *Assessment of [UK] Compliance with OAIS and METS, p.*6

Digital library development started about twenty years ago.[338] Practical digital content management software has been available for more than ten years.[339] Commercial offerings include Web content management,[340] imaging, reports management, digital asset management, e-mail management, and document workflow management—topics that today's cultural heritage literature is beginning to discuss. Reducing costs and organizational risks (regulatory compliance and legal) has stimulated consolidation and moved these services down the storage stack to levels at which they can scale and support multiple applications with centralized services. The ability to connect, enhance, and deliver information across diverse operating systems, applications, legacy systems, and processes is an imperative.

There are many ways of implementing collection housing, responsive to the diverse reasons for distributing components: performance enhancements by parallelism, scalability, reliability, resource sharing, insurance against disasters, and distributed human responsibilities. If the content collection or the client community is large, the repository implementation is likely to be distributed over several computing and storage systems[341] that might not be physically close to each other.

---

[338] Thoma 1985, *A Prototype System for the Electronic Storage and Retrieval of Document Images.*

[339] Lesk 1997, *Practical Digital Libraries.*

Theng 2005, *Design and Usability of Digital Libraries.*

Morgan 2006, *Designing, Implementing, and Maintaining Digital Library Services and Collections with MyLibrary,* http://dewey.library.nd.edu/mylibrary/manual/.

Wilkinson 1998, *Document computing.*

Witten 2003, *How to Build a Digital Library.*

[340] Dougherty 2004, *Taming the Wild West.*

[341] Miller 1988, *A Reference Model for Mass Storage Systems.*

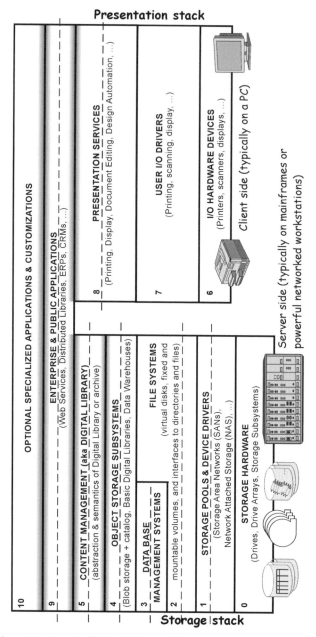

Fig. 24: Software layering for "industrial strength" content management: a solid boundary line between layers depicts a standard interface; a fuzzy boundary (━) suggests possibly proprietary interfaces that might force a installation to choose both components from a single vendor. A dashed line (▬ ▬ ▬) through a component suggests available distributed implementations, whose client and server portions might be at different geographic locations and execute on different computing platforms.

9.1   Software Layering

Deployed digital technologies consist of layers from the most basic and most general services to application-specific layers. The Fig. 24 model suggests how practical software is partitioned for flexibility. Common infrastructure components include

- file storage and replication for bit-strings;
- relational DBMS services for collection catalog, metadata, and administrative rules;
- search index management to speed query responsiveness;
- access control and digital rights management services;
- document management to bind bit-strings to catalog records; and
- content management tailored for each sponsoring institution (§9.3.4).

In addition to serving its primary clientele, an archival institution is likely to foster access by external communities—service without local customization that means little elsewhere. The repository must provide "least common denominator" interfaces to its most basic services—querying its catalog records and retrieving its holdings.

Layering and modularity have become more distinct over time, partly because of design insight and partly because optimization becomes affordable as the number of installations and applications increases. Although great implementation changes have occurred in the quarter century since the Fig. 24 model was first used, its gross structure has been relatively stable. The IBM Content Manager has been stable in layers 2, 3, and 4 since 1993, except that the telecommunications interface and style changed after TCP/IP replaced other network protocols in about 1996 and the WWW came into use in about 1998. The differentiation among today's approximately 80 open source and approximately 20 commercial repository offerings occurs primarily in layers 5 and 9.

Every layer hides details that the designers of higher layers consider irrelevant to their own users. Each lower layer provides functionality required by many realized and potential higher layers. Lower layer design emphasis is on reliability, scalability, and performance. Higher layers implement models that end users want and understand. Their design emphasis includes tailoring flexibility. Every storage layer component can have its own directory, which might or might not be made explicitly visible to higher software layers. This directory might serve many purposes: mapping external object names to internal names and/or locations, managing storage rearrangement, backup and recovery operations hidden from higher service layers, and so on.

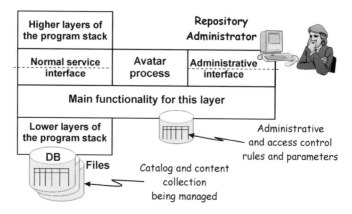

Fig. 25: Typical administrative structure for a server layer
(for any level in the Fig. 24 program stacks)

Automatic, rules-driven administration is essential for all but the smallest collections. For this, a storage stack layer might have two *API* sets—one for normal service and one for administration (Fig. 25). APIs in the two sets are similar; the distinction is enforced by access control that allows only appropriate repository administrators to specify administrative rules. A rule might specify some alteration of part of the catalog and collection, such as backing it up, replicating it to a particular autonomous repository, or fetching a class of Web objects. Another kind of rule might send warnings and recommendations to a repository administrator. Each rule would specify an event that triggers it, such as an anomalous occurrence, a class of date/time occurrences, or an administrator's call for executing that particular rule. The Fig. 25 avatar program, which has no external API, would "listen" for such events, executing actions defined by associated rules when an occurrence is signaled. Each rule sequence would have been specified by a human administrator at some earlier time.

Just as the normal service interfaces can be implemented as a client/server pair, as suggested by the dashed lines in Fig. 24 and the left side of Fig. 25, administrative interfaces are likely to be split, as suggested in the right side of Fig. 25.

Much of the Fig. 25 structure reappears in the Fig. 26 archival storage layer to suggest rules administration for (1) access control, (2) object replication to remote repositories, and (3) validity checking of proposed collection additions. It might further be used for metadata extraction rules to create library catalog records automatically and by users' screen layout preferences for displaying results. Other Fig. 25 applications would probably be implemented low in the storage stack to manage preservation processes—detecting system, network, and media degradation and failures, managing migration to newer storage devices, auditing object integrity by sampling the collection, and so on. There are many tailoring opportunities.

9.2 A Model of Storage Stack Development

Storage stack design is guided by something like the physicians' oath, "First of all, do no harm!" For software engineers, it is, "First of all, lose no information." In a good design, every reasonable measure is taken to avoid losing users' data. Software complexity comes from combining this objective with demanding performance, scale, and flexibility objectives.

Software development history can be described as finding universally attractive abstractions and representing them in reusable modules that eventually replace specialized implementations. The Fig. 24 software stacks gradually evolved with experience about what worked well and pleased the technical community.

What software engineers do to support knowledge workers can be characterized as (1) identifying certain human work as "merely clerical"; (2) choosing a frequently used subset of this for automation; (3) generalizing this to be broadly useful; and (4) implementing the generalization as a new software layer or module that supports autonomous applications. Generalizing software starts by identifying functionality to be removed because it does not contribute to a new abstraction. In these design processes, the questions addressed include:

- What do many kinds of users and applications do in common? Can we express this as a procedure?
- Within an existing software layer, what modularization is possible?
- How should functionality be divided between servers and clients? How can we separate the design of potential modules from methodology for combining such modules to create "solutions."
- Is the usage of what is proposed sufficiently large to justify the cost of a new implementation and its integration into solutions? If the functionality will be visible to end users, can we explain it to them?
- What standard interfaces would allow integrators to mix and match components from competing providers?
- What abnormal situations must be anticipated to achieve "industrial strength"?
- What "home-grown" code can be eliminated because generic components have become available?
- What performance bottlenecks appear or might appear, and how can we mitigate these?

9.3   Repository Architecture

Commercial digital content managers are layered with a core implementing functionality needed by every installation and every collection model—the document storage subsystem in Fig. 26—nested within an application modeling layer—the archival storage layer—with flexible options to help installations add or acquire the functionality to tailor to their institutions' idiosyncratic needs and wishes.[342]

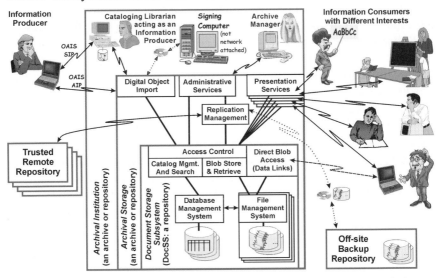

Fig. 26: Repository architecture suggesting human roles in the use of networked, nested repositories. Components are described in §§9.3.2 to 9.3.5.

The figure illustrates that document preparation activities and management of accession into a collection occur on different machines than those housing the collection and providing access to information consumers. This partly occurs naturally because it responds to the different human roles illustrated and the available software tools. It is partly in order to mitigate well known security risks. For good security, the off-site backup repository should never be connected to a network.

Fig. 26 reminds us that the words 'archive' and 'repository' are ambiguous, particularly if it is compared to the widely reproduced *OAIS* diagram of Fig. 1. One of several distinctions made is whether we are talking about a repository level that includes human archive managers or a more primitive construct. At the *document storage subsystem* level, an archive is a set

---

[342]   The architectural description that follows is drawn primarily from personal experience with IBM Content Manager, particularly from Gladney 1993, *A Storage Subsystem for Image and Records Management*. Competitive repository offerings are similar.

of tables and files accessible only by way of software that protects this information according to rules imposed by administrators. At the *archival store* level, a repository or archive is an information collection managed in certain objectively specified ways. At the enterprise level, an *institutional repository* is the execution of practices that implement policies about what is to be stored, who is to be served, what service is to be provided, and administrative and legal constraints such as the dictates of intellectual property law.

A slightly different organization than that depicted, with machines sharing repository holdings in separate machines for accession, for preservation preparation, and for serving information consumers, is used by the National Archives of Australia (NAA). It passes holdings among these machines only on storage media (not over a communication network) to protect against external security risks.[343]

9.3.1 Lowest Levels of the Storage Stack

> All of our digital recording media require active management in order to avoid problems due to media degradation and failure. The only approach to this generic problem is for the repository manager to put in place policies for periodically migrating content and to make sure that there is ample redundancy via routine backups, off-site backup, and the use of mirrored sites or other types of redundancy options to ensure that there is always another digital "place" where one can find the original object.
>
> Jantz 2005, *Digital Preservation*

Storage virtualization services (Fig. 24 layers 0, 1, and 2) are available from many vendors, structured as modules that can be combined differently in different installations.[344] Configurations can be changed as collections grow, often without disrupting user service. Virtualization layers separate how higher software layers and their users "see" storage from the characteristics of storage volumes (tapes and disks), except that data access times, total space available, and reliability characteristics are likely to depend on actual implementations.

The dominant virtualization architecture—*SAN* (*Storage Area Networks*)—is rapidly being associated with standards so that installations can choose interconnected components from competing vendors. Storage

---

[343] Wilson 2002, *Access Across Time: How the NAA Preserves Digital Records,*
http://www.erpanet.org/events/2003/rome/presentations/Wilson.ppt.

[344] Laird 2006, *The Virtues of Virtualized Storage,* http://www.zangogroup.com/d/clips/
IW03SRfstorvirt.pdf.

The range of available components is illustrated by *IBM TotalStorage* offerings; see
http://www-03.ibm.com/servers/storage/ and the tutorial at
http://www-03.ibm.com/servers/storage/software/virtualization/tutorial/.

Networking Industry Association (SNIA) and Distributed Management Task Force standards use a common protocol called the Common Information Model (CIM) to enable interoperability. It uses XML to define CIM objects and process transactions within Web sessions. Standardizations win customers' confidence that an installation's capacity and performance can be improved with additional devices whenever needed. Customers can realistically expect that the cost of expansion will decrease as the vendors refine their offerings and marketplace competition exerts its influence.

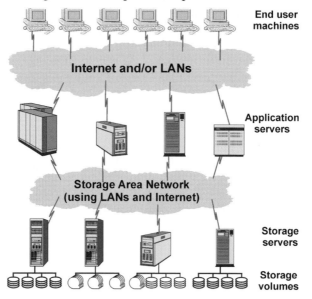

Fig. 27: Storage area network (SAN) configuration

A SAN provides physical connections, storage elements, server systems for secure and robust data transfer (Fig. 27), interconnecting storage volumes with servers that each work on many users' behalf, and a management layer that organizes these. It replaces dedicated connections between application servers and storage, eliminating the concept that any single application server "owns" storage devices. It also increases how much data an application server can access by allowing heterogeneous storage servers to share a pool of disk, tape, and optical storage volumes. Using a SAN can offer the following: [345]

---

[345] Garfinkel 2006, *AFF: A New Format for Storing Hard Drive Images*.

Preston 2005, *Data Security as a Service,* http://www.infoworld.com/article/05/08/11/33FEbackup_1.html?s=feature.

Tate 2005, *Introduction to Storage Area Networks,* http://www.redbooks.ibm.com/Redbooks.nsf/RedbookAbstracts/sg245470.html?Open.

- Improvements to application availability because storage is accessible through multiple data paths for better reliability and serviceability;
- Improved application performance by off-loading storage processing from application servers, with storage traffic on a separate network; a further enhancement, application of the Data Links technology (§9.3.3), would avoid most of the delay and load associated with passing large files through the Fig. 27 application servers; this is yet to appear;
- Simplified consolidated storage management and administration, including the ability to replace HDDs and tapes that are failing or becoming obsolete, and to add new storage volumes for scalability, doing so without interrupting ongoing service; and
- Storage services to remote sites, including replication and conventional backup for protection against malicious attacks and data loss caused by local disasters.[346]

Storage technology and SAN architecture are evolving rapidly in available scale, functionality, and the cost for storing a terabyte of data. SANs are also becoming capable of handling all the widely used storage interface protocols with reduced cabling, technical support, and electricity. A single subsystem might combine nearly every kind of storage volume, while hiding their differences from higher system levels at which they would interfere with concise data models.[347]

File backup and recovery services are becoming sophisticated, perhaps because an immense amount of business-critical information is still exposed to loss.

9.3.2 Repository Catalog

Today's only practical implementation for a large repository catalog is a relational database. Whatever model might be implicit in a relation resides in the semantics of its data values. This can be represented as relations and in optionally linked programs (rules). Furthermore, a database can readily be dumped to Unicode files with simple encoding to handle variable-length fields. In other words, there is a simple scheme with which a database can be preserved. However, many databases are so much larger than typical individual works (often many gigabytes in size rather than a few megabytes) that specialized copying methods might be needed.

Relations are the quintessential structuring abstraction because their content can be freed of most accidental information.

---

[346] Van Drimmelen 2004, *Universal access through time.*

Lovecy 2005, *Disaster Management for Libraries and Archives.*

[347] Riedel 2003, *Storage Systems.*

Databases excel at supporting large numbers of records. For instance, the Transaction Processing Council D benchmark measures query performance for database sizes ranging from one gigabyte up to three terabytes and from six million to eighteen billion rows. A blob can be linked to any database cell. This blob can reside either within the database, or within an external file system. In the latter case, an identifier stored in a DB field points to the blob's location. This helps for aggregating blobs in virtual containers. Aggregation can be done at the file level, using utilities such as the TAR program, at the database level through database tablespaces, or at an intermediate data handling level through the use of software controlled caches. The database can maintain the blob descriptions, as well as sequences within containers and container locations within storage subsystems. A file system supports database access to storage hardware.

A relational DBMS can manage consistency constraints. Imagine the simplest kind of banking transaction—transfer of $100 from an account A to another account B—implemented in an accounting database by the obvious sequential algorithm—first reducing the A balance by $100 and then increasing the B balance by $100 or, alternatively, first increasing the B balance and then reducing the A balance. If this were be programmed naïvely and if the system failed after the first change occurred and before the second change, the accounting database would not merely be in error, but would represent an impermissible situation. In the first case money will have been destroyed, and in the second case money would have magically been created. I.e., these failures have the same effects respectively as burning a $100 bill and counterfeiting a $100 bill. In modern banking, certain database records are money.

Reliable DBMS offerings avoid this flaw by using a protocol called *two-phase commit*.[348] What constitutes a logically complete set of database changes—a *unit of work*—is expressed in an application program. The unit of work is "transfer of $100 from account A to account B." Conceptually, the protocol is simple, ensuring that, from the perspective of an external observer, execution of each unit of work is synchronized in the sense that either all the changes it calls for are committed or that all are rolled back (voided). This external observer would inspect the affected databases using a querying program that executes autonomously from any program effecting database changes. No other operational definition of "inspect" would be sensible. The two-phase commit protocol is fundamental support for consistent database snapshots.

Gray 1993, *Transaction Processing*, §7.5.2.

More generally, modern DBMS offerings are sophisticated programs created by large programming teams. Much of the effort has gone toward convenient programming interfaces, hiding the details of advanced functionality, high performance, and scaling to immense record collections, all with high reliability. There is no practical alternative to using such software for the catalog portion of a digital library. Each of DB2 and DocSS (§9.3.3) have been compiled from a single code base for the smallest computers to the largest, fastest machines. This permitted an IBM customer to test its digital library application programs on a single PC—puny in 1993 by today's measures—before installing them in a production environment months later.

9.3.3   A Document Storage Subsystem

Even though a DB cell can hold a blob, we cannot create a practical DL without combining file management services with a DBMS. The reason is overhead associated with program stack depths and conventional subroutine parameter passing, in which string values are copied rather than pointed to. Copying works well for strings up to a few hundred bytes in length. However an active library would create a heavy DBMS CPU load for 100,000-byte blobs, and an impossible load for 10-Mbyte blobs.[349]

The *document storage subsystem* (DocSS) (box 4 in Fig. 24 and the third largest box in Fig. 26) creates a basic library abstraction, combining a catalog represented by a distributed relational database with files that might be stored locally or in remote computers,[350] and providing referential consistency between the catalog and the document collection.[351] It also enforces access control and other rules defined by the Fig. 26 Archive Manager—rules that define how the repository may be used and by whom.

In 1993, the consistency requirement forced the IBM Digital Library to hide its files from other applications, making it impossible to share them directly with unmodified legacy applications. This restriction hampered

---

[349]   David Choy taught this to the IBM Research digital library team in 1987. At that time, IBM's high performance machines ran OS/MVS, which passed strings with an MVC (move character long) loop. Choy counted seven subroutine calls needed to copy a value from a database field to a network port, and pointed out that "if we do that with digital images, we will freeze IBM's fastest machine to the tracks!"

[350]   The first IBM Digital Library release implemented remote file servers in response to a state highway department need. This department had 12 regional offices distributed across California, with approximately 640 miles separating the most distance offices. It wanted a single catalog for all its bridge maintenance records. In 1993, the Internet was slow and expensive. The solution was to house blobs in regional offices, with a central catalog managing collection integrity and access control.

[351]   To understand how this is accomplished, compare the storage subsystem box in Fig. 26 with in Gladney 1993, Fig. 5 and related text.

using digital libraries in large production installations, such as those of Boeing's airframe design and manufacturing divisions. This was because their massive management and control application systems had been programmed some years earlier, so that the program authors were no longer available. It would have been difficult and expensive to change these applications to use a digital library instead of calling file systems directly.

A 1995 invention, Data Links, allows the DBMS to control files accessible to previous applications using conventional file input/output interfaces, ensuring referential integrity and access control.[352] This permits unmodified legacy application programs to access library-controlled files. This is accomplished by a file system plug-in that traps "open" calls to check permissions and consistency rules represented in DB tables.[353]

Data Links can also be used to accelerate performance-sensitive applications by storing library-controlled files so that read/write operations encounter much reduced system overhead. An example is multimedia streaming of video performance data to users' workstations. Updates to each video file and its metadata can be managed with the same DB that implements a library catalog, while heavy, timing-sensitive data traffic bypasses the DBMS software.

As the number of content repository software offerings increased in recent years, a common programmatic interface became desirable. Industrial partners defined the *Content Repository API for Java* (JSR 170), a standard interface whereby applications can exploit a DL.[354] This specification lists its goals as:

- not being tied to any particular underlying architecture, data source, or protocol, with enough flexibility in the API for both hierarchical and nonhierarchical repository models;
- making programming easy by representing the core functionality without venturing into "content applications";
- allowing easy implementation on top of a wide variety of existing content repositories; and
- standardizing complex functionality needed by advanced applications.

---

[352] Narang 1995, *DataLinks - Linkage of Database and FileSystems.*

Bhattacharya 2002, *Coordinating backup/recovery and data consistency between database and file systems.* See also DB2 Data Links Manager at http://www-306.ibm.com/software/data/db2/datalinks/.

[353] To understand how this works, see Bhattacharya 2002 (loc. cit.)

[354] Nuescheler 2005, *Content Repository API for Java technology API,* http://www.jcp.org/en/jsr/detail?id=170.

A large current European project is using JSR-170; see Risse 2005, *The BRICKS Infrastructure - An Overview,* §4.2; http://www.ipsi.fraunhofer.de/%7Erisse/pub/eva2005.pdf.

This Java specification provides for two repository API compliance levels. Level 1 defines read-only functionality: reading of repository content, inspection of content-type definitions, support for namespaces, export of content to XML, and searching. Level 2 adds methods for writing content, assignment of types to content, and importing content from XML. The specification also defines optional features: atomic transactions and locking, versioning, access control, and extensions for searching.

JSR 170 implementations, perhaps with modest extensions to existing content management code, can readily achieve the stated goals. Application developers will be able to avoid the costs associated with learning a particular API of a conforming repository supplier when they develop content application logic. Enterprises will benefit by being able to replace their repositories without reprogramming applications (Fig. 28).

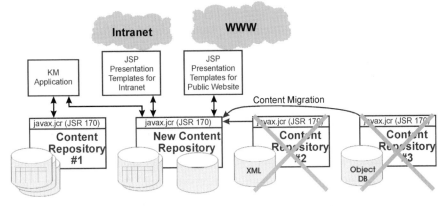

Fig. 28: Replacing JSR 170 compliant repositories

Since the standard is new, not many supporting offerings are available. In 2005, the Apache Foundation began to build an open source API implementation.[355] A version 2 specification team is considering aspects deferred in the approved Java Content Management API.[356] It therefore seems reasonable to recommend that JSR 170 support be regarded as a sine qua non requirement for any institution's repository software acquisition, even if it somewhat delays DL implementation.

---

[355] *Apache Jackrabbit Open Source Content Repository for Java*,
http://incubator.apache.org/jackrabbit/.

[356] *Content Repository for Java Technology API Version 2.0*, http://jcp.org/en/jsr/detail?id=283.

9.3.4   Archival Storage Layer

§9.3.3 functionality is primitive, implementing only what is common to any kind of library or archive. The next higher layer (box 5 in Fig. 24), an *archival storage* service (the second largest box in Fig. 26), implements a functionally richer, but more narrowly applicable, model. For instance, today's preservation literature is mostly about managing research library collections and long-term retention of national government records. In contrast, IBM's first repository service implemented a model requested by insurance companies and state agencies—a folder manager modeling documents within folders that were within filing cabinets. Whatever the model, the archival storage level must accommodate every kind of information and every reasonable policy repository managers might promise to administer for the benefit of institutional and external users.

A single organization may have multiple repositories with different missions. While each repository should provide full *OAIS* functionality, specific functions could be shared between archives or even between different organizations. Repositories might exhibit differences in scale, in ingestion data stream types, in user community expectations, in organizational training, in software applications that must interface seamlessly with storage subsystems and catalog management software, and so on. Such differences lead to variations of repository architecture and processes.

The archive will have a server for receiving data from information producers. This server must accept *OAIS* SIPs, testing them for syntactic validity and submission authorization, advising both the information producer involved and the archive administrator of exceptions. As Fig. 26 suggests, producers internal to the archival institution neither need nor should be distinguished from external producers by this interface, though access control and administrative rules will allow some privileged services to archive administrators.

The business controls of all archive storage services are managed through an Administrative Services module (Fig. 25) in the archival storage layer. For the Fig. 26 Digital Object Import module, this includes not only the specification of who may modify the repository's holdings, but also the definition of TDO acceptability criteria, which will mostly be constraints on metadata in each TDO's Protection Block. This module might route proposed, but unacceptable, archive submissions to the Cataloging Librarian at the same time as it sends exception information to the (external) Information Producer. The End User Service might generate *OAIS* DIPs that differ from the corresponding AIPs.[357]

---

[357]   Van de Sompel 2005, *aDORe: a Modular, Standards-based Digital Object Repository*, §5.2.

9.3.5 Institutional Repository Services

An *institutional repository* (the largest box in Fig. 26) is an information retention and access service consisting of automatic components and human services managed by a single administration primarily for the benefit of a specific *designated community*. The purpose, scope, and contents of such repositories are under active debate, because any large library must serve many interest groups—researchers, students, enterprise management, librarians, and the general public.[358] Whatever the outcome of debates might be, Fig. 29 suggests the activities of an institutional repository layer.

In many cases, such a repository serves an external community that is seldom heard directly about either the service or the content served. This external community makes itself known primarily by its repository transactions. If the offering is attractive and publicly visible, the external community traffic will be large and the service and content will gradually come to be mentioned in publications.

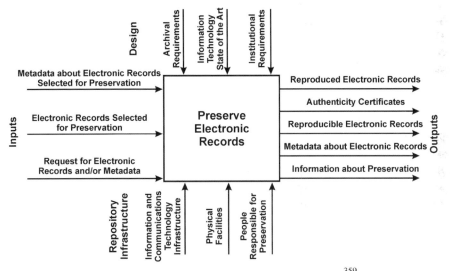

Fig. 29: Preservation of electronic records context[359]

---

358 Poynder 2006, *Clear blue water,* is a history of institutional repositories. See http://dialspace.dial.pipex.com/town/parade/df04/BlueWaterMain.pdf.

359 From InterPares *Authenticity Task Force Final Report* 2001, p. 99; http://www.interpares.org/ documents/atf_draft_final_report.pdf.

9.4   Archival Collection Types

The emphasis and jargon in articles about preserving government records are so different from those about preserving cultural works that readers might think different methodologies are needed. For instance,

> Unlike other types of information objects … records are created within a universe of discourse where there is often a high degree of shared information and expectations among participants. … In such contexts, important information is often conveyed by form, as well as by substance.   … [P]articipants expect certain forms to be used for certain types of transactions ... Common knowledge … provides a systemic check … on the reliability of their records. … To enable parties who were not participants in a process to understand the records of that activity, … an archival system should contain and convey information about the types of records typically produced, the elements of intrinsic and extrinsic form of each type, the relationships between processes and records, and also the implied knowledge … common to participants.
>
> Thibodeau 2002, *Overview of Technological Approaches*

Different collection classes vary most in the work required to populate a repository. This affects the level and type of knowledge management participation by archival institutions and the professional staff they employ. The dividing line is the §3.7 distinction between syntax and semantics. Collection classes also differ in other qualitative and quantitative characteristics that determine the work style needed to create a repository.

9.4.1   Collections of Academic and Cultural Works

A typical research library holding is a work of individual authorship that some professional cataloger accessioned into the collection without having received much evidence of its historical significance or of its relationships with other holdings, and without personal contact with the author's agent. Historical information and relationships are typically added to library contents to a limited extent by a library employee (a cataloger) and perhaps more comprehensively by scholars years later, possibly in finding aids.

The Fig. 30 author of a cultural work is likely to want to convey original conceptual structures as well as complex relationships with previous works. Much of his effort will have been to represent mental constructs in ways that help readers achieve similar mental constructs. A diligent reader will want to tease the author's ideas from the written representation.

Scientific data collections will often include individual holdings that are much larger than those of other collection types.[360] For such collections, lower levels of the Fig. 24 layering will require special measures.

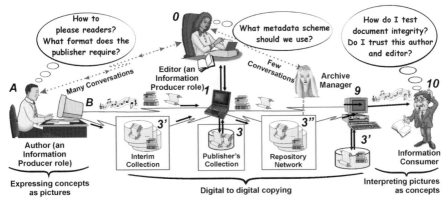

Fig. 30: Workflow for cultural documents

9.4.2   Bureaucratic File Cabinets

The preceding chapters have been oriented toward preserving works of individual authorship—cultural works—without much attention to preserving business and government records that include audit trails, descriptions of historic events, and legally mandated records. The practices surrounding such office records are often different from those for cultural works.

An office file cabinet (physical, or its digital counterpart) typically contains many relatively small files that share context, structure, and administrative constraints. In particular, the format and jargon of individual records within each cabinet is likely to be constrained by agency rules and a common culture shared by employees.[361] An information consumer's request for records is likely to be for a closely related subset of records from some cabinet, such as a chronological sequence for some period or all the records alluding to some corporation, or such record sets from several cabinets. The number of records in a bureaucratic archive is likely to be much greater than the number in a cultural archive, perhaps three orders of magnitude greater, as illustrated by the case of the U.S. National Archives and Records Administration (NARA).[88] Their management will be influenced by the following facts.

---

[360] Hey 2003, *The data deluge.*

[361] Suderman 2002, *Defining Electronic Series.*

- The content of business archives is evidence of its source agencies' work quality.
- Losing almost any archival collection would have readily identified legal and practical consequences.
- Government collections are mostly not encumbered by third-party copyright.
- Collection portions are often subject to confidentiality constraints.
- Since preservation is often mandated, funding for the archive is relatively secure.
- The cost of creating each office record tends to be much less than that for most cultural works.
- Access control will be required, for instance, for records about individuals and military information.

Fig. 31: Workflow for bureaucratic documents

Fig. 31 illustrates that, for commercial and national archives, each accession is likely to be a collection of related office records that has been subject to agency procedures and accumulated under administrative control similar to archival controls. Each collection member is a *record* in the sense meant by professional archivists, i.e., information about a specific historical event whose context is communicated by metadata and by the member's position among siblings, just as each paper record might have a proper place in a filing cabinet. The metadata include format and content rules that often antecede individual records and that might include business control statements such as retention rules. Individual office records are likely to be similar to other office records in the same collection, and their details are likely to be understood by records administrators.[362]

The purposes and structure of each agency collection are likely to be documented, and the accessioning archivists will almost surely have the opportunity to collaborate with agency records administrators to refine metadata, to enhance ontologies,[363] to determine the bounds of each collection, and to augment information about the collection's significance. Each office record collection is likely to be large (many thousand records) to contain only records that conform to a few well known schema, making accessioning affordable. Similar favorable quantitative circumstances are unlikely for the accessioning of cultural works, because libraries are not likely to be provided similar information by the authors of cultural works.

A bureaucratic collection is likely to have many occurrences of each phrase pattern and object layout. The number of relationship instances within such a collection is likely to be much greater than that within a cultural collection. The specific words (symbols) used in office records are of interest if each is used similarly wherever it occurs. Uniform jargon occurs because employees share culture; they might even be required to select terms from an agency glossary. Effective search might depend on the information consumer's knowing and using this jargon. Such circumstances tend to make ontological analysis interesting for office collections and suggest why knowledge management is a high priority in office record investigations.[364]

People rarely care as much what an authoring bureaucrat thinks as they do about how the record is related to the agency's objectives. The written representation tends to be more important than authors' intentions. In some cases, the originator's thoughts about his output are administratively pre-empted by the content. For instance, in contract litigation, conventional interpretation of written words has unconditional priority over what the agreeing parties might have intended.

9.4.3 Audio/Video Archives

As with bureaucratic collections, preservation of any audio/video (A/V) archive will, in the near future, be dominated by the effort required to handle large numbers of existing holdings. However, unlike most other content discussed in §9.4, most performance records are likely to be analog

---

[362] Berkman 2003, *Automated Granularity of Authentic Digital Records in a Persistent Archive*, http://www.sdsc.edu/NARA/Publications/EvREsearch_TR-2003-1_17sep0.doc.

[363] Edgington 2004, *Adopting Ontology to Facilitate Knowledge Sharing*.

[364] Srikantaiah 2000, *Knowledge management*.

recordings rather than digital representations. Many of these recordings will have degraded from what they were when first accessioned. Some will be at risk of becoming unusable within a decade or two. For such materials, the first objectives will not be merely preservation of what exists, but will include conversion to digital representations in order to halt content degradation.

Recording quality possible fifty years ago was not nearly as good as today's audiences are accustomed to and might have come to expect. Modern processing might include restoration of the content to what curators suppose it might have been, or even better.[365] This is common for music performances and films that will be reissued or broadcast on television; how to accomplish it is well known and carefully documented. The applicable authenticity criteria will not be mechanical, but artistic instead. This will often be legally practical, either because the archival copy is held by the copyright owner or because the commercial value of a restoration is sufficient to pay for locating and negotiating with owners.

An aspect of A/V archives that is different from other collections discussed is the raw cost of handling each holding. The unit of work appropriate is an information transfer—fetching an item from its shelf for mounting on a reader that is likely to be old machinery that is expensive to maintain, activating the hardware to view the item and create a content copy and associated metadata, and eventually returning the item to its shelf. Such handling is so expensive that the overall cost of maintaining the archive will be reduced by planning to avoid fetching anything more than once. This is one of the most useful recommendations in a guide being prepared by the managers of the BBC archives.[366]

A consequence of the above factors, and of the size of institutional A/V archives, is that project planning becomes unusually important. The BBC team recommends, as an early project phase, that an A/V archive be mapped (not cataloged). Specifically, it recommends as follows:

> Once the types have been decided, the next step is to evaluate the collection and to get information on each type.
>
> 1. Divide the whole collection into physical format types
> 2. Count the number of items in each format type (counting shelves is the usual method)

---

[365] Consider the handling of the 1927 film, *Metropolis,* discussed at http://www.filmforum.org/archivedfilms/metropolis.html.

[366] This is derived from a "best practices" guide under development by the PrestoSpace project for WWW publication. We are grateful to BBC's Richard Wright for sharing the February 2006 draft and permitting, on behalf of PrestoSpace, publishing this derivative of what it teaches. See http://www.prestospace.org/.

3. While counting shelves, estimate the age of each type—not the age of each item. Where necessary, you will already have subdivided the format type into age groups (i.e., 1950s audiotape and 1980s audiotape), so while counting shelves, estimate the number of items in each age group—for each format.

4. Another task while counting shelves is to estimate the storage history (life history). Again, where necessary, you will already have subdivided the format type by storage conditions as needed (e.g., items that have mainly been in controlled storage vs. items that have mainly been in uncontrolled storage).

With such a map available, it is possible to plan, before any item class is touched, what should be done with each member, and to organize the tools and human work needed. Given the high cost of reading a content object once, processing should be planned to exploit the small incremental cost of additional outputs for each information transfer.

As this excerpt illustrates, the BBC work necessarily focuses on factory aspects not addressed in this book. A project based on Presto technology has a detailed model for estimating costs of massive transfer.[367] The PrestoSpace team concludes, "that current media may last for 20 years more or longer, but format obsolescence and the advantages of digital technology are pushing ALL collections to adopt digital technology—even film, where digital restoration and digital access copies (DVDs) are the motivations."

9.4.4 Web Page Collections

Any topically rational and comprehensive Web page collection is likely to include pages from many administratively unrelated information creators. The individual who assembles such a set is unlikely to have any administrative relationship to most of its page creators, or any proof of permission to republish the retrieved Web pages.

The number of independent pages in a typical WWW collection is likely to be so large—57,000 in the Archive Ingest and Handling Test (AIHT) experiments—that automated processing of each page is essential preparation for repository ingestion.[368] Rule-driven processing (Fig. 25) will be needed both for ingestion and to monitor the WWW for page changes and additions to keep the collection up to date, because Web pages change rapidly and disappear more rapidly than other uncurated resources.[369] The

---

[367] *Presto Preservation Technology*, http://presto.joanneum.ac.at/.

[368] Shirky 2005, *AIHT: Conceptual Issues from Practical Tests*, and other AIHT articles in D-Lib Magazine 11(12).

[369] Kenney 2002, *Preservation Risk Management for Web Resources*.

original Web page creators will have provided little metadata, so that each collection aggregator will need to decide what metadata will be important to eventual consumers and how to accumulate parts of that information from page originators who are hard to locate and possibly unresponsive—a challenge that has not been carefully investigated.

Any Web page collection is likely to include a small number of pages with technically problematic formats.[370] The aggregator cannot ignore these without biasing the collection so that its content (the selected *extension*) is an unfaithful representation of its announced scope (its *intension*). However, if many independently selected Web page collections are constructed, some of these problematic formats might be encountered in several collections. If this is indeed found to be the case, a repository of problematic formats could be accumulated to help later aggregators.

9.4.5 Personal Repositories

Individual scholars or, more realistically, small research groups will find it easy and affordable to construct search databases better suited to their particular interests than those that libraries provide. Automatic means could keep such databases up-to-date. In fact, it has become practical for a small group to create and maintain its own digital library.

Technology for consumers' personal digital libraries is also nearing widespread availability.[371]

For about five years, a Microsoft Research project has been exploring what it would take for a private individual to record "everything" that he encounters.[372] Almost surely, the human interfaces to software like Greenstone[373] will in the next decade be refined sufficiently to organize this "everything" to be readily accessible. Such private resources could effectively overcome some librarians' preservation worries.[374]

9.5   Summary

Digital repository design is best thought through almost separately from collection organization, digital object and catalog structure, or preservation. Each institution will need repository configuration behavior adjusted

---

[370] Anderson 2005, *The AIHT at Stanford University.*

[371] Gardner 2006, *Digital Libraries Come of Age.*

[372] Gemmell 2006, *MyLifeBits: A Personal Database for Everything.*

[373] Witten 2003, *How to Build a Digital Library*; also *Greenstone Digital Library Software*, http://www.greenstone.org/.

[374] Rusbridge 2006, *Some Digital Preservation Fallacies.*

for local requirements that are not entirely like those of any other institution. It is therefore unlikely that prepackaged repository solutions will be entirely satisfactory. For each repository, someone might have to combine layered software components from different sources and tailor these to accommodate institutional requirements.

Good components are available for many Fig. 24 layers. The current cultural heritage community literature is mostly about layers 5 and 9.

The number of items in practical collections will be too large for administration on a per item basis. The opportunity to tailor repository behavior for generic circumstances whose parameters differ among institutions occurs in many places within the Fig. 24 storage stack. Some current tools have such support, but no effort has been applied to making the human factors similar across tools. Software engineers could help archive managers by finding or devising a rules language or interactive interface style that avoids idiosyncratic variations.

Business record circumstances differ from those for cultural collections in many ways (Table 10), and Web page aggregations differ from either of these. Large collections of scientific data, statistical data, and broadcast multimedia data are likely to have quite different characteristics; however, how these might best be accommodated does not seem to have been carefully thought through. Articles about preserving bureaucratic records tend to deal with processes for constructing the metadata describing record sets, whereas articles about preserving cultural works address diverse topics, including document file representations and metadata schema. For bureaucratic, cultural, and Web page collections, salient characteristics are contrasted in Table 10. However, the basic preservation technology can and should be the same for all record classes.

Table 10: Different kinds of archival collection

	Business or government archive	Cultural or research library	Harvest from WWW
Typical ingestion source	The records manager of a government agency or commercial enterprise	A publishing house editor or an individual author	A set of Web pages defined by a query predicate
Typical unit of accession	An ordered collection of administratively related documents	A single work	Autonomous Web pages selected by querying
Repository managers' focus	Conformance to archival principles of what it means to be a historical record	Content description to help patrons find each holding and anticipate its content	Editing the works to meet technical quality criteria
Data file formats	Uniform within a collection, and often relatively simple	Possibly several relatively complex data formats and rendering programs	Probably a dozen dominant forms
Metadata	Shared by the records of a collection	Unique for each work	Must be extracted from the works automatically
Historical context	Mostly records coming from the same collection, or at least from the same agency	Mostly works by authors not affiliated with the author of the work at hand	Almost as many distinct authors as works
Original cost of creating each content object	Relatively low (0.1 man-hour to five man-days, e.g., for a contract)	Relatively high (one man-day to ten man-years, e.g., for a book)	Relatively low, but mostly unknown
Number of distinct records/collection	$\sim 10^3$ to $\sim 10^7$	$\sim 10^2$ to $\sim 10^5$	$\sim 10^2$ to $\sim 10^8$
Fraudulent change risk	High, including by institutional insiders	Low for documents of many topics, but potentially very damaging if it occurs	Low because people's low expectations of Web pages.
Intellectual property rights	The rightsholder is typically the enterprise creating the archive	Permission to copy and distribute should be from rightsholder (part of managing metadata)	Difficult because many original sources do not clearly identify themselves

Part IV: Digital Object Architecture for the Long Term

Age-old preservation practices can be adapted for digitally represented information with effective and pleasing results. Storing copies in widely dispersed, autonomous repositories is both effective and easily applied to digitally represented works. The §1.2 objectives suggest solution components that can be almost independently addressed:

- Content servers that store packaged works, and that provide search and access services to their holdings.
- Replication mechanisms that protect against the loss of the last remaining copy of any work.
- Packaging each work together with metadata that includes provenance assertion and reliable linking of related works, ontologies, rendering software, and package pieces with one another.
- Representing content in language insensitive to irrelevant and ephemeral aspects of its environment.
- A few socially communicated languages and standards for encoding starting points.
- Topic-specific ontologies defined, standardized, and maintained by professional communities.

Chapters 10 through 12 reflect an uncompromising attitude toward information integrity, seeking what will always work. For issues of authenticity, this means designing for documents most at risk from felonious misrepresentation. For issues of comprehensibility, this means creating representations that do not depend on irrelevant ephemeral aspects of either today's or any future computing system. It also means creating the possibility of multiple future renderings that help eventual readers distinguish between essential and accidental information. Such caution helps avoid differing subjective opinions about what might be good enough.

Any information provider can choose some less reliable method in the light of his risk assessment. Choosing a riskier alternative will make sense if that alternative is significantly less expensive than the best method. It might be necessary if information essential for avoiding every possible error is not available. This occurs for data whose schema are trade secrets or encumbered by intellectual property constraints. The most prominent cases for which this currently seems to be the case are Adobe Acrobat and the components of Microsoft Office.

We believe that implementation of the TDO method can be designed to be inexpensive in end user expertise and time, so that alternative methods will not be worthwhile. However, this has not yet been demonstrated.

Different repository institutions have different priorities, collection and service scales, histories, and environments. Preserved digital objects are more homogeneous than repositories in the aspects to which software needs to be sensitive because information representation rules must be widely known for communication. The value of packaging each digital object's metadata as part of the object has been known for about twenty years. If such packaging were widely used, any repository could construct its catalog and search support semiautomatically as part of ingestion.

What makes preservation somewhat more difficult than other information services is that producers (authors, artists, programmers, etc.) must anticipate and provide for every important consumer need, without being sure what the consumers' objectives will be, and without having technical information about their computers. Automation software must also anticipate and be prepared to mitigate every likely aberration before it occurs. This has often forced reexamination of concepts that we take for granted, and does so once again for information preservation.

Repositories' desire to exploit improvements in technology will be stimulated mostly by daily service choices that have little to do with preservation. Old concerns have been reexpressed: "The regular, and costly, upgrades of repository hardware and of software are generally still very painful, especially migration of information holdings from old system to new. The same considerations apply for the movement of holdings between organizations."[375] The data migration needed because of finite media lifetimes is merely replication of files, which modern systems manage almost automatically. Repeatedly updating file formats to mitigate software obsolescence can be avoided by encoding each file in a format that can forever be interpreted. It is also possible to move collections between organizations almost automatically.

Digital repository service should be considered a different challenge than digital preservation. It includes all aspects of creating, maintaining, and serving from a collection. This might include long-term digital preservation measures, but might not extend to deliberate action for that.

In contrast to other topics discussed in Chapters 10 through 12, metadata for long-term records presents unsolved problems. Given a body of works to be preserved, what must be added for preservation can be specified by objective rules and syntactic conventions that editors and curators should follow. However, many metadata choices are subjective judgments, be-

---

[375] Warwick Workshop 2005, *Digital Curation and Preservation*. p. 7.

cause creating metadata is an act of authorship as much as is creating the content being described.

Perfect preservation is feasible for digital representations, but not for other kinds of artifacts, because perfect copying is possible, practical, and inexpensive only for digital artifacts.

10 Durable Bit-Strings and Catalogs

> Truth is embedded in the symbols and artifacts that we create and then keep by choice or by accident. And yet, as we approach the end of the twentieth century, we find ourselves confronting ... a vast void of knowledge filled by myth and speculation. Information in digital form—the evidence of the world we live in—is more fragile than the fragments of papyrus found buried with the Pharaohs.
>
> Conway 1996, *Preservation in the Digital World*

Pessimism about digital preservation is sometimes accompanied by a comparison of the durability of paper-like media with the durability of magnetic and optical media of the kinds used to hold digital bit-strings and analog recordings. While there is truth in what Conway asserts, nobody seriously proposes that digital information be stored forever on today's media, which are designed for high-density storage and for rapid access to what they hold. The survival of a few papyri teaches something about the likely survival of paper records, but little about the durability of digital content.[376]

- What fraction of original papyri have been lost? We do not know, but it might be large. For instance, recent television accounts of the Egyptian pyramids suggest very sophisticated engineering design that must have been written, but none of this content seems to have survived.
- Papyrus that survived was probably of the best quality and might have had durability treatment as good as that applied to deceased pharaohs. A modern digital counterpart would be nickel disks.[377]
- By the time that many of the surviving papyri were created, their technology had been refined for several centuries. Digital documents were first created about 40 years ago. Who knows how durable digital media will become?
- Paper needs to be durable partly because it is so difficult to copy its contents to another carrier. Since they make copying easy, digital media are useful without long-term durability. Good digital content is replicated many times, increasing its likelihood of survival. Did the Egyptians create even five copies of important papyri?
- Storage spaces for surviving papyri—Egyptian monuments in a dry climate—were engineered for durability, not for ready access. The modern

---

[376] Huttenlocher 2000, *On DigiPaper and the Dissemination of Electronic Documents*, shows how to record digital information on paper at several times the density of conventional printing, but still much less densely than is routine with magnetic recording. It seems unlikely that a business case will ever be made for developing the machinery and infrastructure to deploy this technology.

[377] Robertson 1996, *Digital Rosetta Stone*.

comparison might be a sealed stone cavern. Special physical facilities are used for archives based on paper. It therefore seems reasonable to consider caverns for digital archives if doing so diminishes the risks.

- Some paper is durable; other paper is not.[378] For instance, books printed between about 1880 and about 1930 are on "acid paper," which contains residual sulfuric acid that is gradually burning it up.
- Color photographs fade.

Thus, the specifics do not support a firm assertion that "information in digital form is more fragile than … papyrus" or paper. A realistic comparison test for durability of a digital medium might be to write something onto each of 100 nickel crystals, to seal and store each crystal under 50 feet of nearly solid rock, and to inspect their contents a century later. Sampling the stored data in 100 years would be accelerated testing, since the assertion is 3,000 years of storage.

A plausible comparative statistic would be storage effectiveness—integrating content amount over time. Some paper has stored about 3,000 characters per page for 500 years, i.e., for a 300 page book the retention has been about 10^9 character-years. A hard disk drive (of roughly the same size, weight, and price as a book) can be counted on to save about 200 gigabytes for about five years, i.e., about 10^{12} character-years. By this measure, today's magnetic technology is 1,000 times more effective as a storage medium than is paper.

10.1 Media Longevity

As in every engineering discipline, failure prediction enables responsive policy and action.

Lifetime predictions of storage media are complicated and controversial.[379] They are complicated because many chemical and physical conditions contribute to degradation and eventual failure. They are difficult to predict because the only forecast mechanism is accelerated aging at high temperatures with moisture and contaminants. However, the specific chemical mechanisms by which polymers and composite materials deteriorate are rarely known. Even if they were known, to determine how their rates change with temperature would be difficult and expensive. Even less is known about the prediction of physical degradation mechanisms, such as cracking, delaminating, and the effects of particulate contaminants.

---

[378]   Langendoen 2004, *The Metamorfoze Project.*

[379]   Van Bogart 1998, *Storage Media Life Expectancies.*

10.1.1 Magnetic Disks

Computer centers have long known that all media fail, some sooner than others, some more predictably than others. Data should be copied to new media when sampling tests suggest doing so to be timely, and replicated to multiple locations.[380] Whether the lifetime of a digital storage volume is five years or 20 years is of little importance. Maintaining large numbers of digital objects requires the ability to migrate data to new media. A regimen of media refreshing has value beyond avoiding information loss because of the finite media lifetimes.

New media typically store at least twice as much data as the previous versions, usually for roughly the same cost per storage volume. Copying a collection onto new media requires half as many cartridges, half the floor space, and lower ongoing expenditures for electricity and cartridge handling. The lifetime media cost for an existing collection will forever remain bounded, being approximately twice the original media cost. (This is because the series $1 + \frac{1}{2} + \frac{1}{4} + \ldots$ sums to 2. The projection is somewhat optimistic, since the current rate with which storage density is improving will not continue forever. Today's exponential increase in the amount of data will probably also abate.) The dominant cost to support a continued migration onto new media is the operational support needed to handle them.

Many data collections are doubling in size more quickly than annually. For them, copying the entire collection to new media will take less effort than storing the new data of a single year. Migration to media with faster access and read/write rate and increased parallelism (Fig. 27) is the only way to ensure accessibility of archived data. The governing metric for a collection is the time required to read the entire collection. If this is not less than a day or two, a collection will become unmanageable.

Except for very large collections, the current best digital preservation medium might be the HDD because we can easily automate error and failure testing, making a problem with any library holding apparent soon after it occurs, and remedying this with a backup copy. We can limit such remedial action to the blobs at risk.

10.1.2 Magnetic Tapes

Predicting lifetimes of magnetic tapes is particularly difficult. Acetate-based tapes and microfilm[14] rapidly burn up; the smell of vinegar signals their imminent demise. Many polyester-based tapes are at risk from dete-

---

[380] Tabata 2005, *A Collaboration Model between Archival Systems ... by an Enclose-and-Deposit Method*, http://www.iwaw.net/05/papers/iwaw05-tabata.pdf.

rioration of the binder holding their magnetic particles. No tape end-of-life predictions are reliable, partly because of variations within single products dependent on each tape's unique history.

Some vendors are claiming multiple decade tape life, e.g., IBM for LTO tape media.[381] For large users, automated tape libraries with quality monitoring software does make sense within the context of a refreshing regimen. Whatever the lifetime of the tape, a repository needs to plan for the fact that the tape drive mechanism and storage subsystem enjoy only a limited guarantee of device compatibility with future products.

10.1.3 Optical Media

Much has been written about how long a compact disk (CD) will survive with its data intact.[382] Published reports suggest that the topic is controversial.[383] CDs are so new that historical information about their durability is not available. Laboratory testing of CDs under conditions that stress them in ways that resemble aging[384] suggest that the best quality CDs might reliably retain their data for decades or longer[385] if stored optimally. (Media lifetimes depend on chemicals used, physical structure, storage temperature, humidity, light exposure, mechanical stress, air quality, and manufacturing conditions. The quality of the recording machine and the copying speed also affect lifetimes.)

Volume reliability is measured as error or failure rates. Specification of safe duration periods is likely to mislead. That different error correction encodings can be applied improves an already good situation at the cost of making prediction even more difficult to explain to most people.

RW (read-write) disks are known to fail early, and should not be used for archival storage. Recordable CDs use dyes that change color or reflectivity when heated by lasers. Phthalocyanine, azo, and cyanine dyes are common; different products have different life expectancy and stability.[386]

---

[381]   IBM, *Tape Storage,* http://www-03.ibm.com/servers/eserver/xseries/storage/tape.html.

[382]   This section is informed by private communications with Richard Hess, an audio engineer whose practice includes recovering the content of magnetic tapes at risk.

[383]   *Life Expectancy of Recordable CD Disks*, suggesting a life of only two to five years, http://blog.eogn.com/eastmans_online_genealogy/2006/01/life_expectancy.html..

[384]   Audio Engineering Society 2000, *Standard for audio preservation*.

Hartke 2001, *Measures of CD-R Longevity,* http://www.mam-a.com/technology/quality/longevity.htm, exemplifies manufacturer's specifications.

Slattery 2004, *Stability Comparison of Recordable Optical Discs.*

[385]   The Optical Storage Technology Association suggests that optical recordable media will last 50 to 200 years, http://www.osta.org/technology/cdqa13.htm.

[386]   Iraci 2005, *The Relative Stabilities of Optical Disc Formats.*

Factory pressed CDs are made by pressing data as pits in the reflective material. These pits are stable unless the disk is mechanically damaged or over-heated.

10.2 Replication to Protect Bit-Strings

Copies matter, and digital copies have the advantage that they can be made quickly, remotely, and without loss. For computing professionals this argument seems so overwhelmingly reasonable that it can be difficult to understand how fragile the whole interlocking system of duplicate copies and anticipated failures sounds to those schooled in the common sense principle that valuable materials should be stored on durable media. It is not unusual to see high-quality "gold" CDs (which were once actually made with an actual gold reflective layer) filling the role in today's grant proposals that reel-to-reel analog tape would have had several years ago as the true archival form. The media-based preservation mindset is hard to break.[378]

Preservation replication is somewhat simpler than computing installation backup because what is to be remembered are *bit sequences,* the unchanging values of the bit-strings the installation has been entrusted to protect. In other words, the bit sequence of a retrieved bit-string should be equal to the bit sequence of the string handed to the protection infrastructure at some earlier date. More simply, the information conveyed by a preserved bit-string is a value, not a frequently changing object. Replication management software can be set up to be extremely robust, providing access to nearly all network content even when a large fraction of the Internet is inaccessible to the client at hand. It can also provide each digital librarian with full autonomy to control which objects he makes available.[387]

Replication management in Fig. 26 provides bit-string safety using methods pioneered by the Stanford University DL group.[388] The Stanford implementation, a tool called LOCKSS (for "Lots of Copies Keeps Stuff Safe"), allows libraries to run Web caches for specific periodicals. Like the Import and End User Services modules, it operates according to rules specified and stored by an archive manager or database administrator. Interposing access control between it and the storage subsystem is necessary

---

[387] Software for preservation replication has similarities to that for peer-to-peer networks such as Kazaa and Gnutella.

[388] Crespo 1998, *Archival Storage for Digital Libraries.*

Cooper 2001, *Peer to peer data trading to preserve information.*

Reich 2001, *LOCKSS: A Permanent Web Publishing and Access System.* See also http://lockss.stanford.edu.

See also Weatherspoon 2001, *Silverback: A Global-Scale Archival System*, http://oceanstore.cs.berkeley.edu/publications/papers/pdf/silverback_sosp_tr.pdf .

to enforce mutual administrative autonomy of this repository and others, which might be distant and controlled by independent institutions.

LOCKSS was designed for a specific application—protecting images of scholarly periodicals held by academic libraries in the context of their financial agreements with scientific publishers. It seems that, as a consequence, it has built-in conformance to constraints for that application—constraints that might be inappropriate for other digital content classes. What other repository services will want is generalizations for librarians to specify content-class dependent rules (Fig. 25) for access control and other subscribers' limitations, replication rules, frequency and method of automatic checking for the integrity of originals and replicas, actions to be taken when the reliability of replica access falls below predetermined thresholds, and more. If we permit users access to replicas, we can provide reliable access paths to those instances.[389]

10.3   Repository Catalog ↔ Collection Consistency

Any repository manager (Fig. 26) can choose how to organize its catalog. He will not be hampered by the constraints of physical catalogs that used to be implemented with 3" × 5" index cards. He might accomplish this by choosing terms and indices to use in building a relational database that represents the catalog. He is likely to try to please the *designated community*—his most important clients, who are probably members of his own institution. For a large public library that caters to clients who expect its catalogs to be similar to those of other libraries, he will surely continue to choose in collaboration with colleagues in sister libraries.

We can create the catalog entries for any repository holding either by catalog DB updates originating in some information producer's interactive session or by extracting information from the holding itself. The former procedure is common in conventional libraries. This procedure is supported in many DL offerings. Often its agent is not the author of the holding, but a library administrator—a cataloger. Its reliability depends on the correspondence between the author's actions in preparing his submission and the cataloger's actions. While a third party could check for consistency, doing so would be so tedious that it might seldom be done. An error will probably be corrected only if some library patron discovers an inconsistency and reports it to a librarian.

---

[389]   Hildrum 2004, *Finding Nearby Copies of Objects in Peer-to-Peer Networks*, http://www.eecs.berkeley.edu/~samr/TheorySeminar/Abstracts/3-1-04.html.
Zhao 2005, *Tapestry: A Resilient Global-scale Overlay.*

The alternative, constructing catalog records from repository holdings, does not seem to have received the attention it merits.[390] Ideally, a repository would accept only accessions that meet its completeness criteria, including its requirements for accompanying metadata, requiring each information producer (as suggested in Fig. 26) to provide conforming metadata for his repository submissions. Then the catalog entries for accessions prepared this way could (and should) be built automatically as part of the object ingestion process.

This alternative has some valuable advantages, starting with automatic catalog/collection consistency. It also makes catalog rearrangement easy. Whenever the institution decides to improve information discovery convenience, search performance, or content accessibility by enhancing the catalog, it can choose whatever catalog DB table changes would effect the improvements and build the replacement catalog by running its digital object import service (Fig. 26) for each of its current holdings—a procedure that we can readily design for execution without disrupting ongoing repository service. This procedure would merely be a variant of what might be done for other purposes—copying digital object extracts into separate storage in order to arrange them conveniently for applications other than normal library services.

10.4 Collection Ingestion and Sharing

Information *ingestion* is the process whereby a repository accepts information properly, with careful checking that what is accepted conforms to published rules. *Metadata harvesting* is a process whereby metadata is extracted from information that has been received and possibly ingested into other repositories than the one of interest. Ideally, the metadata to be extracted would be what some metadata standard calls for, and the information source objects would conform to known, standardized formats. If these conditions are not met, the extracted metadata will almost surely be imperfect—perhaps so much so that human help is essential. Meeting them will probably not in all cases be sufficient for satisfactory automatic metadata generation.

The technologies for sharing metadata, for transferring collections between repositories, and for repository information ingestion are closely related.[391]

---

[390] It is, however, done at the Los Alamos National Laboratory. See Van de Sompel 2005, *aDORe: a Modular, Standards-based Digital Object Repository,* §3.

[391] Bekaert 2005, *A Standards-based Solution for the Accurate Transfer of Digital Assets.*
Witten 2005, *StoneD: A Bridge between Greenstone and DSpace.*

The Open Archives Initiative Protocol for Metadata Harvesting (OAI-PMH) is a lightweight protocol enabling access to Web accessible material from repositories interoperable for metadata sharing, publishing, and archiving.[392] It helps information providers make their metadata available to services using HTTP and XML by a community process that defines metadata formats for sharing. With it, metadata from multiple sources can be gathered into one database from which access is provided for these harvested, or aggregated, data.

However, an expensive pilot instance based on over 100 National Science Digital Library (NSDL) repositories suggests that early hopes for semiautomatic aggregation of large collections were unduly optimistic. The stumbling block has been the quality of metadata provided outside the professional culture of institutional libraries. The experimenters, who criticize their own work,[393] suggest that the difficulty has been lack of personnel who combine (1) domain expertise that includes knowledge of the resources collected and their pedagogical application; (2) formal cataloging experience that includes application of controlled vocabularies and proper formatting of data such as names and dates; and (3) computing expertise that includes use of XML, formal schema, Unicode and UTF-8, and HTTP.

Pessimism about the long-range prospects for infrastructure illustrated by this NSDL experiment would be premature. Many of the difficulties in (2) and (3) could be mitigated by metadata preparation tools that parsed inputs for comparison with BNF representations of the applicable standards and conventions. This could be repeated within repository ingest filters (suggested by the Digital Object Import module of Fig. 26)—filters that refuse to ingest flawed submissions, returning error analyses to information producers and/or cataloging librarians. Since the disappointing results from this NSDL experiment have only recently been reported, it is too early to expect reports of solutions, but the potential remedies are so obvious that attempts will almost certainly be launched.

We cannot help wondering whether the skills gap highlighted above is a transitory problem. As suggested in §2.8, our children are more comfortable with digital technology, and more skilled in its use, than we are. Over time, the digital librarians who participated in the NSDL experiment will be trained in routine use of digital technology and/or replaced by younger staff members who grew up with computers. Authors of original materials

---

[392]   Van de Sompel 2004, *Resource Harvesting within the OAI-PMH Framework*. For an *OAI-PMH tutorial*, see http://www.oaforum.org/tutorial/. Software tools supporting OAI-PMH are described at http://www.openarchives.org/tools/tools.html.

[393]   Lagoze 2006, *Metadata aggregation and "automated digital libraries"*.

might also become more skilled, particularly if repositories reject objects that do not meet higher syntactic standards than have been commonplace heretofore.

Some effort is being expended to extract metadata (semi)automatically from documents,[394] but independent evaluations of such efforts do not yet seem to have been written. The initial promise of semiautomatic library creation has not been realized.[393]

10.5 Summary

Recent disasters around the world highlight the need to improve planning and preparation to ensure the survival of library collections and cultural materials.

Contrary to opinions expressed so often that they might be accepted as realistic, the storage effectiveness of magnetic recording is greater than that of paper. The appropriate measure combines storage capacity and likely duration for equivalent cost and space.

Halting or reversing the deterioration of media is neither a likely prospect nor required for digital preservation.[395] This fact might contradict preservation specialists' training, perhaps even seem an attack on their professional culture. Although one must replace digital substrate from time to time, repositories can manage media inexpensively, reliably, and almost automatically. The labor involved is roughly commensurate with that for maintenance of book and media stacks.

During this book's manuscript final editing phase, a UNESCO report summed up opinions of using optical storage media for preservation with:

> "While recordable optical discs are viable tools in the access to and dissemination of digital information of all kinds, it is strongly recommended that professional data storage methods, as developed by the IT industry, should be used. All digital carriers are to some extent unreliable, however, data tape and hard disc systems are made reliable because technological testing, copying and management systems are implemented to support the data carrier and the quality of its content, maintain and manage the integrity of the data. These systems are feasible for storing critical data even under climatically and financially sub-optimal conditions. No viable automatic testing and management system exists to make optical disc reliable, and

---

[394] Greenberg 2005, *Final Report for the AMeGA (Automatic Metadata Generation Applications) Project.*

National Library of New Zealand Metadata Extraction Tool, http://www.natlib.govt.nz/en/whatsnew/4initiatives.html#extraction.

Aiolli 2002, *Semiautomatic Annotation in E-business Applications.*

[395] Seadle 2004, *Sound Preservation: From Analog to Digital.*

consequently any archival use of optical systems must depend on a manual approach using people and testing equipment ..."[396]

What is to be remembered are *bit sequences,* the unchanging values of bit-string objects that repositories are entrusted to protect, not the carrier objects. What we really want—bit-string longevity—is a different challenge than media longevity.

Locating a record depends on identifier-to-location mapping—a catalog function. Error-free retrieval depends on consistency between a repository's catalogs and its collection. To achieve high performance information discovery, it might from time to time be necessary to rearrange a catalog's metadata and other content extracts, and to derive other search indices, without changing any document received. A reliable way to avoid inconsistency between a repository catalog and its holdings is to mechanize catalog creation by copying information from annotated digital objects. To minimize errors and labor costs, human beings should not be required to type metadata that can be copied.

The disappointing results of early experiments in semiautomatic library creation[393] might not be a good indicator of future performance. Current methods can be bolstered by better metadata editors and filters. It would help to have personnel truly comfortable with and sensitive to the strengths and weaknesses of computing tools.

---

[396]   Bradley 2006, Risks [of] Recordable CDs and DVDs as Reliable Storage Media.

11 Durable Evidence

On the digital landscape … it is still relatively easy for a creator to alter or retract previously released information. Such actions can eliminate or overlay significant content and thereby corrupt the record. It is also relatively easy in an on-line environment—and equally confusing for purposes of preserving information integrity— … to make available concurrently multiple representations of [what someone] considers to be the same work, …

To address these problems, a wide range of cryptographic techniques … exist … These could serve well to mark and identify specific, canonical versions and editions of textual, audio and visual works, and to establish trusted, protected channels of distribution for those objects.

Garrett 1996, *PDITF* p.14

From the perspective of the most demanding consumer, every change to recorded information introduces risk that what he depends upon will have been distorted significantly—perhaps an asserted truth will be transformed into an asserted falsehood, or the decimal point of a number will be shifted, sending astronauts to the sun instead of the moon. That the author of a change might be the agent of an archival institution is irrelevant, as are the possibilities that this editor has the best of intentions or that the change might be only an additional metadata attribute or document reference.

Concern about technology impairing authenticity is hardly new. Robert Cecil, Lord Salisbury, at the time Prime Minister of the U. K., was an enthusiastic tinkerer.

Salisbury quickly appreciated the political implications [of] an increase in the speed of communications …. When he was staying at the home of one of his MPs … in February 1893 prior to switching on the world's first full-gauged electric railway in Liverpool, the house was connected up to the chamber of the Commons. "I can hear someone talking about Uganda," Salisbury announced delightedly. He later told his host: "I hate political functions; but this was a very different occasion. It was one of the most interesting twenty-four hours I have passed." He did not trust the telephone altogether, however, … for transacting official business, "as there was nothing to vouch for its genuineness."

Roberts 1999, *Salisbury: Victorian Titan*

The current chapter focuses on technical design to manage records to be *evidence*—a design that satisfies archivists' criteria for prudent custody of socially important evidence.[397] Solutions developed for content that is mostly represented by paper documents, however, lend themselves poorly to adaptation for digital content. This is partly because of technical

---

[397] Adaptation of Gladney 2004. Compare Hackel 2005, *ArchiSafe … recordkeeping strategy.*

reasons, and partly because methods used for works on paper require more professional attention than is likely to be affordable for the flood of digital content people will want to preserve.

Risks to end users of cultural documents are mostly low. However, how can we today know how future readers might use and depend on repository holdings? The question is practical if somebody's finances, health, or reputation could be impacted by flawed information.

Answers must address the concern that the easy mutability of digital documents creates reliability exposures. Audit procedures (§8.1.5) would need to discover whether some unscrupulous or careless repository administrator has altered any records in the decades that they have been held. Since the number of digital holdings is likely to be very large, this procedure needs to be (semi)automatic.

11.1 Structure of Each Trustworthy Digital Object

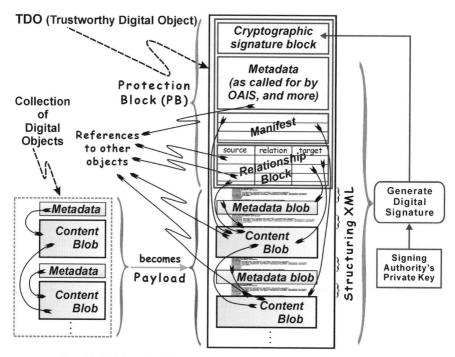

Fig. 32: MAC-sealed TDO constructed from a digital object collection.
(Notice that some links are to blobs and other links are into blobs.)

An input file set (left-hand side of Fig. 32) might be scholarly manuscripts, or artistic performances, engineering specifications, a medical history, government embassy records, a computer program with its documentation, military commands, or any expression of ideas that somebody wants to save as history. However, such a file set would not, without certain additions, be evidence of the authenticity of its own content—or of any other content.

The auditor's phrase "indelibly recorded as a collaboration of two or more people," together with some consumers' need for documented contextual information (§1.2), suggests what is needed. Each information producer should include as much contextual information as he believes is needed to persuade the eventual consumer of this information's authenticity. This should include information about the creation of the record itself. Furthermore, "indelibly recorded" implies that the record should be sealed to prevent undetectable tampering. Thus, each producer should make each DO the payload of a TDO, as suggested by the right-hand side of Fig. 32, with a *protection block* (*PB*), and should seal this bundle with a *message authentication code* (*MAC*) that he signs. The structure of each TDO conforms to the MPEG-21 standard for digital multimedia objects (§7.2.7). A concrete syntax for its depicted structuring XML has been described.[398]

The large number of links and the Relationship Block of Fig. 32 are responsive to Wittgenstein's and Carnap's teaching that any structure is a set of relationships.

Any TDO might itself be a payload portion. In other words, TDOs can be nested; this contributes to document version management and to control of essential document interdependencies.

Most digital objects will have related versions in the repository network. We can signal this special kind of relationship by a shared attribute that has the semantics of an identifier—a *digital resource identifier* (DRI §7.3.4). Each producer must decide whether to use a new DRI or the DRI of some existing TDO. (Only producers have the authority and insight to estimate when users will appreciate that a new document is sufficiently closely related to a prior document to do this; machines cannot do it without human guidance.)

A TDO without payload can communicate metadata. For instance, it might convey identity certificates or descriptions of individuals.

Fraud-resistant preservation depends on the infrastructure described in §11.2. The security and integrity of each preserved TDO depends on the secrecy of the signing cryptographic key. Consumers' ability to test the authenticity and provenance of a TDO further depends on evidence that the producer's corresponding public cryptographic key is indeed associated with the purported producer.

---

[398] Bekaert 2003, *Using MPEG-21 DIDL to Represent Complex Digital Objects.*

Building a TDO can be made convenient by embedding the creation process within the Fig. 30 workflow from author to editor, to publisher, and so on.

11.1.1 Record Versions: a Trust Model for Consumers

What might lead a Fig. 2 consumer to consider a bit-string to be an authentic version of an archival record? He is likely to require that all the following characteristics seem to be truly satisfied:

- That neither sloppy handling nor deliberate mischief has impeached the authenticity of the record copy delivered to him;
- That the underlying record (document) is described by a credible provenance assertion that represents enough of the record's history;
- That at least two well informed people who are unlikely to collude in misrepresentation have agreed that the record content is honestly described by the corresponding provenance assertion; and
- That all the information just mentioned is reliably bound to evidence that it has not been changed since this event of agreement.
- Such consumer's decisions will contain many subjective elements that cannot be replaced by objectively testable assertions (§3.3).

An archival institution is likely to assert that its content deliveries meet such requirements. If it manages paper-based records, it is further likely to mention business controls protecting its records against alteration during delivery to any client or by any client. However, such methods are poorly suited to serving Internet clients.

The TDO structure and the §11.1.3 discipline for saving the derivative of a work suffice for choosing a 'version' definition that avoids the §5.0 difficulties with "the original." We define *version* by saying that a new version of a work is created whenever a custodian certifies a representation of the work and turns this over to a new custodian who validates the embedded provenance information and signals his validation by certifying also. In other words, custody transfer is the event that defines an archival version, and the first such transfer defines when the work is "born digital." (The reader who does not immediately see that this choice is socially appropriate might consider how human birth dates are chosen.)

11.1.2 Protection Block Content and Structure

Each TDO is a MAC-sealed[399] package of a protection block and a payload that represents the information of interest (Fig. 32). The payload is a

---

[399]   Herzberg 2002, *Securing XML,* describes how to do this for XML packages.

multifarious sequence of content and metadata blocks that might include interconnecting links. The embedded *protection block* (PB—Fig. 33) represents metadata that might include references into the payload and to external objects.[400]

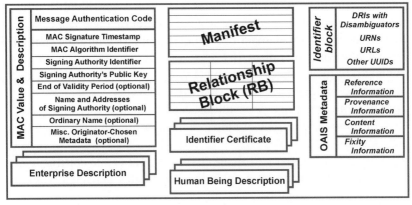

Fig. 33: Contents of a protection block (PB)

A protection block consists of the following:

- An identifier block containing at least one URN, and any number of other self-identifiers; an object might be a member of several families and indicate this with a DRI for each family.
- A MAC description block containing fields for essential and optional information related to signing, perhaps extending what is specified for X.509; the essential information includes a time stamp, a signature algorithm identifier, a signing authority identifier, and the signing authority's public key value.[401] Each item of nonessential information can be any scalar, including, but not limited to, the signing authority's name, address, e-mail address, etc.; a date beyond which the signer believes the digital object will not be useful; and a text specification of what TDO properties are certified and what facts and commitments are not certified, including liability disclaimers and the like.
- A *manifest*. Each manifest element is a value set (§6.4.3) describing the corresponding payload block, e.g., the nth manifest element describes the nth payload block; it might also identify an external object, such as another digital object or a material object.

---

[400] Compare Hackel 2005, *ArchiSafe*, pp. 19–22, http://europa.eu.int/comm/secretariat_general/edoc_management/dlm_forum/doc/26_Hackel_06-10-05pm.pdf.

[401] XML packaging for signing with a time stamp is standardized in W3C's *XML Advanced Electronic Signatures,* http://www.w3.org/TR/XAdES/. See also *XML-Signature Syntax and Processing*, http://www.w3.org/TR/xmldsig-core/.

- An optional *relationship block* (*RB*) with any number of 3-cell rows. (§4.5) The first and last cells in a row typically identify some blob in the TDO or some external object, or are a bookmark into such an object. The middle cell, describing the relationship between these objects, is typically encoded as a value set (§6.4.3) that might identify other objects, and might also include descriptions of the first and last cells.
- More generally, any element of a relationship block might be the identifier of any kind of object (§7.3.5), a collection identifier (§7.3.4), a bookmark into an object or an object extent (§6.4.1), a scalar value such as a number or character string, or a value set (§6.4.3).
- Zero or more enterprise descriptions, each formatted as a value set.
- Zero or more descriptions of human beings or human roles, each formatted as a value set.
- Zero or more identifier certificates, which might create certificate chains that authenticate signers of included certificates sufficiently for large eventual user populations.
- A standard metadata block, perhaps conforming to and extending METS.

A PB might further contain or refer to documents that contribute integrity and provenance evidence, such as information about digital watermarks and fingerprints applied to payload elements, and might identify standards and programs used for encoding content blob renderings.

11.1.3 Document Packaging and Version Management

To prepare a preservation version, an author might package his book draft as a TDO. The Fig. 30 editors might package their extensively revised version as a TDO reusing the DRI chosen by the author. The publisher might share this version with a copyright depository library and request a new TDO with standard cataloging metadata and endorsed with the library's signature. The library could reuse the DRI first provided by the author in creating a new TDO that it returns to the publisher; this would be a good version for the publisher to disseminate (Fig. 34).

When the time comes for a new edition, the participants might repeat these steps with a revised manuscript, and reuse the DRI of the original manuscript. Each participant might include new information to enhance the work. If the book is about computation, the author might include new sample programs, the publisher might include new links to Web sources for related software, and the library might include new links to specialized bibliographies. Reusing the earlier DRI value would facilitate intellectual property management and would help readers who care to audit the work's history.

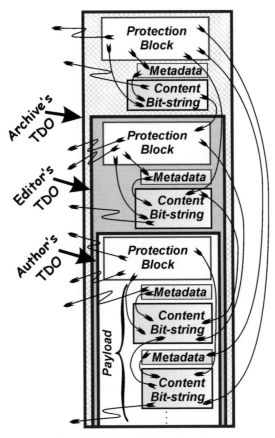

Fig. 34: Nesting TDO predecessors

Many years later a reader who finds a version could request all works with the same DRI. If both editions have been stored in widely accessible repositories, he would receive, after filtering out duplicates, two versions each including its own provenance metadata (Fig. 32 and Fig. 33). From the library's time stamped signatures he might believe that both were valid. From the protection information described in §11.1.2 he would learn additional parts of the work's history. Furthermore, he could compare their payloads to gain confidence that both were trustworthy, and also to glean change details that scholars sometimes find interesting.

As Fig. 34 suggests, later document versions might replace a payload bit-string by an edited version. Because this relationship cannot be verified reliably by bit-string comparison, it should be recorded with a row entry in the Relationship Block.

In the most secure application of trustworthy packaging, each successive producer would include in the TDO he creates the entire TDO he received.

If every producer does this, the latest TDO will reflect the entire history of the work. (From an audit perspective, the significant events in a history are the transfers of a work from each producer to his successor in the chain of custody. These are the only occasions in which two people assuredly "see" the same version of the work.) Although this structure will often speed and sometimes simplify a consumer's examination of document history and of any certificates he wants to examine as part of authenticity testing, it will not always be convenient. Certain information helpful, or even essential, for interpreting TDO content will be so widely used that it will almost certainly be saved as independent objects to which many TDOs refer. For instance, this will be done with schema information and with UVC programs (§12.2.2) needed to render complex blobs. For such information, we can use pointers as in the structure suggested by Fig. 35.

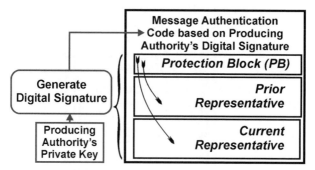

Fig. 35: Audit trail element—a kind of digital documentary evidence

In the basic audit trail element scheme (Fig. 35), a *representative* is a complete TDO, a reference to a TDO, or a reference to a TDO portion. A producer adding metadata to some TDO he received might package this new TDO with only a link to the previous TDO. If this new TDO is given the same DRI value as that of the previous TDO, consumers will still find it relatively easy to retrieve the prior TDO and assess how it and the new one are related.

It might seem expensive to carry a growing set of versions through every transfer of control and into eventual repositories. However, by the time the kinds of transactions illustrated occur, it is already known that the work is sufficiently valuable to deserve careful business controls and preservation. Each transfer version will probably represent a significant effort by an author, editor, or archive employee, so that the implied incremental expense to make it as useful as possible will be relatively small. Decreasing prices for digital storage and communication bandwidth will make doing this economically favorable for end user convenience.

References to the prerequisites for TDO interpretation would introduce a security loophole if they were used without further ado. Were such a referent to be improperly altered before its use, the result could mislead the eventual TDO consumer. Conceivably, some clever criminal could exploit this weakness to perpetrate widespread fraud. Doing so would be particularly easy with unprotected UVC programs. However, this loophole is readily addressed. Wherever the TDO architecture described above calls for an included TDO identifier, it should be accompanied by the associated MAC and the public portion of the asymmetric key pair used to sign it. With this, a suspicious consumer could immediately check whether the referenced TDO is what the producer referred to. Such checking could, and perhaps should, be built into TDO retrieval procedures.

11.2 Infrastructure for Trustworthy Digital Objects

A certification—an unforgeable signed sealing with a message authentication code, can make a bit-string reliable for some applications. Authenticity evidence must be based on the security and credibility of records of producers' identities and their cryptographic private keys. These, in turn, must be based on facts that people—the public at large—trust. The intended clients of a certifying institution might include the entire citizenry of a large geography. We can engender their trust by grounding claims on relatively simple public assertions by some institution that has little to gain and much to lose by misrepresentation of the information it publishes—an institution, such as a national library, that is widely trusted to handle documents like the one in question correctly and faithfully. We call such an institution a *trustworthy institution* (TI).

A TI assertion might be represented by a WWW and newspaper publication of its own public key, which it announces will be used in signing certificates and message authentication codes, and an offer to issue identifier certificates to certain organization classes. For instance, each of a dozen or more national libraries or archives might advertise something like, "La Bibliothèque nationale de France (BNF) offers certification of the public key of any [some class of institution] that provides [certain information about itself] by a visit of its accredited representative to BNF premises. The BNF public key from [beginning date] to [end date] is [key value]." From a few such starting points, we could create a network of interdependent facts that will allow a TDO recipient to evaluate claims of veracity and authority made in and about the TDO.

Part of what a TI must do to qualify itself is to publish its certification criteria and to persuade its intended clients that the institution depends in essential ways on its reputation for integrity and competence.

Furthermore, it should submit to occasional independent audits of the adequacy of its external commitments and its compliance in its internal workings with these commitments. This would be a much simpler audit than that called for by RLG (§8.4). It would check adherence to the quality specifications for acceptable input and production of new TDOs, as well as the management controls on the use and protection of the institution's private keys. Many programmers have the knowledge needed to perform such an audit.

The certification criteria would typically include specific requirements for each document's metadata, and also submission by an agent the TI knows and trusts for such submissions. To help manage a large traffic of certification requests, compliance testing can be at least partially automated (in the Digital Object Import module of Fig. 26). Each proper TDO would include or refer not only to a MAC signed by its producer, but also to descriptions and identifier certificates of every individual producer in its history (or cryptographically secured references to such certificates). Each TI agent who certifies a document acts as producer who should diligently judge the authenticity of information that he will certify. Flawed certifications will jeopardize the reputation for integrity and quality that creates and maintains the trusted status of his employer.

A TI can enlarge the community that might trust the works that it certifies by persuading other TIs to certify its public keys using public key identifier certificates conforming to the X.509 standard.[402] Each such TI would participate in creating a web of trust (§8.1.4) by publishing the public key certificates it has signed to endorse the public-key-to-identity mapping of its sister TIs. Such mutual endorsement can be made safe against "man in the middle"[403] attacks by institutional agents exchanging public keys in face-to-face meetings. The benefit to each participating TI would be a reciprocal endorsement.

11.2.1 DO Certification by a Trustworthy Institution (TI)

After a TI receives information from its producer, it must test this input and its knowledge of the producer to determine whether these satisfy its own published criteria for document certification. If they do, it should create a new DO by copying, editing, and augmenting the input metadata with a new metadata block that conforms to standards and to its own published specifications. When this editing is complete, it should copy the resulting DO into a signing computer (SC in Fig. 26) that it can detach

---

[402] Gerck 1998, *The Unabridged X.509 Certificate.*

[403] Schneier 2000, *Secrets and Lies: Digital Security in a Networked World,* p. 48.

from the Internet in order to protect the sensitive signing step and its private key from Trojan Horse attacks.

Whenever it contains a sufficient input batch, its operator must detach the SC from all networks and then load it with the TI's private (secret) key. The operator will then start a utility program that (1) tests that each input meets all TI-required quality criteria, (2) fills in missing PB portions into each input, including metadata for the pending MAC, and (3) computes and adds the MAC, thereby finishing the TDO construction. Finally, the operator must remove the private key from the SC before he reattaches that computer to networks to send the newly certified TDOs to wherever they are wanted.

To assure users about the age of the TDOs it has sealed, and to protect its private key further, the TI could choose a new public/private key pair periodically—annually for instance—and destroy all copies of the expired private key. It should further publish the history of its public key values.[404] This mimics an eighteenth and nineteenth century Japanese practice, in which the censors of ukiyo-e ("pictures of a floating world") changed their seals approximately annually, doing so over a period of 200 years, and published these keys (Fig. 36) so that each became evidence of the print date of the pictures on which it recurred.[405]

| 15. 1842 | 16. 1842 | 17. 1843-5 | 18. 1843-5 | 19. 1843-5 | 20. 1843-5 | 21. 1843-5 |

Fig. 36: Japanese censor seals: ancient practice to mimic in digital form

The SC should be exclusively devoted to creating institutional MACs that convert DOs into TDOs as a security measure for protecting the private key of the TI. Whenever it is attached to any network, the SC must be guarded against containing any TI private key. It might more securely protect the private key never to attach this security computer to the network. Instead, one can transfer objects requiring certification onto a Write-Once CD, using this as input for sealing, and transfer the resulting TDOs back to a networked machine with a fresh Write-Once CD. By checking that the input CD contains no stowaway files, this procedure would make virus invasions unlikely. (The input files need never be executed on the SC, so that the risk of virus entry opportunity is avoided.)

---

[404] Maniatis 2002, *Enabling the Archival Storage of Signed Documents,* suggests a different solution. See also Wallace 2000, *Trusted Archive Protocol,* http://middleware.internet2.edu/pki04/proceedings/trusted_archiving.pdf.

[405] Illing 1980, *The Art of Japanese Prints,* p. 170.

A TI would make misappropriation of TI private keys difficult if it followed the above procedures and also conformed to administrative security controls. How carefully this process and related procedures need to be managed will depend on the kinds of information that the private key will be used to certify, for example, keys for military applications will require more care than keys for scholarly publications.

11.2.2 Consumers' Tests of Authenticity and Provenance

Accumulating certificate signing events described will elaborate Fig. 23 to create a Fig. 37 web-of-trust-based certificate forest.

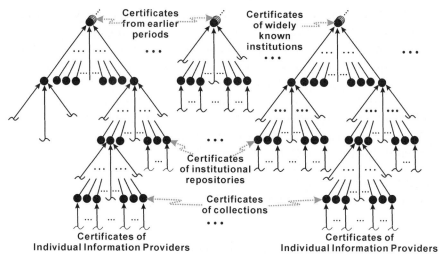

Fig. 37: A certificate forest

A cautious consumer will not judge a received TDO to be authentic unless he believes certain things:

- That the enclosed MAC demonstrates that the TDO has not been altered after it was certified;
- That the enclosed identifications of the most recent MAC signatory and date are authentic;
- That the producer of each stage in the TDO's history had the authority to make her/his changes;
- That the final signatory's procedure for generating TDOs is sound and includes judging the authenticity of information it includes in any TDO it creates; and
- That the TI (trustworthy institution) signing procedure has been correctly executed.

As evidence, the consumer will have the published public keys of the world's TIs, endorsed by other TIs' cross-certifications, and the certified public keys and known identities and roles of TDO producer chains, which are carried in TDOs. If each TDO embeds all its prior versions, the consumer will quickly be able to identify the specific changes made by each producer. The consumer might additionally be able to judge the TDO payload (Fig. 32) as corroborative evidence and might also use the context provided by other documents that he knows professionally.

Locating such certificates, certificates for signatories of each interesting identifier certificate, and producer descriptions whose content the consumer chooses to inspect are graph traversals.[406] That each document referred to is the correct object is validated by comparing its MACs to the MAC value stored within the link at the time it was constructed.

The correct rendering (for human consumption) of a collection member is likely to depend on the correctness of other information objects, some of which might not be in the collection. Even if an object is protected so that its bit-string source is known to be authentic, changes in the objects on which its rendering depends might mislead its user. For sensitive objects, this poses a security risk that should be mitigated by time stamped MACs within the rendering tools used and checked.

A software tool is needed to help the consumer inspect a TDO and extract portions of interest. He might have received the TDO in e-mail from its producer or from a third party. With the appropriate tool he will be able, without further ado, to extract and exploit blobs that interest him. He will also be able to use PB contents together with published key values and published TI acceptance policies to assess to what extent he will trust TDO payload components. This task can be automated if the endorsing TI has expressed its quality criteria as production rules of the kind used in artificial intelligence applications.

This tool might be a Web browser application similar to today's interactive research library interfaces. The challenge is to make it intuitively convenient for untutored users, who should not need even help text to formulate queries or traverse reference and certificate networks. Such a search service crawler would exploit other information in each PB immediately, including its semantic relationship information.

Search services should provide for returning URL sets of at least three different kinds: (1) URLs satisfying the query; (2) all URLs of (1) augmented by URLs whose DRIs coincide with those found in the response (1); or (3) the response (2) pruned to remove URLs for duplicate TDOs. The graphs of related documents would be easily constructed.

---

[406] Caronni 2000, *Walking the Web of Trust* discusses optimal traversal algorithms.

Graphical interfaces might be convenient to browse and traverse relationship networks.[407]

11.3 Other Ways to Make Documents Trustworthy

§11.2.2 suggests basing consumer's authenticity testing on the validity of a cryptographic key. This key is recursively testable for validity according to an acyclic graph of public keys that are rooted in the published keys of a few widely known institutions (Fig. 37). Each step of the certification chain can be tested to check that it has not been falsified. This method works because its execution is easily controlled administratively, because it is easy and inexpensive to apply, and because responsibilities are partitioned so that it would be against the interests of certifying institutions to permit fraud.

Waugh suggests another method of showing that a particular public key belonged to a particular signer at the time a preserved object was signed.[408] A well known publisher might use the same certification key-pair for many works. The user interested in the authenticity of a work issued could check whether its public key value is identical to that of a body of works from the publisher. This is likely to be acceptable to a user who is satisfied with knowing that the work is truly from the alleged source.

As an example of why this makes sense, consider the outré case of someone who wants evidence that a certain play is by William Shakespeare rather than by Christopher Marlowe. Unless this reader is interested in the narrow historical question of whether the true author of all Shakespeare's plays was in fact Marlowe, nobody really cares about the connection of the plays to a particular collection of buried bones. What might be interesting is whether the author of *Cymbeline* is the same as that of *Hamlet*.[409]

Yet another method of time certification is based on the administrative independence of repositories belonging to and managed by unrelated institutions. If the same document has been independently stored in several individually credible repositories, its eventual consumer can test whether the supposedly independent instances are sufficiently similar. For this to be proof against fraud, there must be accessible, unforgeable evidence that the document's producer himself delivered each instance to a credible inde-

---

[407] *Aduna Autofocus* exemplifies such graphical browsers; http://aduna.biz/products/autofocus/.

[408] Waugh 2002, *On the use of digital signatures in the preservation of electronic objects.*

[409] For amusement, see the Christopher Marlowe anagrams at Shakespeare's grave, available at http://www.geocities.com/chr_marlowe/shakespeare_epitaphs.html.

pendent repository, rather than that a single deposited instance was copied among repositories.

This might be made verifiable by the firm binding of each repository's credible assertion that it received its instance from the producer rather than from some third party—a provenance certificate for its holding. For cautious consumers, the solution must be proof against independent misbehavior by anyone, including any repository employee. Any reader who cares to do so can surely work out the details whereby a repository can test, prove, and certify that the provider of a document copy is also its producer.

11.4 Summary

When information is cryptographically packaged together with its own provenance assertion, and this evidence shows itself to be intact, a consumer can be confident that the information is authentic. We call a data object packaged this way a Trustworthy Digital Object (TDO).

One can transfer the loci of trust from numerous objects that are individually relatively large to a few small objects—from document copies to a few cryptographic keys whose secret portions are the private keys of a few widely trusted institutions. These private keys can be protected easily and inexpensively against improper disclosure. The TDO method binds three generic sources of trust—information with which a consumer can decide whether to trust the provenance and integrity of a TDO, i.e., the context of cited documents, especially linked TDOs, whose contents can be judged for consistency with the content at issue; access to previous TDO versions, either by including them in the TDO payload (Fig. 34) or by their availability by Internet searches based on shared resource identifiers; and links to descriptors of each TDO's producers and, through them, to a network of identity certificates rooted in the public keys of respected institutions.

Most documents will rely on other documents for their reliable interpretation. Such dependencies will be highly recursive, but can be grounded in a small number of documents that articulate data processing standards, such as ISO Unicode, and ontologies for the topics at hand. This leads to heavy use of links and to our needing graphic programs for conveniently navigating dependency graphs to show the values represented within each node.

Object encapsulation and sealing are not new ideas. TDO properties that make it possible to test authenticity include the following:

- Each TDO package includes all metadata needed as evidence of its content blobs' provenances; these metadata are *OAIS*-compliant.

- Each TDO contains its own worldwide eternal and unique identifier, a URN, and ideally also a DRI denoting all the versions of a single work.
- Each TDO is cryptographically sealed to prevent undiscoverable changes.
- The cryptographic key management uses the Web of Trust model grounded in keys that widely trusted institutions publish and periodically replace with new keys, so that each key is evidence for the approximate date of signing.
- Each reference to an external object is accompanied by its referent's message authentication code.
- Each human being who edits a work being prepared for long-term storage nests or links to the version with which he started, thereby creating a reliable history;
- Each participant in the creation sequence usually is, or readily can become, acquainted with his predecessor and his successor. Thus, the public keys that validate authorized version deliveries can readily be shared without encountering well known PKI security risks.
- Any interesting collection can be defined by the links in a document. This is the precise digital equivalent of what research librarians have long called a *finding aid*.
- If each TDO carries sufficient metadata, we can build library catalogs and search indices automatically.

Such packaging is the digital equivalent of an ancient practice in which rulers certified their decrees with wax seals and formal information (dates, authority claims, etc.) within important documents. Adaptation of time-honored methods minimizes reliability dependencies on human processes.

The tree approach of Fig. 37 is both workable and efficient because it is grounded in a few root nodes, each anchoring many users' certificates, and because certificates can be published, with the publication records packaged within objects replicated in many repositories. The combination of having every object include or reference information needed to test its authenticity and of widespread replication among autonomous repositories can be managed so that the survival and testability of any included object does not depend on the survival of any repository institution—not even the institutions that provided the root certificates.

12 Durable Representation

We want unambiguous communication with future generations with whom dialog is impossible, without restricting what today's authors can communicate. For this, we need language that we can confidently expect our descendants to understand easily. This challenge is the kind of language problem that has been central to computer science since it emerged as a discipline in the 1960s. Its core can be restated as, "ensure that an arbitrary computer program will execute correctly on a machine whose architecture is unknown when the program is saved."

> The English logician A. M. Turing showed in 1937 (and various computing machine experts have put this into practice since then in various particular ways) that it is possible to develop code instruction systems for a computing machine which cause it to behave as if it were another, specified, computing machine. ...
>
> A code, which according to Turing's schema is supposed to make one machine behave as if it were another specific machine ... must do the following things. It must contain, in terms that the machine will understand and (purposively obey), instructions ... that will cause the machine to examine every order it gets and determine whether this order has the structure appropriate to an order of the second machine. It must then contain, in terms of the order system of the first machine, sufficient orders to make the machine cause the actions to be taken that the second machine would have taken under the influence of the order in question.
>
> The important result of Turing's is that in this way the first machine can be caused to imitate the behavior of any other machine.
>
> von Neumann 1956, The Computer and the Brain, pp.70–71

Durable encoding, described in this chapter, represents difficult content types with the aid of programs written in virtual machine code—the code of a machine we call a *UVC* (*Universal Virtual Computer*). This Turing-Machine-equivalent virtual machine[410] is simple compared to the designs of practical hardware. Its design can be specified completely, concisely, and unambiguously for future interpretation.[411]

Objects to be preserved might consist of several source files, each represented as a bit-stream in a Fig. 32 digital object collection, with labeled links between parts of the complete package. Much of each TDO will be encoded using XML, relations, encryption algorithms, and

---

[410] A concise account of Turing's invention of universal computers can be found in Davis 2000, *Engines of Logic*, Ch. 7.

Virtual machines have many uses. See Rosenblum 2005, *The Reincarnation of Virtual Machines*.

[411] This chapter adapts Gladney and Lorie 2005.

identifiers. These are governed by relatively simple standards that are widely used—standards that we can be reasonably confident will be completely and correctly understood many years into the future. As described in §11.1, metadata can, and should, record the representation of each TDO component.

The means for making each Fig. 32 content blob interpretable forever remains to be provided. What follows describes how this can be accomplished for a single content blob.

12.1   Representation Alternatives

We want information representation methods that can be embodied in tools whose use would be practical for information producers and consumers who do not have specialized skills or equipment.

12.1.1 How Can We Keep Content Blobs Intelligible?

Any information we want to save can be represented as a set of computer files—a set of bit-strings. In repositories, a digital entity is registered under a certain name, a bit-string copy of the entity is stored in a safe place, and an entity description is saved in a database that points to the stored bit-string. This pattern mimics the organization of ordinary libraries. However, unlike what happens with a physical book, the consumer cannot extract the information without a computer and, seeing it in raw form, would not know its meaning, since his schooling probably did not include the bit-string language.

Suppose that in 2005 we had created digital information, saving this on a storage volume called D2005. (For brevity, we use "2005" as a surrogate for "at the current time," and "2105" as a surrogate for "too long from now for any conversation between information consumers and information producers." Similarly, "M2005" denotes a current computer and "M2105" denotes its eventual successor.) Suppose further that, a century later, some information consumer wants to use it. What must happen to make this possible and effective? Four things must be true in 2105:

Condition 1: A storage volume D2105 containing bit-strings that are true copies of what had been on D2005 must be found.

Condition 2: D2105 must be sufficiently intact to be read.

Condition 3: A device must be available to read the raw bit-strings from D2105 into a machine M2105.

Condition 4: M2105 must render each bit-string, making it comprehensible to the consumer, or executable if it represents a computer program.

Keeping obsolete machines in working order is difficult and expensive. This particular difficulty is made moot by moving bit-strings onto media accessible by some then-modern computer, doing this before computers of the previous generation become inoperable. (§10.1.1)

12.1.2 Alternatives to Durable Encoding

Prompt work for preservation is not always essential. Choosing to prepare a document for retention is an economic decision that depends on the expected number of retrievals, the cost of preparation, and whether one is willing to invest on behalf of unknown future beneficiaries.

Digital archeology leaves rescuing content to (agents for) whoever wants it.[412] This approach might be chosen for some content, or become necessary because we cannot persuade people to prepare works for preservation. However, although digital archeology might be reasonable for some kinds of information, it cannot be reliably used for computer programs because they contain insufficient redundancy for sure human translation.

What methods might we use for making a Fig. 32 content blob durably intelligible? Apart from durable encoding as described in this chapter, only the following possibilities and their combinations present themselves.

- Natural language contains too many ambiguities to be used alone for precise communication. It also changes too rapidly for unqualified confidence in it as a preservation foundation.
- Formal semantics[413] such as denotational semantics[414] might mitigate weaknesses of natural language. However, its methods seem to be understood only by formal language theorists.
- Standards expressed in a combination of natural and formal (mathematical) languages are essential starting points but, used alone, are practical only for relatively simple data types.
- Transformative migration[415] has been carefully considered for almost ten years.[416] Historically, such format conversions have been lossy. Apart from having highly skilled software engineers inspect many ex-

---

[412] Ross 1999. *Digital Archaeology: Rescuing Neglected and Damaged Data Resources*, http://www.ukoln.ac.uk/services/elib/papers/supporting/pdf/p2.pdf.

[413] Bjørner 1982, *Formal Specification and Software Development*.

[414] Gordon 1979, *The Denotational Description of Programming Languages*.

[415] Mellor 2002, *Migration on Request*.

Oltmans 2005, *A Comparison Between Migration and Emulation in Terms of Costs*.

[416] Lawrence 2000, *Risk Management of Digital Information: A File Format Investigation*, http://www.clir.org/pubs/reports/pub93/contents.html.

amples of each migrated file type, no one has devised a reliable method of eliminating translators' errors.[417] ASCII is the only format that has stood the test of time, but ASCII text carries neither semantics nor application behavior.

- Preservation emulation[418] has been considered as an alternative to migration. It tries to preserve obsolete technical environments— information that is both difficult to capture correctly and also mostly irrelevant to authors' objectives. Furthermore, emulated objects would present difficulties for collection users who do not have ready access to emulation machinery or the expertise to use it.

Multiple formats combined with "digital archeology" might be practical for relatively simple data formats. Future readers' problems can be eased by the Rosetta Stone lesson; it was the redundancy of multiple languages expressing the same information that enabled Young and Champollion to decipher the Egyptian hieroglyphic language.[419]

12.1.3 Encoding Based on Open Standards

Three generic methods emerge as promising from critical analyses of the §12.1.2 possibilities. Each assumes durable understanding of the saved specifications of a few relatively simple digital representation standards: Unicode/UCS and UTF-8; a small subset of XML standards[420], and a few others identified in §6.2 and §7.3. Bit-strings conforming to a few extremely simple formats can be safely saved "as is." Any bit-string whatsoever can be safely preserved with the §12.2 *Durable Encoding* method, but "industrial strength" software to do so has not yet become available.[421] An intermediate course is to convert bit-strings into representations depending only on a small set of standards that enable the rendering of conforming data into comprehensible forms at any future date.

---

[417] For rescuing data that have been neglected for years, transformative migration can be an option. See Green 1999, *Preserving the Whole: A Two-Track Approach to Rescuing Social Science Data and Metadata,* http://www.clir.org/pubs/abstract/pub83abst.html.

[418] Rothenberg 1995, *Ensuring the Longevity of Digital Documents.*

[419] Donoughue 2002, *The Mystery of the Hieroglyphs.*

[420] The specifications for XML 1.0, for XML Namespaces, for XPath, and for XPointer are the core needed by information consumers' agents. See IBM 2004, *A Survey of XML Standards,* http://www-128.ibm.com/developerworks/xml/library/x-stand1.html.

[421] That such software is not today available is merely a funding issue. IBM Research, which invented and tested the UVC methodology, has decided not to develop it into a practical offering just yet because no plausible business case has been advanced to support the investment needed. Public sector institutions investing in digital preservation do not yet seem to have yet taken much interest in saving programs and other data for which simpler methods would be inadequate.

Evaluation criteria for a file format to be used for long-term preservation are outlined in a 2005 presentation.[422] This intermediate tactic has been adopted by the National Archives of Australia (NAA), at least for the time being,[423] is proposed for electronic periodicals by the Library of Congress and the British Library,[424] and is called for in a British study[425] for audiovisual performance records:

> The key requirements that emerged from [a survey of curators] were:
> - an agreed set of standard formats for the preservation of moving image and sound;
> - an agreed set of significant properties for preservation purposes;
> - an agreed, flexible, metadata set to cover all aspects from search and retrieval to preservation metadata;
> - adequate storage for large volumes of content; this is particularly acute for uncompressed content; and
> - adequate funding!

Audiovisual data differ from other data types in ways that influence how their preservation might be managed: (1) their datasets tend to be very large, both individually and in comprehensive collections of broadcasts; (2) they always involve lossy data compression, if only because they are discrete representations of continuous source content; (3) their users are relatively insensitive to small data losses and errors; and (4) they constitute the most valuable asset of entertainment and news enterprises. These circumstances favor the search for standard representations for the content and metadata of audiovisual data called for in the recent AHDS study.[425]

Preserving data in the format of XML files whose content blobs conform to a few widely used representation standards has been implemented in an extensible prototype that is used internally in the NAA. Its saved file structure has some similarity with the right-hand side of Fig. 32, without apparently providing the kind of linking suggested by that figure.[426] Its currently supported file types are summarized in Table 11.

---

[422] C. Huc et al., *How to Evaluate the Ability of a File Format to Ensure Long-Term Preservation for Digital Information*, http://www.nesc.ac.uk/action/esi/download.cfm?index=2823,

[423] Wilson 2002, *Access Across Time: How the NAA Preserves Digital Records*, at http://www.erpanet.org/events/2003/rome/presentations/Wilson.ppt.

[424] Library of Congress news release, http://www.loc.gov/today/pr/2006/06-097.html.

[425] U.K. Arts and Humanities Data Service [AHDS], *Moving Images and Sound Archiving Study*, http://www.jisc.ac.uk/index.cfm?name=project_movingimagesound.

[426] The NAA XML data schema are accessible at http://www.naa.gov.au/recordkeeping/preservation/digital/xml_data_formats.html.

Table 11: NAA content blob representations

Blob classes	Supported file types	Standards used
Office documents: text, spreadsheet, presentation, and project management	MS Word, Excel, Powerpoint and Project; OpenOffice.org Writer, Calc, and Impress; RTF	OASIS OpenDocument[427]
Electronic mail	PST, TRIM, MBOX	Standards applicable to message format, such as RTF
Address files	CSV files	
Static image files	JPG, GIF, TIFF, PNG, BMP, PC	JFIF JPEG File Interchange Format[428]
Page images	PDF	PDF[429]
Simple Web pages	HTML	XHTML[430]

This approach risks that transformations might introduce errors that misrepresent authors' intentions. This is most obvious with translation of MS Office files to OpenOffice files that implement the OpenDocument standard, because one can detect small differences in the renderings of source and transformed versions. For most information consumers' purposes, such differences are unlikely to be problematic. Similarly, errors that might occur in image transformations are likely to be small and not problematic. Nevertheless, NAA emphasizes keeping source files as insurance against translation errors that might be discovered and judged to be significant.

Part of what makes this transformation approach possible and practical today is that the needed programs are readily available, inexpensive, and have been devised for other purposes than digital preservation, and so have effectively been tested by many users. This is because these formats are widely used, which also makes them prime targets for preservation development.

---

[427] http://www.oasis-open.org/committees/download.php/12572/OpenDocument-v1.0-os.pdf. The transformation from MS Office documents is built into the free OpenOffice program offering.

[428] *JFIF JPEG File Interchange Format*, http://www.digitalpreservation.gov/formats/fdd/fdd000018.shtml.

[429] PDF is not a formal standard, but is so widely used that people have confidence in its durability. A PDF subset, PDF/A, is standardized specifically for preserving documents. See http://www.digitalpreservation.gov/formats/fdd/fdd000125.shtml.

[430] *XHTML Extensible HyperText Markup Language*, http://www.w3.org/TR/xhtml1/.

12.1.4 How Durable Encoding is Different

A 1970s *compiler* was a computer program that accepted a file in some source language (e.g., COBOL) and produced a new file in some target language, which might be the *machine language* for the hardware on which the program was to execute. Its output conformed to *principles of operation* that describe the *instruction set* of some computer. The core of any compiler is a parser that decomposes input mostly into source language primitives—phrases from a rigidly constrained vocabulary. The rest is a target language generation subroutine for each kind of source language phrase; each such subroutine produces part of an output bit-string. The compiler itself is a program in the code of some computer, which might or might not be the target machine for execution of the compiler's output programs.

A programming language *interpreter* differs from a compiler primarily in its output timing. Instead of producing an output string of target machine instructions, it immediately executes each instruction an equivalent compiler might have written to an output file.

Modern programming language translators are more complicated than the previous paragraphs suggest. This is to facilitate translation for several otherwise incompatible hardware platforms and to permit late binding of resources, such as data files and drivers for otherwise incompatible printers and display devices. To reduce the cost of supporting incompatible instruction sets, compilation might be partitioned, with a "front end" producing code for a virtual computer (such as Sun Microsystem's Java Virtual Machine (JVM)[431]) and, for each target machine, with a "back end" compiler or interpreter that translates or executes the virtual machine instructions. To support late binding of input sources and output targets, the compiler produces subroutine call stubs with free variables and a symbol table of these variables, along with expressions of constraints on the values that can be bound to each variable. Each such stub calls a *driver* program interface that is generic for a service class (e.g., printers). At the time the compiled program is invoked, or during its execution, an opportunity is provided to choose or change the specific resource bound to each variable encountered.

Durable encoding changes these well known practices only slightly: in 2005, we would write programs in UVC code that will be interpreted or compiled in 2105. Writing such a translator will be easier than writing most compilers. Many compiler complexities are irrelevant, because each input will be static (no longer being changed by programmers), because it

---

[431]   *The Java Virtual Machine Specification,* http://java.sun.com/docs/books/vmspec/.

can be assumed to be without error, and because optimizing execution performance is relatively unimportant.

It is prudent to save a copy of the source object together with its versions transformed for preservation, together with metadata describing the provenance and technical relationships of the versions. (Fig. 8 and Fig. 32) Doing so might enable recovery from any transformation error.

12.2 Design of a Durable Encoding Environment

Every kind of persistent digital object will have a linear (one-dimensional) encoding—an equivalent bit-string. Operating systems or application programs provide for converting such bit-strings to other forms and for creating bit-strings from other forms. We therefore treat only bit-strings. Furthermore, without reducing generality, we can treat files as bit-strings in which any bit can be accessed independently of other bits. We distinguish methods for cases of increasing difficulty.

Case 1: The blob is readily understandable by a human reader without specialized expertise, aided only by programs available on almost any computer. Practical examples are ASCII-encoded text and binary raster images represented without compression. The latter can be preserved without encoding beyond text declarations of field types and dimensions.

Case 2: The data are too complex for human beings to understand without sophisticated assistance. Some 2105 programmer must write a decoding program, using a 2005 program specification in natural language and the BNF conveyed in some TDO referred to. This program must be able to render for a (human) consumer the interpretation of every important DO aspect. A line drawing might be conveyed this way, because its presentation algorithm is simple and amenable to a natural language description.

For objects represented by some file types, especially widely used ones, transformation to file types corresponding to international data standards might be judged to be sufficiently safe, i.e., to have low risk of transformation errors that affected information consumers will deem essential.

Case 3: The content is too complex for reliable Case 2 treatment. This includes tables, complex graphics, and engineering designs. Conveying one or more rendering programs is the only way to ensure that the consumer will be able to comprehend the blob. Whatever language this program is written in must be sufficiently understood in 2105 for writing an interpreter or compiler at that time.

Case 4: The content is a program or system to be saved for its own sake. We must ensure that this program will execute in the M2105 machine. For instance, if we want to preserve the look and feel of an Apple Macintosh or the user interface of a Computer-Aided Design (CAD) system, we must save the M2005 programs together with instructions for executing these programs in M2105.

Case 5: Programs with concurrency and critical timing relationships can be represented by modest extensions of the Case 4 mechanism. Real-time input can be represented by memory locations and triggers that accept changes from outside. The most complex programs will be simulations, such as virtual reality programs and aircraft pilot trainer control programs. For instance, a pilot-training program must respond to numerous cockpit controls, provide a video simulation of what the pilot would see in many dials and in flight path displays such as those used for landing when runways are hidden by fog, and mimic the reaction times of the aircraft, even though future computers will run at different speeds than today's.

Case 1 and **Case 2** instances present no problems needing discussion in the current chapter. They could be handled with **Case 3** procedures, but people might prefer simpler methods. In **Cases 3** and **4**, we must save a program. The difference is that for **Case 4**, we must interpret M2005 machine language, because we cannot save program behavior reliably except by saving the program itself. **Case 5** has not yet been handled. The case of nondeterministic programs still needs to be considered.

No conceptual difficulties that have not yet been worked out are expected in any of these cases.

12.2.1 Preserving Complex Data Blobs as Payload Elements

For **Case 3** we save the data itself in whatever form it was produced and/or is usually used, together with a UVC program that provides intelligible or otherwise useful renderings of data (Fig. 38). Optionally, we transform the input **Data** to some **Data'** in order to simplify the programming work. We also would save the original **Data** in order not to interfere with new purposes whose nature we cannot today predict.

The program, written in UVC code, consists of a parser and subroutines for producing some number of result bit-strings. More than one result string might be wanted in order to reduce ambiguity (§4.1). More than one result string might be needed to represent information not included in the single string that might otherwise be chosen. We might even decide to produce several result strings simply for consumers' convenience; for instance, we might produce a form for printing tables, a file of commands to load a relational database, and instructions for drawing a directed graph.

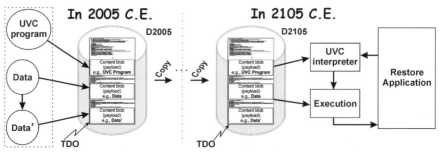

Fig. 38: Durable encoding for complex data

This 2005 UVC program will be interpreted in 2105 by a UVC interpreter written to operate in a M2105 environment and to process the saved data. The **Data** file, the **Data'** file, and the **UVC program** are each a 2005 blob that we might package into a single TDO (Fig. 32), together with metadata that might be needed by the restore application execution in 2105. We would store this TDO on the volume D2005. Repository managers would cause this TDO to be copied to replacement disks whenever older disks approach the ends of their useful lives (Fig. 38).

We can test the correctness of the UVC program in 2005 by comparing the results of an emulation on M2005 with those from a UVC emulator running on a computer incompatible with M2005 (such as an Apple Macintosh if we started with an IBM PC). Another good test would be to translate exemplary results and observe whether independent human readers understand the information to be conveyed in the future.

To prepare for using the preserved bit-strings, our 2105 successors must write a UVC emulator that executes on some M2105, and create a restore application. The restore program must pass the locations of the saved UVC program, saved **Data** and **Data'** strings (there might be several of the latter), and addresses where results should be stored. These would be the call parameters for invoking the emulator. It also needs to print or otherwise handle the results.

Fig. 38 suggests that the UVC program is stored in the same blob as **Data** and **Data'**. We would more likely have the blob reference a single stored program copy (Fig. 35).

Recently a variant encoding procedure has appeared, targeted for saving compressed files for as long as CPUs implementing descendants of the Intel x86 instruction set are available, which is likely to be for several decades.[432] Both to achieve high performance and to enable reuse of

---

[432] Ford 2006, *VXA: A Virtual Architecture for Durable Compressed Archives*, http://arxiv.org/abs/cs/0603073.

existing compression and decompression software (so-called *codecs*), this procedure replaces Lorie's UVC with a virtual machine that implements a subset of the x86 machine instructions. This subset omits input/output and all operating system calls and triggers so that it is insensitive to specifics of the environment, making it similar in this respect to the UVC definition in Appendix E. Its execution environment is close to what Fig. 38 suggests.

12.2.2 Preserving Programs as Payload Elements

In Case 4, we save the input **Data**, the **Application program** (an M2005 program), and an **M2005 emulator** written as a UVC program. We package these 2005 objects and their relationship specifications into a TDO, and copy this bit-string from volume to volume over the years (Fig. 39).

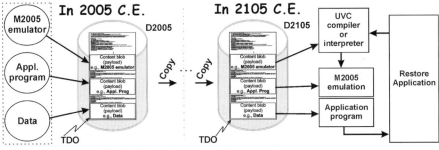

Fig. 39: Durable encoding for preserving a program

In 2105, a restore application uses a UVC interpreter written in M2105 code to execute or compile the **M2005 emulator**. This output executes the 2005 **Application program,** taking as input the 2005 **Data.**

12.2.3 Universal Virtual Computer and Its Use

A single UVC definition would be enough, but nothing precludes developing a new version if this is really needed; each TDO identifies the UVC it uses. Since an M2105 emulator for a particular UVC would be suitable for many object instances, it will be shared just as compilers are shared.

The UVC could be as simple as a Turing machine. However, this choice would make UVC programming tedious. More practical is a machine with generous memory and register structures. An IBM prototype suggests that it will cost less than a man-year to create an emulator for such a virtual computer and any real machine architecture. Of course, a UVC emulator for M2105 would work for any saved information, i.e., it needs to be written only once for each future machine architecture. The

UVC description that follows (for more detail see Appendix E) suggests how 2005 and 2105 programmers would accomplish their responsibilities.

- The machine has an unlimited number of registers, each of unlimited length, supporting any number of variables of any length.
- The memory has an unbounded number of segments, each of unbounded length. Thus, its programmers need be little concerned with data sizes.
- The memory is bit-addressable. A typical reference is to a bit offset from the origin and a bit length. Thus, the UVC is not biased toward any particular machine word or byte length.
- Fewer than 40 UVC instruction definitions provide the usual kinds of copying between registers and memory segments, integer arithmetic, and tests comparing values in two registers.
- The UVC includes a branch operation. A UVC programmer needs to create loops and other high level flows "by hand," as all programmers did before high-level programming languages were invented. (It would be easy to add a conventional looping statement equivalent to '`for I = 1 to N while F(I)`', where **F** is a simple function.)
- IBM's prototype UVC supports only a single programming thread. More complex examples than have been prototyped would need UVC instructions that read a clock, handle interrupts, fork to implement multiprogramming, and provide latches for synchronization.

UVC documentation, application program documentation, and input and output descriptors are ASCII and BNF files that include the following:

A: Natural language description of the alphabets used in **B**, **C**, **D**, and **E**.
B: Natural language description of each program, and its inputs and outputs.
C: A UVC program **U,** with a terminal parse tree node branching to a result method for every input token.
D: Schema for the input and output bit-strings of **U**.
E: Description of the invocation and return sequences of **U**. This might specify into which address segment the restore program (Fig. 38 and Fig. 39) needs to load the data, in which memory segments it will find the various renderings provided by **U**, and how to print these results or pass them to other 2105 programs that would use them as their 2005 producers intended.

A restore application would read the UVC program **U** and each input bit-string into a different memory segment (without any transformations) and then call the emulator, which would execute **U**, put its results into some number of different segments, and call back the restore application either many times (for a UVC interpreter) or when complete (for a UVC compiler). The restore application can be written to handle results as the 2105 programmer wants, using access methods described by the 2005 UVC programmer.

It might be impractical to apply the UVC method completely to every object to be preserved before it is ingested into an archival repository, perhaps because UVC programs have not been created for the types of some of its content blobs. It would be sufficient to do so shortly before the data types at issue become obsolete. Part of what might be necessary is timely discovery that certain objects are at risk. A tool to help with this is being developed.[433]

12.2.4 Pilot UVC Implementation and Testing

The IBM prototype UVC has been fully implemented. This implementation is being used at the National Library of the Netherlands.[434] A demonstration is available for download.[435]

An important question is "how can we be sure that an archived program is bug-free?" There are two correctness issues. The first one is making sure that a given UVC implementation is correct. To that effect, an extensive UVC test program has been developed that covers the whole functionality of the machine:

- Initial loading testing—whether sections and global constants are loaded correctly in the UVC.
- Activation of sections, passing arguments and results, and returning control to the invoking section.
- Bit addressability tests of different bit-oriented and segment/memory mechanism memory references.
- Instruction set, testing every instruction, making sure that no unwanted side effect (such as overflow) occurs.
- Communication channel, through the use of the IN and OUT instructions.

The second correctness issue concerns the UVC application programs. For this, each UVC programmer will need to demonstrate that his work will correctly handle all potential blobs for which it is intended to create durable representatives. This kind of test is similar to testing the correct-

---

[433] Hunter 2004, *PANIC—An Integrated Approach to the Preservation of Complex Digital Objects using Semantic Web Services*, http://www.iwaw.net/05/papers/iwaw05-hunter.pdf.

[434] Lorie 2002. *The UVC: A Method for Preserving Digital Documents: Proof of Concept*, http://www.kb.nl/hrd/dd/dd_onderzoek/reports/4-uvc.pdf.

[435] IBM, *Digital Asset Preservation Tool*, http://www.alphaworks.ibm.com/tech/uvc/download.

ness and completeness of a program compiler, which is usually impractical to accomplish completely.

Another kind of testing is possible by using two computers of different architecture, A and B. For each kind of content blob originating in A machine environments and to be preserved with a UVC program, one can use the B machine in lieu of the Fig. 38 2105 C.E. machine, testing that the outputs are indeed what they should be.

The sections above treat only relatively simple digital objects—static data files and the class of programs called *filters*. Static data files and filters are sufficient for a large fraction of the resources at risk. No one has yet described how to handle either nondeterministic programs or **Case 5** instances sufficiently for confident exposition.

12.3 Summary

The current chapter describes digital representation methods that are independent of the architecture of any particular computing machinery or programs. Such a method is based on relatively simple, widely used standards and the notion of a *Universal Virtual Computer* (UVC).

Before submitting any information for preservation, its producers should ensure that it is not unnecessarily confounded with irrelevant details of today's information technology—details that are difficult to define, extract, and save completely and accurately.

Critics of UVC methodology might argue that this mechanism is more difficult than required, because scholars in centuries to come would have available not only the works we specifically preserve, but also many works that have not been so preserved—an information collection that can be used to guide interpretation that does not depend on the UVC mechanism. For much content, such an argument has merit; it is an assertion that *digital archeology*—an almost "do nothing for the time being" tactic that leaves most of the work to whoever is interested in each saved document far in the future—will often work satisfactorily, even if accomplishing it might be tedious. This works only for documents belonging to a corpus for which there is sufficient redundancy and contextual information to perform a Rosetta Stone feat. One needs more for any case in which the correctness of some critical fact cannot reliably be determined from available context, as often occurs in computer programs.

For simple digital objects, standards that do not depend on ephemeral technology suffice, since they can be specified precisely and intelligibly. For more complex digital objects in other data formats, the instruction set of a relatively simple virtual machine can be used to encode any kind of file to be durably intelligible or useful. This is accomplished by creating

UVC programs that accompany today's content to render it for our descendants. Durable encoding uses current hardware and software information in rewrite routines whose outputs exclude irrelevant information from preservation bit-strings.

The UVC definition is simple enough that its complete specification can be written to be correctly understood whenever needed. One can in fact test a durable encoding solution by porting information between incompatible computing platforms. Every step of creating and emulating UVC programs can be executed by programmers of basic competence.

The amount of UVC code needed is small compared to the amount of information to be preserved, and also small compared to other document management programs. A single UVC definition can be sufficient for all data types and for all time. A single set of UVC programs can be sufficient for every type of file that people might want to preserve. A single UVC interpreter is all that is needed for every computer execution architecture of interest.

Objects represented with proprietary file types might be impossible to preserve reliably with this method either because their owners choose to conceal their representations or because they insist on copyright limitations prohibiting creation of derivative works. This seems to be the case today for files produced by Microsoft Office. The National Archives of Australia has chosen to preserve such objects by transforming them to XML formats conforming to relatively simple standards for a heavily used XML subset.[436]

A part of each preservation package can be today's bit-strings. No bit need be discarded. No detail should be altered. Thus, durable encoding will not interfere with any invention for exploiting the saved information in new ways (repurposing), because all essential details about today's context can be saved.

---

[436] NAA 2006, *Digital Preservation: Illuminating the Past, Guiding the Future,* http://www.naa.gov.au/recordkeeping/preservation/digital/XENA_brochure.pdf.

Part V: Peroration

13 Assessment and the Future

More information is more readily available today, and more people use it, than ever before. Almost all of it now originates in digital form: public records, engineering designs, legal documents, medical patients' charts, and artistic and scholarly works. The amount of digital information will increase greatly in years to come. People expect more ready access, better content quality, and better content fidelity than has historically ever been the case. They will be critical of information deliveries that do not manifest these attributes because they know that the quality they want can readily be achieved and inexpensively delivered.

Digitization of analog materials is increasing around the world because digital infrastructure is more responsive than the analog means it is replacing.[437] This is favorable for long-term preservation because bit-strings can be copied perfectly and therefore pattern representations need not deteriorate simply because chemical polymers gradually decompose.[438]

OAIS and related expositions[439] address the question, "What architecture should we use for a digital repository (the people, resources, processes, and content for long-term preservation)?" *Preserving Digital Information* asks, "What characteristics will make saved digital objects useful into the indefinite future?" Such different questions of course have different answers.

Many of the cultural heritage community's difficulties with what it means by long-term digital preservation are digital content management issues that would exist even if material carriers, digital hardware, and computer programs had unbounded practical lifetimes. *Preserving Digital Information* has therefore separated, as much as possible, considerations of durable document structure, of digital collection management, and of repository management. It says little about internal repository workings that

---

[437] Morgan 2006, http://infomotions.com/musings/mass-digitization/, reporting on a symposium called *Scholarship and Libraries in Transition: A Dialog about the Impacts of Mass Digitization Projects,* summarizes the best talks with "mass digitization allows libraries to rethink the role of physical space, but more importantly, it allows libraries to rethink what libraries do regarding collections. Both of them alluded to the possibilities of enhanced, value-added services against collections of electronic texts, but when pressed for elaborations none were forthcoming."

Institute of Museum and Library Services, *Status of Technology and Digitization in the Nation's Museums and Libraries,* http://www.imls.gov/publications/TechDig05/.

[438] DeWitt 1998, *Going Digital.*

[439] Verheul 2006, *Networking for Digital Preservation ... in 15 National Libraries.*

relate eventual outputs to histories of inputs. Instead it focuses on information package structure, responding to a 2003 challenge:

> There is no clear solution or set of solutions to meet the challenges of digital
> preservation. The unpredictability of technological development ... and
> [of] the global political environment ... contribute to the challenge of plot-
> ting a course ...

NDIIPP Plan, p.19

Taking "long-term digital preservation" to mean "remedies for technology
obsolescence and fading human memory," previous chapters offer a clear
solution to this challenge.

13.1 Preservation Based on Trustworthy Digital Objects

Archival service users care only about finding helpful documents and
about the data characteristics of works delivered. For them, quality can be
expressed entirely in terms of the functional relationship between the
inputs received by each repository and its observed and potential outputs
(deliveries of packaged information and of answers to catalog queries).
Archive managers would gain flexibility and freedom of action for internal
matters by making only input/output behavior commitments, discussing
their repositories with outsiders only with a black box approach.

13.1.1 TDO Design Summary

The core proposed for long-term preservation of digitally represented
works is document packaging employing lightly coupled software components. Requirements expressed by the digital heritage community can be
satisfied by conventions and infrastructure consisting of the following:

- A few socially communicated languages and standards (§6.2) that are
  not themselves parts of the technical solution, but that are needed starting points.
- Naming whereby any resource (digital, analog, or physical) can be
  uniquely identified for all time, with extensions for uniquely identifying
  locations and extents within any resource (§7.3).
- A scheme for representing relationships of any kind whatsoever, useful
  not only to manage bibliographic and other references, but also to represent any information collection (§6.4.1).
- Encapsulation of digital works in which each complying instance is
  called a TDO. To meet archival standards, TDO-embedded metadata
  must document provenance and also relationships binding TDO pieces
  with one another and with external resources.

- Encoding to represent patterns in language insensitive to irrelevant and ephemeral environmental details (§4.1), protecting what is essential from the ravages of technology obsolescence and fading human memory (§12.2).
- Certification that provides authenticity evidence, with certificate validity evidenced by other certificates recursively grounded in a few widely known public encryption keys tightly bound to their own creation dates (§§8.1.4 and 8.1.5).
- Repositories to store TDOs and to help information consumers find and obtain what interests them (Chapter 9).
- Replication mechanisms that protect against the loss of the last remaining copy of any TDO (§10.2).
- Topic-specific ontologies provided and maintained by academic and other professional communities (§6.5).

To prepare any digital work for preservation, an editor would encode each payload bit-string to be durably intelligible and would collect the results, together with standardized metadata, to become a Fig. 32 payload. In addition to its payload, each TDO would contain a protection block within which a human editor would record relationships among its parts, and between these parts and other objects. The final construction step, executed at a human agent's command, would be to sign and seal all these pieces as a single package with a cryptographic *message authentication code*.

Only four things can properly happen to a digital object X that is encapsulated in this fashion: (1) X can be reused within other objects; (2) parts of X can be extracted, making them data that no longer have as much evidentiary status; (3) identical replicas of X can be archived anywhere in the world, where they will continue to be as useful as X if they can be found; and (4) X and every X-replica might be lost, making all references to X worthless. The pattern represented by X cannot be changed without the result being some not-X pattern and this fact being manifest.

13.1.2 Properties of TDO Collections

Firm assertion of TDO packaging superiority would be premature. Ideally, we would compare TDO design to alternatives. However, as far as we know, no alternative design has been proposed.

A TDO implementation along the lines just summarized will not only satisfy the §1.2 objectives, but additionally will exhibit the following desirable characteristics.

- Consumers will be able to evaluate TDO content authenticity without help from administrators.
- Unintended metadata-to-object dissociation will occur at most rarely, and will be discernible when it happens.
- Information delivery correctness will be insensitive to Internet security risks. Objects might disappear, but if a TDO is delivered, the recipient will be able to evaluate its integrity.
- Collection management will be simplified by exploiting TDO link reliability. If metadata are sufficiently standardized, research groups and individual users will be able to use automatic tools to create digital library catalogs that suit their special needs and preferences.
- Library catalogs can themselves be preserved as TDOs.
- TDO software can be brought into service without disrupting installed digital libraries. Preserved objects can be stored, cataloged, and served by almost any widely distributed content manager.
- Industries will be able to streamline conformance with regulatory requirements that demand accountability and audit trails, such as those of the U.S. Food and Drug Administration (FDA), by linking the history of each document within the package conveying the current version.
- Good XML tools exist to make implementations easy to tailor. Recursive TDO schema and extensive linking can be used to make TDO collections scalable.

13.1.3 Explaining Digital Preservation

TDO methodology can be explained to almost anyone by reminding him of close analogies between its core methods and long established practice for preserving works represented on paper:

- Any information pattern can be made durable against loss by replicating its carrier object in multiple independent repositories.
- Helping consumers find any preserved document can be achieved by making accessible, for each information genre, a relatively small number of readily discovered inventories or catalogs that might themselves be replicated for reliability and rapid access.
- Ensuring that consumers can use any preserved document can be achieved by augmenting its source version with representations in the lingua franca appropriate to its genre. Ideally, this would be done in collaboration with the document's author.
- Making a document trustworthy can be achieved by firmly attaching evidence, which might include signatures, and which must be embedded in a socially acceptable infrastructure. The latter must include relation-

ships with individuals and/or enterprises that have little to gain and much to lose by allowing their names to endorse misrepresentations.

- Hiding information technology complexity from end users can be achieved by a combination of education that is most effective with young participants and of refined design for artifact usability.

Most of what is needed for preserving digital documents can be adaptations of age-old procedures for managing works on paper. Of course, the specific means whereby these objectives are best achieved is different for different information genres and different physical carriers.

13.1.4 A Pilot Installation and Next Steps

> Good design is very hard to do. It is easy and understandable to make fun of bad technologies. It is not easy to make good ones. ... Too often, information technology design is poor because problems have been redefined in ways that ignore the social resources that are an integral part of this socialization process. By contrast, successful design usually draws on these social resources, even while helping them change.
>
> Brown 2002, *The Social Life of Information*

The Koninklijke Bibliotheek (KB, the national library of the Netherlands) has deployed an electronic publication deposit system based on a prototype developed by IBM using the *Universal Virtual Computer* (*UVC*) mechanism to encode JPEG files. Using this, IBM and the KB conducted a joint proof of concept study, showing how the UVC can be used to archive information from a PDF file.

We must still work out careful designs for nondeterministic applications,[440] time-sensitive applications and simulations (§12.2 **Case 5**). Practical **Case 3** and **Case 4** pilots are still needed for the usual reasons—testing the soundness of ideas, exposing design errors and oversights, and estimating costs and the operational skills required. Furthermore, we need to inspect and assess announcements of prominent office automation vendors that their offerings will produce XML files directly, as this might make UVC use unnecessary for very large numbers of documents. Finally, we need to position the current work relative to emerging standards directed at digital preservation and file format information.[441]

A TDO implementation with tools that the preservation community finds practical and convenient to use still needs to be provided. Its bit-string encoding subroutines must be written only once for every file type

---

[440]   Ronsse 2003, *Record/Replay for Nondeterministic Program Executions.*

[441]   Darlington 2003. *Domesday Redux: The rescue of the BBC Domesday Project videodiscs.*
Waibel 2003, *Like Russian Dolls: Nesting Standards for Digital Preservation.*

of interest. Another step would be to build client workstation tools that ordinary users[442] will find convenient for packaging TDOs sealed with authenticity certificates, for extracting TDO payloads, and for inspecting evidence contained in TDO certificates and in the digital objects cited by archived TDOs.

There is little doubt that everything needed is technically feasible. Prototyping would have two objectives: (1) demonstrating that the technical complexities can be hidden so that ordinary users find the package convenient; and (2) as a step toward pilot installations.

If we find it difficult to make every TDO mechanism easy enough to use for all kinds of data, we can consider simplifications for relatively simple data types. As part of this it will be necessary, for each Table 2 threat class, to trade off the cost of defense against the level of system degradation at risk. The degradation may be evaluated in terms of the following questions:

- What fraction of the system's content might be irrecoverably lost?
- What fraction of the user population might suffer delays in accessing the impaired, but recoverable, fraction of the system's content?

An open question is, "What information renderings do we want to convey to our descendants?" For relatively simple data, such as organizational hierarchies, photographs, legislative text, or tables of numbers, the answer is often obvious. Other cases are more difficult, partly because they involve questions of authenticity. Planning optimal action is sufficiently important and subtle to merit careful treatment.

13.2 Open Challenges of Metadata Creation

Metadata is the special case of information that describes primary information for managers and clients of libraries and archives. Without constraints, it might become be as diverse and as complicated as other intellectual works. Since metadata is created for administrative purposes, conventions and standards have been the subject of many articles and conferences in the last ten years. However, conversations do not seem to have reached the consensus needed for acceptance widely used schemata and tools that make metadata use easy.

As shown in Chapters 10 to 12, most TDO content originating with authors can be handled objectively by editors, records administrators, librarians, and archivists. This is because curators try to avoid changing any au-

---

[442] By 'ordinary user' we mean a service client who is not a computing specialist and who has not been specially trained to use the applications in question. (Colloquial English does not yet have a term for this relationship to computer applications.)

thor's meaning or style. The situation is less favorable for metadata because the work of librarians and archivists includes information generation and choosing ways of communicating widely shared meaning. There is no apparent consensus about what is to be conveyed (except for the simplest facts, such as the name of an author).

It took many years to reach today's level of consensus for library subject classifications. There is thus little reason to expect rapid consensus for the more complicated choices available for metadata structure and semantics.

There are three metadata challenges: finding the "Semantic Holy Grail"; coming to agreement on structural and syntactic standards; and persuading authors and editors to complement their works with standard metadata. The first of these is outside the scope of digital preservation, but is briefly discussed below because support for constructing ontologies is sometimes cited as justification for metadata creation.

The first metadata challenge, which is beginning to be called "the Holy Grail of technical communication," is to create semantically enabled, topic-based documentation. Without knowledge theory far beyond anything known today, this cannot be achieved. For hopes summarized by Warren[443] the underlying thinking has not factored in distinctions between idiosyncratic, subjective judgments and objective designs that can be mechanized. It would be unrealistic to expect the Semantic Holy Grail to be discovered much sooner than the original Holy Grail, or to expect any large community to accept claims that it has been discovered.

Fixing on firm community meanings for structural and semantic standards for describing relationships between objects seems a far-fetched objective. Authors would find that such standards tend to inhibit their originality, and would avoid their use. This is because relationships within and among the texts of any scholarly topic are themselves a topic of discussion, with the discovery of new kinds of relationships a scholarly goal.

Just how difficult it will be to achieve metadata exploitation that some people are seeking is illustrated by efforts to combine collections whose metadata have been assembled by different teams. Such teams are likely to have chosen different metadata standards and conventions.[444] To make a collection efficiently searchable, one needs to reconcile metadata from different sources into a single scheme. (This need not be realized by a database with a single schema. An alternative is that the reconciliation scheme is inherent in search software used by collection clients.)   The

---

[443]   Warren 2006, *Knowledge Management and the Semantic Web,* suggests that the only successful uses of shared ontologies have been in the area of e-commerce.

[444]   Chan 2006, *Metadata Interoperability and Standardization,* http://www.dlib.org/dlib/june06/ zeng/06zeng.html.

simpler parts of achieving this are normalization of formats (e.g., for dates and representations of proper names) and choices of field subsets, but the challenge encounters the ambiguities of natural language.[445]   The core problem is that what is essential to any information representation is a subjective choice that depends on what some human being is trying to achieve and on other unstated circumstantials. Solutions that please large communities seem unlikely.   Compromises that specialized communities find workable are likely to be achieved only with discussions that take years to consummate, and that even then might not fully please anybody.

Often syntax and document image layouts provide good hints about meanings; good accuracy for automatic selection of document titles, authors, dates, and citations is feasible for works represented with known formal layouts, such as the articles that appear in a specific scientific periodical. In contrast, automatic extraction of meanings from mostly unstructured text, such as from the abstracts of the same articles, will probably not be achieved in the foreseeable future. One of the earliest artificial intelligence challenges addressed by computer scientists was automatic translation between natural languages. Forty years have elapsed without much progress.

We can automate much of syntax management, but not the extraction of descriptive metadata that positions a document within collections. We do, however, agree with Warren's opinion that semiautomatic procedures are promising for managing and applying ontologies. Building them to automate the clerical parts of syntax management and thesaurus lookup would allow human beings to focus on semantic choices.

Relative to the second metadata challenge, there is consensus that we need good tools to minimize the cost of metadata generation and to maximize the quality of what is generated.[51] The designers of such tools should consider both the information producers who will generate metadata and the information consumers who will depend on it for searching and other applications. The tools might include schema validators, online thesauri, vocabulary controls, and metadata authenticators that contribute to better quality metadata. The tools should, of course, support formal preservation metadata schema. To design them well we need improved insight into the preparation, transmission, receipt, unpackaging, and ingestion of TDOs in multiple system environments. The tools might best be constructed to be modules that application developers, such as the authors of Fig. 26's outer software layer, would be pleased to embed.

To persuade the generation and use of such tools, good understanding of the benefits of and costs for metadata would be helpful. "We do not know

---

[445]   Wasow 2005, *The Puzzle of Ambiguity*.

how to estimate the cost of producing adequate metadata. We do know, however, that the increasing demands for ever more metadata mean that traditional hand-crafted approaches (as in Library MARC records) are no longer affordable."[446]

The third metadata challenge remains a dilemma. Notwithstanding many years' effort toward metadata design, few authors or editors generate metadata, even when the cost of doing so is only a small fraction of their cost of preparing the works these metadata would describe.

Nobody thinks that generation of metadata by professional librarians and archivists could effectively replace what we believe authors and their supporting editors should do; the number of works to be handled is far too great. Even though librarians and archivists would probably do a better job than authors at creating metadata conforming to standards and syntactic conventions, they would rarely have the authors' expertise with semantic and social aspects, such as the informal conventions of professional communities or target audiences.

Although the lack of good tools is sometimes cited as the barrier, it is not at all certain that the challenge would be handled just by making tools available. We might be faced by a "chicken and egg" situation. Almost nobody creates metadata, because information consumers do not habitually use metadata. And nobody depends on metadata, because there is so little of it that what exists has not been organized. To make progress, repository managers need to decide how to persuade authors to participate in creating effective metadata infrastructure.

13.3 Applied Knowledge Theory

That the §13.1.1 design choices are close to optimal is made plausible by the epistemelogical analysis of Chapter 3 through Chapter 6.

If a choice is subjective, important to the discussants, and needed for information sharing within a community larger than a few friends, it will not be agreed to quickly, and possibly never settled to most people's unqualified satisfaction. For this reason some information systems standards discussions last for a decade or longer, and sometimes result in competing standards that few people use as their authors intended.

That it has taken so long to come to grips with digital preservation is partly because of misunderstandings of the logic of our language. What can be preserved is illuminated by philosophical insights achieved over 50 years ago. The basic ideas have been absorbed into everyday scientific and engineering methodologies so thoroughly that they might seem mere

---

[446] W2005, §A 2.5.

common sense to scientists. If they have been absorbed by people not trained as scientists, they are apparently ignored.

Knowledge theory needed for digital preservation methodology can be distilled to a surprisingly small number of ideas. Without pretending to explain again what philosophers have meticulously analyzed and effectively taught, we can list principles guiding what this book suggests.

- We cannot communicate with certainty that the listener or reader achieves the same conceptual models as the speaker or writer might intend. The world is more complex than the language used to describe it. Even topical boundaries tend to be subjective and fuzzy.
- Objective description and analysis of its representation is possible for anything that has been written. Except for observations about the simplest facts, the acts of writing, speaking, designing, and learning are laden with subjectivity (§3.3).
- Every communication contains accidental information that is irrelevant to the originator's intentions (§4.1).
- Facts are apparent to most people who observe them. Expressions of such facts can be tested for objectivity. We can address a question to people thought to be honest and competent observers, and be confident that a factual base is involved if they agree (§3.4).[447]
- Facts are statements of structure. Structure can be objectively communicated as a set of relationships (§4.5).
- Most information is a surrogate for something other than itself (§3.5). Every assertion, predicate, noun phrase, or mathematical function definition has two senses. One is a set of denoted entities, sometimes called the *extension* (§3.6). The other is a class of relationships within some social and language context, sometimes called the *intension*. The abstraction of a structure is sometimes called a *pattern* (§4.6).
- Careful scientific communication is mostly objective, signaling its subjective portions (opinions, values, and beliefs). Any subjective comment can be replaced by an objective assertion of its provenance, along the lines of, "In a 1 January 2000 speech in Philadelphia, X said that ..." (§5.2).
- Often a computing infrastructure, or even a single computer, contains several versions of an object. These are distinct objects. Commonly, some of them are ephemeral. To avoid absurdities, such as that in §5.3.2, we must carefully distinguish which objects are the subject of the conversation of the moment.

---

[447] The test for objectivity suggested is similar to those taught by Ryle 1950, *The Concept of Mind,* for instance in his Ch. 2, §(8).

- Communication is full of confusion that cannot be completely avoided. In conversation, we commonly deal with the most obvious and troublesome confusion by questioning and answering (§3.2). In contrast, recorded communication—this book, for instance—cannot include interactive dialog. We can partially compensate for this by careful language choice (§4.2), and by multiple ways of communicating the same pattern (§4.1). However, careful language can be tedious; reporting a welter of contingencies can obscure a key message.

In addition to the above principles from knowledge theory, we can apply certain software engineering practices to simplify the preservation solution structure. Such practices will minimize implementation cost by enabling extensive program module reuse.

- Focusing first on data schemas (§6.4), and only secondarily on programs (§9.3) that manipulate, manage, and exploit the conforming objects.
- Using recursion to minimize the number of data schema, e.g., in TDO structure, in information whose interpretation depends on other information, and in authenticity certificate trees.
- Recognizing that catalogs and collection descriptions are specialized document instances, so that a single schema suffices for both documents and collections.
- Using references (pointers, links) extensively, and avoiding semantic inference from reference strings (§7.3).
- Using ternary relations for communicating structure because their graphical depictions represent key aspects, and for data processing because they avoid technical constraints of SQL (§6.4.1).
- Using administrative rules and avatars extensively (§9.1).

It would be impractical to assign to people work that machines can do as well or better. The number of digital objects repository managers will want to save is too large for them to ignore any automation opportunity.'

13.4 Assessment of the TDO Methodology

Communicating without contaminating intended information with accidental content seems to be impossible (§4.1). We cannot speak without using some voice pitch; any paper document has paper and ink colors that are usually irrelevant to its message. This observation suggests two questions: (1) Given some record to be preserved, what is the best that can be accomplished toward communicating what encoded information is intended and what is accidental? (2) Recognizing that few people will understand UVC programs, what tools can we provide to ordinary users without confronting them with the complexities?

Good repository software offerings have existed for ten years. Some are almost adequate for their digital preservation roles, needing at most small extensions for long-term content. However, even perfect repositories would not be sufficient to achieve digital preservation. Information producers' and curators' actions described in §13.1.1 are essential.

The TDO methodology addresses only the technical portions of digital preservation. It focuses on the most difficult anticipated cases for which preservation might be wanted—file types for which perfect rendering is difficult and records for which chicanery (record or provenance falsification) is tempting and can create large risks for legitimate users. For relatively simple file types and for records not associated with large risks, other mechanisms than those we describe might be more economical.

For documents of probative value in legal proceedings, the standing of digital versions in general and digital signatures in particular is problematic.[448] Undoubtedly, this uncertainty will be addressed in the context of specific legal disputes. Clear rules based on precedents will probably emerge only slowly.

For proprietary software that produces widely used information of lasting value, intellectual property rules pose a bigger practical challenge than any technical problem.[449]

To understand this, consider the difficulties that might arise in preserving a version of the Microsoft Word program. (This example is chosen because so many readers will know the program, not to suggest that preserving MS Word would be worthless. A century from now, people are likely to be interested in MS Word documents without wanting the MS Word program.) The would-be conservator with unfettered access to source code would need highly technical expertise to decide what code is part of MS Word and what should be considered part of the MS Windows operating system and therefore out of scope. He would also face a high cost for translating Word to UVC code—probably between 5% and 50% of the creation cost of the Word product. However, such practical challenges pale in comparison to legal risks.[450]

Source code for proprietary software is typically held as a trade secret. As long as business conditions remain much as they are today, upgrade versions of Word will be a large revenue source. Even if Microsoft were

---

[448] Scoville 1999, *Clear Signatures, Obscure Signs.*

[449] National Research Council 2000, *Digital Dilemma: Intellectual Property in the Information Age.*
Samuelson 2001, *Intellectual Property for an Information Age.*
Aoki 2006, *Bound by Law?*

[450] Besek 2003, *Copyright Issues Relevant to the Creation of a Digital Archive.*

to make source code available, it would almost surely oppose translation, treating it as a violation of its copyright privilege of creating derivative works. In fact, Microsoft might plausibly argue that its future versions of Word provide what is needed for preservation of both the program and the universe of MS Word files.

TDO's novel features have been published, informally starting in 2000 A.D., and formally in refereed periodicals later. No criticism questioning any part of this solution has appeared.

Notwithstanding our confidence in what *Preserving Digital Information* presents, we believe it premature to relax about TDO methodology correctness or its optimality. Critical readers, particularly those who intend to contribute to achieving widely available digital preservation services, might consider three questions. Is the reasoning presented correct and, if not, what specific flaws does it conceal? Are its methodological recommendations optimal and, if not, what specific improvements might be made? What are the next practical steps toward convenient and relatively inexpensive preservation of digitally represented information?

13.5 Summary and Conclusion

Current progress is breathtakingly rapid toward widely accessible shared information infrastructure that will include many public sector institutional repositories, and will include information discovery tools of convenience and power beyond what we already enjoy. In contrast, work on technology for long-term preservation of digital objects has not much progressed since 1996, except for what *Preserving Digital Information* reports.

The open problems discussed in this book and the articles it references are likely to be resolved in about ten years. We know of no outstanding conceptual problem. Those identified in published articles are all plausibly answered in this book. Good methods for managing digital documents mimic those for works on paper. Conflicting interests in intellectual property pose a bigger barrier than technical or cost challenges.

Early twentieth century scientific philosophy, also called *epistemology* or theory of knowledge, provides an adequate intellectual foundation for digital preservation—a foundation called for by cultural heritage community spokespersons. Applying it helps identify and avoid published confusions about digital objects and the patterns they convey. It helps to distinguish between information and knowledge, and to signal assertions that are subjective rather than objective.

Gaps exist between what is known and our having the tools that the cultural heritage community seems to want. The apparent functional needs have been addressed by plausible solutions, but are not yet represented by practical implementations. Commercial software suppliers seem to have no plans to provide them, perhaps because they do not see a viable document preservation marketplace emerging in the near future.

Any set of files can be collected and packaged as a bit-string that represents what is commonly called *a work*. Anything written, drawn, photographed, or performed can be represented by a bit-string—a sequence of 0s and 1s. Any set of relationships can be represented by a ternary table. Collection preservation will be achieved if we do the following:

- Save the bits so that somewhere a copy survives and can be found.
- Identify relationships by a recursive network of reliable references.
- Include library catalogs among the set of saved documents.
- Make the bits trustworthy by reliably associating sufficient metadata.
- Ensure that the bits can be interpreted.

If all works of long-term interest are packaged for preservation and managed as suggested, the world's preservation objectives will be satisfied. When a clear solution is proposed for an acknowledged need, responsible action would include critical assessment and prompt deployment if assessments made reveal no insurmountable flaws. This is particularly so when solution deployment seems likely to be relatively inexpensive and rapidly feasible, as is the case for the methodology described in Chapters 10 through 12.

We believe the TDO methodology to be correct and, in principle, sufficient for preserving anything that can be preserved, including so-called "dynamic" information. It defines quality against which any proposed digital preservation method should be judged. We invite anyone who believes otherwise to produce an objective demonstration that our confidence is premature.

Appendices

Appendix A: Acronyms and Glossary

A few works are cited so often or are so important that it has been convenient to indicate them by abbreviations:

LSW   Rudolf Carnap 1928, *Logical Structure of the World.*

NDIIPP   Library of Congress 2003, *Preserving Our Digital Heritage: Plan for the National Digital Information Infrastructure and Preservation Program.*[451]

OAIS   CCSDS 2001, *Reference Model for an Open Archival Information System.*[452]

PDITF   John Garrett et al. 1996. *Preserving Digital Information: Report of the Task Force on Archiving of Digital Information.*[453]

PI   Ludwig Wittgenstein 1956, *Philosophical Investigations.*

PK   Michael Polanyi 1958, *Personal Knowledge.*

RLG   RLG-OCLC 2002, *Trusted Digital Repositories: Attributes and Responsibilities.*
          RLG-NARA 2005, *An Audit Checklist for the Certification of Trusted Digital Repositories.*[454]

TLP   Ludwig Wittgenstein 1918, *Tractatus Logico-Philosophicus.*

W2005   Final report of the 2005 *Warwick Workshop on Digital Curation and Preservation.*

In this book a few phrases are used so often that it is convenient to represent them with acronyms. Also some common words are used as technical terms to convey what is intended as precisely as possible. These are:

abstract   (noun) summary of a statement, document, or speech; (verb) reduce by eliminating all properties not essential to the concept in question; (adj.) expressing a characteristic apart from any specific object or instance.

access   (noun) specific type of interaction between a subject and an object that results in the flow of information from one to the other; in general, the right to enter or make use of; (verb) to achieve the status of having access.

---

[451] *NDIIPP Plan* via http://www.digitalpreservation.gov/.

[452] *OAIS*, http://ssdoo.gsfc.nasa.gov/nost/wwwclassic/documents/pdf/CCSDS-650.0-B-1.pdf.

[453] Available via http://www.rlg.org/ArchTF/.

[454] *Trusted Digital Repositories,* http://www.rlg.org/longterm/repositories.pdf and http://www.rlg.org/en/pdfs/rlgnara-repositorieschecklist.pdf.

access control	(noun) security component which defines who may do what and administers these rules; (from *ISO/IEC 10181–3*) the process determining which uses of resources within an open system environment are permitted and, where appropriate, preventing unauthorized access, which is frequently subdivided into classes known as unauthorized use, disclosure, modification, destruction, and denial of service.
access path	(noun) means of referring to an entity by identifying positions in (a nest of) containing entities, e.g. John Doe in the San Jose office of the Acme Corp. A name is a special kind of access path; the containing object is a context. An index into an array is another kind of access path.
accession	(noun) new item added to a library or museum collection; (verb) acquiring additional property.
activation	(noun) executable combination of an operation and a state; the state includes an indication of the next step to be executed. Each activation of an operation is distinct from other activations associated with other states.
address space	(noun) directly accessible memory of a process, typically segmented and partially shared with other processes.
agent	(noun) person or machine that provides a particular service, as a surrogate for some other entity; person or automatic process that takes an active role or produces a specified effect.
age-old	(adj.) alluding to practice and methodology for information communication, management, and preservation before widespread use of digital information technology.
aggregation	(noun) synonym for *collection*; in this work, any of a collection, a set, or a class, when we want to avoid implying any particular method for identifying what is aggregated.
algorithm	(noun) finite sequence of steps by which some data manipulation may be accomplished.
API	(acronym) application programming interface.
architecture	(noun) abstraction of design, hiding features not of interest in a conversation about high level aspects; rules for interfaces provided for some collection of entities and services; the choice and structuring of what can be viewed and what manipulations can be performed through these interfaces.
Archival Information Package (AIP)	(noun phrase) information unit that is preserved within an OAIS, consisting of Content Information and associated Preservation Description Information.
archival storage	(noun phrase) *OAIS* entity of services and functions used for the storage and retrieval of Archival Information Packages.
archive	(noun) persistent storage used for long-term information retention, typically inexpensive per unit stored and with a long response time, and often in a different geographic location to protect against equipment failures and natural disasters; organization that intends to preserve information for access and use by a *designated community*; temporary backup collection of computer files.
archiving	(noun) administrative procedure to achieve economy, efficiency, and effectiveness in the selection, maintenance, preservation, access, and use of records that have been selected for long-term preservation.
assertion	(noun) a statement about some fact, expressed in marks on paper, or in some other manifestation that could be transformed to marks on paper by a finite sequence of mechanical steps.
asymmetric cryptography	(noun phrase) (also *public-key cryptography*) encipherment based on algorithms that enable the use of a *public key* to encrypt a message and a different, but mathematically related, key (a *private key*) to decrypt such a message.

atomic	(adj.) intended not to be decomposed, at least within the discussion of the moment. For instance, the integer 2 is atomic and the list '2 4 6' is compound (not atomic).
atomic unit of work	(noun phrase) set of data changes managed so that either all of the changes take effect or none take effect, and so that anything read from these data has values as if no concurrent data changes were occurring in other units of work.
attribute (of a digital object)	(noun) synonym for *property*; mathematical value that is a mathematical function of the object..
audit	(verb) conduct independent review and examination of system records and activities; (noun) the process of such a review, or its result.
audit trail	(noun phrase) record sequence describing events deemed important to determine whether or not a set of resources has been used in accordance with guidelines defined by appropriate authorities; results of monitoring operations on objects.
auditor	(noun) human being with responsibility for checking that resources are not being misused or misappropriated and/or mechanisms to prevent misuse are in place and being used as prescribed.
authentic	(adj.) having the purported relationship to historical events and circumstances, particularly those that change the object.
authenticate	(verb) verify the identity of a person (or other agent external to the protection system) seeking service (see *CCITT Rec. X.800* or *ISO/IEC 7498–2*); verify the integrity of data that has been exposed to possible unauthorized modification.
authentication	(noun) mechanism for establishing with known confidence that a token passing between processes belongs to a set of allowed tokens; typically each such token identifies a subject and also contains some secret that could only come from the single user authorized to use the subject; (verb) checking the assertion of identity of persons or documents in order to establish it is what it purports to be and has not been altered or corrupted at any time. (See *ISO 15489-1:2001*, §7.2.2.)
author	(noun) person who writes a novel, poem, essay, etc.; the composer of a literary work, as distinguished from a compiler, translator, editor, or copyist; the maker of anything; creator.
authority	(noun) privilege and responsibility to utilize and/or control some resource; quality of special value of information stored or conveyed, because of either knowledge or official right to comment, as in "spoken with authority"; especially valuable commentator by virtue of superior knowledge, diligence, or scholarship.
avatar	(noun) incarnation of a Hindu deity (such as Vishnu); embodiment (as of a concept or philosophy) often in a person; virtual representation of a user on a network, typically in text or graphic form; process which implements human-specified rules whenever stimulated by some event originating in the external world or in another computing component; cf. *agent*.
bag	(noun) generalization of a mathematical set, with the difference that the members of a bag may be identical objects or values. For instance, {1 2 3 3} denotes a bag, but not a set.
binding	(noun) association of entities, such as a name with an object, or a name in one context with a name in another context.
bit	(noun) contraction of *binary digit*; one of the two elementary values (0 and 1) in the binary number system.
bit sequence	(noun phrase) order of *bits* within a *bit-string*. Whereas a bit-string is an object, a bit sequence is a value.
bit-string	(noun) finite sequence of bits representing information; unit of data whose meaning and interpretation are not pertinent to the discussion at hand. Cf. *blob*.

black box	(noun phrase) machinery or process whose operational properties are discussed without "opening it up" to inspect its inner workings.
blob	(noun) acronym for binary large object; data unit whose representation and meaning are not pertinent to the discussion at hand, such as the objects stored and cataloged in a library. Cf. *bit-string*.
BNF	(acronym) Backus-Naur form, which is a method of describing the syntax of a formal language; alternatively, Bibliothèque nationale de France.
catalog	(noun) table relating names to names, objects, or locations of objects, and possibly also to object descriptions; synonym for *directory*; among librarians, a specific kind of finding aid with one or several entries for each collection element and conforming to carefully documented standards.
certificate	(noun) unforgeable object that attests to the accuracy, correctness, completeness, and provenance of some information.
certification	(noun) administrative act of approving a computer system, component, or dataset for use in a particular application.
certification authority (CA)	(noun) organization that manages certificate processes by issuing, distributing, revoking, and verifying certificates to advertised policies.
channel	(noun) means for passing a message from a source to a target.
codec	(acronym) bit-string compression and decompression software that is typically oriented toward specific file types; more generally, any coding and decoding software to help transmit information across networks; hardware that accomplishes the same function.
collection	(noun) set of intellectual works related by some announced or discoverable attributes. Cf. *aggregation.*
collision	(noun) unintended and perhaps undesirable equality of independently chosen bit-strings.
compiler	(noun) computer program that translates programs written in some specific formal language into an instruction sequence that can be executed by a particular kind of computing machine.
compliance	(noun) fulfilling official and legislative requirements; in archival context, the usual recordkeeping requirements relate to legislation such as the Data Protection Act, Companies Act, Taxes Management Act, and Freedom of Information.
component	(noun) entity which is a part of something larger.
concrete	(adj.) related to the reduction of an abstraction to practice; including details not necessary for a concept, but necessary for a realization.
concurrent	(adj.) simultaneously occurring or, of computer processes, simultaneously executing.
consistent	(adj.) of a data collection, conforming to rules for relationships among elements defining collection correctness.
constraint	(noun) rule relating permissible (values of) two entities.
consumer	(noun) role of a person or enterprise that interacts with *OAIS* services to find and access preserved information; *information consumer.*
contain	(verb) have as a constituent part; X contains Y if X has Y as a component, or if a component of X contains Y.
content	(noun) set of objects held in some vessel, book, etc., possibly considered together with the location of each contained entity.
content management	(noun phrase) topic that used to be called *digital library*, extended to include record services and constraints beyond those traditionally associated with *library*.

context	(noun) setting for an event, statement, or idea from which it can be understood; passages that immediately precede and follow a word or passage and clarify its meaning. For instance, the meaning of "bald" depends on the context. If the context is English, "bald" means "without hair"; if it is German, "bald" means "in kurzer Zeit" ("in a short time").
continuous	(adj.) of a mathematical sequence, the property of having a value between any two values; hence, a similar property of space, signals, and objects.
correlation problem	(noun phrase) ambiguity inherent in pointing at any object, since almost every object is part of larger objects and, in turn, consists of smaller objects.
cryptography	(noun) originally the science and technology of keeping information secret from unauthorized parties by using a code or a cipher; today, similar techniques used for applications that might not involve confidentiality.
cultural history community	(noun phrase) as defined by *OAIS*, the staffs of museums, archives, and research libraries, and also the research and development communities that focus on tools and methods for such institutions.
curate	(verb) care for an object, whether physical or digital, of historical significance in a managed environment.
custodian (in an archive or library)	(noun) human being or organization holding or managing resources for beneficial use by others, such as the data and programs of a library service. To offer a library service is to make explicit or implicit contracts with information owners and users. To each owner, a custodian commits to preserve the information entrusted with specific promises of data integrity and security. To each user, a custodian offers means of searching for and rapidly retrieving information.
Dark Web a.k.a. Deep Web	(noun phrase) Internet content not found in most search engines because it is not stored on HTML pages. Viewing Dark Web content is accomplished by going to the Web site's search page and following its query protocol.
data	(noun) information represented suitably for communication, interpretation, or processing. Examples include bit-strings, tables of numbers, characters on a page, and sound recordings.
data dictionary	(noun) formal repository of terms used to describe data.
data integrity	(noun phrase) state of a bit-string that conforms to the state of its source documents and has not suffered alteration.
data object	(noun phrase) entity valued for the information it might represent.
database	(noun) set of records, sometimes called *tuples,* each with a few fields. A relational database has a number of tables; the tuples of each table share a format. Typically, most fields are relatively short (up to 256 bytes). However a DBMS might allow longer fields for which operations are curtailed in comparison to what it supports for short fields.
dataset	(noun) synonym, in the context of computing, for *file.*
date/time stamp	(noun phrase) record of when a transaction or document is initiated, submitted, changed, read, logged, or archived. Often it is important that the stamp be certified by some authority to make it trustworthy.
DBMS	(acronym) database management system
decidable	(adj.) propositional property of having a bounded procedure for determining truth or falsity. (A procedure or algorithm is said to be bounded if it can be completed in a finite number of steps for any valid input data whatsoever.)
designated community	(noun phrase) group of potential consumers that a repository intends to serve especially well, possibly by providing services attuned to the group's special needs or purposes. For example, for a university library, the institution's undergraduates typically constitute such a designated community.

DIDL	(acronym) in the MPEG-21 standard, *Digital Item Declaration Language.*
digest	(noun) much condensed message version produced by processing the message by a hash algorithm.
digital archeology	(noun phrase) painstaking recovery of digital information by some future scholar or technician, needed because the content in question has not been prepared for withstanding time's ravages when doing so would have been inexpensive.
digital curation	(noun phrase) neologism for all of the actions needed to maintain digital objects and data over their entire life-cycle and over time for current and future generations of users, including digital archiving and digital preservation; the processes needed for good data creation and management, and for adding value to data to generate new sources of information and records of knowledge.
digital library (DL)	(noun) digital analog of a conventional library; integrated services for capturing, cataloging, storing, searching, protecting, and retrieving information.
Digital Object (DO)	(noun phrase) object composed of bit-strings, metadata, and structuring XML.
digital preservation	(noun) organized actions to ensure usefulness of digital objects for many years; key elements include ensuring digital objects are never lost or damaged, are trustworthy, can always be found, and can always be understood, notwithstanding technological obsolescence.
DRI	(acronym) digital resource identifier (§7.3.4)
digital signature	(noun) data appended to a message to assure the recipient of its origin and integrity; digitized analog of a written signature, commonly produced by a cryptographic procedure acting on a digest of the message to be signed.
digitization	(noun) process of selecting, preparing, and capturing analog signals into a digital format, adding metadata, providing archival and derivative formats, performing quality assurance, and delivering files.
directory	(noun) table relating names to names, objects, or object locations. For instance, a directory could define the mapping from the names of programs to the location of their entry points in computer memory. Cf. *catalog.*
distributed	(adj.) descriptor of a system with several points of control, knowledge, storage, or processing.
document	(noun) (1) structure of text objects, images, or other data objects, such as (digital representations of) the pages of a book; (2) information sequence that could be inscribed onto paper; (3) some number of sheets of paper or similar material fastened together and inscribed with one or more of text, pictures, numerical tables, engineering drawings, photographs, drawings, mathematical formulae, or any other collection of symbols. Cf. *record.*
driver	(noun) in the context of computer operating systems, a program for a specific input-output device model that hides from the operating system those device characteristics that might be different from their counterparts for other devices of the same class—e.g., hiding the unique characteristics of a printer so that a generic printer invocation will work with any of many printers, including printers produced by different manufacturers.
electronic record	(noun phrase) in the context of the federal government, any information that is recorded by or in a format that only a computer can process and that satisfies the definition of a *federal record* in 44 U.S.C. 3301.
emulation	(noun) system process that performs in the same way as another system of a different type in order to run its programs.
end user	(noun) human being obtaining service from computing processes.

entity

(noun) something that exists, especially when considered as distinct, independent, or self-contained; a member of a set; in the context of object-oriented systems, *entity* is used when one does not wish to distinguish between *object* and *value*.

environment

(noun) relative to an activation, the set of objects (and their values) reachable for a function evaluation.

epistemology

(noun) branch of philosophy that deals with the origin, nature, methods, and limits of human knowledge; theory of knowledge (in contrast to belief or opinion). Epistemological works analyze the possibilities and limitations of answers to, "What do people know? What can be known?" and "What can they communicate, and how can they minimize misunderstandings?"

essence

(noun) for a digital document, the core matter provided by originators.

essential

(adj.) of an entity property, required for the entity to serve its subjectively chosen purpose; of a word's or phrase's property, being required for that locution to have its intended meaning.

ethical

(adj.) having to do with the branch of philosophy treated by, e.g., Moore's *Principia Ethica*; moral, aesthetic, or evaluative, in contrast to empirical.

evidence

(noun) in the archival sense, information about the processes, activities and events that led to a record's creation or alteration, being important for legal, historical, and other purposes.

extension

(noun) the range of a term or concept as measured by the objects which it denotes or contains. Cf. *intension*.

fact

(noun) thing done; action performed or incident; event or circumstance; actual happening in a time and space; observable relationship. A fact is either a state of things—an existence, or a motion—or an event.

faithful

(adj.) of a data copy, conforming accurately to some earlier data instance, usually identically bit by bit.

filter

(noun) mechanism that accepts a finite number of finite input strings and produces a finite number of finite output strings.

finding aid

(noun) librarian's term for an information collection that is not a *catalog*, but serves a similar purpose as a catalog to the extent that something simpler (and less expensive) can do.

fond

(noun) archival term for a collection of papers or other ephemera that originate from a single source.

form

(noun) document with blanks to be filled up; that which makes anything a determinate species; shape, arrangement of parts, visible aspect.

formal

(adj.) pertaining to, or emphasizing, organization or composition of the constituent elements. In a formal mathematical system the elements of discourse are not associated with meanings; interest is limited to relationships between elements, which are deduced from simpler relationships (axioms) on the basis of combining forms.

function

(noun) relation defined on two sets, called the domain and the range, consisting of a set of pairs whose first component is from the domain and second component is from the range with no two pairs having the same first component. (Note: any element can be either simple or compound, and of any type whatsoever.)

genre

(noun) category of artistic, music, or literary composition characterized by a particular style, form, or content.

glyph

(noun) picture for a character of printed or written language.

grammar

(noun) collection of rules/specifications describing the valid strings of a particular language.

granularity	(noun) measure of the detail with which some data object set is accessible or is controlled by some process or program.
graph	(noun) picture, or its abstract counterpart, describing the connections among a set of entities. If the direction of the edges is significant, the graph is called *directed*. If names are associated with its nodes and/or edges, it is said to be *labeled*.
ground	(verb) provide a basis for (a theory, for instance); justify; provide a starting point for a recursive definition.
harvesting	(noun) gathering data from several distributed repositories into a combined store.
HDD	(acronym) hard (magnetic) disk drive.
holding	(noun) in a library, archive, or museum, an object that is administered.
identification	(noun) process of ascertaining an identifier associated with a specific object, or sending the identifier from an agent that knows it to an agent that needs it.
identifier	(noun) short string distinguishing an entity from other entities. Names and locations are identifiers. Cf. *name*.
index	(noun) value distinguishing a structure component from other components. *Key* is a synonym; *index* is used when a noniterative algorithm is available for component location, and *key* is used when a variable number of comparisons is required.
indirection	(noun) instance of referring (cf. *reference*); commonly used in the phrase "a level of indirection" because resolution might require following a chain of several pointers. Indirection is essential to recording each datum only once so that its changes will be accessible from many information collections.
information	(noun) the portion of *knowledge* (q.v.) which is, or can be, communicated in speech, signals, pictures, writing, other artifacts, and perhaps even with body language.
ingest	(verb) in the context of a library, accept information and validate it to become a holding. *OAIS* ingest accepts Submission Information Packages from producers, prepares Archival Information Packages for storage, and ensures that Archival Information Packages and their supporting Descriptive Information become established within the *OAIS*.
instance	(noun) specific case from a set of cases; for instance, 8 denotes an instance of integer.
institutional repository	(noun phrase) set of services that an enterprise offers to its community members for the storage, management, and dissemination of informational materials, possibly with emphasis on those created by the institution's staff, with a commitment to the stewardship of these materials, possibly including long-term preservation, as well access to members.
intension	(noun) the internal content of a concept, having some meaning within a context. Cf. *extension*.
interchange	(noun) with respect to information, the action of sharing content across the boundary of two systems that might be incompatible except for this sharing ability.
interface	(noun) convention set permitting cooperation between two purposeful units which are otherwise independent; a sort of contract between two programmers; surface (with keyboards, screen images, audio output) on which a computer user can display, enter, and modify representations of stored objects.
interoperability	(noun) of a computing service, being able to interchange data with computers from different vendors without any special conversion or interfacing tools that users must understand, usually achieved by defining standard formats and protocols.
interpreter	(noun) computer program that, in sequence, translates each statement in a program written in some specific formal language into an instruction sequence for the computing machine on which it is executing and then submits the translated sequence for immediate execution on that machine.

ISO (acronym) International Standards Organization.

key (noun) hard-to-guess token shared only with a few processes or individuals, and sometimes not shared at all, and used as the secret element of a scheme to keep other information secret; see also *index*.

knowledge (noun) that which is contained in human memories (and, to a lesser extent, in animal memories) and which, when used together with reasoning, enables action and communication; cf. *information*.

knowledge management (noun phrase) use of technology to make information relevant and accessible wherever that information may reside, incorporating systematic processes of finding, selecting, organizing, and presenting information in a way that improves an employee's or client's comprehension and use of business assets.

legacy application (noun phrase) an existing computer application which must continue in service in new environments and interact with new kinds of data and service without its program being modified.

library (noun) collection of books, papers, pictures, and other reading materials together with a catalog to this collection; room or building in which such a collection is housed; information service institution with people and other resources that include physical premises, a collection, and a catalog for this collection; electromechanical device to hold and manage a data collection; electronic analog of a collection and catalog that are presumed to be long-lived. The difference between a library and a set of readables is organization conforming to communicated rules.

lingua franca (noun phrase) language used as a common language between speakers whose native languages are different.

link (noun) digital reference that may be external (to a document other than that within which the link itself is found) or internal (to some place in or extent of the document within which it occurs).

locator (noun) string that denotes where a resource is to be found.

logic (noun) study of inference, of what sets of premises support or justify by virtue of the formal relations between their parts, and irrespective of their particular meaning or content.

long-term (noun) relative to the usefulness of an asset, time period long enough for there to be concern about the impact of changing technologies, including support for new media and data formats, and of a changing user community.

map (noun) synonym for *function*; (verb) relative to a *function*, replace the domain entity with the corresponding range entity.

MARC (acronym) MAchine-Readable Cataloging, a standard [for] exchanging bibliographic, holdings, and other data among libraries.

meaning (noun) for a language element or expression, an expression in simpler terms of the same language, or else an associated entity in some other language or model which itself is assumed to be understood..

message authentication code (MAC) (noun phrase) message digest which reliably establishes the identity of the message originator and that the message has not been tampered with.

meta- (prefix) from Greek, and meaning "beyond." For instance, metadata describe a document and related administrative circumstances such as permissions to use.

metadata (noun) descriptive information about other data's content, quality, and other characteristics. Often metadata is provided by people other than the work's authors, and is either in a separate file or a clearly demarked portion of the main file.

METS (acronym) Metadata Encoding and Transmission Standard.

migration	(noun) transfer of digital materials from one hardware/software configuration to another, or from one generation of computer technology to a subsequent generation. *OAIS* defines digital migration as transfer of digital information, while intending to preserve it, distinguished from transfers in general by three attributes: a focus on the preservation of the full information content; a perspective that the new archival implementation of the information is a replacement for the old; and an understanding that full control and responsibility over all aspects of the transfer resides with the *OAIS*.

Digital migrations are identified in the *OAIS* model by four main categories:

> *refreshment* - replacement of a media instance with one of the same type;
>
> *replication* - copying a complete object to a new media instance of the same or different type;
>
> *repackaging* - copying with information content, but some change to packaging information; and
>
> *transformation* - copying with some change to the full information content.

model	(noun) representation showing the structure of or serving as a copy of something, suppressing details deemed irrelevant; (verb) serve as a model, or construct a model. Typically, mathematical representations model computing processes.
name	(noun) string identifying an object in context, not necessarily uniquely. A global name identifies an object uniquely in the world, but not all objects have global names. A local name identifies an object in a limited context, e.g., within a protected resource, with a resource directory mapping local names to embedded objects. Cf. *identifier*
NAS	(acronym) network-attached storage. A NAS device is dedicated to file sharing. NAS allows more storage volumes to be added to a network without disrupting service.
number	(noun) arithmetic value, depicted or expressed by a word, symbol, or figure and representing a particular quantity.
numeral	(noun) figure, work, *glyph*, or group of figures denoting a number.
object	(noun) in this book, following Carnap's *LSW,* anything that can properly be denoted by the subject of a sentence.
objective	(adj.) (opposite of *subjective*), undistorted by emotion or personal bias; based on observable phenomena, as in "objective evidence"; expressing things as perceived without distortion of personal feelings or interpretation; belonging to immediate experience of things or events, as in "there is no objective evidence of anything of the kind." Cf. *subjective.*
one-way hash	(noun phrase) function that produces a message digest that cannot be deciphered to obtain the original.
ontological commitment	(noun phrase) promise to use certain vocabulary in some limited conversations in which it is supposed that the participants understand the same meanings.
ontology	(noun) branch of metaphysics concerned with the nature of being; formal description of the concepts, roles, and relationships that exist for a community of agents. Ontologies provide a shared understanding of a domain that can be communicated across people and applications, and play a major role in supporting information exchange and discovery.
open	(adj.) describing computing characteristics that allow competitive supply of equivalent function that replaces the component in question.
Open Archival Information System (OAIS)	(noun phrase) organization of people and systems that accepts responsibility to preserve information and make it available for a *designated community.* The term 'Open' in *OAIS* implies that its concepts and standards are developed in open forums, rather than that archive access is unrestricted.

operating system   (noun phrase) program that provides basic services for applications running on some computer. Such functions might include screen displays, file handling, and encryption. Microsoft Windows and Linux are examples.

ostensive   (noun) describing a way of defining by direct demonstration, for example, by pointing.

overloaded   (adj.) describing a name that, considered alone in the current context, has two or more distinct meanings.

owner   (noun) relative to some resource, human being or surrogate with the benefits of the existence of that resource, including the right to permit or deny others its use.

paradigm   (noun) Thomas Kuhn's conceptual tool set that a community uses to study a specific topic. The paradigms of theoretical physics, for instance, encompass equations embodying the relevant laws of physics, many specific problems that have been solved with those equations, and pictures or diagrams with a matching vocabulary.

pattern   (noun) set of relationships between elements, abstracted from any physical manifestation.

payload   (noun) information or goods prepared somewhere for use elsewhere; message portion that is the reason for the message.

persistent   (adj.) descriptor of information which outlasts the process manipulating it.

philosophy   (noun) inquiry into and commentary on the most basic and puzzling aspects of human existence and the world.

picture   (noun) in this book, a synonym for *representation* (q.v.) and for *model.*

pointer   (noun) data type whose instances inform about the location of other data, e.g., used for linear stores, where instances are cell numbers.

portability   (noun) property of a program or data, allowing it to be run on or used on several different computer systems.

predicate   (noun) something affirmed or denied concerning the argument of a proposition.

private key   (noun phrase) in an asymmetric cryptographic application, the part of the key that a message originator should share with no-one.

procedure   (noun) method for realizing an operation, expressed as a sequence of steps each of which accomplishes some part of the operation. For programming languages, a program segment viewed as a unit. See also *abstraction* and *rule.*

process   (noun) synonym for activation; program or procedure in execution either by a machine or by an organization. A process is completely characterized by a single current execution point (represented by the machine or organizational state) and the content of an address space or the internal disposition of the organization and its resources.

program   (noun) representation of a set of rules and/or a sequence of operations, expressed as a combination of identifiers of other (simpler) rules and/or operators. Cf. *procedure.*

property   (noun) essential or distinctive attribute of a thing, as in "the color of a pigment"; existence or possibility of an operation for which the thing is an operand, e.g., "measure the color" for a "pigment."

proposition   (noun) assertion that evaluates either to "true" or to "false."

protection block (PB)   (noun phrase) metadata portion that is part of the TDO archiving proposal.

protocol   (noun) prescription of rules which must be followed if two processes are to exchange information intelligibly.

provenance	(noun) account of circumstances of the creation of some resource, including metadata that needs to be conveyed to gain the trust of an eventual user that the resource will meet his requirements.
public key	(noun phrase) in an asymmetric cryptographic application, the part of the key that is shared with the world.
public key certificate	(noun phrase) unforgeable statement that affirms a relationship between a named individual (or organization) and the public part of an asymmetric key pair.
record	(noun) (1) information created, received, and maintained as evidence by an organization or person, in pursuance of legal obligations or in the transaction of business (*ISO 15489*); (2) in computer engineering, a row of a file or a database, or the information that might conveniently be stored in such a row; (3) in business and accounting, information about a single event; (4) in archival science or history, information about a closely related set of events; (5) any interrelated information that might be collected into a single document. Cf. *document*.
recursive	(adj.) with self-reference; describing an entity or relationship whose definition refers to itself either directly or indirectly.
reference	(noun) symbol or string that identifies a resource or another reference; in scholarship, a synonym for *citation*.
reference model	(noun phrase) framework for understanding significant relationships among the entities of some environment, and for the development of standards or specifications supporting the environment, based on a few unifying concepts; representation of an *ontological commitment*.
reliability	(noun) ability of a machine or service to perform consistently, correctly, and precisely according to its specifications, so that people depending on it can be confident about its services; for information, dependability, even for applications whose users risk loss should the object not be precisely what it purports to be.
render	(verb) display a digital object to be intelligible to human beings—a specialized form of *interpret,* for instance, using a browser to display a Web file, or the BBC micro emulator to present Domesday Project results.
replication	(noun) process making one or more data copies to protect against loss of an inherent pattern.
repository	(noun) institution, building, or location where things are deposited and organized, or the digital analog of such physical repositories; implemented resources and processes for managing an organization's or an individual's content collection, consisting of software, machines, housing, and human beings used to manage some collection, with these resources optionally construed as including the collection managed. In the cultural heritage literature, the term is ambiguous as it can refer to an institution, a portion of an institution, an infrastructure for holding materials, or the digital core of such an infrastructure.
represent	(verb) express, designate, stand for, or denote, as a word or symbol does; symbolize; making such an association.
representation	(noun) pattern associated with a meaning; format used for a document, e.g., RTF, XML, MS Word 97, LaTeχ, TIF, JPG.
resolution	(noun) act of using the reference or pointer to understand or fetch whatever it references.
resolve	(verb) find the referent of an identifier.
resolver	(noun) network service that accepts an object name and, either alone or in cooperation with other resolvers, returns the locations of objects with that name; service that maps names to network locations, either by itself or in cooperation with other resolvers. See IETF RFC 2276.

reversible	(adj.) for a transformation, neither adding nor removing any *essential* information; of a mathematical function, having an *inverse*—a related function that, operating on the result, returns the original value.
rewrite rules	(noun phrase) rules which, applied to a character string, might replace some substrings by other strings.
risk	(noun) the likelihood that a vulnerability may result in damage, or that something threatening may become harmful.
role	(noun) relationship of an individual to a social situation, as in "secretary to"; specifically for a library service, the temporary exercise of a proxy, created by claiming as part of establishing a library session.
SAN	(acronym) storage area network. See §9.3.1.
scalar	(adj. or noun) without internal structure relevant to the current discussion.
schema	(noun) pattern or definition of information characterizing the format or structure for all instances of the characterized information.
scope	(noun) set of entities accessible from some active program; a well-defined part of a source program text in which each name is related to a specific meaning; for a topic of discussion, a characterization of what is included and what is intended to be excluded.
security	(noun) property of having controls limiting the circumstances under which resources may be used or modified; conformance to proper authorizations for the movement of data between stores, and for changes made in one store responsive to instructions originating outside its domain.
semantics	(noun) study of meaning; in connection with programming languages, language specification in terms of some other language which is itself assumed to be known. Informal semantics is usually framed in a natural language, such as English. Formal semantics is based on a mathematical language.
server	(noun) process which responds to requests from other processes in a network, usually executing in its own address space and often communicating with other processes only by network messages; machine that executes one or more such processes.
service	(noun) abstract specification of some actions to be performed, possibly implemented as a client part and a server part; process which responds to certain requests for information or action.
side effect	(noun phrase) any change induced by an operation other than the production and delivery of a result.
signal, analog	(noun phrase) information transmission by means in which the intensity is proportional to the value of interest—for instance, as a voltage that is at every instance proportional to the amplitude of a sound.
signal, digital	(noun phrase) information transmission by means of a bit sequence, possibly constructed by periodic sampling of a physical value, with sampling at small time intervals—small compared to the time in which the physical value is expected to change by a significant amount. Except for the errors implicit in sampling, digital transmission can be accomplished with an error rate as small as what the application at hand requires.
signature, electronic	(noun phrase) data in electronic form that is bound to other electronic data to provide authentication.
snapshot	(noun) in a database management system, a query result conveying database state at a particular moment; in a conventional financial reporting system, a balance sheet. (The analog of a database log is a financial journal.)

specification	(noun) artifact description, sufficient so that a newly constructed conforming implementation instance would be deemed satisfactory.
SQL	(acronym) Structured Query Language, a programming language for expressing database queries and update commands.
state	(noun) internal condition of an object, or set of objects. The state of a computing machine is the content of its storage and registers.
store	(noun) in the abstract, a map from locations to values; in the concrete, a means of realizing the abstraction, such as a suitably structured collection of digital circuits. The abstraction describes the means by which data entities may be located; concrete examples are a storeroom and a computer's main storage.
structure	(noun) pattern of organization of entities into larger entities; set of principles describing an organization of entities, for example, "sequence" is the common property of all sequence instances, with one of several organizing principles being that each sequence component, except for the first component, has a predecessor; anything composed of parts arranged together in some determinate way.
subject classification	(noun phrase) set of class names or labels in which each label has as its context relationships with the other classes denoted in the set. Very useful subject classifications are associated with professional societies and their periodicals. For example, see the ACM Computing Classification System description at http://en.wikipedia.org/wiki/ACM_Computing_Classification_System.
subjective	(adjective) not *objective*; having to do with personal opinions, tastes, judgments, purposes or feelings that can be talked about but not shared, except perhaps incompletely. Cf. *objective*.
surrogate	(noun) individual acting for another, with a subset of the privileges of the latter individual; entity replacing or denoting for another, e.g., a business agent is a surrogate for an actor.
syntax	(noun) originating from the Greek words συν (sun, meaning "together") and ταξις (taxis, meaning sequence/order), is the study or use of rules governing the arrangement of words in speech or writing, such as the rules of a programming language for construction of meaningful programs from character strings.
system	(noun) careful combination of smaller elements that is talked of as a whole and provides some service.
TCB	(acronym) Trusted Computing Base.
TDO	(acronym) Trustworthy Digital Object.
transaction	(noun) process carried to a stage of completion; unit of processing carried out by a program activation starting from and ending with a dormant state of relatively long duration; in database systems, a unit of processing that is guaranteed either to complete a specified set of state changes or to leave the database unchanged; see *atomic unit of work*.
tree	(noun) directed graph in which each node has exactly one incoming arc, except for a single node, called the root, which has no incoming arcs.
trusted computing base (TCB)	(noun phrase) protection mechanism within a computer system, including hardware, firmware, and/or software, the combination of which enforces a security policy.
trustworthy	(adj.) describing information and/or services that deserve people's confidence for announced purposes.
trustworthy Institution (TI)	(noun phrase) organization that can be trusted, for any document that it certifies with a message authentication code, to have faithfully tested that the document conforms to properties it asserts or communicates.

tuple	(noun) member of a set of records, usually used when the set constitutes a row of some table in a relational database.
Turing machine	(noun phrase) symbol manipulating device that, despite its extreme simplicity, can be programmed to simulate any feasible single-thread computer. Described in 1936 by Alan Turing, such machines were intended to be feasible without necessarily being practical. Instead, they are used for thought experiments about the limits of mechanical computation.
two-phase commit	(noun phrase) protocol for maintaining consistency in a database.[455]
unit of work	(noun phrase) procedure or process portion constituting a database change from one valid state to another valid state.
URI	(acronym) Uniform Resource Identifier.
UVC	(acronym) Universal Virtual Computer.
value	(noun) magnitude, quantity, number; point in the range of a function corresponding to a particular point in its domain.
version	(noun) one of a set of representations of approximately the same information, often a member of a time-sequence of successively improved instances, but versions are created for other purposes; examples are a formatted version of marked-up text, a low-resolution derivative of a portrait, and a two-dimensional projection of a three-dimensional design.
volume	(noun) physical object on which data is stored; computer disk or tape.
work	(noun) distinct intellectual or artistic creation. Shakespeare's *Macbeth* is considered a *work*. An *expression* is the realization of a work in the form of alpha-numeric, music, or choreographic notation, sound, image, and movement, or any combination of such forms. *Macbeth* in the form of English language text is an expression of the work *Macbeth*. Finally, a *manifestation* is a physical embodiment of an expression of a work. The Folger Shakespeare Library edition of *Macbeth*, published in paperback by Washington Square Press in 2004, is a distinct manifestation of the work *Macbeth*.
XML	(acronym) eXtensible Mark-up Language, which allows document originators to specify the structures in their documents and have these understood and displayed by browsers and other programs.
XML namespaces	(noun phrase) collection of names, identified by a URI reference, which are used in XML documents as element identifiers, types, and attribute names.

---

[455] Gray 1993, *Transaction processing*, §7.5.2.

Appendix B: Uniform Resource Identifier Syntax

What follows[456] is supplied both for its value in itself and as a practical illustration of regular expressions (§6.2.1).

URI-reference	= [absoluteURI | relativeURI] ["#" fragment]
absoluteURI	= scheme ":" (hier_part | opaque_part)
relativeURI	= (net_path | abs_path | rel_path) ["?" query]
hier_part	= (net_path | abs_path) ["?" query]
opaque_part	= uric_no_slash *uric
uric_no_slash	= unreserved|escaped| ";" | "?" | ":" | "@" |"&" | "=" | "+" | "$" | ","
net_path	= "//" authority [abs_path]
abs_path	= "/" path_segments
rel_path	= rel_segment [abs_path]
rel_segment	= 1*(unreserved | escaped | ";" | "@" | "&" | "=" | "+" | "$" | ",")
scheme	= alpha *(alpha | digit | "+" | "-" | ".")
authority	= server | reg_name
reg_name	= 1*(unreserved|escaped| "$" | "," | ";" | ":" | "@" | "&" | "=" | "+")
server	= [[userinfo "@"] hostport]
userinfo	= *(unreserved | escaped | ";" | ":" | "&" | "=" | "+" | "$" | ",")
hostport	= host [":" port]
host	= hostname | IPv4address
hostname	= *(domainlabel ".") toplabel ["."]
domainlabel	= alphanum | alphanum *(alphanum | "-") alphanum
toplabel	= alpha | alpha *(alphanum | "-") alphanum
IPv4address	= 1*digit "." 1*digit "." 1*digit "." 1*digit
port	= *digit
path	= [abs_path | opaque_part]
path_segments	= segment *("/" segment)
segment	= *pchar *(";" param)
param	= *pchar
pchar	= unreserved | escaped | ":" | "@" | "&" | "=" | "+" | "$" | ","
query	= *uric
fragment	= *uric
uric	= reserved | unreserved | escaped
reserved	= ";" | "/" | "?" | ":" | "@" | "&" | "=" | "+" | "$" | ","

---

[456]   From Berners-Lee 1998, *Uniform Resource Identifiers (URI)*, IETF RFC 2396.

unreserved	= alphanum | mark
mark	= "-" | "_" | "." | "!" | "~" | "*" | "'" | "(" | ")"
escaped	= "%" hex hex
hex	= digit | "A" | "B" | "C" | "D" | "E" | "F" | "a" | "b" | "c" | "d" | "e" | "f"
alphanum	= alpha | digit
alpha	= lowalpha | upalpha
lowalpha	= "a" | "b" | "c" | "d" | "e" | "f" | "g" | "h" | "i" | "j" | "k" | "l" | "m" | "n" | "o" | "p" | "q" | "r" | "s" | "t" | "u" | "v" | "w" | "x" | "y" | "z"
upalpha	= "A" | "B" | "C" | "D" | "E" | "F" | "G" | "H" | "I" | "J" | "K" | "L" | "M" | "N" | "O" | "P" | "Q" | "R" | "S" | "T" | "U" | "V" | "W" | "X" | "Y" | "Z"
digit	= "0" | "1" | "2" | "3" | "4" | "5" | "6" | "7" | "8" | "9"

Appendix C: Repository Requirements

The cultural heritage community has been paying a great deal of attention to descriptions that would figure in repository quality certification. A challenge with such specifications is to make each listed requirement as objective as possible so that auditors' appraisals would not depend on the human biases. To discover the extent to which this is possible, we have drafted such a statement focused on museums. This continues as a work in progress that is available on application to the author.

Although a formal requirements analysis is usually written only when information technology services or products are about to be purchased, it can be extremely helpful for an institution to distinguish among today's needs, needs that can wait for several years, and generic needs that are irrelevant to that institution. It can also expedite informing the institution what is available from existing tools and offerings, what needs to be integrated into the institutional environment, which needs require research and development, and what specific training is needed for staff members.

- Ideally, such a document would have sufficient quality and detail to be useful first in an RFP, and later as part of a services contract. In the latter role, it should be useful to test compliance by the vendor.
- Ideally, every specified requirement would be such that shortfalls would be clear to an objective critic.
- A response should further address all portions of some explicitly identified and clearly defined enterprise objectives, and, for any "line item" requirement, specify broad aspects of the expected deliverable (e.g., "this is expected to be a software component".)
- Finally, each requirement would be specific to a real situation in a real institution. For instance, if the archiving service had to use particular software to interoperate with preexisting services, or because personnel were trained in some particular family of application programs, this would be stated.

We expect a plan to articulate concisely each objective, the resources needed to meet it, commitments to specific actions, a schedule for each technology or service delivery, and a prescription for measuring outcomes and quality. If the plan is for a large project, we expect it to be expressed in portions that separate teams can address relatively independently, and expect that a plan document exists for each team. We further expect concise descriptions of the environment—business and social circumstances that the participants cannot substantially change. If an environmental factor is adverse, we expect the plan to indicate how the team will bypass or mitigate its effects. If the resources currently available are inadequate, we expect the plan to identify each shortfall. Finally, if the team has already worked on the topic, we expect its plan to list its previous achievements.

Engineers want questions that can be answered objectively by testable facts. They expect documents clear enough so that every participant and every qualified observer can understand what is committed and what work is not authorized, and can judge whether committed progress is being achieved.

Any comprehensive requirements analysis faces a perplexing challenge. Next to no one wants to use such checklists. We recognize that doing so would surely be tedious.[457] However, most repositories need to accommodate many detailed requirements. Since "the devil is in the details," there would seem to be no alternative to working with and refining careful detail lists, discussing their individual items with the eventual software users, and using such lists both for software development and software selection.

The dilemma is far from new. Numerous 1980s software development studies resulted in "best practices" expositions that next to nobody either objected to or followed, even though the business press had many articles about software project cost overruns, schedule disappointments, and outright failures partly caused by inadequate appreciation of requirements. This dilemma is still with us.[458]

In a *Fortune* interview, Fred Brooks observed that, while technology managers widely quote his 1975 book, *The Mythical Man-Month*, few actually follow its recommendations.[459] Brooks, who managed IBM's OS/360 software development, argued that adding more people to a software project that is behind schedule slows it even further. This is because adding people increases bureaucracy and needed training. It can be better to slip the schedule, limit the scope, and/or phase features into later versions. Brooks was not surprised that managers continue to make the same mistakes.

---

[457] The Web page draft is about 50 pages long and far from reading like popular literature. However, nobody seems ready to say that it is more complicated than warranted by the technical issues. The experience is not new; after the 1995 transfer of IBM Digital Library from the IBM Research Division to the IBM Santa Teresa Development Laboratory, the new project owners were little interested in anybody's analyses of product shortfalls—not even analyses written by its IBM Research originators.

[458] An example is a recent scandal of a U.S. FBI expenditure of over $200M for a system it has discovered is unusable.

[459] Roth 2005, *Quoted Often, Followed Rarely.*

Appendix D: Assessment with Independent Criteria

Readers might reasonably ask how TDO methodology measures up against independently articulated objectives. For the most part, they would have to make such assessments themselves with such aid as the book's citations provide. However, a start for such an assessment is provided by the following two tables, whose early columns are excerpts respectively from a long-running task force on preservation authenticity[460] and a workshop of library managers.[461]

Table 12: TDO conformance to InterPARES authenticity criteria

InterPARES authenticity requirement	How TDO methodology would handle it
§1.2 Assessing Authenticity: the preserver's inference of the authenticity of electronic records must be further supported by evidence … that they have been maintained using … procedures that either guarantee their continuing identity and integrity or at least minimize risks of change from the time the records were first set aside to the point at which they are subsequently accessed.	Each TDO carries or reliably links to its authenticity evidence. Surreptitious TDO changes are prevented.
§1.3 Production of Authentic Copies of Electronic Records: After the records have been [appraised as] authentic, and have been transferred from the creator to the preserver, their authenticity needs to be maintained by the preserver [by] … producing copies according to procedures that also maintain authenticity.	Other than bit-stream backup, TDO custodians should do nothing. Action other than including a TDO in the payload of another TDO will destroy authenticity evidence!
Any [type] of copy is authentic if attested to be so by the official preserver.	See §11.1.1 about authenticity assertions.
2.2 Verification of Authenticity: verification of authenticity [establishes] a correspondence between known facts about the record and the various contexts in which it has been created and maintained, and the proposed fact of the record's authenticity.	TDO validation is by establishing that its seal is valid and resealing only TDOs from trustworthy acquaintances. See §11.2.2.
§A.1 Expression of Record Attributes and Linkage to Record: attributes [specified elsewhere must] be expressed explicitly and linked inextricably to the record … to establish a record's identity and demonstrate its integrity.	See §11.1.2.
§A.2 Access Privileges: the creator [manages] access privileges concerning the creation, modification, annotation, relocation, and destruction of records. Effective implementation … involves the monitoring of access through an audit trail.	Not needed because sealing prevents surreptitious alteration.
§A.3 Protection against loss or corruption: the creator [manages] procedures to prevent, discover, and correct loss or corruption of records.	Replication (§10.2). The seal makes evident any inappropriate change.

---

[460]   From MacNeil 2002, *Providing Grounds for Trust II.*

[461]   The first two columns of this table are copied from Report of the Warwick Workshop November 2005, *Digital Curation and Preservation*, §2.1, "Common research issues identified across all three discussion groups" (items 1 to 15) and §2.2, "Specific research topics" (items 16 to 32).

Table 12 continued

InterPARES authenticity requirement[462]	How TDO methodology would handle it
§A.4 Protective procedures, Media and Technology: the creator [manages effective] procedures to guarantee the continuing identity and integrity of records against media deterioration and across technological change;	Computer file backup provides this to compensate for hardware and media deterioration and change.
§A.5 Establishment of Documentary Forms: the creator has established the documentary forms of records ...	Record forms are established by published standards or community conventions.
§A.6 Authentication of Records: ... specific rules regarding which records must be authenticated, by whom, and the means of authentication. [A]uthentication is understood to be a declaration of a record's authenticity ... by [an official].	By sealing, an producer converts a digital object into a signed TDO.
§A.7 Authentication of Authoritative Record: if multiple copies of the same record exist, the creator has established procedures that identify which record is authoritative ... as one of the components of a records retention schedule.	Not required, because digital copying is perfect, including maintaining all seals.
§A.8: if ... records [move] from active status to ... inactive status, which involves the removal of records from the electronic system, the creator [manages transfer of] documentation ... to the preserver along with the records.	Producers convert ordinary digital objects to TDOs before of sending them to an archival repository.
§B.1 Controls over Records Transfer, Maintenance, and Reproduction: the procedures ... used to transfer records to the archival institution must be [under business controls that] guarantee the records' identity and integrity.	Rules for converting digital object into TDOs and transferring these to an archival repository must be managed.
§B.2 Documentation of Reproduction Process and its Effects: is an essential means of demonstrating that reproduction is free from pretence or deceit.	Part of the previous requirement.
§B.3 Archival Description: the archival description of the fonds containing the electronic records includes ... information about changes the electronic records of the creator have undergone since they were first created.	TDOs are never changed except by destroying their TDO property.

The item numbering in the following table is from the Warwick report, with gaps for items calling for "virtualization." These are omitted because what the Warwick report means by virtualization is either murky or refers to representing digitally something that is inscribed or performed in some nondigital fashion. In the latter case, there exists no outstanding conceptual problem hindering virtualization.

---

[462] From MacNeil 2002, *Providing Grounds for Trust II.*

Table 13: Comments on a European technical research agenda

2005 Warwick Workshop on *Digital Curation and Preservation*		Relationship to the current book
Discovery and location	1. Adopt or develop an agreed, **persistent, actionable, identifier for digital objects,** with associated name resolvers which are themselves persistent.	§7.3	It might be convenient to have persistent resolvers, but is not strictly necessary.
	2. Continue to develop **search and discovery tools** in partnership with relevant user groups.		Not a preservation topic.
	3. Develop more **detailed Data Models** for each domain and abstract out intra-domain and inter-domain commonalities.	§6.4	Not a preservation topic.
Trust	4. Develop and integrate **DRM, provenance and authenticity** checking into ingest processes.		Not a preservation topic.
	5. Prototype and test national certification "badges" as **prototypes of certification processes.**		No comment.
Cost	6. Continuing **data collection and modeling of costs,** with adequately complex parameterization, over the life cycle of different data types.		Mostly a digital library challenge.
Automation	7. Develop language to **describe data policy** demands and processes, together with associated support systems.		Not a preservation topic.
	8. Develop **collection oriented description** and transfer techniques.	§10.4	OAI-PMH development addresses this. However, the need for domain knowledge has created practical limitations.[393]
	9. Develop data description tools and associated generic migration applications to **facilitate automation.**		The number of digital objects will be so large that every promising opportunity for automation should be explored.
	10. Develop **standardised intermediate forms** with sets of coder/decoder pairs to and from specific common formats.		Perhaps the UVC is what the Warwick participants meant by an intermediate form.
	11. Develop **code generation tools** for automatically creating software for format migration.	§12.1.2	Format migration risks unacceptable errors that are not discovered in time for repairs.
	13. Management and policy specifications will be need to be formalised and virtualised.		
	15. Develop **automatic processes for metadata extraction**	§13.2	Much progress is possible, but full automation is infeasible because metadata choice will require subjective decisions.

The numbers with §7.3 and similar column values relate to relevant sections of the current book.

Table 13 continued

2005 Warwick Workshop on *Digital Curation and Preservation*		Relationship to the current book
Virtualization 16. Continuing work on ways of **describing information all the way from the bits upwards,** in standardised ways – "virtualization".		Almost every case for which this helps everyday information exploitation will be addressed by the IT community.
18. Develop use of **data format description languages** to characterize the structures present within a digital record, independently of the original creation application.	§6.2.2	BNF is such a language, and is known address this adequately.
19. It is important to make significant progress on dealing with **dynamic data including databases,** and object behavior.	§5.4	No unsolved technical problem exists.
20. **Representation Information tools,** probably via layers of virtualization to allow appropriate normalization, including mature tools for dealing with dynamic data including databases.		Nobody has identified any unsolved conceptual problem; good tools would be valuable.
21. Additional work on **preservation strategies and support tools,** from emulation to virtualization.	§12.2.1	We need UVC representations for the most interesting data types.
Automation 23. Develop protocols and information management exchange mechanisms, including synchronization techniques for indices, etc., to **support federations.**		Not a preservation issue.
24. **Standardized APIs** for applications and data integration techniques	§9.1	Not a preservation issue.
25. Fuller development of **workflow systems and process definition** and control.		Sophisticated tools are available from commercial content management vendors, but have neither been tailored for cultural repositories nor is there evidence that these have been considered by the cultural heritage community.

Table 13 continued

2005 Warwick Workshop on *Digital Curation and Preservation*		Relationship to the current book
Support	26. Develop simple semantic **descriptions of Designated Communities.**	§8.1.5	The functionality desired can probably be accomplished with role-based access control.
	27. **Standardize Registry/Repositories for Representation Information** to facilitate sharing.	§11.1	This would be accomplished if the repositories alluded to were to choose and use a subset of existing metadata standards.
	28. Develop **methodologies and services for archiving personal collections** of digital materials.		Not a preservation issue.
Hardware	29. Develop and **standardize interfaces** to allow "pluggable" storage hardware systems.		Not a preservation issue.
	30. **Standardize archive storage API,** In other words, standardized storage virtualization.	§9.1	Repositories should use only content management offerings conforming to the JSR 170 standard
	31. Develop **certification processes for storage systems.**		It is unclear what is called for beyond what storage managers and commercial customers already do.
	32. Undertake research to characterize types of read and **transmission errors** and the development of techniques which detect and potentially correct them.	§9.3.1	This topic is well handled by the vendors of storage hardware.

Appendix E: Universal Virtual Computer Specification

Raymond Lorie has designed a Turing-complete computer with powerful and flexible bit-string instructions that exploit the fact that performance is of secondary importance.[463] This UVC architecture relies on the oldest computer science concepts without secondary features commonly used to improve performance. It tries to be natural; for instance, a negative number is a positive number with a sign (rather than using 2's-complement form). It has no notion of byte or word length, but instead implements bit-level addressing. This UVC consists of a CPU, a status (condition flag and error indicator), an instruction counter, and a memory (Fig. 40). Its programs are machine language sequences, with little glue to hold their pieces together. The instruction set includes input/output commands to exchange data between a UVC emulator and a Restore Application. The emulator and restore application cannot be written until the architecture of the eventual target machine is known.

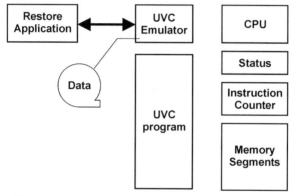

Fig. 40: Universal Virtual Computer (UVC) architecture

It would be unrealistic to expect that the proposed UVC will never change. Any preserved document using the UVC mechanism should contain the UVC version identification.

E.1 Memory Model

The UVC memory model is that of a segmented store in which each segment contains an arbitrarily large *register* set and a bit-addressable *sequential memory*. A register may contain a value or a pointer to a particular se-

---

[463] Appendix E is adapted from IBM Research Report RJ 10338 (2005) with the kind permission of the IBM Almaden Research Center.

quential memory bit (actually the displacement from the beginning of the segment). Registers are of unlimited length. An integer value occupies as many bits as necessary at the right of the register. The sign is a separate bit (0 for plus, 1 for minus). The UVC itself maintains the length of the value internally. The only operations involving a segment's memory move information from/to memory to/from registers or communicate with the external world. A segment is uniquely identified by a *Physical Segment Number.*

A UVC program is composed of interacting sections, each stored in a segment. An individual section can address all segments that are in its *address space*. During an execution, the UVC emulator manages a mapping of physical segments to logical segments. (All segment numbers below are logical segment numbers.) A section's address space contains segments 0, 1, and 2, plus a segment that contains the section code, plus an arbitrary number of segments containing variables and data. If a section is called recursively, the code is stored only once, but each instantiation has its own address space.

Segment 0   is accessible by any section (it belongs to all address spaces). It contains a collection of shared constants and variables. There is a mechanism to load the constants initially (see *archive module,* below).

Segment 1   is accessible by the section to which it belongs. If the section is invoked recursively, segment 1 can be addressed by all instantiations; it acts as a shared memory to communicate between multiple activations of the same section.

Segment 2   There is one such segment per address space; its function is to handle data exchange during invocations (calls) among sections. If a section A invokes a section B, A will see the results of B in A's segment 2. (The UVC will adjust the mapping, avoiding a need to copy the results from one segment to another.)

Segments   are shared. Each belongs to the address spaces of all sections. For instance,
3 to 999   if two sections refer to a segment 4, both see the same segment 4.

Segments   are private. If two sections refer to segment 1,000, the emulator maps them
>= 1,000   onto different physical segments. When such a section is invoked recursively, each invocation receives its own instance.

E.2 Machine Status Registers

The status of the UVC after an operation is conveyed by a *condition flag* reflecting the result of the last comparison operation, and a 32-bit *error indicator* identifying the error that occurred. Error values are specific to each UVC emulator implementation. They are intended to assist debugging that implementation.

An *instruction counter* indicates the address of the next instruction to be executed, and is updated by the CPU each time an instruction completes.

The address is composed of two integers (each of 32 bits): the number of the segment containing the section, and the bit-offset of the instruction inside that segment.

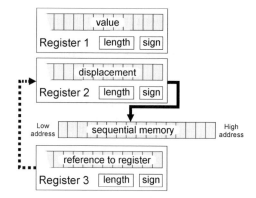

Fig. 41: Exemplary register contents in UVC instructions

In any instruction, the specification of a register R may include an indirection flag (R*). When the emulator encounters a register R*, the content of R* is a register number which identifies the register containing the operand. The various cases are illustrated in Fig. 41.

E.3 Machine Instruction Codes

Most UVC instructions have the same format: an eight-bit operation code followed by zero, one, two, or three 64-bit strings. Each 64-bit string designates a register: the first 32 bits identify a segment; the next 32 bits are decomposed into an indirection flag and a 31-bit value that identifies a register in that segment.

In the example that follows, the operation code expects two operands: Reg1 and Reg2. Reg1 stands for a pair (s1, r1), denoting the content of register r1 in segment s1. The content of a register may be a value or an address (a displacement) in the sequential memory, if that is what the instruction expects. The specification of an operand is a 64-bit string, composed of a segment number (seg) and a register number (reg) with its indirection flag. If that flag is 0, the register contains the operand; if it is 1, the register contains the number of the register (in the same segment) that contains the operand (the lengths are shown in parentheses):

Op (8 bits)	Segment (32 bits)	Flag (1 bit)	Register (31 bits)	Segment (32 bits)	Flag (1 bit)	Register (31 bits)

Only a few instruction formats differ from this. All instructions are shown in the following table.

In a register, the rightmost bit is the least significant. When the register length is automatically updated as the result of an operation, leftmost bits appear or disappear (the length is updated accordingly). When a register is transferred to memory, the leftmost bit of the register is copied at the bit position indicated in the instruction; the next bit in the register is copied to the next bit (higher bit address) in the memory, and so on. The inverse operation is clearly defined. The process is depicted in Fig. 42.

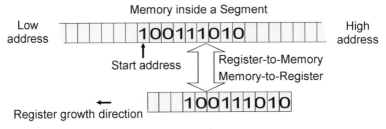

Fig. 42: UVC bit order semantics

When data is transferred from memory to the communication channel (details below), the bit at the address specified in the instruction is sent first, then the bit at that address +1, +2, and so on. The inverse operation stores the first bit received on the channel at the address supplied in the instruction, the next bit at the address +1, and so on.

The sequential memory can be initialized by first loading a value in a register and then storing the register value in the memory. A register can also be initialized by loading a value from the sequential memory.

Register manipulations

0A	*load*	Reg1, Reg2, Reg3	Load from memory to register.
			Insert into Reg1 a k-bit string from memory, starting at address in Reg2; the length k is in Reg3.
			The length of Reg1 is set to k.
0B	*store*	Reg1, Reg2, Reg3	Store from register into memory.
			Store the rightmost k bits from Reg1 into memory at address in Reg2. The length k is given in Reg3.
0C	*lsign*	Reg1, Reg2	Load sign.
			Set the sign of Reg1 to 0 (or 1) if the single memory bit at address in Reg2 is 0 (or 1).
0D	*ssign*	Reg1, Reg2	Save sign.
			Set the memory bit at address in Reg2 to 0 (or 1) if the sign of Reg1 is 0 (or 1).

	14	*loadr*	Reg1, Reg2	Load register.
				Copy the content of Reg2 into Reg1 (including the sign).
				After the operation, the lengths of Reg1 and Reg2 are identical.
	15	*psign*	Reg1	Set sign to positive. Set sign of Reg1 to 0.
	16	*nsign*	Reg1, Reg2	Set sign to negative. Set sign of Reg1 to 1.
	17	*loadc*	Reg1, k, string	Insert in Reg1, right justified, the k bits of the given string;
				k is a 32-bit integer denoting the length of the string.
				The length of the register is set to k. The sign of Reg1 is unaffected.
	18	*rlen*	Reg1, Reg2	Get register length.
				Store the length of Reg2 into Reg1. If an operand is expected to be a 32-bit integer but is actually shorter, it is padded with zeros on the left; if it is larger, an error condition is raised. Since some of instructions change the length of a register, this instruction provides access to the length.

Numeric Instructions

These instructions may cause the lengths of registers to change to accommodate the result. The sign is set to the result sign; if the result is zero, the sign is set to 0 (positive). All numeric instructions are performed according to the laws of binary arithmetic.

Addition	**1E**	*add*	Reg1, Reg2	The sum of the values in Reg1 and Reg2 is computed and stored in Reg1. The size of the register r1 is set to the order of the leftmost 1 bit in Reg1.
Subtraction	**1F**	*subt*	Reg1, Reg2	The value in Reg2 is subtracted from the value in Reg1 and the result is stored in Reg1.
				The size of the register r1 is set to the order of the leftmost 1 bit in Reg1.
Multiplication	**20**	*mult*	Reg1, Reg2	The product of the values in Reg1 and Reg2 are computed and stored in Reg1. The sign of Reg1 is also updated.
				The size of Reg1 is set to the order of the leftmost 1 bit in Reg1.

Division	**21**	*div*	Reg1, Reg2, Reg3	The division of the value in Reg1 by the value in Reg2 is computed; the quotient is stored in Reg1.
				The size of Reg1 is set to the order of the left-most 1 bit in Reg1. The remainder is stored in Reg3. The sign of Reg1 is also updated, and the sign of Reg3 is set to the original sign of Reg1.

Comparison instructions

Greater than	**28**	*grt*	Reg1, Reg2	Set the condition flag to 1 if the value in Reg1 is larger than the value in Reg2; (the signs are taken into account).
Equal to	**29**	*equ*	Reg1, Reg2	Set the condition flag to 1 if the value in Reg1 is equal to the value in Reg2; (the signs are taken into account).

Logical instructions

Negation	**32**	*not*	Reg1	All bits are inverted in Reg1.
				The post-execution length of Reg1 is the same as the pre-execution one.
Inclusive or	**33**	*or*	Reg1, Reg2	The bits in Reg1 and Reg2 are or'ed bit by bit and the result is stored in Reg1.
				If the pre-execution length of Reg2 is less than that of Reg1, Reg2 is virtually left-padded with 0s (the post-execution length of Reg2 remains unchanged). If the pre-execution length of Reg2 is larger than that of Reg1, Reg1 is left-padded with 0s (the post-execution length of Reg1 becomes equal to the length of Reg2).
	34	*and*	Reg1, Reg2	The bits in Reg1 and Reg2 are and'ed bit by bit and the result is stored in Reg1.
				If the pre-execution length of Reg2 is less than that of Reg1, Reg2 is virtually left-padded with 1's (the post-execution length of Reg2 remains unchanged). If the pre-execution length of Reg2 is larger than that of Reg1, Reg1 is left-padded with 1's (the post-execution length of Reg1 becomes equal to the length of Reg2).

Instructions that alter the flow of execution

Unconditional branch	**3C**	*br*	Reg1	Set the instruction pointer to the displacement of the target instruction in the same section.
Conditional branch	**3D**	*brc*	Reg1	The instruction acts as the previous one (br) if the condition flag is on. Otherwise, the execution proceeds sequentially.

Subroutine invocation	**3F**	*call*	Reg1, Reg2, Reg3	Invoke code section identified by Reg1;
				Reg2 identifies the starting address of the first instruction to be executed; Reg3 identifies the segment used to submit parameter(s).
	3E	*break*	--	Return control to the calling section at instruction following the call.
	40	*stop*	--	Stop execution and return the emulator to its initial state, waiting for a new input.
Communication with the outside world (I/O)				The communication makes use of a simple channel abstraction. The abstract channel behaves as a half-duplex communication channel. Any "message" traveling on the channel is composed of three components:
				1) Message Type (a 32-bit integer) identifies the role of the data being transferred. It may be a tag for a piece of data or simply a code that is used for synchronization between the UVC program and the application.
				2) Message Length (a 32-bit integer) is the length of the data being transferred.
				3) Message Body is the actual bit-string to be transferred.
Fetch data (Fig. 43)	**46**	*in*	Reg1, Reg2, Reg3	The contents of Reg1 and Reg2 before the operation are irrelevant.
				Reg1 will be set to the message type received.
				Reg2 will be set to the length of the message.
				Reg3 specifies the starting memory address where the data will be stored.
Deliver data (Fig. 43)	**47**	*out*	Reg1, Reg2, Reg3	Reg1 contains the message type.
				Reg2 contains the length of the data to be transferred.
				Reg3 contains the starting memory address where the data resides.

The UVC convention requires a half-duplex abstract channel that must be enforced by all specific implementations. Fig. 43 illustrates the only valid communication patterns.

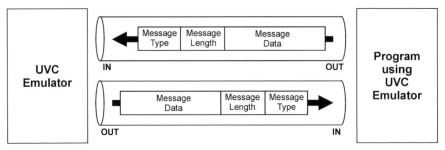

Fig. 43: Valid UVC communication patterns

The UVC convention imposes no additional requirement on the use and/or specific implementation of the channel. For instance, if the bit-string to be transferred is larger than the maximum allowed, it can be split into multiple messages; the exchange can be controlled by introducing message types such as message start, message continuation, and message end. Similarly, synchronization between the UVC emulator and the outside application can be established by sending specific user defined messages types with no data. (When the message length is zero the memory address specified in Reg3 is ignored.)

E.4 Organization of an Archived Module

A program is built of multiple sections that call each other. Sections can be written independently, using symbolic names for segments. An ordinary compile and link process transforms these symbolic references into segment numbers. The module is then obtained by concatenating items according to the following hierarchical structure:

> **Stream:**   **Nconstants, Constant*, Nsections, Section***
> **Constant:**   **Reg#, Sign, Length, string**
> **Section:**   **Segment#, Length, Code**

Nconstants (a 32-bit integer) is the number of constants that must be loaded in segment 0; it is followed by Nconstants structures of type Constant, followed by Nsections (a 32-bit integer), the number of program sections to be loaded, followed by Nsections structures of type Section.

The structure of type Constant is the concatenation of a register number (a 32-bit integer), a sign bit, a string length L (a 32-bit integer), and the L-bit string itself.

A structure of type Section is the concatenation of a segment number (a 32-bit integer), the length of the code in bits (a 32-bit integer), and the code itself. The segment number indicates in which segment the section code must be loaded. By definition, the first section in the archived module is the starting section of the program.

E:5 Application Example

In many applications, the function of the UVC program will be to decode a
file format to return the results according to a predefined logical view. In
more general cases, the UVC program can also implement any arbitrary
logic, using some input parameters and/or some input file(s). The following program is simple but still illustrates the more general case. Instead of
processing a file, it generates the results of a recursive computation.

```
int a = 10; // introduced to illustrate sharing
void main ( )      {
     int x, y, w; scanf ("%d", &x);
     y = factorial(x);
     w = a * y;
     printf ("%d\n", w);
     }
int factorial (int x) {
     int z;
     if (x == 1) return (1);
     z = x * factorial(x-1);
     printf ("%d %d\n", a, z);
     return (z);
     }      }
```

The execution of this C program produces:

```
10 2
10 6
10 24
240
```

For a simple output, the documentation may easily explain to the future
user what the output represents. But, in general, the future user will want
to process the data and it is therefore preferable to return the data elements,
one by one, and tagged. If tag=1 identifies the output for a, tag=2 identifies
the output for z, and tag=3 identifies the output for w, the results would be:

```
1    10
2    2
1    10
2    6
1    10
2    24
3    240
```

This is what is implemented in the UVC program below. The documentation might explain the format by using a simple specification (such as a
DTD in XML):

Result: Line*, W
Line: A, Z
A (1)
Z (2)
W (3)

in which the values in parentheses indicate the tag values.

Constants.asm

```
# Constants to be defined in segment 0
# Entry format:
# register   sign (plus: 0, minus: 1)   length (in bits)   value (in hex)

# Constants used for communication
0 0 1 0x0         # default entry address into a section
1 0 1 0x1         # constant 1 = the message tag for a
2 0 2 0x2         # constant 2 = the message tag for z
3 0 2 0x3         # constant 3 = the message tag for w
4 0 16 0xFFFF     # constant is memory address of message to be output

# Global variables
5 0 4 0xA    # a = 10
```

Main.asm

```
Main
1001              # segment number for Main section
0,1002,1003       # segments this section references (for assembler only)

# Program: Main, to compute the factorial of a given number
# This program computes the factorial of a value received over the
# communication channel. It outputs the result as binary values.
# These values are tagged as mentioned in the simple specification above;
# the tags themselves are communicated as message types.
#
# By convention, the argument to the factorial section is loaded in register
# 1 of the segment containing the argument. The result is communicated
# back in register 2 of the same segment.

# section uses 1002 as working segment
# Set input address in register (1002,12): 255
LOADC 1002 1 8 0xFF

# Get argument and load it in argument section (1003)
IN 1002 2 1002 3 1002 1      # only (1002,1) is an input argument
LOAD 1003 1 1002 1 1002 3 # save input value x in (1003,1)
```

```
# Set up arguments to call Factorial (seg 1010) with arguments (seg 1003)
LOADC 1002 4 12 0x3F2    # set (1002, 4) to value 1010
LOADC 1002 5 12 0x3EB    # set (1002, 5) to value 1003

# Call the factorial section
CALL 1002 4 0 0 1002 5

# z = a * factorial(x)
LOADR 1002 6 0 5          # copy value of a in (1002,6)
MULT 1002 6 1003 2        # multiply a by the result of factorial
RLEN 1002 3 1002 6        # store length of result in (1002,3)
STORE 1002 6 0 4 1002 3   # store result in output area - at address
                         # specified in (0,4)
OUT 0 3 1002 3 0 4        # message type = 3 (0, 3)
STOP
```

Appendix F: Software Modules Wanted

A repository manager is likely to want effortless addition of all repository components of a preservation solution to his existing software infrastructure (level 10 in Fig. 24). Providing such support would today be difficult because there exist about 100 viable repository software offerings and because every institution will want behavioral and appearance tailoring that is different from the tailoring even in similar institutions. A good alternative is a modular suite delivering widely useful functionality with parametric and interface options that are easily exploited by local software engineers, as suggested by Fig. 25.

In contrast, we can easily provide[464] personal computer components pleasing in the light of most people's expectations and skills, because almost everybody uses one of three operating systems and everybody will be able to share a single family of office document formats. As end users, we tend to value familiar interfaces over personal customization.

Preservation components for execution in personal computers should include:

- An editor with which information producers can create and update TDOs whose structure is described in §11.1.
- Fig. 38 and Fig. 39 encoding and rendering tools for each blob file type requiring UVC assistance for producing programs suggested in Appendix E. §4.2 of Gladney 2005 suggests how to estimate the cost of this work.
- Protection block creation and editing tools which are modest extensions of metadata editors.
- A tool with which information consumers can browse the certificate signature forests. Ideally, this would have a pictorial interactive displace looking something like Fig. 37, with each node labeled to identify its signature owner, and colored to distinguish nodes accepted and rejected from each other and from nodes not yet inspected.[465] Whenever a certificate is accepted, its identity should be added to a local cache together with an expiry date for this notation of validity.

Much of this software can be harvested for reuse from recent open source offerings. What is already available would tip the scales, if there were

---

[464] What follows is speculative, since I have had insufficient time for software development. Nor have I commanded resources to create and distribute the packages contemplated. The funding needed would be only for 1–2 man-years of framework programming, and additionally for resources estimated in §4.2 of Gladney 2005 for UVC application development (§12.2).

[465] The *Piccolo toolkit for Java* programming to present 2D graphics that include zoomable interfaces and editability is promising. See http://www.cs.umd.edu/hcil/jazz/.

otherwise doubt about what programming language to use, in favor of programming with Java and XML.[466]

Since TDO structure conforms to both the OpenDocument Format[467] and the MPEG-21[468] standards, TDOs can be created and refined with OpenOffice Writer[469] complemented by a suite of XML templates and Writer macros. The use of free integrated development software, such as Eclipse, has much to commend it.[470]

---

[466]   Promising sources of these XML schema and Java code segments include the open-source program packages and articles of the *Los Alamos aDORe project* (http://african.lanl.gov/aDORe/projects/adoreArchive/), the Florida Center for Library *Automation DAITSS project* (http://www.fcla.edu/digitalArchive/pdfs/DAITSS.pdf), the [U.S.] National Library of Medicine *Archiving and Interchange DTD* (http://dtd.nlm.nih.gov/), and the *CNRI Handle System* (http://www.handle.net/). The *METS Implementation Registry* (http://sunsite.berkeley.edu/~rbeaubie/metsimpl/) contains descriptions of METS projects planned, in progress, and fully implemented.

[467]   OASIS 2005, *The OpenDocument Format for Office Applications (OpenDocument) v1.0 Specification*.

[468]   *MPEG-21 Standard*, http://xml.coverpages.org/ni2002-08-26-b.html.

[469]   *OpenOffice*, http://www.openoffice.org/.

[470]   D'Anjou 2005, *The Java Developer's Guide to Eclipse*.

Bibliography

Abrams, Stephen L. "The role of format in digital preservation." Vine 34 (1999): 49–55.

Abrams, Stephen L. and David Seaman. "Towards a global digital format registry." World Library and Information Congress: 69th IFLA General Conference. 2003.

Alexandra, Moreira, Lidia Alvarenga, and Oliveira Alcione De Paiva. "'Thesaurus' and 'Ontology': A study of the definitions found in the computer and information science literature, by means of an analytical-synthetic method." Ariadne 31 (2004): 231–244.

Anderson, Dave. "You Don't Know Jack about Disks." ACM Queue 1 (June 2003): 20–30.

Anderson, Richard, Hannah Frost, Nancy Hoebelheinrich, and Keith Johnson. "The AIHT at Stanford University." D-Lib Magazine 11 (December 2005).

Anderson, Ross. *Security Engineering: A Guide to Building Dependable Distributed Systems.* Wiley, 2001.

Anonymous. *The National Digital Information Infrastructure and Preservation Program (NDIIPP).* Library of Congress, 1975.

Aoki, Keith, James Boyle, and Jennifer Jenkins. *Bound by Law? Tales from the Public Domain. Center for the Study of the Public Domain*, 2006.

Arthur, Kathleen, Sherry Byrne, Elizabeth Long, Carla Q. Montori, and Judith Nadler. "Recognizing Digitization as a Preservation Reformatting Method." Microform and Imaging Review (June 2004).

Asadi, S. and M.H.R. Jamali. "Shifts in search engine development: A review of past, present and future trends." Webology 1 (2004).

Ashley, Kevin. "The preservation of databases." Vine 34 (2004): 66–70.

Atkins, Derek, Paul Buis, Chris Hare, Robert Kelley, Cary Nachenberg, Anthony B. Nelson, Tim Ritchey Paul Phillips, and William Steen. *Internet Security Professional Reference.* New Riders, 1996.

Ayre, Catherine and Adrienne Muir. "The Right to Preserve: The Rights Issues of Digital Preservation." March Magazine 10 (1999).

Barrows, Ryan and Jim Traverso. "Search Considered Integral: A combination of tagging, categorization, and navigation can help enterprise search." ACM Queue 4 (May 2006): 30–36.

Barton, Jane, Sarah Currier, and Jessie M. N. Hey. "Building Quality Assurance into Metadata Creation: an Analysis based on the Learning Objects and e-Prints Communities of Practice." Proceedings 2003 Dublin Core Conference: Supporting Communities of Discourse and Practice - Metadata Research and Applications. 2003.

Bauer, Friedrich Ludwig. *Decrypted secrets: methods and maxims of cryptology.* Springer Verlag, 2002.

Bayer, D., S. Haber, and W. S. Stornetta. "Improving the Efficiency and Reliability of Digital Time stamping." Communication, Security, and Computer Science. Ed. R. Capocelli, A. DeSantis, and U. Vaccaro 1992, 329–334.

Beagrie, Neil. "Plenty of Room at the Bottom? Personal Digital Libraries and Collections." D-Lib Magazine 11 (May 2005).

Bearman, David and Jennifer Trant. "Authenticity of Digital Resources: Toward a Statement of Requirements." D-Lib Magazine (June 1998).

Beedham, Hillary, Julie Missen, Matt Palmer, and Raivo Ruusalepp. "Assessment of UKDA and TNA compliance with *OAIS* and METS Standards." JISC (2005): http://www.data-archive.ac.uk/news/publications.asp.

Bekaert, Jeroen, Patrick Hochstenbach, and Herbert Van de Sompel. "Using MPEG-21 DIDL to Represent Complex Digital Objects in the Los Alamos National Laboratory Digital Library." D-Lib Magazine 9 (November 2003).

Bekaert, Jeroen and Herbert Van de Sompel. "A Standards-based Solution for the Accurate Transfer of Digital Assets." D-Lib Magazine 11 (June 2005).

Besek, June M. "Copyright Issues Relevant to the Creation of a Digital Archive." Microform and Imaging Review 32 (2003): 86–97.

Besser, Howard. "The Next Stage: Moving Isolated Digital Collections to Interoperable Digital Libraries." First Monday 7 (June 2002).

Bhattacharya, Suparna, C. Mohan, Karen W. Brannon, Inderpal Narang, Hui-I Hsiao, and Mahadevan Subramanian. "Coordinating backup/recovery and data consistency between database and file systems." Proceedings of the 2002 ACM SIGMOD international conference on Management of data. 2002, 500–511.

Birrell, Andrew D., Butler W. Lampson, Roger M. Needham, and Michael D. Schroeder, "A Global Authentication System without Global Trust." IEEE Symposium on Security and Privacy (1986): 223–230.

Bjørner, Dines and Cliff B. Jones. *Formal Specification and Software Development.* Prentice-Hall, 1982.

Bradley, Kevin. "Risks Associated with the Use of Recordable CDs and DVDs as Reliable Storage Media in Archival Collections—Strategies and Alternatives" UNESCO Memory of the World Programme (October 2006).

Brown, Adam. "Automating Preservation: New Developments in the PRONOM Service." RLG DigiNews 9 (2005).

Brown, John Seely and Paul Duguid. *Universities in the Digital Age.* Heldref Corp., 1995.

Brown, John Seely and Paul Duguid. *The Social Life of Information.* Harvard U. P., 2002.

Buchman, Johannes et al. "Perspectives for Cryptographic Long-Term Security." Comm. ACM 49(9) (2006): 50–55.

Bulterman, Dick C.A. "Is It Time for a Moratorium on Metadata?" IEEE Multimedia 5 (December 2004).

Burmester, Mike and Yvo G. Desmedt. "Is Hierarchical Public-Key Certification the Next Target for Hackers?." Comm. ACM 47 (2004): 68–74.

Calas, Marie-France and Jean-Marc Fontaine. *La conservation des documents sonores.* CNRS Editions, 1996.

Carnap, Rudolf. *Meaning and Necessity.* U. Chicago Press. 1946. 25–32.

Carnap, Rudolf. *The logical structure of the world and pseudoproblems in philosophy.* Originally published in 1928 as *Der Logische Aufbau der Welt.* U. Chicago Press, 1967.

Caronni, Germano. "Walking the Web of Trust." Proc. 9th Workshop on Enabling Technologies. 2000.

Carroll, Lewis The Annotated Alice: the definitive edition, W.W. Norton, 2000 (originally 1872).

Cassirer, Ernst. *The problem of knowledge: philosophy, science, and history since Hegel.* Yale U.P., 1978. Originally published as Erkenntnisproblem in der Philosophie, v. 4, circa 1941.

Chamberlin, D.D. *Using the new DB2: IBM's object-relational database system.* Morgan Kaufmann, 1996.

Cipra, Barry. "Electronic Time stamping: The Notary Public Goes Digital." Science 261 (July 1993): 162–163.

Codd, E.F. "A Relational Model of Data for Large Shared Data Banks." Comm. ACM 13 (1970): 377–387.

Conway, Paul. "Preservation in the Digital World." Council on Library and Information Resources, 1996.

Cooper, Brian and Hector Garcia-Molina. "Peer to peer data trading to preserve information." ACM Transactions on Information Systems 20 (2001): 133–170.

Coyle, Karen. "Descriptive metadata for copyright status." First Monday 10 (2005).

Crespo, Arturo and Hector Garcia-Molina. "Archival Storage for Digital Libraries." Proc. 3rd ACM Conference on Digital Libraries. 1998, 69–78.

Dam, Kenneth W. and Herbert S. Lin. *Cryptography's Role in Securing the Information Society.* National Academy Press, 1996.

D'Anjou, Jim, Scott Fairbrother, Dan Kehn, John Kellerman, and Pat McCarthy. The Java Developer's Guide to Eclipse, Addison-Wesley, 2005.

Darlington, Jeffrey, Andy Finney, and Adrian Pearce. "Domesday Redux: The rescue of the BBC Domesday Project videodiscs." Ariadne 36 (July 2003).

Darlington, Jeffrey, Andy Finney, and Adrian Pearce. "PRONOM-A Practical Online Compendium of File Formats." RLG DigiNews 7 (2003).

Davis, Martin. *Engines of Logic: Mathematicians and the Origin of the Computer.* W.W. Norton, 2000.

DeLoache, Judy S. "Mindful of Symbols." Scientific American 293 (August 1999): 72–77.

Denning, Peter J. "Accomplishment." Comm. ACM 46 (2003): 19–23.

Denning, Peter J., Jack B. Dennis, and Joseph E. Qualitz. *Machines, Languages, and Computation.* Prentice Hall, 1978.

DeWitt, Donald L. *Going Digital: Strategies for Access, Preservation, and Conversion of Collections to a Digital Format.* Haworth Press, 1998.

Donoughue, Carol. *The Mystery of the Hieroglyphs: The Story of the Rosetta Stone and the Race to Decipher Egyptian Hieroglyphs.* Oxford U.P., 2002.

Dougherty, Michael S. "Taming the Wild West, Part 2." DB2 Magazine Quarter 3 (2004): 17–20.

Drucker, Peter F. *Management Challenges for the 21st Century.* Harper, 1999.

Duranti, Luciana. "The Long-term Preservation of the Dynamic and Interactive Records of the Arts, Sciences and E-Government: InterPARES 2." Documents Numrique 8 (2004): 1–14.

Eastlake, Donald, Joseph Reagle, and David Solo. *Secure XML: The New Syntax for Signatures and Encryption.* Addison-Wesley, 2002.

Edminster, Judith R. *The Diffusion of New Media Scholarship: Power, Innovation, and Resistance in Academe.* PhD thesis, Univ. South Carolina, 2002.

Edmonds, David and John Eidinow. *Wittgenstein's Poker: The Story of a Ten-Minute Argument Between Two Great Philosophers.* Faber and Faber, 2000.

Edmonson, Ray. *Audiovisual Archiving: Philosophy and Principles.* UNESCO, 2004.

Ellison, C. "Naming and Certificates." Proceedings of the 10th Conference on Computers, Freedom, and Privacy: Challenging the Assumptions. 2003, 213–217.

Ellison, C. and B. Schneier. "Risks of PKI: E-Commerce." Comm. ACM 43 (2000): 152.

Engelmann, Paul. *Letters from Ludwig Wittgenstein*. Blackwell, 1967.

Entlich, Richard. "Too Close for Comfort? The Case for Off-site Storage.." RLG DigiNews 9 (2005).

Fagin, Ronald. "Multivalued dependencies and a new normal form for relational databases." ACM Transactions on Database Systems 2 (1977): 262–278.

Fallows, James. "File Not Found." The Atlantic 298(2), September 2006, 142–5.

Feghhi, Jalal, Jalil Feghhi, and Peter Williams. *Digital Certificates: Applied Internet Security*. Addison-Wesley, 1998.

Fluit, Christiaan, Marta Sabou, and Frank van Harmelen. "Ontology-based Information Visualization." Visualizing the Semantic Web 2002. Springer Verlag, 2002.

Fox, Edward A. and Shalini R. Urs. "Digital Libraries." *Annual Review of Information Science and Technology*. Volume 36 . "Online Information Review," 2002. 503–589.

Frege, Gottlob. *The foundations of arithmetic; a logicomathematical enquiry into the concept of number*. Originally published in 1884 as *Die Grundlagen der Arithmetik*. Philosophical Library, 1950.

Garfinkel, Simson L. "AFF : A New Format for Storing Hard Drive Images." Comm. ACM 49 (2006): 85–87.

Garrett, John, Donald Waters, P.Q.C. Andre, H. Besser, N. Elkington, H.M. Gladney, M. Hedstrom, P.B. Hirtle, K. Hunter, Robert Kelly, D. Kresh, M. Lesk, M.B. Levering, W. Lougee, C. Lynch, C. Mandel, S.B. Mooney, A. Okerson, J.G. Neal, S. Rosenblatt, and S. Weibel. *Preserving Digital Information: Report of the Task Force on Archiving of Digital Information*. The Commission on Preservation and Access, 1996.

Gardner, Pam Frost. "Digital Libraries Come of Age" IEEE Computing in Science and Engineering 8(5), (October 2006).

Gauravaram, Praveen, Adrian McCullagh, and Ed Dawson. "The legal and practical implications of recent attacks on 128-bit cryptographic hash functions." First Monday 11 (2006).

Gemmell, Jim, Lyndsay Williams, Ken Wood, Gordon Bell, and Roger Lueder. "MyLifeBits: A Personal Database for Everything." Comm. ACM 49 (1999): 88–95.

George, Gerald W. "Difficult Choices: How Can Scholars Help Save Endangered Research Resources?" Council on Library and Information Resources, 1995.

Gillmor, Dan. *We the Media*. O'Reilly, 2004.

Gladney, H.M. "A Storage Subsystem for Image and Records Management." IBM Sys. J. 32 (1993): 512–540.

Gladney, H.M. "Digital Intellectual Property: Controversial and International Aspects." Columbia-VLA Journal of Law and the Arts 24 (2000): 47–92.

Gladney, H.M. "Trustworthy 100-Year Digital Objects: Evidence After Every Witness is Dead." ACM Transactions on Info. Sys. 22(3), 406–436, 2004.

Gladney, H.M. and R.A. Lorie. "Trustworthy 100-Year Digital Objects: Durable Encoding for When It's Too Late to Ask." ACM Transactions on Info. Sys. 23(3), 299–324, 2005.

Gordon, Michael J. *The Denotational Description of Programming Languages*. Springer-Verlag, 1979.

Goth, Greg. "XML: The Center of Attention Up and Down the Stack, IEEE Distributed Systems Online." IEEE Distributed Systems Online 7 (2001): art. no. 0601–o1003.

Gracy, Karen F. and Michle Valerie Cloonan. "The Preservation of Moving Images." Advances in Librarianship 27 (2004): 49–95.

Gradmann, Stefan. "Cataloguing vs. Metadata: old wine in new bottles?" 64th IFLA General Conference (1998).

Grandison, Tyrone and Morris Sloman. "A Survey of Trust in Internet Applications." IEEE Communications Surveys and Tutorials (4th Quarter 2000).

Granger, Stewart. "Emulation as a Digital Preservation Strategy." D-Lib Magazine 6 (October 2000).

Granger, Stewart. "Digital Preservation and Deep Infrastructure," D-Lib Magazine 8 (February 2002).

Gray, Jim and Andreas Reuter. *Transaction processing: concepts and techniques*. Morgan Kaufmann, 1993.

Hackel, Siegfried. "ArchiSafe: a legally secure and scalable long-term recordkeeping strategy." Electronic Records Supporting e-Government and Digital Archives: DLM Forum. 2005.

Hart, John L. "Digitizing hastens at microfilm vault." LDS Church News 2006 (March 2006): 1–5.

Heidegger, Martin. *Being and Time* (originally *Sein und Zeit*). Harper and Row, 1962.

Hersh, Reuben. *What Is Mathematics, Really?* Oxford U.P., 1997.

Hertz, Heinrich. *The principles of mechanics, presented in a new form* (originally *Prinzipien der Mechanik*, 1894). Dover, 1956.

Herzberg, Amir. "Securing XML: Ensuring confidentiality, authentication, authorization, and more." Dr. Dobb's Journal (March 2002): 56–62.

Hess, Richard L. "The Jack Mullin/Bill Palmer Tape Restoration Project." J. Audio Engineering Society 49 (2001): 671–674.

Heuscher, Stephan, Stephan Jaermann, Peter Keller-Marxer, and Frank Moehle. "Providing Authentic Long-term Archival Access to Complex Relational Data." Symposium: Ensuring Long-Term Preservation and Adding Value to Scientific and Technical Data. Ed. European Space Agency. European Space Agency, 2004.

Hey, Tony and Anne Trefethen. "The data deluge." Grid computing: making the global infrastructure a reality. Ed. Fran Berman, Geoffrey Fox, and Tony Hey. Wiley, 2003.

Hilbert, David. "On the Infinite." In Paul Benacerraf and Hillary Putnam. *The Philosophy of Mathematics,* Prentice-Hall, 1964, pp. 134–151. Originally in Mathematische Annalen (Berlin) no. 95 (1925), pp. 161–190.

Hunter, Jane. "MPEG-7 Behind the Scenes." D-Lib Magazine 5 (September 1999).

Huttenlocher, Dan and Angel Moll. "On DigiPaper and the Dissemination of Electronic Documents." D-Lib Magazine 6 (June 2000).

Illing, Richard. *The Art of Japanese Prints*. Calmann and Cooper, 1980.

Iraci, Joe. "The Relative Stabilities of Optical Disc Formats." Restaurator 26 (2005): 134–150.

James, William. "Does 'Consciousness' Exist?." J. Philosophy, Psychology, and Scientific Methods 1 (1904): 477–491.

James, William. "A World of Pure Experience." J. Philosophy, Psychology, and Scientific Methods 1 (1904).

James, William. *Essays in Radical Empiricism*. Longmans, Green, 1912.

Janik, Allen and Stephen Toulmin. *Wittgenstein's Vienna*. Ivan R Dee, 1997.

Jantz, Ronald and Michael J. Giarlo. "Digital Preservation: Architecture and Technology for Trusted Digital Repositories." D-Lib Magazine 11 (June 2005).

Jordan, Ken, Jan Hauser, and Steven Foster. "The Augmented Social Network: Building identity and trust into the next-generation Internet." First Monday 8 (2003).

Just, Mike. "Some Time stamping Protocol Failures." Internet Society Symposium on Network and Distributed System Security. 1998.

Kahn, David. *The Codebreakers*. Scribner, 1967.

Kant, Immanuel, Paul Guyer (ed.), and Allen W. Wood (ed.). *The Critique of Pure Reason*, Cambridge U.P. 1998. First published as *Kritik der reinen Vernunft*, 1787.

Kenney, Anne R., Nancy Y. McGovern, Peter Botticelli, Richard Entlich, Carl Lagoze, and Sandra Payette. "Preservation Risk Management for Web Resources: Virtual Remote Control in Cornell's Project Prism." D-Lib Magazine 8 (January 2002).

Knudsen, Jonathan. *Java Cryptography*. O'Reilly, 1996.

Koltun, Lilly. "The Promise and Threat of Digital Options in an Archival Age." Archivaria 47 (Spring 1999): 114–135.

Kripke, Saul A. *Wittgenstein on Rules and Private Language*. Harvard U.P., 1984.

Lampson, Butler, Martin Abadi, Michael Burrows, and Edward Wobber, "Authentication in Distributed Systems: Theory and Practice." ACM Transactions on Computer Systems 10(4) (1992): 256–310.

Langendoen, Andrea. "The Metamorfoze Preservation Program." Microform and Imaging Review 33 (2004): 110–5.

Lawrence, Gregory W., William R. Kehoe, Oya Y. Rieger, William H. Waters, and Anne R. Kenney. Risk Management of Digital Information: A File Format Investigation. Council on Library and Information Resources, 2000.

Lazinger, Susan S. *Digital Preservation and Meta-data: History, Theory, Practice*. Libraries Unlimited, 2001.

Lekkas, D. and D. Gritzalis. "Cumulative notarization for long-term preservation of digital signatures." Computers and Security 23 (2004): 413–424.

Lemieux, Victoria L. "Let the Ghosts Speak-An Empirical Exploration of the "Nature" of the Record." Archivaria 51 (Spring 2001): 81–111.

Lesk, Michael. *Practical Digital Libraries: books, bytes, and bucks*. Morgan Kaufman, 1999.

Lessig, L. "The Law of the Horse: What Cyberlaw Might Teach." Harv. L. Rev. 113 (1999): 501.

Levy, David M. "Heroic Measures: Reflections on the Possibility and Purpose of Digital Preservation." Proceedings of the Third ACM Conference on Digital Libraries. 1998. 152–161.

Levy, David M. "The Universe is Expanding: Reflections on the Social and Cosmic Significance of Documents in a Digital Age." Bull. ASIS 25 (1999): 17–20.

Levy, David M. *Scrolling Forward: Making Sense of Documents in the Digital Age*. General, 2003.

Littman, Justin. "A Technical Approach and Distributed Model for Validation of Digital Objects." D-Lib Magazine 12 (May 2006).

Lorie, Raymond A. and Raymond J. van Diessen. "A Universal Virtual Computer for Long-term Preservation of Digital Information." IBM Research Report RJ 10338 (February 2005).

Lossau, Norbert. "Search Engine Technology and Digital Libraries: Libraries Need to Discover the Academic Internet." D-Lib Magazine 10 (June 2004).

Lovecy, Ian. "Disaster Management for Libraries and Archives." Ariadne 44 (July 2005).

Ludäscher, B., R. Marciano, and R. Moore. "Preservation with Self-Validating, Self-Instantiating Knowledge-Based Archives." ACM SIGMOD Record 30 (2001): 54–63.

Lynch, Clifford. "Identifiers and Their Role in Networked Information Applications." ARL Newsletter of Research Library Issues and Actions 194 (October 1997).

Lynch, Clifford. "Canonicalization: A fundamental tool to facilitate preservation and management of digital information." D-Lib Magazine 5 (September 1999).

Lynch, Clifford. "Where Do We Go From Here? The Next Decade for Digital Libraries." D-Lib Magazine 11 (July/August 2005).

Lynch, Clifford A. and Joan K. Lippincott. "Institutional Repository Deployment in the United States as of Early 2005." D-Lib Magazine 11 (2005).

MacNeil, Heather. "Trusting Records in a Post-Modern World." Archivaria 51 (Spring 2001): 36–47.

MacNeil, Heather. "Providing Grounds for Trust II: The Findings of the Authenticity Task Force of InterPARES." Archivaria 54 (Fall 2002): 24–58.

Magee, Bryan. Talking Philosophy, Oxford U.P., 1978.

Maly, Kurt, Michael L. Nelson, and Mohammed Zubair. "Smart Objects, Dumb Archives: A User-Centric, Layered Digital Library Framework." D-Lib Magazine 5 (March 1999).

Maniatis, Petros and Mary Baker. "Enabling the Archival Storage of Signed Documents." Proc. of the FAST 2002 Conference on File and Storage Technologies (January 2002).

Mann, Thomas. "Why the cybergurus are wrong about libraries." Logos 13 (2002): 190–198.

Marcum, Deanna and Amy Friedlander. "Keepers of the Crumbling Culture: What Digital Preservation Can Learn from Library History." D-Lib Magazine 9 (May 2003).

Marcum, Deanna B. "Research Questions for the Digital Era Library." Library Trends 51 (Spring 2003).

Maurer, Hermann and Klaus Tochtermann. "On a New Powerful Model for Knowledge Management and Its Applications." J. Universal Computer Science 8 (January 2004).

McClelland, Marilyn, David McArthur, and Sarah Giersch. "Challenges for Service Providers When Importing Metadata in Digital Libraries." D-Lib Magazine 8 (April 2002).

McDonough, Richard M. The Argument of the Tractatus: Its Relevance to Contemporary Theories of Logic, Language, Mind, and Philosophical Truth. SUNY Press, 1986.

McKemmish, Sue, Michael Piggott, Barbara Reed, and Frank Upward. Archives: Recordkeeping in Society. The Recordkeeping Institute, 2004.

Mellor, P., P. Wheatley, and D.M. Sergeant. "Migration on Request: A practical technique for digital preservation." Research and Advances Technology for Digital Technology : 6th European Conference, ECDL 2002. Ed. M. Agosti and C. Thanos. LNCS Volume 2458 . Springer, 2002. 516–526.

Meloan, Steve. "No Way to Run a Culture." Wired (February 1998).

Menezes, A.J., P.C. van Oorschot, and S.A. Vanstone. *Handbook of Applied Cryptography.* CRC Press, 1997.

Millar, Laura. "The Spirit of Total Archives: Seeking a Sustainable Archive System." Archivaria 47 (Spring 1999): 46–65.

Miller, Paul. "Toward the Digital Aquifer: introducing the Common Information Environment." Ariadne (April 2004).

Miller, Steven W. "A Reference Model for Mass Storage Systems." Advances in Computers 27 (1988): 157–210.

Miller (ed.), David. *A Pocket Popper.* Oxford U.P, 1983.

Mintzer, F. "Developing Digital Libraries of Cultural Content for Internet Access." IEEE Comm. Mag. (Jan. 1999).

Mintzer, F.C., L.E. Boyle, A.N. Cazes, B.S. Christian, S.C. Cox, F.P. Giordano, H.M. Gladney, J.C. Lee, M.L. Kelmanson, A.C. Lirani, K.A. Magerlein, A.M.B. Pavani, and F. Schiattarella. "Toward On-Line Worldwide Access to Vatican Library Materials." IBM J. Research and Development 40 (March 1996): 139–162.

Mitchell, William, Alan S. Inouye, and Marjory S. Blumenthal. *Beyond Productivity: Information Technology, Innovation, and Creativity.* National Academies Press, 2003.

Mohan, C., Don Haderle, Bruce Lindsay, Hamid Pirahesh, and Peter Schwarz. "ARIES: a transaction recovery method supporting fine-granularity locking and partial rollbacks using write-ahead logging." ACM Transactions on Database Systems 17 (1992): 94–162.

Moore, G.E. *Principia Ethica.* Cambridge U.P., 1903.

Morrison, Michael et al. *XML Unleashed.* Sams Publishing, 2000.

Mylonopoulos, N.A. and V. Theoharakis. "Global perceptions of IS journals." Comm. ACM 44 (1999): 29–33.

Naor (ed.), Moni. "Theory of Cryptography: First Theory of Cryptography Conference." LNCS Volume 2951. Springer Verlag, 2004.

Narang, I. and R. Rees. "DataLinks - Linkage of Database and FileSystems." Proc. Sixth Int Workshop on High Performance Transaction Systems. September 1995.

National Research Council (ed.). *Digital Dilemma: Intellectual Property in the Information Age.* National Academies Press, 2000.

National Research Council (ed.). Trust in Cyberspace. National Academies Press, 1999.

Neal, James G. "Chaos Breeds Life: Finding Opportunities for Library Advancement During a Period of Collection Schizophrenia." J. Library Administration 28 (1999): 3–17.

Nelson, Michael L., Johan Bollen, Giridhar Manepalli, and Rabia Haq. "Archive Ingest and Handling Test: The Old Dominion University Approach." D-Lib Magazine 11 (Juanuary 2005).

Nimmer, David. "Adams and Bits: of Jewish Kings and Copyrights." S. Cal. L. Rev. 71 (1998): 219–245.

Odlyzko, Andrew. "Silicon dreams and silicon bricks: the continuing evolution of libraries." Library Trends 46 (1997): 152–167.

O'Donnell, J.J. *Avatars of the Word: from Papyrus to Cyberspace.* Harvard University Press, 1998.

O'Hara, Kieron et al. "Memories for life: a review of the science and technology." J. Royal Society Interface 3(8) (2006): 351–365.

Ouksel, A.M. and A. Sheth. "Semantic Interoperability in Global Information Systems." ACM SIGMOD Record 28 (1999): 5–12.

Payette, Sandra and Carl Lagoze. "Policy-Carrying, Policy-Enforcing Digital Objects." Proceedings of the 4th European Conference on Research and Advanced Technology for Digital Libraries. Springer Verlag. 2000. 144–157.

Peat, F. David. *From certainty to uncertainty: the story of science and ideas in the twentieth century*. Joseph Henry Press, 2002.

Perkings, John, David Dawson, and Kati Geber. "Beyond Productivity: Culture and Heritage Resources in the Digital Age." D-Lib Magazine 10 (June 2004).

Peters, Thomas A. "Digital repositories: individual, discipline-based, institutional, consortial, or national?." J. Academic Librarianship 28 (1999): 414–417.

Plato and R. Hackworth (ed.). *Phaedrus*. Cambridge U.P., 1972.

Pohlmann, Ken C. *Principles of Digital Audio*. McGraw-Hill, 2000.

Polanyi, Michael. *Personal Knowledge*. U. Chicago Press, 1958.

Polanyi, Michael. *The Tacit Dimension*. Doubleday, 1966.

Pratt, Wanda, Kenton Unruh, Andrea Civan, and Meredith Skeels. "Personal Health Information Management." Comm. ACM 49 (2006): 51–55.

Pulkowski, Sebastian. "Intelligent Wrapping of Information Sources: Getting Ready for the Electronic Market." Proceedings of the 10th VALA Conference on Technologies for the Hybrid Library. 2000.

Quine, Willard Van Orman. *Word and Object*. M.I.T. Press, 1960.

Raskin, Jef. "Silicon Superstitions." ACM Queue 1 (2004).

Riedel, Erik. "Storage Systems: Not Just a Bunch of Disks Anymore." ACM Queue 1 (June 2003): 32–41.

Roberts, Andrew. *Salisbury: Victorian Titan*. Weidenfeld and Nicolson, 1999.

Robertson, Steven B. *Digital Rosetta Stone: A Conceptual Model for Maintaining Long-Term Access to Digital Documents*. Master's thesis, Air University, 1996.

Ronsse, Michiel, Koen de Bosshere, and Mark Christianens. "Record/Replay for Non-deterministic Program Executions." Comm. ACM 46 (2003): 62–67.

Rosenthal, David S. H., Thomas S. Robertson, Tom Lipkis, Vicky Reich, and Seth Morabito. "Requirements for Digital Preservation Systems: A Bottom-Up Approach." D-Lib Magazine 11 (November 2005).

Ross, Seamus and Andrew McHugh. "Audit and Certification of Digital Repositories: Creating a Mandate for the Digital Curation Centre." RLG DigiNews 9 (2005).

Roth, Daniel. "Quoted Often, Followed Rarely." Fortune 152 (1999): 151.

Rothenberg, Jeff. "Ensuring the Longevity of Digital Documents." Scientific American 272 (1995): 42–47.

Rusbridge, Chris. "Excuse Me... Some Digital Preservation Fallacies." Ariadne 46 (February 2006).

Russell, Bertrand. "Mathematics and the Metaphysicians." Repr. in Russell, Bertrand, *Mysticism and Logic*, London: Long-mans Green, 1918, 74–96. International Monthly 4 (1901): 83–101.

Russell, Bertrand. "On Denoting." Repr. in Russell, Bertrand, *Essays in Analysis*, Allen and Unwin, 1973, 103–119. Mind 14 (1905): 479–493.

Rust, Godfrey. "Metadata: The Right Approach: An Integrated Model for Descriptive and Rights Metadata in E-Commerce." D-Lib Magazine (July/August 1998).

Ryle, Gilbert. *The concept of mind.* New York: Barnes and Noble, 1949.

Sandhu, R.S. "Role-based Access Control." Advances in Computers 46 (1998).

Schäfer, Günter. Security in Fixed and Wireless Networks. dpunkt Verlag, 2003.

Schechter, Bruce and Michael Ross. "Leading the Way in Storage." IBM Research (1997): 16–21.

Schilpp, Paul Arthur. *The Philosophy of Rudolf Carnap.* Open Court Pub., 1963.

Schlatter, M., R. Furegati, F. Jeger, H Schneider, and H. Streckeisen. "The Business Object Management System." IBM Systems Journal 33 (1994): 239–263.

Schneier, Bruce. Applied Cryptography: Protocols, Algorithms, and Source Code in C. Wiley, 1996.

Schneier, Bruce. Secrets and Lies: Digital Security in a Networked World. Wiley, 2000.

Schwartz, Ruth Bolotin and Michele C. Russo. "How to Quickly Find Articles in the Top IS Journals." Comm. ACM 47 (2004): 98–101.

Searle, John R. *Mind, Language, and Society.* Basic Books, 1998.

Seadle, Michael. "Sound Preservation: Analog to Digital." Advances in Librarianship 27 (April 1999).

Shankaranarayanan, Ganesan and Adir Even. "The Metadata Enigma." Comm. ACM 49 (2006): 88–94.

Shepard, Thom. "Universal Preservation Format." D-Lib Magazine 5 (May 1999).

Shepherd, Elizabeth. and Geoffrey Yeo. *Managing Records: A handbook of principles and practice.* Neal-Schuman Publishers, 2002.

Shirky, Clay. "AIHT: Conceptual Issues from Practical Tests." D-Lib Magazine 11 (November 2005).

Singh, Simon. *The Code Book: the Evolution of Secrecy from Mary, Queen of Scots, to Quantum Cryptography.* Random House, 1999.

Slattery, Oliver, Richang Lu, Jian Zheng, Fred Byers, and Xiao Tang. "Stability Comparison of Recordable Optical Discs-A Study of Error Rates in Harsh Conditions." J. Res. Natl. Inst. Stand. Technol. 109 (2004): 517–524.

Snow, C.P. The Two Cultures. Cambridge U.P., 1964.

Society, Audio Engineering. "Standard for audio preservation and restoration?Life expectancy of information stored in recordable compact disk systems? Method for estimating, based on effects of temperature and relative humidity." J. Audio. Eng. Soc. 48 (2000): 679-705.

Sowa, John F. *Knowledge representation: logical, philosophical, and computational foundations.* Pacific Grove: Brooks/Cole, 2004.

Srikantaiah, T. Kanti and Michael E.D. Koenig (ed.). *Knowledge management for the information professional.* Information Today, 2000.

Stanat, D.F. and D.F. McAllister. *Discrete Mathematics in Computer Science.* Prentice-Hall, 1977.

Suderman, Jim. "Defining Electronic Series: A Study." Archivaria 53 (Spring 2002): 31–45.

Teets, Michael and Peter Murray. "Metasearch Authentication and Access Management." D-Lib Magazine 12 (June 2006).

Teruggi, Daniel. "Can We Save Our Audio-visual Heritage?" Ariadne 39 (April 2004).

Theng, Yin-Leng and Schubert Foo. *Design and Usability of Digital Libraries: case studies in the Asia Pacific.* Info. Sci. Publishing, 2005.

Thibodeau, Kenneth. "Overview of Technological Approaches to Digital Preservation." The State of Digital preservation: An International Perspective. Ed. Council on Library, Information Resources, and the Library of Congress ISBN 1-887334-92-0, 2002.

Thoma, G. R. et al. "A Prototype System for the Electronic Storage and Retrieval of Document Images." ACM Transactions on Office Information Systems 3(3) (1985): 279–291.

Tomaiuolo, Nick. "Building a World Class Personal Library with Free Web Resources." Information Today (February 2004).

Thompson, D. A. and J. S. Best. "The future of magnetic data storage technology." IBM J. Res. and Dev. 44 (1999): 311–322.

Trevedi, Bijal P. "The Rembrandt Code." Wired (December 2005).

Ubois, Jeff. "New approaches to television archiving." First Monday 10 (2005).

UNESCO. "Memory of the World: General Guidelines," prepared by Ray Edmondson. Paris: UNESCO, 2002. UNESCO has created and is generating supporting documents that can be located via http://portal.unesco.org/ci/en/ev.php-URL_ID= 1538&URL_DO=DO_TOPIC&URL_SECTION=201.html

Vacca, John. Internet Security Secrets. IDG Books, 1996.

Van Bogart, John W. C. "Long-Term Preservation of Digital Materials." Conference on Preservation and Digitization: Principles, Practice and Policies. Ed. National Preservation Office 1996.

Van Diessen, Raymond J. and Titia vander Werf-Davelaar, "Authenticity in a Digital Environment," IBM/KB Long-Term Preservation Study Report Series #2 (2002).

Van de Sompel, Herbert, J. Bekaert, X. Liu, L. Balakireva, and T. Schwander. "aDORe: a Modular, Standards-based Digital Object Repository." Computer Journal 48 (2005): 514–535.

Van de Sompel, Herbert, Michael L. Nelson, Carl Lagoze, and Simeon Warner. "Resource Harvesting within the OAI-PMH Framework." D-Lib Magazine 10 (December 1999).

Van de Sompel, Herbert, Jeffrey A. Young, and Thomas B. Hickey. "Using the OAI-PMH Differently." D-Lib Magazine 9 (July/August 2003).

Van Drimmelen, Wim. "Universal access through time: archiving strategies for digital publications." Libri 54 (2004): 98–103.

Vitiello, Giuseppe. "Identifiers and Identification Systems: An Informational Look at Policies and Roles from a Library Perspective." D-Lib Magazine 10 (January 2004): 85–96.

Von Neumann, John. The Computer and the Brain. Yale U.P., 1956.

Waibel, Günter. "Like Russian Dolls: Nesting Standards for Digital Preservation." RLG DigiNews 7 (2003).

Wang, Roland. "Enterprise Search: The Next Frontier.." Software Development 12 (2004): 36.

Warren, Paul. "Knowledge Management and the Semantic Web: From Scenario to Technology." IEEE Intelligent Systems 21 (2006): 53–59.

Wasow, Thomas, Amy Perfors, and David Beaver. "The Puzzle of Ambiguity." Morphology and The Web of Grammar. Ed. O. Orgun and P. Sells. CSLI Publications, 2005.

Waters, Donald. "Good Archives Make Good Scholars: Reflections on Recent Steps Toward the Archiving of Digital Information." The State of Digital preservation: An International Perspective. Ed. Library of Congress. Council on Library and Information Resources, 2002.

Waugh, Andrew. "On the use of digital signatures in the preservation of electronic objects." @ccess and preservation of electronic information: best practices and solutions. DLM Forum Proceedings of the 2002 Workshop, 2002. 510–517.

Webb, Colin. *Guidelines for the Preservation of Digital Heritage*. UNESCO, 1999.

Weibel, Stuart. "Border Crossings: Reflections on a Decade of Metadata Consensus Building." D-Lib Magazine 11 (July/August 2005).

Westrienen, Gerard van and Clifford A. Lynch. "Academic Institutional Repositories: Deployment Status in 13 Nations as of Mid-2005." D-Lib Magazine 11 (November 2005).

White, Michael. *Acid Tongues and Tranquil Dreamers: Eight Scientific Rivalries That Changed the World*. Harper Perennial, 2002.

Wilkinson, Ross. *Document Computing: technologies for managing electronic document collections*. Kluwer Academic, 1998.

Winchester, Simon. *The Meaning of Everything: The Story of the Oxford English Dictionary*. Oxford U.P., 1999.

Witten, Ian H. and David Bainbridge. *How to Build a Digital Library*. Morgan Kaufmann, 1999.

Witten, Ian H., David Bainbridge, Chi-Yu Huang, Katherine J. Don, and Robert Tansley. "StoneD: A Bridge between Greenstone and DSpace." D-Lib Magazine 11 (September 2005).

Wittgenstein, Ludwig. *Tractatus LogicoPhilosophicus*. Routledge, 1921.

Wittgenstein, Ludwig. *Philosophical Investigations: The English Text of the Third Edition*. Blackwell, 1958.

Wittgenstein, Ludwig and Cora Diamond (ed.). *Wittgenstein's Lectures on the Foundations of Mathematics*, Cambridge 1939. Library of Congress, 2003.

Wolf, Milton T. "By the Dawn's Early Light." J. Library Administration 28 (1999): 19–32.

Wright, Richard. "Digital preservation of audio, video and film." Vine 34 (1999): 71–76.

Zhao, Ben Y., Ling Huang, Jeremy Stribling, Sean C. Rhea, Anthony D. Joseph, and John D. Kubiatowicz. "Tapestry: A Resilient Global-scale Overlay for Service Deployment." IEEE Journal on Selected Areas in Communications 22 (2004): 41–53.

Friedrich L. Bauer, Munich Institute of Technology, München, Germany

Decrypted Secrets
Methods and
Maxims of
Cryptology

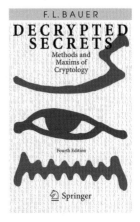

2007 4th edition
XIV, 525 p. 191 Illus., 16 in color
ISBN 3-540-24502-2

Cryptology, for millennia a "secret science", is rapidly gaining in practical importance for the protection of communication channels, databases, and software. Beside its role in computerized information systems (public key systems), more and more applications within computer systems and networks are appearing, which also extend to access rights and source file protection.
The first part of this book treats secret codes and their uses – cryptography. The second part deals with the process of covertly decrypting a secret code – cryptanalysis – where in particular advice on assessing methods is given. The book presupposes only elementary mathematical knowledge. Spiced with a wealth of exciting, amusing, and sometimes personal stories from the history of cryptology, it will also interest general readers.
Decrypted Secrets has become a standard book on cryptology. This 4th edition has again been revised and extended in many technical and biographical details.

Uwe M. Borghoff, Peter Rödig, Lothar Schmitz, Universität der Bundeswehr München ("University of the Federal Armed Forces"), Munich, Germany; Jan Scheffczyk, International Computer Science Institute, Berkeley, CA, USA

Long-Term Preservation of Digital Documents

2006 Approx. XV, 274 p. 67 illus.
ISBN 3-540-33639-7

Key to our culture is that we can disseminate information, and then maintain and access it over time. While we are rapidly advancing from vulnerable physical solutions to superior, digital media, preserving and using data over the long term involves complicated research challenges and organization efforts.

Uwe Borghoff and his coauthors address the problem of storing, reading, and using digital data for periods longer than 50 years. They briefly describe several markup and document description languages like TIFF, PDF, HTML, and XML, explain the most important techniques such as migration and emulation, and present the OAIS (Open Archival Information System) Reference Model. To complement this background information on the technology issues the authors present the most relevant international preservation projects, such as the Dublin Core Metadata Initiative, and experiences from sample projects run by the Cornell University Library and the National Library of the Netherlands. A rated survey list of available systems and tools completes the book.

With this broad overview, the authors address librarians who preserve our digital heritage, computer scientists who develop technologies that access data, and information managers engaged with the social and methodological requirements of long-term information access.

Contents: Part I: Methodology - 1) Long-Term Preservation of Digital Documents - 2) OAIS and DSEP Organizational Models - 3) Migration - 4) Emulation - 5) Document Markup - 6) Standard Markup Languages - 7) Discussion.- Part II: Recent Preservation Initiatives - 8) Markup: Current Research and Development - 9) Migration: Current Research and Development - 10) Emulation: Current Research and Development - 11) Software Systems for Archiving.- References - Index.

Julien Masanès, European Web Archive, Paris, France (Ed.)

Web Archiving

2006 VII, 234 p. 28 illus.
ISBN 3-540-23338-5

The public information available on the Web today is larger than information distributed on any other media. The raw nature of Web content, the unpredictable remote changes that can affect it, the wide variety of formats concerned, and the growth in data-driven websites make the preservation of this material a challenging task, requiring specific monitoring, collecting and preserving strategies, procedures and tools.

Julien Masanès, Director of the European Archive, has assembled contributions from computer scientists and librarians that altogether encompass the complete range of tools, tasks and processes needed to successfully preserve the cultural heritage of the Web. His book serves as a standard introduction for everyone involved in keeping alive the immense amount of online information, and it covers issues related to building, using and preserving Web archives both from the computer scientist and librarian viewpoints.

Practitioners will find in this book a state-of-the-art overview of methods, tools and standards they need for their activities. Researchers as well as advanced students in computer science will use it as an introduction to this new field with a hopefully stimulating review of open issues where future work is needed.

Contents: Web Archiving: Issues and Methods.- Web Use and Web Studies.- Selection for Web Archives.- Copying Web Sites.- Archiving the Hidden Web.- Access and Finding Aids.- Mining Web Collections.- The Long-Term Preservation of Web Content.- Year-by-Year: From an Archive of the Internet to an Archive on the Internet.- Small Scale Academic Web Archiving: DACHS.

Springer
the language of science

springer.com

Carlo Batini, Università di Milano Bicocca, Italy;
Monica Scannapieco, Università di Roma La Sapienza, Italy

Data Quality

2006 XIX, 262 p. 134 illus.
ISBN 3-540-33172-7

Poor data quality can seriously hinder or damage the efficiency and effectiveness of organizations and businesses. The growing awareness of such repercussions has led to major public initiatives like the "Data Quality Act" in the USA and the "European 2003/98" directive of the European Parliament.

Batini and Scannapieco present a comprehensive and systematic introduction to the wide set of issues related to data quality. They start with a detailed description of different data quality dimensions, like accuracy, completeness, and consistency, and their importance in different types of data, like federated data, web data, or time-dependent data, and in different data categories classified according to frequency of change, like stable, long-term, and frequently changing data. The book's extensive description of techniques and methodologies from core data quality research as well as from related fields like data mining, probability theory, statistical data analysis, and machine learning gives an excellent overview of the current state of the art. The presentation is completed by a short description and critical comparison of tools and practical methodologies, which will help readers to resolve their own quality problems.

This book is an ideal combination of the soundness of theoretical foundations and the applicability of practical approaches. It is ideally suited for everyone – researchers, students, or professionals – interested in a comprehensive overview of data quality issues. In addition, it will serve as the basis for an introductory course or for self-study on this topic.

Springer
the language of science

springer.com

Ian Gorton, National ICT Australia, Everleigh, NSW, Australia

Essential Software Architecture

2006 XVIII, 283 p. 93 illus.
3-540-28713-2

Job titles like "Technical Architect" and "Chief Architect" nowadays abound in the software industry, yet many people suspect that "architecture" is one of the most overused and least understood terms in professional software development.

Gorton's book helps resolve this predicament. It concisely describes the essential elements of knowledge and key skills required to be a software architect. The explanations encompass the essentials of architecture thinking, practices, and supporting technologies. They range from a general understanding of software structure and quality attributes, through technical issues like middleware components and documentation techniques, to emerging technologies like model-driven architecture, software product lines, aspect-oriented design, service-oriented architectures, and the Semantic Web, all of which will influence future software system architectures.

All approaches are illustrated by an ongoing real-world example. So if you work as an architect or senior designer (or want to someday), or if you are a student in software engineering, here is a valuable and yet approachable source of knowledge.

"Ian's book helps us to head in the right direction through the various techniques and approaches... An essential guide to computer science students as well as developers and IT professionals who aspire to become an IT architect". (Anna Liu, Architect Advisor, Microsoft Australia)

Contents: Understanding Software Architecture.- Introducing the Case Study.- Software Quality Attributes.- A Guide to Middleware Architectures and Technologies.- A Software Architecture Process.- Documenting a Software Architecture.- Case Study Design.- Looking Ahead.- Software Product Lines.- Aspect-Oriented Architectures.- Model-Driven Architecture.- Service-Oriented Architectures and Technologies.- Software Architecture and the Semantic Web.- Software Agents: An Architectural Perspective.

Printing: Krips bv, Meppel
Binding: Stürtz, Würzburg